MACROMEDIA® FLASH®
PROFESSIONAL 8
GAME DEVELOPMENT

MACROMEDIA® FLASH®
PROFESSIONAL 8
GAME DEVELOPMENT

GLEN RHODES

CHARLES RIVER MEDIA

Boston, Massachusetts

Cover Design: Tyler Creative
Cover Image: Chris Hildenbrand

CHARLES RIVER MEDIA
25 Thomson Place
Boston, Massachusetts 02210
617-757-7900
617-757-7969 (FAX)
crm.info@thomson.com
www.charlesriver.com

This book is printed on acid-free paper.

Glen Rhodes. *Macromedia Flash Professional 8 Game Development.*
ISBN-13: 978-1-58450-4870   ISBN-10: 1-58450-4870

Library of Congress Cataloging-in-Publication Data
Rhodes, Glen.
  Macromedia Flash professional 8 game development / Glen Rhodes.
     p. cm.
  Includes index.
  ISBN 1-58450-487-0 (pbk. with cd-rom : alk. paper) 1. Computer games--Programming.
2. Computer animation. 3. Flash (Computer file) I. Title.
  QA76.76.C672R532 2004
  794.8'1526--dc22
                              2006014500

  07 6 5 4 3

CHARLES RIVER MEDIA titles are available for site license or bulk purchase by institutions, user groups, corporations, etc. For additional information, please contact the Special Sales Department at 800-347-7707.

This book is dedicated to those whose eyes fall upon these words.
Thank you for reading this book and I hope that I can help
you get to where you want to be in your game development career.
Oh, and also to Nurp.

CONTENTS

PREFACE

With Macromedia Flash Professional 8, the Flash Games genre has once again been redefined. We now have more power and more tools at our fingertips to make things run faster, look cooler, and play better. I wrote this book because I wanted to "spread the word" about the powerful possibilities with Flash 8, and to make it clear that this platform rivals the best and most established platforms out there, like C++ and Java.

Never before has there been such a powerful yet simple means of delivering game content to the world. We can start developing a game at 5:00, and by 8:00 ten million people could be playing it.

Gone are the distribution roadblocks. The information now flows freely across the world, and anyone with the latest Macromedia Flash Player installed on their computer can participate in our creations and visit our worlds.

This book is intended for anyone who would like to take their Macromedia Flash Professional 8 skills to a new level, producing games that rival anything available on the web today. Perhaps you're a game developer in another language, or perhaps you're a Macromedia Flash developer and you need to start creating games for your clients. Whatever the case, this book is for you.

We'll be covering many advanced topics in this book, but we'll be covering them in a simple and easy to understand way. We'll be covering many different aspects of game design with Macromedia Flash Professional 8, including:

- Understanding the elements of game design and what makes a good game, including challenge, reward, plot, story and motivation.
- The simple point and click "whack-a-mole" game, popular to many Macromedia Flash game developers.
- The bouncing ball block breaking game.
- The high-speed top-down view space shooter.
- Creating sounds for games.
- Saving data to the disk with the built in SharedObject.

- Physics for games that include many different types of motion such as bounce, gravity and circular motion.
- The side-scrolling, fast-paced game with advanced vehicle physics.
- Learning the specifics and tricks of game optimization, including the "bitmaps versus vectors" argument, and the steps that can be taken to dramatically improve the performance of a game.
- Creating an optimized action game to make use of the optimization techniques covered.
- Using the new BitmapData class and all of the speed and performance enhancements that have been introduced thanks to the bitmap overhaul in Flash 8. It has never been easier to get right down to the pixel level and manipulate things at blazing speeds, making previously impossible games a breeze to make.
- Developing standalone games to be played off of the web, as executable files on the computer. We'll look at using a 3rd party tool to generate the EXE files, as well as the many useful functions that are offered to Macromedia Flash when embedded inside these third party tools.
- Developing games for standalone devices, with specific attention to new Pocket PC systems, which have the Macromedia Flash 6 player built in.
- Understanding the different techniques for producing fast 3D effects, and the ways that they can be used along with various "cheat" techniques to produce powerful results at a maximum of speed performance.
- Creating a large-scale 3D game using the techniques covered.

So sit at the computer, insert the CD-ROM, and prepare to begin your journey into the world of Macromedia Flash Professional 8 game development.

1

THE FLASH 8 RENAISSANCE

Since the first edition of this book, written for Macromedia® Flash™ MX 2004 Professional, things have come a long way in the world of Flash. Flash 8 is a complete overhaul of Flash MX 2004, and luckily for us, the most significant improvements are in areas that directly affect the art of Flash game development. Flash Professional 8 is poised to usher in a renaissance in Flash game development. This is a good time to get on board.

INTRODUCTION TO GAMES

Creating games in Flash Professional 8 is one of the most rewarding endeavors that an aspiring, or seasoned, programmer can pursue. Anyone who chooses to develop games for Macromedia Flash Professional 8 will do so for any number of reasons. It could be for the sheer enjoyment of seeing a creative idea come to life, it could be a specific project for a client, it could be to learn the details of programming Macromedia Flash Professional 8, or it could simply be a way to express oneself.

Before we look at the motivation, let's briefly look at the history of computer games in general.

THE HISTORY OF GAMES

Ever since the early days of humankind, games have been an integral part of our existence. Games allow us to escape from reality, while at the same time they allow us to mimic reality in ways that we might never be able to. The perfect examples are running around the fields as a child playing soldier in a war or exploring far off lands in your own backyard. These experiences allow us to try things we might never actually get to and let us live the fantasy of what we think it would be like.

Enter the computer. The computer allows us to delve into worlds like never before. The computer can be a portal into distant lands and can place us in the storylines of the greatest science fiction and fantasy stories.

Before the electronic game era, we had the old fashioned pinball machines, which can be seen as a precursor to modern video games and as the catalyst that spawned the first general interest in computer games. Looking back at the history of games, it is amazing just how far they have come in a relatively short period of time.

In 1958 Willy Higginbotham, a physicist who worked on the Manhattan Project in 1947, created the world's first electronic game. It was a basic tennis game, rightly called, *Tennis for Two*. In the 21st century the use of the third dimension in games is almost a necessity. However, over 50 years ago this 2D game revolutionized computers and showed how the computer could transition from a purely functional role to entertainment.

The origins of the modern computer game can be traced back to the early days of computer science and the invention of the transistor. At this point the computer became accessible to enough people to warrant the first games and allow the use of these machines for more than just business tasks. These games were very simple, and the earliest example, *Spacewar!*, was created in 1961 to run on the first PDP-1 computer at MIT. This game consisted simply of a few dots on screen meant to represent spaceships, but even then the potential was evident.

Ralph Baer, considered the father of video games, was at the forefront of early video game development in the 1960s. A pioneer of the television, his goal was to merge the computer and television to create the home console video game. His earliest achievement was the chase game, which consisted of two objects moving along the screen, such as a fox and a hound. By the late 1960s, Baer and his team of developers created a shoot the dots style of game and followed that with a ping-pong game for two players. Ultimately, what Baer developed was what he referred to as the brown box, which was the original incarnation of the home-based console, which today is embodied in the Playstation®, Playstation 2, and the Nintendo GameCube™.

By the 1970s a new, yet humble, computer game industry had emerged. Games such as *Pong*® and *Space Invaders*™ became conversation pieces in many homes. One of the largest companies that emerged from this revolution was Atari®. Behind it all was video game pioneer, Nolan Bushnell. Although other creators, such as Baer, believed that the idea for *Pong* was taken from earlier forms, it was Atari that marketed the game first. To this day, *Pong* is still a landmark, a milestone in the advancement of the gaming industry.

The 1970s also saw the exponential rise of other games such as *Pac Man*® and *Frogger*®. The emergence of the handheld games (today's equivalent being the Nintendo Game Boy®) unfortunately did not help the already growing stigmatism that video games were antisocial; the very consciousness of those who oppose video games today originated during the 1970s. Nevertheless, all these achievements paved the way for advancement in the computer gaming industry in the coming decade.

By the 1980s arcade games were the central hub of an entire generation. Children filled the arcades, spending most of their pocket money to try the new *Donkey Kong* or *Ms. Pac Man* or the improved version of *Space Invaders*, *Galaga*™, or *Galaxian*™.

More importantly, the personal computer became an affordable household item. In early 1982 the Commodore 64 was considered *the* home computer to have. Many games had become a permanent fixture on the Commodore 64, for example, *The Olympics* and *Mission Impossible*. Ultimately, the PC allowed for the ordinary person to learn and use computer programming at home, thus opening the door to many aspiring programmers to begin creating their own PC games and play at home rather than solely at the arcades.

In the years that have followed, games have expanded into many areas of life and have spawned many genres from fiction and nonfiction. Today the latest and greatest games feature real-time rendered 3D graphics with thousands of polygons of detail, millions of colors, lighting, reflection, and full surround sound. In this book we'll be looking at several genres of games, from top-down action, to side-scroller, to behind-the-player 3D. We'll be pushing Macromedia Flash Professional 8 to its limits.

MOTIVATION

Whatever your reason for making games, Macromedia Flash Professional 8 provides the perfect medium to do so. Its interface is straightforward and easy to use, while its programming language is robust and powerful, yet simple once you get the hang of it.

Macromedia Flash Professional 8 introduces so many new features that the doors have literally opened up for a whole new level of Flash game development. What Flash once struggled with, it now does with ease. Effects such as blur and drop shadow that were once created in separate programs and saved as images can now be easily applied at run time to objects on the stage, with little or no overhead. Having direct access to the bitmap at the pixel level allows us to create games that are blazingly fast, with lots of things going on, yet never having to worry about the overhead processes of creating hundreds of instances of processor-intensive objects like movie clips. Flash has always been known as a vector renderer, but the speed at which it copies and displays pixel bitmap data is much faster, and now we can take full advantage of these improvements.

On top of all that, creating a game with Macromedia Flash Professional 8 allows you to deploy your games to millions of people within minutes, giving game developers today more opportunity to make a name for themselves and gain exposure than ever before.

Enjoyment

There's no denying it; it's fun to make games. Once you've overcome the technical hurdles, nothing is more satisfying than watching your creations and ideas come to life.

Potential

One of the most critical roles that Macromedia Flash Professional 8 plays today in the online world is to entertain an audience, and in the online world of mass marketing, this audience translates to advertising revenue. When this happens in a medium, we inevitably see an emergence of corporate clients who want to make use of that technology. In the case of Flash 8, games are a perfect example of this application.

Craig Swann, CEO of CRASH!MEDIA, had these words to say on the importance of games in Macromedia Flash in the modern online world. CRASH!MEDIA can be visited online at *www.crashmedia.com*.

VALUE OF GAMING IN TODAY'S INDUSTRY

There should be no doubt about the importance of gaming in the online community. In an industry where content is king and the medium is nearly as flexible as thought itself, there is almost no limit to what exactly content can be. Since the birth of the Worldwide Web, we have seen a shift in people's experiences. Before the Web we were living in a world where we received our content in a "lean-back" form of communication. Very little was expected of us. So there we sat on our couches, in a vegetative state, leaning back and accepting whatever was broadcast to us as information, the only interaction the clicking of the remote. When the Web came along everything changed. We entered the age of "leaning forward." We began leaning into our screens, searching for information. We were slowly gaining some control—and more important interest in getting involved with data, information, images, text, videos, and of course games.

I was lucky enough to have been born alongside the birth of mainstream video games in the early 80s. *Pacman*, *Donkeykong*, *Frogger*, *Space Invaders*—I was there popping quarters into the arcade on my tippy-toes when they first came out. I've seen these classic games transformed over the decades into games that are now very close to real-life multiplayer simulations. It's incredible, and the one thing that has continued to advance is the interactivity of the games: the feeling of the games and how they are played.

Games take us into a world. The world of the developer. Through the clever use of motion, sound, music, animation, and most importantly interactivity, entire worlds are created. Games take us to another place, our mind focused on the environment of the game—everything else fades out in our perceptions. It really is amazing how mentally involved and focused we become when we play games. This is one of the main reasons games can play an important role in online development of interactive brands. Games *give* something. Anytime, as developers, we create something that goes online we are vying for a piece of a person's life. Think about that; their time; their existence. Yet games are something that we are all guilty of spending hours and hours playing. Escapism.

Without a fancy survey to back me up, and going only on my personal experience of eight years on the Web as both a developer and surfer, I would have to say that as far as entertainment on the Web goes, games take the cake. In my experience, online games are the number one overall activity for people around the world looking for fun on the Web. Clean fun that is! This is largely due to the very existence of Flash. People have been producing the most amazing variety of games using Flash for years now. Flash, due to its ubiquitous nature, has evolved rapidly to become the number one platform for online game development.

Advantages of Flash as a Platform for Games

Macromedia Flash is an excellent tool for creating games because of a combination of factors. First, its scripting environment is sophisticated enough to enable real life physics and motion elements to games. Second, being a vector-based application allows for the creation of TINY graphic elements. This means that sophisticated interactive games can be created and experienced with a very little footprint on bandwidth. Whether on an ultra-fast optical T3 connection or on a 28.8 dial-up modem, Flash games can be experienced just the same—if they are created properly.

One of the unique aspects of games is that they take us into a world where, as developers, we create the rules. We create the characters and the environment. When you have the ability to code an environment with its own sets of natural laws and physics, you truly do create unique interactive experiences. Through the rich integration of sound and music, games allow you to go even further and create strong experiences tying in all of the senses, as they are ultra-focused on gameplay.

This sort of intense user focus can be channeled to help strengthen a brand or concept to the user. Unlike general visiting times to sites, users will often spend as much as an hour playing games. This unusual length of time on an Internet property offers many ways to communicate to the user, whether it is through the game concept itself, or through interstitials, ads, and marketing.

The Internet by its very nature is viral. We tend to hear about things and check them out. The ease of communication on the Internet allows us to easily pass along ideas as well as share things that we find in this seemingly never-ending universe. Games are an amazing way to get people to talk about something and participate. Contesting for high scores has proven to be an excellent way to generate traffic to a site. What better way to win something than by playing fun games?

With Flash we don't have to stop at single-player games either! There are many ways now possible including XML sockets and the Flash Communication Server to facilitate REAL-TIME multiplayer games. This is where things start to get really interesting! Today we can create games and environments that can involve any number of people based on the concept of the game. From our experience, we had the opportunity to create a multiplayer game as part of contesting for a large beverage distributor. The game allowed people from around the world to play and battle each other head to head in real time. The ability to experience an event with someone halfway across the world is something new to us, something that is continuing to grow and flourish. This is the direction we are headed. To communicate, collaborate, and most importantly PLAY with each other. We are living in fabulous times—where the power is truly in our hands to create the very things we envision. It blows my mind to imagine what sort of ways we'll be gaming and sharing our lives with people through the amazing ways we can create games and experiences with Macromedia Flash Professional 8.

Let's move on as we start looking at the first step, the elements of game design, in the next chapter.

2

THE ELEMENTS OF GAME DESIGN

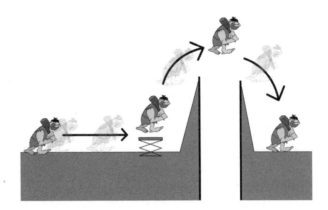

So you've decided that you would like to make a game. The game design process can be one of the most rewarding experiences in computers today. It's the one field that calls for the perfect fusion of creativity and technical expertise. The game maker must be a storyteller, an artist, and a technician. This book doesn't presume that most game designers will have all three of these talents rolled; it focuses mainly on the technical aspect of game coding.

Before you start coding you should be aware of a few things in the overall process of game design. These are the fundamentals—the set of guidelines by which the majority of games are written. There will always be exceptions, of course (a flight simulator, for example, doesn't rely heavily on character development and plot), but on the whole, these are the simple rules by which most good games are made, and following them will ensure that your audience is satisfied.

THE PROCESS

In general, the game creation process consists of several steps, from initial idea to a release-ready product.

1. The Game Idea

This is the first step in good game design. This is when you sit down at a table, most likely away from a computer, and start sketching out ideas for a game design. This is where you ask yourself the big question, "What's this game going to be *about*?" At this stage you decide what *type* of game it is, with a general thought given to your target audience.

For example, the creators of the popular game *Donkey Kong* originally started out saying, "Let's make a game similar to *King Kong*, about a giant ape or gorilla who kidnaps a girl, and you have to rescue her." That would be the extent of the game idea. The specifics of exactly how this idea is presented to the user would be decided in the next step.

2. Genre

This is a simple but important step. This is where you decide exactly what the genre of this game will be. Will it be a first-person shooter like *Doom* or *Half-Life*? Will it be a trivia game? Will it be a puzzle game with blocks? You have to look at your basic idea and decide what type of genre it best fits.

3. Story or Plot Elements

At this stage you sit down and decide exactly what happens in the game. Is it about a rogue soldier on the run from an evil commander? Perhaps it's going to be about an explosion at the fruit factory, wherein you have to catch all the falling fruit in a basket before the timer runs out. These would be two *very* different genres of game. One could be a first person, or side-scrolling action game, while the other could be a *Tetris*-like puzzle game.

If the game follows a specific storyline, or a plot that calls for a series of scripted events, then at this point you have to sit and write out this script. Something like this:

```
Level 1: The Player, Rex Macro, arrives at the missile base. When he WALKS
UP, the guards at the large steel front door stop him. There is a large
hook on a chain attached to the ceiling on a railing.

GUARD 1
Stop! State your name and your reason for being here.

PLAYER
My name is Rex Macro, and my reason for being here is to do this…
```

```
The player must then GRAB THE HOOK and send it hurtling at the guards. It
hits the first one, knocks him out and continues toward the second guard
and hits him, but not before he can sound the alarm.
```

It's almost like a film screenplay, but rather than containing camera instructions, it contains a general list of actions, as well as the details of some interactivity points that the player must be responsible for carrying out for the script to proceed. The points the player is responsible for are capitalized.

This script also contains dialog, so it's easy to see where actors could be hired to read these voices, and animations must be made to illustrate the scene. Alternatively, the dialog could be produced using text overlaid on screen.

4. Game Design Document

Many people would be inclined to skip this step, but this is a critical part of the game design process. The game design document is a culmination of the creative efforts of both the design and the programming team. It puts the entire scope of the game in writing. The game design document should clearly lay out all of the pieces that will come together to make the game, including:

- Theme or plot outline.
- List of locales or environments and a detailed list of what they entail.
- Sketches of maps, bonuses, and puzzles.
- Cast of characters, including player controlled and computer controlled, what they do, how they behave, how they look, and so on. The idea is to give both programmers and artists a clear guideline to follow.
- Storyboards for animations and scripted sequences.
- Technical problems such as sketches of motion paths, formulas, and so on. These are designed to be visual representations of some of the more complex concepts.

The goal of the game design document is to give the programmers something to use as a basis upon which to build the game engine. The document can never be *too* detailed; the more information it contains, the less room there will be later on for conflict arising from misinterpretation (see step 6).

The creation of the design document should be a joint process between producers, programmers, and artists. During its creation, the producers should be at meetings to outline the requirements, programmers should be there to outline the technical requirements and any possible limitations on design, and the artists should be there to suggest creative ideas, as well as determine any visual limitations. This part of the process is more a technical step than a creative step. It is to determine what exactly can and cannot be done. At this point the programmers would speak up and say that the artists must design their art to have, for example, no more than 400 vectors per element. Without this communication, one may end up with a lot of beautiful but impractical artwork.

This is also the opportunity for the artists to suggest ideas the programmers may not be considering. Can we make the background scroll? Can we make the stars change over time? Can we make the flames from the engine flare when the player is accelerating? The programmer would say yes or no, and a good programmer would try and accommodate as many ideas as possible, as these will ultimately contribute to the creation of a great game.

This process will result in a clear, concise design document that all parties can use as a reference. It also provides a nice checklist for the developers to follow.

5. The Core Engine

This where the programming begins. In any game, before story and special effects are fused into the code, a general *engine* must be programmed. In a Nintendo-style side-scroller, for example, a basic engine to draw tile-based levels, scroll them around, and provide collision for the player object and enemy objects must be built.

This would usually be built with a very simple and straightforward test level, perhaps just a few screens wide, with tile blocks that are simply solid colors and a player that is a static, one- or two-frame animation. The key objective in building the core engine is to create a framework upon which the rest of the game can be built and added.

Once you have a game engine that loads in levels, displays enemies, moves them according to scripts, and has a generic collision-handling system, building the game is a matter of level and graphic design. The programmer creates the mold upon which the rest of the game can be built. This means the player can be given a 15-minute game or a 40-hour experience that takes place over multiple sessions, all with the same engine. The difference between these two would be the extent of the level and graphic design, the next step.

6. Level and Graphic Design and Integration

Once the core engine is created, the process of filling out that core engine with game material begins. While the programmer may have created a game that loads a JPEG of his dog as a background image, the artist must take this JPEG and replace it with an actual game background (much to the protest of the programmer, of course). The programmer created the functionality, and the artist creates the actual content; the code provides the tools the artist uses to create the world. Both jobs are equally important, although both often undervalue the other—but that's for another book: *The Politics of Programmer–Artist Interaction*.

The artist has been creating all of the graphics for the game and has been following the game design document, as well as any technical limitations that may be imposed by the engine. It is up to the programmer to create his engine so that it is modular and expandable—so that the artist can create one animation or 100 animations and the code will not break. At the same time, it is up to the programmer to clearly define the parameters and limitations of the engine, so that the artist doesn't waste time designing or creating something that is not technically possible to implement.

This step is a back-and-forth process, as the programmer says, "OK, the engine allows each monster to fire up to two moving projectiles. And for collision purposes, each monster may only move left and right on a given path." Then the artist says, "We want the monster to shoot a solid energy beam as well as a force wave, every so often jumping into the air to add some variation." At this point the programmer has a dilemma: his engine supports discreet projectiles but doesn't currently support the concept of a solid "beam" or a "wave," which are not projectiles and don't fit into the engine structure. His engine also supports simplistic left-right motion for each monster, not jumping, as the artist has suggested. This is possibly due to a technical limitation; perhaps the addition of jumping means the monster requires a completely different and more complex collision scheme, and perhaps this will have a detrimental effect on game performance. Or perhaps it's simply due to a programming oversight. The artist has asked for something because he, as an artist knows it will be great for the game, even though the programmer has specified what the limitations of the engine are. How does the programmer convey to a nontechnical team member something that is highly technical in nature? Who has to yield? There are two options:

- The artist can recognize this limitation and modify his design accordingly. Rather than asking for a beam, he could find a way to make the projectiles look really, really cool (possibly cooler than the beam would *ever* have been), and the player would certainly never know the difference.
- The programmer can recognize the importance of adding beams to the engine and take the time to expand the code to allow this. Once this is done, if it's coded right, all monsters, players, turrets, sentries, and so on, would have the ability to support a variety of beam-type weapons; this is the principal behind an *engine*. The programmer could also explore expanding the monster's collision code to allow for vertical motion or perhaps find a way to emulate vertical motion through trickery and animation, thus not requiring any collision detection.

So, which of these two options would you follow? The answer depends upon several factors that are all very important to consider in game design:

Scope: Does the design call for something that's outside of the original scope of the game? Does it overtly ignore the game design document? If so, then it can be said that the *scope* of the game has begun to grow, and this usually translates to changes in deadlines, dollars, and so on.

Deadline: Is there enough time to put in the requested changes? This is often a straightforward yes or no and allows the decision to be simple.

Priority: If it turns out that beams are going to become a major part of the game, across the board, then it's probably a good plan to build them in because they're of a higher priority and have the added bonus of being reusable.

This step can be fraught with difficulty as opinions and egos can collide; two people believe that two opposite things are correct. The programmer believes the artist can modify his design enough to fit within the programmatic structure, and the artist believes the programmer can expand his program easily to accommodate the new artistic design. Don't get caught in this trap. By far, the best solution is to have a good solid team who *communicates* clearly. Communication is paramount. Many good ideas have ruined a game because they had such a detrimental effect on game performance. Conversely, many great games were only made great because features like advanced lighting, reflections, and weapon effects were added at the end, which really made the game engine shine.

7. Game Play

At this point in the game creation process, the specific elements of the game play are programmed and solidified. While a great engine may have been created, that engine should have been built so that game play elements could be added in. For example, imagine one level that calls for a church bell to come crashing down the bell tower just as the player dives out of the way. Where does "falling, crashing bell" fit in the game engine? Probably nowhere, because this happens only once and is a special case. This is a game play element that must be coded. Ideally, objects in general will have an open-ended control scripting set-up so that they can be expanded and modified to allow them to take on specific roles and actions.

In the game play stage the programmers and artists would also be adding things like power-ups, bonuses, and general things that help to fill in the game and take it from being an engine to being a developed, professional game. While the core engine may consist of running around and shooting a variety of weapons at enemies, the game play step is where we add that special bonus you can pick up to make yourself invincible.

8. Computer A.I.

This step doesn't necessarily come *after* the previous steps, but it generally is focused on later in the development. This is where we concentrate on making the enemies behave like enemies—giving them their brains, or artificial intelligence (A.I.). Here we code some logic into them, so that they don't just walk around and shoot blindly, but actually wait until they've got you lined up in their sights and then shoot. Or perhaps if your weapons are injuring them, they'll flee and try to find safety.

At this point all the attributes and logic points of A.I. are programmed. Most of these should have been defined in the game design document. What is this enemy's threshold for damage? What's their aim like? How aggressive are they? How smart are they? Do they respond to your sound or just your sight? A.I. is an entire field of study unto itself, and much research has gone into the creation of realistic A.I.

The bottom line is that it all depends on the technical limitations and the time limitations. Making an enemy who constantly monitors your movements, constantly checks for exits, and constantly looks at different paths for moving around objects is a fun programming exercise, but the computer processing required to run it can be restrictive to the game performance. Add onto that the physical computation required for each enemy, for basic collision, and for physics and motion, and adding even a few of these super-enemies can make a game unplayable.

9. Story Elements

Remember that movie-like script we looked at earlier? This is the point when these elements are implemented. We're talking about elements that don't necessarily make use of the core engine but are a critical part of the overall game play *experience*. Perhaps these are movies that play between each level or small animations meant to play when the player reaches a certain trigger point in the level. This step can be thought of as the glue that binds everything else together and gives the visuals and game experience that finished polish.

The story elements are necessary to increase the player's attachment to the game and give a *point* to all this running and shooting.

10. Sound and Music

This step is done at two different stages in the production processes. When it comes to voices and character acting, the audio is usually recorded very early on in the creative process so animators can take those voices and create lip synching to the animation.

The music and sound effects are often done toward the end of the game production because it's only when you have the visuals and the feel of the game that you can truly determine what type of music you want to use to give the game its sense of emotion. While the visuals may be powerful and striking, it is music that the human mind tends to assimilate into the mix to determine just how a scene should be making it feel. The combination of stirring music and powerful imagery can be enough to make a game an instant classic.

The sound effects are also a multistage process. Toward the beginning of production, simple sound effects, or *placeholder* sound effects, are used to allow the audio engine to be tested, as well as to give the designers and coders an elementary sense of how the final game will feel. Once the look and feel has been established, a sound designer will usually go through the game's sound effects and modify them and expand them to give them the extra edge. Very much like film production, this can be seen as the postproduction process.

11. User Interface

This is one of the final elements in game creation and is often overlooked. Generally, the programmers will build a rudimentary user interface at the very beginning to facilitate their testing and development of the game. Toward the end, the artists must take the user interface experience and make it really cool. Remember, the user interface is the first thing the player will see, and you never get a second chance to make a first impression. The user interface generally consists of the following:

Play button: This is probably the most important part of the user interface and generally comes in a number of different flavors. It can say Play, Start, or any number of different things. It could be a series of interactive doorways, for example, or a series of screens asking the player to create a character or select a difficulty level. No matter what the implementation, this part of the user interface has one purpose: to let the user start playing the game.

Load/Save: Games that allow the user to load or save their games usually allow the user to perform these actions from some sort of user interface. A list, or table, of saved games or an input field asking for a name by which to save usually follows this.

Quit: Yes, eventually most players will end up needing to leave the game.

Options: Many games have a slew of options available and are highly configurable. From key mappings, to quality settings to simple things like sound on/off, options are very important to the average user.

Remember, the user interface is your first opportunity to hook the player into your game universe. The look and feel of the user interface will often emulate a specific element within the game. For example, a futuristic military game may present all of its options on battle-worn display screens, set to a backdrop of explosions and orchestral music.

12. Testing and Debugging

That's generally it for the design part of the game creation process. At this point the game will be mostly finished and the product will usually be ready for some heavy alpha and beta testing. Some say this stage is when the real work begins for the production team.

It's a good idea to perform a thorough series of tests on your games, because testers will be far more forgiving than end-users when the main character suddenly becomes stuck between a rock and a juniper bush. Have the testers try to break the game. They should test game play and the user interface.

Testers will find all sorts of things you never even thought of, or things that you never discovered because you, as a developer, specifically avoided doing them. For example, the tester may walk into a particular wall and find a way to walk through it. You would have never discovered this because you would never waste precious development time walking into walls. These are the obvious bugs that need to be fixed.

On the other hand, testers will give you reports that are more opinions than bugs. A tester may say, "I can't jump high enough from this platform. I keep dying." You may have intended that or perhaps there's a secret solution that the tester hasn't discovered. When the game is behaving as designed but testers still complain, perhaps it's time to reconsider the design. In this way, testers are not just looking for bugs; they're your test screening audience as well. You may find yourself having to make hard decisions to get rid of something that you spent hours coding, because players are finding it difficult or inhibitive to game enjoyment. The most important thing is that games must be fun. Listen to the feedback of testers (who could simply be friends and family) and see how you can modify your game to enhance the experience. This is the step when the game design document often goes out the window, mainly because it's impossible to completely predict what will be good and what will be bad when designing a document on paper eight months before the game even exists.

It has been said that it takes 10% of the time to do 90% of the work (development process) and then 90% of the time to do the remaining 10% of the work (testing and debugging). Be prepared for this. This step can make developers hate their own games. When you've performed a particular jump or maneuvre for the 500th time because a single tester caused it to crash once on that jump and you absolutely cannot reproduce the crash, you will soon find yourself never wanting to see that jump again. Multiply that by the entire length of the game, and you may be happy to squash that last bug and then never look back.

What's in a Game?

What exactly makes a good game? Why do critics and players alike hail some games, while other games end up in the bargain bin after a few weeks? Usually, the good games are separated from the bad games by only a few simple criteria. Generally, with bad games, one can easily locate the problem from the following items and see exactly where things went wrong.

Technical Performance

This is probably one of the most important things in a game, period. This is a look at how well your game actually plays: how responsive it is, how smooth it is, the frame rate, and so on.

Let's imagine a scene where the player is supposed to run along and then jump over a waterfall to a ledge on the other side. Let's say, however, that the programmers didn't do the waterfall code very well, and whenever a waterfall is on screen, the game performance suffers. So, the player is running along, and the waterfall begins to come onto the screen. As it does, the frame rate drops from a smooth 30 frames per second, to about 5 frames per second. As this happens, the player's temporal perceptions go all out of kilter and he ends up jumping early. At the old 30 frames per second that would have been fine, but the sudden drop in game performance meant that he misjudged and fell to his death.

The player will probably say a few unkind words and possibly turn off the game, never to return, especially if this is an online game, where the visitation of a user is as whimsical as hitting Back or clicking on another link. Performance *is* the difference between a playable game and an unplayable game. Let's face it: bad performance looks *unprofessional*.

Who is responsible for ensuring that this doesn't happen? Well, we could say that the programmer who made the waterfall didn't do a very good job of optimizing the game engine. Or perhaps the programmer knew of this but still allowed it to be put in the game. Or perhaps the programmer knew and said something, but the artistic or management team insisted on putting it in regardless. In each case, someone forgot that the most important part of the game experience is performance. It doesn't matter how beautiful the graphics are; it doesn't matter how stirring the music is; it doesn't matter which actors were hired to do the voices; it doesn't matter how lifelike the physics are. If the game becomes unplayable at *any* time, then something has to be changed. In our example getting rid of the waterfall would have been the *only* solution if its performance could not be improved.

In games developed with C/C++ using the latest DirectX technology, playing on the latest computers, performance is becoming less and less of an issue. With Macromedia Flash Professional 8, however, things are a little bit different. Many strides have been made in this version to allow us to make things much, much faster than Macromedia Flash MX 2004, but we're still in a position where we always have to consider game performance issues. We'll look at this in detail later in the book, in optimizations and in bitmaps in Chapter 10 and 11.

Interactivity and Control

Interactivity and control are ways of describing the act of *using* the game. It is looking at how the player causes the character to move and shoot. Control is a way of describing the ease with which the player can make the game do what it is primarily designed to do; it's very controllable. Interactivity is a way of describing the mechanical process by which the player performs that control.

Looking at today's most popular games, one only has to take five minutes to realize why they're so popular. They're very interactive and easy to use, and the player has a high level of intuitive control over the character. In a first-person shooter running, jumping, and turning to the left and then shooting are a complex series of actions, but because of the interactivity of these games, they're easy to control, and as a result these actions are simply a matter of pressing the W key and the spacebar and moving the mouse to the left while pressing the left mouse button.

The player's actions should produce the results he expects, and those results should be smooth, fluid, and realistic. In some ways this is similar to the previous point on performance; bad control can make the game performance appear to be unrealistic and not lifelike. In real life we move in curves and arcs, and motion tends to have momentum and recoil associated with it—the basic Newtonian laws of action and reaction. When a game appears not to follow these, the player doesn't necessarily know *what* is wrong, but he knows that something just feels *weird*.

Control is not just about keyboard and mouse interactivity; it can also be about good and bad physics. Imagine this hypothetical situation. Most players expect horizontal and vertical momentum to be treated independently, and in real life they generally are. So when a player is running along and he hits a springboard on the ground, he expects to be catapulted upward, but he also expects to maintain the horizontal motion he had before hitting the springboard. Let's imagine that the programmer made a mistake here and programmed it so that the player gains a lot of vertical motion but loses all horizontal motion when he hits the springboard. We have a player who was running at 10 miles per hour suddenly stop moving to the right and start flying straight up. The motion has lost its curve—its arc. The player has made an L shape with the ground, which is very unnatural, like in Figure 2.1.

Let's look at the same example with good control. The player is running along and sees the springboard ahead. He runs toward it and then hits it. His vertical velocity is suddenly injected with a huge boost and he starts to move upward. Because he was already moving horizontally, the two motions superimpose and the player performs a nice, smooth arc—up and over the pit he was trying to get past, like in Figure 2.2.

FIGURE 2.1   Bad control resulting in unnatural motion.

FIGURE 2.2   Good control resulting in naturally arced motion.

Story

It is the storyline of the game that will extract emotion from a player. Through the story, the player will maintain a greater interest and a higher sense of purpose in a game. The story provides the motivation to progress and work toward the resolution.

In a typical game with a strong story, the player is the hero, or lead character, like the protagonist in a film. The player is usually entrusted with an important task, not the least of which is saving the universe, or on a slow day, the world. Some games rely largely on plot, while others only require a simple peripheral plot. In a

World War II shooter, your character is part of a great story, which is nothing short of the triumph of good over evil on a global scale. You will be given missions, your character will have a name, and you will take on that character and all of the aspects of his personality.

In a puzzle game that consists of clearing blocks from an on-screen grid, the plot is not so much the focus. Perhaps something as simple as "There has been an explosion at the cardboard box factory and boxes are falling all over the city. Can you help the city clean them up before it's too late and everyone is swallowed up in a corrugated sea of recyclable cardboard?" The plot does little except help give the game a sense of meaning, possibly trying to explain the presence of these falling boxes. The player may also gain a sense of purpose from this as he tries to work toward the eventual goal of freeing the city.

Goal, Challenge, and Reward

There is a famous phrase that goes something like, "Nothing worth having is easily attained." This general life philosophy also applies to games. All games must be challenging to the player, and overcoming these *challenges* allows the player to have a sense of *reward* from achieving his *goals*. A good challenge should always make itself known to the player and give the player a clear indicator that there's a definite way to beat it and what the goal is.

A giant wall may look impossible to scale, except for the nicely placed bricks that jut out slightly from its surface. These give the player the clues as to what the goal is (getting over the wall), the challenge (jump from brick to brick without falling), and the reward (access to whatever is on the other side of the wall).

Take for example the screen full of gems that must be cleared. The goal is to clear the board, the challenge is doing it without losing, and the reward is the bonus associated with successfully completing the goal at the end of the level.

The rewards must be worth the effort, or players may tire of doing the same thing over and over. Sometimes a bonus, such as an extra life or a stronger weapon, may be awarded. These are rewards that have a distinct functional application. Be careful of rewards that have no particular purpose, such as watching the character do a victory dance. These rewards will quickly lose their appeal to the player because they will be perceived as simply *eye candy*. The player may feel shortchanged for all his hard work if he doesn't get something he can *use* toward his game experience.

Goals, challenges, and rewards should always feed back into the game to produce more goals, challenges, and rewards—something that eye candy does not do. The money (reward) your character won in the sword battle (challenge) will be usable later to buy the jetpack that will allow you to get past the dragon (challenge) to the top of the mountain (goal) and find the super word (reward). With this, you can continue on to overcome more challenges and win more rewards and ultimately achieve more goals. It's easy to put in a hundred eye candy rewards, but it doesn't make a good game. However, to put in hundreds of rewards that are all part of a large plot is hard to do but makes a very good game.

How about something that's not fictional, like a flight simulator? The goal is to become a good pilot, the challenge is in mastering the technique of flying and controlling the aircraft, and the reward is a successful take off, flight, and landing.

Repeatability

A good game is a game the player can enjoy many times. These are the games we come back to time and time again because they make us feel good and we love to get into them all over again, just like movies we love to watch over and over.

One of the ways a game can be made repeatable is to add enough game play options so that playing it once does not let the player experience everything. Perhaps there were two or three paths the player could have taken at one point. Perhaps the player could have joined one of four different races and therefore had one of four different experiences. Perhaps the player could have played a good or evil character. Perhaps the game offers easy, medium, and hard difficulty options.

Whatever the game, there are many ways of making it so that the player will come back and replay it. Unlike a movie, which is unchanging once it is released, a game is interactive, and because of that it inherently has replay all over it.

SUMMARY

In this chapter we looked at the fundamentals of game design and development. Though we didn't look at any code, we did look at what needs to be done *before* the code starts and the pixels are painted. In the next chapter, we're going to start looking at coding.

- We looked at the key steps behind the creation of a game from the game idea to testing and debugging.
- We looked at the different elements that must come together to make a *great* game.

WHACK A CAPSULE

In this chapter we begin our journey down the long and exciting road of making games with Macromedia Flash Professional 8—a road that will be both smooth and bumpy. Over the next five chapters, we're going to be creating some games and learning the fundamental programming techniques that will allow us to create bigger, more complex games.

In this chapter we're going to take a classic amusement park game and recreate it in Flash Professional 8. This is going to be the first in our series of five simple games, each one getting progressively more complex. After we've gone through these five games, we'll start getting into some *really* complex games, with a larger scope and combination of Flash 8 programming principles and general game programming fundamentals. Our first game is going to be called *Whack a Capsule*.

ABOUT THE GAME

Most of us have seen this game before in real life. Whether it's in the midway of an amusement park, or the play area at a children's theme restaurant, this game is the same. It comes under many names, but the most famous iteration of it is the classic *Whack-a-Mole*.

The idea behind the game is simple. There are nine holes in a playing surface. Within each hole is a plastic mole (the animal) on the end of a hydraulically activated pole. At random, these poles rise quickly up so that the mole is protruding from the hole. When this happens, the player must take a mallet or hammer of some sort and whack the mole hard on the head, sending it back down into the hole. If the player is fast enough and strikes the mole, he scores some points, but if he's not fast enough, the mole will drop back down into its hole, and the opportunity to score will be lost. With nine holes going, and nine moles shooting quickly in and out of the board, it can become quite a hilarious (and frustrating) venture trying to hit them fast enough.

Now, it's true that this game has been remade into Flash many times, but we're going to do it here just to say we've done it, get it out of the way, and learn a few great Flash game development principals.

In the development of this game we're going to be creating the simple Flash animations and the code, but the graphics are up to you. You can load and use the sample graphics that were created for this chapter, but as you'll soon see, the graphics that we're using were created in an external 3D application. This is an important concept that many Flash developers miss. Sometimes it's good to do all the graphics in Flash, but on many occasions the best results are achieved in an external graphics package and then imported as bitmaps or vectors into Flash. In this example, we've used 3ds Max to create a bitmap background and PNG (bitmap with transparency) game pieces. Figure 3.1 shows the game in action:

FIGURE 3.1   Whack a Capsule in action.

Our rendition is called Whack a Capsule because rather than whacking moles, we whack blue plastic capsules that move in and out of the red plastic tubes—same game, different colorful and friendly look. Feel free to make your own graphics, but for now we're going to give instructions as if you're using our graphics, which have been provided in the folder for Chapter 3 on the accompanying CD-ROM.

ON THE CD

BUILDING THE GAME

We call it building because it's more than just coding: with Flash, we have to create the graphical elements as well as write the code in order for anything useful to happen. In the case of Whack a Capsule, we can build these graphics ourselves, but as most programmers are not professional artists, in a fully produced commercial game it is probably best to get a skilled artist or animator to create your images. You can use the 3D graphics included or you can make your own.

We're assuming that Flash 8 is already installed on your computer and that you know how to open and navigate around Flash for the most part. So, for starters, make sure that Flash 8 is open.

1. When Flash Professional 8 first opens up, choose Flash Document, from underneath the Create New section.
2. Alternatively, if Flash is already open, press Ctrl-N to create a new document. In the New Document dialog box that appears, ensure that the General tab is selected and choose the Flash Document from the Type list and then click OK, as indicated in Figure 3.2.

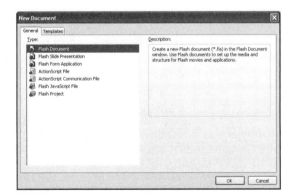

FIGURE 3.2   The New Document dialog box.

At the bottom of the screen we can see the Properties panel for our new movie. This is where we set certain details about our movie such as Size, Background color, and Frame Rate, as shown in Figure 3.3. If this doesn't appear at the bottom of the screen, you must make sure that you have the Properties panel visible by pressing Ctrl-F3. If the Properties panel is visible, but you do not see Size,

Background, and Frame Rate, you must be sure to have nothing else selected. To do this, simply click with the selection tool on the gray area that surrounds the stage.

FIGURE 3.3   The movie Properties panel.

3. On the Properties panel, click on the Size button to open up the Document Properties dialog box. You can also open the Document Properties dialog box at any time by pressing Ctrl-J.
4. In the Document Properties dialog box set the Width to 640, the Height to 480, and the Frame Rate to 31 fps, as shown in Figure 3.4.

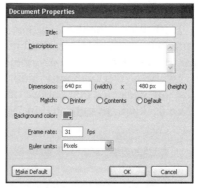

FIGURE 3.4   The Document Properties dialog box.

5. Close the dialog box by clicking OK.

Our movie is now ready to begin building Whack a Capsule. First, we must create the background. If you want to create your own background image, you must create your image to be 640 × 480 in size.

6. Create a new layer by pressing the New Layer button. That's the small button with the + symbol in it at the bottom-left corner of the timeline.
7. There should now be two layers in the timeline. The bottom one should be called Layer 1. Double-click on the text that says Layer 1 and type in the new title, Background.

From now on, we will refer to these steps simply by saying "Create a new layer and name it, 'whatever,'" where the word whatever would be replaced with the name of the new layer we're creating.

8. *With the background layer selected,* open the File menu and choose Import > Import to Stage or press Ctrl-R (see Figure 3.5).

FIGURE 3.5   Importing the background image.

9. In the dialog box that appears navigate to the sample graphics included with this chapter (or to your own file if you wish to make one) and choose the file gamebg.jpg.
10. Click Open. The background image will appear on the stage. The stage should look like Figure 3.6.

FIGURE 3.6   The imported background image.

11. Create the rest of the layers and name them from top to bottom: `Action-script`, `Title`, `UI`, `Front Row`, `Middle Row`, and `Back Row`. `Background` should already be there. The entire thing should look like Figure 3.7.

FIGURE 3.7   The layers for the game.

Now that we have all the layers ready to build upon, let's lock the background layer so that our future selecting and drawing doesn't inadvertently select and move the background jpeg around. Click on the Lock icon, to the right of the word Background on the background layer.

Now we're going to start drawing the game elements. We'll begin with the game title. This is simply a regular movie clip that starts off above everything else. Its purpose is to provide the player with some game instructions as well as act as a device whose mouse press event we will use to start the game (more on that later, when we get to the code for the game).

12. On the `Title` layer, draw a graphic that looks approximately like the one in Figure 3.8. It should be exactly the same size of the stage (640 × 480) and it should completely cover the background layer. I've chosen to make the title movie clip a red box in the middle of the screen, with a larger 50% alpha black box around it.

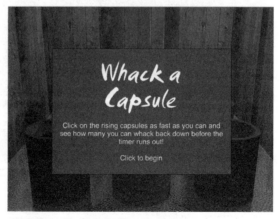

FIGURE 3.8   The game title movie clip.

13. Once the graphic is drawn, select the entire image and press F8.
14. The Convert to Symbol dialog box will appear. In the Name text box type "startScreen." Next to the word Behavior, make sure Movie Clip is selected. Next to the word Registration, make sure the small box in the top middle of the nine boxes is selected (darkened). Take a look at Figure 3.9 to see how things should be.

FIGURE 3.9   Creating the title screen movie clip.

15. Click OK, and the title screen will now be on the stage as a movie clip.
16. Look at the Properties panel and you will see a text field that says <Instance Name> in it. Click inside this text field and type "titleScreen." Now this instance of the startScreen movie clip is called titleScreen.

Now that the title screen is created, we don't need to do anything more with it at the moment, so hide the layer by clicking on the eye icon next to the word Title on the Title layer. The next thing we're going to create is the score display area.

17. Make sure the UI layer is selected.
18. Draw a box near the upper-right corner of the stage, making it approximately 300 wide and 50 high.
19. Select it and convert it to a movie clip by pressing F8 and then make sure it is named scoreDisp.
20. Click on the OK button.
21. With the newly created movie clip selected, right-click and choose Edit. We will now be editing the scoreDisp movie clip.
22. You can create this movie clip to look any way you want, but the most important thing is that there must be two dynamic text fields within it.
23. Select the Text tool from the Tools panel and draw a text field near the left side of the box.
24. With that text field still selected, change its type to Dynamic Text and give it the instance name time_txt, as shown in Figure 3.10.
25. Draw another text field near the right end of the movie clip and set it up the same as the previous text field, but this time give it the instance name whack_txt.
26. Create a label for the right text field. Anything will do, but the word "Whacks" seems most descriptive. The final movie clip should look like Figure 3.11.

FIGURE 3.10   Creating the time display text field.

FIGURE 3.11   The score display movie clip.

27. Return to the main timeline by clicking on the word Scene 1 near the top of the screen next to the word `scoreDisp`.
28. Click on the movie clip and give it an instance name of `scoreDisplay`.

Now that our score display movie clip has been created, it should be placed in the upper-right corner of the game stage, like in Figure 3.12.

FIGURE 3.12   The placement of the score display movie clip.

Now that we're done with that, we're ready to create our "moles." These are the capsules that will move up and down, in and out of the red drums. The following needs to be done:

- Create a simple movie clip that consists of a 20-frame animation.
- From frames 1 to 10, the capsule is rising, and from frames 11 to 20 the capsule is lowering.
- We have some Actionscript code on frame 1 to stop the animation, and we have code on frame 10 to stop the animation.
- We use a mask layer to allow the capsule to appear as if it's actually dropping *behind* the front side of the tube that it's inside of.

Because of the perspective, lighting, and shade difference between them, we have to create three versions of this movie clip. One is for the left column of three, one for the middle column, and the other for the right column. The only difference between these is the bitmap image used for the capsule and the shape of the mask used. We're going to look at creating just one of these, and the other

two can be an exercise for you. If you created your own graphics and didn't create a 3D perspective in your version, you may not need three different perspec-
tives. Either way, let's look at creating the left column perspective capsule.
Because each capsule movie clip is functionally the same, whether you create
three versions, one version, or even nine versions is irrelevant as long as they are
20 frames long and have a stop action on frame 1 and 10.

29. With the `Front Row` layer selected, import the file `leftcapsule.png` to the stage.
30. The blue capsule will appear on the stage. Grab it and drag it down so
    that it is positioned in front of the front, left tube, like Figure 3.13.

FIGURE 3.13   Positioning the first capsule.

31. With the blue capsule selected, convert it to a movie clip and give it the
    movie clip name `leftOne`.
32. Right-click on this new movie clip and select Edit in Place, or simply
    double-click on it. We will now be editing the movie clip so that it's pos-
    sible to still see the background image lightly in the background, like in
    Figure 3.14.

FIGURE 3.14   Editing the capsule movie
clip in place.

33. Name the layer that the capsule is on `Capsule`.
34. Create a new layer above the `Capsule` layer and give it the name `Mask`.
35. On the `Mask` layer use the paintbrush tool to carefully draw so that only the area above the near wall of the tube is covered. The paintbrush drawing should not extend forward beyond the front lip of the tube. There's no real easy way to do this, and it has to be done basically by eye. Remember to paint quite high, as the mask has to cover as much of the capsule as is exposed when it is fully protruding from the tube. Look at Figure 3.15 for an idea of how this is done.

FIGURE 3.15   Drawing the mask.

36. In the timeline, click on frame 20 of the `Mask` layer and press F5. This will extend the mask to cover the entire length of our animation.
37. Right-click on the `Mask` layer label (left of the timeline) and from the drop down menu that appears, choose the word Mask. Now the capsule should appear as if it is sticking out of the top of the tube.
38. Click on frame 20 of the `Capsule` layer and press F6. This will duplicate the capsule's position as a keyframe on frame 20.
39. Click on frame 1 of the `Capsule` layer and from the Properties panel change the Tween type from None to Motion.
40. Click on frame 10 of the `Capsule` layer and press F6. This will be the keyframe that will define the top of the capsule's ascent.
41. Unlock the `Capsule` layer and drag the capsule up so that it is protruding a realistic height from the tube. Notice that unlocking the `Capsule` layer will cause the mask to appear. Simply hide the `Mask` layer if it is getting in the way. To see how the final capsule looks on frame 10, relock the layer and make sure the `Mask` layer is not hidden. Notice that in this case the capsule will need to be dragged up and slightly to the left to follow in line with the angle of the render. It should look something like Figure 3.16.

FIGURE 3.16   The top of the capsule's motion, with masking applied.

42. Finally, insert a new layer above the `Mask` layer and call it `Code`.
43. Click on frame 1 of the `Code` layer and open up the Actions panel by pressing F9.
44. In the Actions panel that appears, type the code `Stop();`.
45. Click on frame 10 of the `Code` layer and press F6 to insert a keyframe.
46. Again, with the newly created frame 10 selected, type the code `Stop();` in the Actions panel. The final timeline for the capsule movie clip should look like Figure 3.17.

FIGURE 3.17   The timeline of a capsule movie clip.

Repeat steps 28 to 46 to create the other two capsule movie clips, middle and right, naming them `middleOne` and `rightOne`. Most of the process will be the same. The only differences will be the mask shape and the imported filename. Rather than `leftcapsule.png`, load `midcapsule.png` and then `rightcapsule.png`. These differ in their rendering angle and lighting.

All done? OK, we're almost there. We've got the front row created: three capsule movie clips. We must copy these movie clips to create the other two rows.

47. Select all three movie clips and press Ctrl-C or choose Copy from the Edit menu.
48. Select the next layer down, called `Middle Row`.

49. Paste the movie clips (Ctrl-V or Edit > Paste) and then line them up such that they're positioned similarly to the first row, but now the copied left, middle, and right movie clips are lined up with the second row.
50. With all three movie clips selected, press Ctrl-T to bring up the Transform dialog box.
51. Within the Transform dialog box, change the horizontal and vertical scale to 80. The movie clips should be sized so that they now fit nicely within the middle row of tubes.
52. Carefully line them up so that the capsules are perfectly lined up with the tubes.
53. Repeat steps 47 to 51, but this time paste the three capsules for the back row. Instead of scaling to 80%, scale them to 60% in the Transform dialog box.

Now there should be nine capsule movie clips on screen, nicely masked and nicely lined up with the tubes that they're supposed to inhabit. Now that these have been created, they need to be given instance names, as they're going to be driven with Actionscript in a short while.

54. Starting with the closest, leftmost capsule, give it an instance name of m0. (Remember, instance names are set by selecting the movie clip and placing the name in the Properties dialog box, which is opened with Ctrl-F3)
55. Going to the right, set the instance names of the rest of the front row to m1 and m2.
56. In the same left to right fashion, name the second row capsules m3, m4, and m5.
57. Again in the same way, name the back row capsule instances m6, m7, and m8.

Now we're nearly ready to begin coding. All of our graphic layers have their necessary items on them, but there's one more graphic that we need to create. This one isn't on the stage already, because it's going to be dynamically placed on stage at runtime. All we need is to make sure it's in the library.

At any time, if you want to make changes to any of the graphics, you can do so from the Library. Open up the Library by pressing Ctrl-L. The Library is a useful tool for navigating through our graphical assets, and at any time, we can drag an item from the Library onto the stage to create an instance of it in our movie. There is a fundamental difference between a movie clip in the Library and a movie clip on the stage: the stage contains instances of movie clips from the library. We can create as many instances as we want of one movie clip from the Library.

The graphic we're going to be creating is simple. It's a small burst graphic used to give the player a visual indication that he has indeed scored a successful whack. The one I created looks like the one in Figure 3.18.

The best way to create this is to go somewhere off stage and start drawing it in the surrounding space.

FIGURE 3.18   Whack! Just like Batman used to make!

58. Start by drawing the starburst background shape. It should be about 150 wide by 120 high.
59. Once it's drawn, select it and convert it to a movie clip by pressing F8.
60. In the Convert to Symbol dialog box, enter whackSign as the movie clip name and make sure the Behavior is set to Movie Clip. In the Registration selection, choose the center box of the nine boxes.
61. If you see a button below this that says Advanced, then click it.
62. In the lower half of the dialog box is a large area called Linkage. Click on the check box that says Export for Actionscript.
63. Once that is selected, the two text fields above it will become editable. In the text field labeled Identifier enter the word whackSign. We can leave the AS 2.0 Class text box empty.
64. Press the OK button.
65. Double-click on the movie clip and go in and add the overlaid text so that it says, "Whack!"
66. Once you are finished, click on the Scene 1 link above the Timeline layers to return to the main movie timeline.
67. Finally, delete this movie clip from the stage. Yes, that's right. It's not needed here anymore. It was just placed there to ease the creation process. The movie clip will be attached at runtime with code.

That's it! Everything needed to create the game is prepared. Now all we need to do is code, but before we do, let's look at what we've done here.

First, we're using the classic combination of animation and code to create an effect. Notice that our capsules' rising and falling motion is animated by hand, rather than being coded. We *could* have coded it, but that would've, in this case, caused more complexity, as each render has a slightly different axis of motion. So we've combined the timeline animation with a few stop frames to create some game-usable graphics.

We've also had our first look at a grid. As we'll see throughout this book (and indeed in the very next chapter), grids abound in games. Grids form the basis of organization for most games from tile-based side scrolling to overhead strategy. The entire concept of an array, be it 1D, 2D, or 3D, is based on a grid. Graphics themselves, being made up of pixels on the screen, are really just a large grid of dots.

Our grid happens to be quite simple, 3 × 3, but it demonstrates this important concept. We could have had one capsule, but that would have made for a boring game. By taking the functionality of one capsule and extending it out to a 3 × 3 grid, we make the game nine times more challenging, yet the core functionality remains expandable. It would be easy, for example, to double or triple the number of capsules on screen if we wanted to make the game even more challenging. The most challenging aspect would be the necessary modifications to the graphics.

CODING THE GAME

We have one layer on our timeline that is as yet untouched. This is the topmost layer, which we labeled Actionscript at the beginning of this chapter. The code for this game is quite simple and it's not heavy on the math end (don't worry, that'll be coming in the next few chapters). Select frame 1 of the Actionscript layer and open the Actions panel by pressing F9 (if it's not already open). Type the following code:

```
titleScreen.onRelease = function()
{
    this._visible = false;
    startgame();
}
```

That's it! Or rather, that's our first function. But what exactly are we doing here? When this code is executed, Flash will create an onRelease function. This simply means that the code within the function will be executed when the player clicks on the item to which it is attached. In this case, that item is the titleScreen movie clip.

Once the player clicks on the titleScreen movie clip (which should be full screen and therefore covering everything else), it will make itself invisible with this._visible = false. This means the title screen will vanish, leaving the game uncovered. At this point, the function startgame will be called. This is the function that we'll be writing next. That's all there is to this opening piece of code.

Next, type the following code:

```
startgame = function()
{
    for (var i = 0; i < 9; i++)
    {
        var nm = "m" + i;

        _root[nm].onPress = function()
        {
            if (this._currentframe == 10)
            {
                this.play();
                whacks++;
                scoreDisplay.whack_txt.text = whacks;
                doWhackAt(_xmouse, _ymouse);
            }
        }

        _root[nm].onEnterFrame = function()
        {
            if (this._currentframe == 1)
            {
                if ((Math.random() * 100) < 1)
                {
                    this.play();
                }
            }
            else if (this._currentframe == 10)
            {
                if ((Math.random() * 100) < 10)
                {
                    this.play();
                }
            }
        }
    }

    whacks = 0;
    scoreDisplay.whack_txt.text = whacks;
    endTime = getTimer() + 30000;

    _root.onEnterFrame = function()
    {
        var etime = endTime - getTimer();

        if (etime <= 0)
        {
            scoreDisplay.time_txt.text = "Time Up";

            for (var i = 0; i < 9; i++)
            {
                var nm = "m" + i;
                delete _root[nm].onPress;
                delete _root[nm].onEnterFrame;
```

```
                    _root[nm].stop();
                    delete _root.onEnterFrame;
                }
            }
            else
            {
                scoreDisplay.time_txt.text = Math.ceil(etime / 1000) + "
    sec";
            }
        }
    }
```

That's our startgame function. What are we doing in this function? We're start-ing off by entering a loop that will see the i variable going through the numbers 0 to 8. We're creating a temporary variable called nm and assigning to it the value of "m" + i. This will cause nm to be m0, m1, m2, all the way up to m8, which correspond to our capsule movie clip names.

We then begin creating functions for each of the capsules. First, we create an onPress function, which is called whenever the player clicks on a capsule. (Not to be confused with onRelease, which is triggered when the player releases the mouse button, onPress is triggered when the player presses down on the mouse button.) This is how we're going to be "whacking" the capsule—by clicking on it. When the capsule is clicked, it's first checked to see if it is on frame 10. Remember, frame 10 is the frame at which the capsule is fully raised. This is the only valid opportunity to strike the capsule and score a whack. Any other moment and you're too early or too late.

If the player *does* click at the right moment, we tell the capsule to play with this.play();. This will cause the capsule to lower back down. We also increment a variable called whacks by 1, with whacks++. Any variable that is a number can be increased by 1 with the ++ operator and decreased by 1 with the -- operator. After the whacks variable is incremented, we display the new value inside the whack_txt text field inside the scoreDisplay movie clip.

The last thing we do upon a successful click is call a function called doWhackAt and pass into that function the current screen position of the mouse cursor. We'll be looking at that shortly. That's it for the onPress function.

Now we create another event function for the capsule movie clip. This time it's an onEnterFrame event, which is called every single frame of our movie. With a 31-frames-per-second movie, onEnterFrame will be called 31 times per second. This function is responsible for giving the capsule some autonomy -- some life. This is the *brain* of the capsule.

It's actually quite simple:

- If the capsule is sitting on frame 1 (down position), choose a random number between 0 and 99.
- If that number is less than 1 (which will happen approximately 1 in 100 times), then this.play(), which will start the capsule on its upward mo-tion. This means each capsule will stay down for an *average* of 3 seconds.

- If the capsule is sitting on frame 10 (the fully extended position), choose a random number between 0 and 99.
- If that number is less than 10 (which will happen approximately 1 in 10 times), then, again, `this.play()`, which will start the capsule on its descent.

The effect is that when the capsule is down, it rises approximately every 3 seconds. If the capsule is up, it will usually begin to drop within a second. This means capsules *can* stay up long enough to get to click, but it's a challenge. And remember, the whack only registers if the capsule is sitting on frame 10. When it's rising (frames 1 to 9) or falling (frames 11 to 20), clicking on it will accomplish nothing. When the movie clip gets to frame 20, it loops back around to frame 1, hits the internal `stop()` action, and then waits for the random command to rise again.

That's all there is to the `onEnterFrame` function. We're done attaching functions to the capsule movie clips. The next thing we do is initialize the `whack` variable to 0 and then display that value in the `scoreDisplay.whack_txt` text field. These lines of code are executed only once per game.

Now we have a line of code that looks like this:

```
endTime = getTimer() + 30000;
```

This line of code is also executed only once per game. By using the `getTimer` function, we create a variable `endTime` to be 30 seconds into the future. Remember, the `getTimer` function returns the number of milliseconds elapsed since the game started to execute. By choosing a time relative to `getTimer`, we can find a nice target time that we'll be using in a moment to determine the amount of time remaining in the game.

Next we create an `onEnterFrame` function that is attached to `_root`. Remember that `_root` is the main timeline and that we can legally attach an `onEnterFrame` function to it. This function is going to be responsible for our timekeeping and determine when the game is over.

The first thing we do is this:

```
var etime = endTime - getTimer();
```

We're creating a temporary variable called `etime`, which is used to keep track of the time remaining between the `endTime` and now (from `getTimer`). The value returned by `getTimer` is constantly changing. The value stored in `endTime` is not. Therefore, `etime` will constantly get smaller and smaller as time elapses.

Based on this fact, we perform a check to see if `etime <= 0`. If `etime` does fall below or equal zero, we know that time's up and we must stop the game. First, we display the text "Time Up" in the `time_txt` text field. Then we step through all 9 of our capsule movie clips and delete the functions that we previously assigned to them:

```
for (var i = 0; i < 9; i++)
{
    var nm = "m" + i;
```

```
    delete _root[nm].onPress;
    delete _root[nm].onEnterFrame;
    _root[nm].stop();
    delete _root.onEnterFrame;
}
```

We delete the onPress and onEnterFrame functions of each capsule and tell the capsule to stop(), no matter where it is in its animation. This will truly create the impression that the game has completely ended. The last line of code is to kill the timer function, which is accomplished by deleting _root.onEnterFrame.

If, on the other hand, etime has not dropped below 0, and therefore the game is still in valid play mode, we simply display the time remaining with the word "sec" in the text field, like so:

```
scoreDisplay.time_txt.text = Math.ceil(etime / 1000) + " sec";
```

Since etime will be a number in milliseconds, we must divide it by 1000 to get a time in seconds. However, we must perform a rounding function for our time remaining reading that will be something like "6.543 sec." We want this to simply say "7 sec." The Math.ceil function causes a number to round up to the nearest whole number.

That's our entire startgame function. Once this code has been executed (by clicking the startScreen and thus calling startgame), the game will spring to life; the capsules will start randomly rising and falling, and the timer will begin at 30 and start counting down. If we wanted to make the timer longer, we would have to change the endTime code to something other than 30000. For example, 60 seconds would be done like so:

```
endTime = getTimer() + 60000;
```

We have one more piece of code remaining. Remember that in our startgame function, on a successful whack we're calling a function called doWhackAt. That's what's left. Enter this code next:

```
wcnt = 0;
doWhackAt = function(x, y)
{
    var nm = "wc" + wcnt;
    _root.attachMovie("whackSign", nm, wcnt + 99);
    _root[nm]._x = x;
    _root[nm]._y = y;
    _root[nm]._xscale = _root[nm]._yscale = 60;

    _root[nm].onEnterFrame = function()
    {
        this._alpha -= 10;
        if (this._alpha <= 10)
        {
            delete this.onEnterFrame;
```

```
            this.removeMovieClip();
        }
    }

    wcnt++;
    wcnt %= 5;
}
```

This code has one specific purpose: to display the "Whack!" graphic at the moment a successful whack has taken place. The function is designed to allow you to place the graphic anywhere on screen, but remember that when the function is called, it is called by passing in the _xmouse and _ymouse variables, which correspond to the position of the mouse cursor. There's no better place to show the graphic than where the player's eye is currently looking—at their mouse cursor. This is also good because if there was a successful hit, you know for sure that the mouse cursor is on the capsule it whacked, making it the correct position to display the "Whack!"

What we're doing here is setting a variable called wcnt to 0. This variable will be used to created instances of the whackSign at run time. We need to keep a counter because it's possible to have more than one whackSign on screen at once (if the player is *really* good at the game), so one fixed name will not work; Flash doesn't allow two movie clip instances to share the same instance name.

Inside the function, the first thing we do is create a temporary variable called nm. Into this we create the string "wc" + wcnt. This means the first instance of the graphic will be named wc0, the next one wc1, then wc2, and so on. Then we use the attachMovie command, which takes a movie clip from the library and attaches it to the stage. In this case we're attaching it to the _root timeline.

- The first parameter attachMovie takes is the linkage identifier (which we specified in the library). In this case, it's whackSign.
- The second parameter is the *instance name* for our new movie clip instance (in this case, the value stored in nm).
- The third parameter is the depth level, which determines the order in which Flash layers things for drawing. Each depth level is rendered on top of the depth levels below it. For good measure, we're adding 99 to wcnt to determine the depth level here, so that our first instance will be at depth 99, then 100, then 101. No two movie clips may be created on the same depth level, so by starting at 99, we guarantee that they're on top and that they'll be far away from any other items that may be around the lower depth levels. By default, the items on the stage at design time will be drawn in the depth order that we specified, so the whackSigns will *always* be on top, even if we started them at 0, but it's still a good practice to attach an unknown number of movie clips in a depth level range that we know is free.

After the movie clip is attached, we set its _x and _y position properties to be the same as the values that were passed in to the function. We then set its _xscale and _yscale properties to 60. This means the movie clip will be scaled to 60% of its original size. This was done because it seemed too big otherwise, so 60% made it size properly. You can play with different values if you want.

We then create an onEnterFrame function for the newly created instance:

```
_root[nm].onEnterFrame = function()
{
    this._alpha -= 10;
    if (this._alpha <= 10)
    {
        delete this.onEnterFrame;
        this.removeMovieClip();
    }
}
```

What we're doing is very simple—fading the movie clip away. We don't want the whackSign to remain on screen forever. We want it to appear quickly and then fade away. Since the _alpha property determined the transparency of a movie clip, subtracting 10 from its transparency value means it will go from 100% to 0% in 10 frames. This is a fast, yet still visible, rate for the whackSign to fade. Once the _alpha value drops below 10 (almost completely invisible), we simply delete the onEnterFrame function and then remove the movie clip altogether with this .removeMovieClip(). Deleting the onEnterFrame function manually like that is a good idea to ensure that no loose, dead processes continue to run, even though they have no context. It's just smart code cleanup.

After this, we have two more lines of code:

```
wcnt++;
wcnt %= 5;
```

This is executed at the end of the doWhatAt function. This simply increments the wcnt variable, allowing the next instance created to have a different instance name. The second line will cause wcnt to "wrap" around at 5 and go back to 0. The value of wcnt will always be 0, 1, 2, 3, 4, 0, 1, 2, 3, 4, and so on, because we're using the %= 5 code. We're using the number 5 because, realistically, it's very unlikely that the player will ever have more than 5 on screen at once, considering that each one fades completely away in 10 frames.

That's the end of that function, and in fact, the end of all the code for the entire game. Now it's time for the fateful test. Press Ctrl-Enter to compile and run the game, or choose Control > Test Movie. If all's well, the game should run, and it's time to start whacking those capsules. My record is 29 capsules in the time period.

EXTENDING THE GAME

How could this game be extended and enhanced? There are several things we could do:

- We could add sound. Sound adds another layer of interactivity to any game, but more of that later in the book.
- We could extend the game into multiple levels. When a round is finished, perhaps move on to a more difficult level.
- Make the game more or less difficult. Increase the randomization odds (change that number 100 to a lower or higher number).
- Make the amount of game time greater than or less than the current 30 seconds.

SUMMARY

In this chapter we have:

- Learned simple concepts such as handling mouse events and user interaction with clicks and releases
- Learned about displaying animated game elements by creating modular movie clips that are both code and animation driven
- Looked at creating simple timers
- Played around with randomness to add some variation to the game play

BLOCK BREAKER

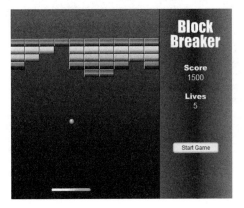

In the last chapter we looked at creating a very simple game with basic mouse-click interactivity. All of our animation was precreated in the Flash design environment, and all of the graphics were prerendered in a 3D rendering program. This allowed for a game that looked pretty cool but lacked somewhat in the game programming fundamentals.

In this chapter we're going to take a step further into the game-programming world and add a few more concepts to our repertoire including simple motion and collision. We're going to recreate a classic called *Breakout* and call it Block Breaker.

ABOUT THE GAME

The idea behind this game is to use a paddle at the bottom of the screen to bounce the flying ball around the stage, causing it to hit the blocks on screen. The paddle moves left and right and is controlled by the mouse. When a block is hit, it will flash and vanish, and 100 points will be added to the player's score. Figure 4.1 shows the game in action.

If the player should miss the ball, it will fly off the bottom of the screen and the player will lose a life. The object of the game is to clear all the blocks from the screen. The game does not begin until the player presses the Start Game button, at which time the score will be set to 0 and the player will be given five lives.

When the game begins, 50 blocks will be created at the top of the screen. They will be placed in 10×5 grid, as shown in Figure 4.2.

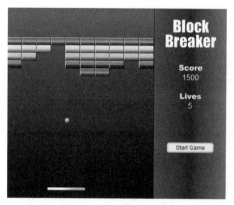

FIGURE 4.2   The grid of blocks created at the start of the game.

FIGURE 4.1   Block Breaker in action.

If this game sounds familiar, that's because there have been many incarnations of it. The original version was called *Breakout*, and it was released in arcades in 1976. It may seem like we're reaching pretty far back for this one, but the best games are often the simplest. These games rely on their simplicity to provide the player with pure, uncomplicated fun.

We're not going to be putting any sound in this game, because we're going to be looking at sound separately, later on in the book (however, it could be a good exercise to come back to this game later and add sound yourself).

BUILDING THE GAME

Now we're going to take a look at putting the whole game together. Make sure Macromedia Flash Professional 8 is open. Create a new, blank Flash document.

We now have Flash 8 looking the way we want it to look to start creating our game. Let's start by creating the graphical elements that our game will require. The graphics are nothing more than boxes and circles, so don't worry—we won't require any major artistic skill.

1. In the Document Properties dialog box (opened with Ctrl-J), set the Width to 480, the Height to 400, and the Frame Rate to 48 fps, as shown in Figure 4.3.

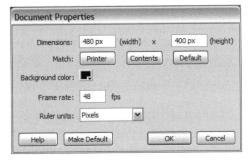

FIGURE 4.3   The Document Properties dialog box.

2. Close the dialog box by clicking OK.
3. We have prepared the stage upon which we will be creating Block Breaker. Let's start by creating the background image.
4. Create a new layer and name it `background`.
5. Draw two boxes on this background layer. One box should be 320 × 400 in size and have its upper-left corner at x position 0, y position 0. The other box should be 160 × 400 and have its upper-left corner at x position 320, y position 0. The colors do not matter, but they should have some differentiation. The left side will be for the game play and the right side will be for the score and lives display. It should look something like Figure 4.4.
6. Create the rest of the layers, and name them from top to bottom: `action-script`, `ball`, `paddle`, and `text`, as shown in Figure 4.5.

FIGURE 4.4   The game background.

FIGURE 4.5   The layers for the game.

Lock the background so that we can no longer select it and inadvertently move it around. Now, let's create the paddle.

7. On the `paddle` layer draw a yellow rectangle that is 80 inches width, and 5 inches height.

To draw an accurate rectangle, use the Properties panel once it has been drawn. Simply draw the rectangle and then select it with the selection tool (draw a box around it or double-click on the shape). Once it's selected, the Properties panel will show information about that shape. You will see four number fields, for Width, Height, x, and y. You can use these to manually set the size and position of any shape you've drawn (see Figure 4.6).

8. Once the paddle rectangle has been created, select it by drawing a rubber band with the selection tool or double-clicking on its center.
9. Convert the rectangle to a movie clip symbol by pressing F8.
10. The Convert to Symbol dialog box will appear. In the Name text box, type "paddle_mc." Next to the word Behavior, make sure Movie Clip is selected. Next to the word Registration, make sure the small box in the top-middle of the nine boxes is selected (darkened). Take a look at Figure 4.7 to see how things should look.

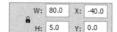

FIGURE 4.6   The manual size and position text fields.

FIGURE 4.7   Creating the paddle movie clip.

11. Click OK, and the paddle will now be created.
12. Back on the main stage, the new paddle movie clip should be selected, but if it is not, click on it to select it.
13. Set its y position to 375. Its x position doesn't matter as much, because at runtime the x position will be determined by the position of the mouse cursor, so place it anywhere on the game play area in x, but at 375 in y.
14. With the paddle still selected, we must give it an instance name. This is the name we will use when manipulating and referring to the object with Actionscript. With the paddle selected, look at the Properties panel and find the text field that says <Instance Name> in it. Click inside this text field and type the word "paddle." Now this instance of the paddle_mc Movie clip is called paddle.

Now we have a paddle sitting on the paddle layer, looking something like Figure 4.8.

At this point it's probably best to lock the paddle layer so you don't accidentally drag and move the paddle. Now we're going to create the ball movie clip. This is done in nearly the same manner as the paddle, with a few minor differences.

15. Make sure the ball layer is selected.
16. On the stage use the Circle tool to draw a white circle that has a width of 10 and a height of 10. The best thing to do is draw a perfect circle of any

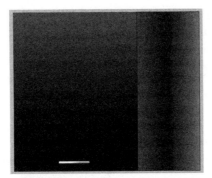

FIGURE 4.8   The paddle and the background.

size by holding down the Shift key while creating the circle. Then select the circle and use the manual numeric entry box in the Properties panel to set its width and height to 10.

17. As with the paddle, convert the circle to a movie clip by selecting it and pressing F8.
18. In the Convert to Symbol dialog box, set the Name of this movie clip to `ball_mc`, set its Behavior to Movie Clip, and this time set its registration point to the tiny black square at the dead center of the group of nine squares, as in Figure 4.9.

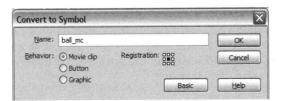

FIGURE 4.9   The symbol properties for the ball movie clip.

19. Press OK.
20. Place the ball somewhere in the middle of the play area and set its instance name (in the Properties panel) to `ball`.

We now have a ball with the instance name `ball` on the screen. We're nearly ready for some code, but first we must create our on-screen text. In the game we make use of two dynamic text fields: one for lives and the other for score. We also have two other text fields that are *not* dynamic (they remain the same for the entire game). These are called *static* text fields and they are merely labels that read "Lives" and "Score," and these go above the dynamic text fields. One more text field at the top of the screen is simply the game's title, Block Breaker, and that too is a static text field.

21. With the text layer selected, choose the Text tool from the tools panel.
22. In the smaller background area at the right side of the stage, draw two text fields of equal width. Place these a good distance apart from each other vertically.
23. In the top text field, type the word "Score" and in the bottom text field, type the word "Lives." For both of these text fields, select a font size of 12 and choose something like Arial Black or Helvetica Black. Also, set the text alignment to center.
24. In the Properties panel for each of these text fields, make sure the Text Type drop-down box (at the far left side) is set to Static Text like in Figure 4.10.

FIGURE 4.10   Setting up the static text fields.

25. Below the Score text field create another text field of approximately the same width.
26. For this new text field, choose the font _sans, 12 point, center aligned.
27. At the left side of the Properties panel, from the Text Type drop-down box, choose Dynamic Text. When this is selected, another entry field will appear below this drop-down box, with the words <Instance Name> inside.
28. Give the new text field an instance name of score_txt.
29. Repeat these steps and create a dynamic text field beneath the Lives text field and give it the instance name lives_txt.
30. Finally, create a big *static* text field at the top right corner of the screen and put the words "Block Breaker" in a big font of your choosing.

Now that we've placed most of the graphical elements on the stage, we need to create a Start button on screen so players can trigger the starting of the game.

31. Open the Components panel by pressing Ctrl-F7.
32. Find the Button component and click and drag it onto the stage. This should be dragged onto the layer called text, because that layer is holding all of our user interface elements.
33. The button will be placed on the stage. Move it so that it is below the lives_txt text field.
34. With the button still selected, look in the Properties panel and give it an instance name of startButton.
35. In the Label property, which can be found under the parameters tab, enter the text "Start Game."

Now we've created all of our on-screen elements. We're almost ready to start coding. There are just two more graphics that must be created: the blocks and "the faders." These, however, will be created differently than the other items.

That's because we're going to be placing them and assigning them instance names dynamically, at runtime, so we won't be starting with any of them on screen at design time.

The blocks are the blocks that we normally see on screen—the objects of the game. The *faders* are the same size as the blocks except that they're only used quickly to create a special visual flashing effect when a block is hit. First, let's create the blocks.

36. In the gray area off the stage, draw a red rectangle that is 31 wide and 15 high. The layer that you draw it on does not matter, because it will not be remaining on stage for long.
37. Select it and convert it to a movie clip by pressing F8.
38. In the Convert to Symbol dialog box, name it `block_mc`, and in the Registration selection choose the upper-left corner box of the 9.
39. Click on the button below this that says Advanced.
40. In the Linkage area choose Export for Actionscript.
41. Once that is selected, the two text fields above it will become editable. In the Identifier text field enter the word "block." Leave the AS 2.0 Class text box empty.
42. Press OK.

Now we have a block movie clip. We want more than just red blocks to appear in our game, so we must go into this movie clip and add a few frames to hold different blocks.

43. Double-click on the block movie clip that is sitting on the stage.
44. We will now be editing the block movie clip. We are considered to be "inside" the block movie clip, as seen by the text next to the words Scene 1 in Figure 4.11.
45. In the timeline at the top of the screen, click on Frame 1 of the only layer in this movie clip, called, by default, Layer 1.
46. Press the F6 key, three times. This will insert three keyframes after frame 1. Each keyframe will contain exactly the same thing. As we can see in Figure 4.12, the movie clip is now four frames in length.

FIGURE 4.11   Editing the block movie clip.

FIGURE 4.12   The block movie clip after inserting three keyframes.

47. Step through the frames and change the color of the block on each frame. In the version contained on the accompanying CD-ROM, the blocks are colored so that frame 1 is red, frame 2 is yellow, frame 3 is green, and frame 4 is blue.

48. Once you are finished with the blocks, click on the Scene 1 link above the timeline layers to return to the main movie timeline.

49. Click on the instance of the block movie clip sitting on the stage and press delete to remove it. We no longer need it on stage at design time. It is sitting safely in the library, ready to be brought into play at runtime, with code.

Now, let's create the final graphical element: the fader.

50. On the gray area off stage draw a single white rectangle that is 32 wide by 16 high.

51. Select it and convert it into a movie clip with F8. Call the movie clip fader_mc and make sure its Behavior is set to Movie Clip and its Registration point is set to the upper-left corner box. In the Linkage area at the bottom select Export for Actionscript and give it an Identifier name of fader. Press OK.

52. Double-click on the movie clip instance on stage, and you'll be editing the fader movie clip.

53. We will have a one-frame movie, containing a single white square. Move to frame 16 and press F6 to insert a keyframe there.

Select the rectangle on frame 16 and change it so that its color remains white but its alpha value is zero; this will cause the rectangle to be *invisible*. To do this, make sure the rectangle is selected and open up the color mixer with Shift-F9. Keep the color as white, but set the alpha to 0, as in Figure 4.13.

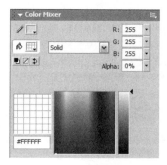

FIGURE 4.13   Creating a color with alpha of zero.

54. Go back to frame 1, and select the frame in the yimeline.

55. In the Properties dialog box, find the word Tween, and in the drop-down box next to it, choose the word Shape.

Now this movie clip will consist of a white rectangle that fades out to invisible over the period of 16 frames. Finally, we have to put a tiny bit of code on the last frame of this movie clip.

56. In the timeline select the last frame again and press F9.
57. The Actionscript box will appear. Click inside it and type the following Actionscript code

```
this.removeMovieClip();
```

This will cause the fader movie clip to play once and then remove itself from existence. This is how we want the fader to work, because it is supposed to just appear to be a flashing effect that occurs once.

That's it! We have created all of the graphical elements and movie clips that will be used to bring our game to life. Now it's time to code.

Coding the Game

Now that all of the graphics and elements have been built, we need to sew it all together and bring it to life with code. Looking back at the timeline, we can see that there's one more layer that we created called actionscript. This layer should contain no graphics. It's a blank layer that we're going to use to attach all of our Actionscript to.

 Remember, we're assuming that you know a thing or two about Actionscript, along with programming concepts like loops, arrays, and variables. This book is not an Actionscript guide but rather a guide to making games with Actionscript. So, if you're completely unfamiliar with it, you should probably grab a quick Actionscript guide and brush up because we're about to dive headlong into the world of Actionscript.

To begin, click on frame 1 of the actionscript layer and press F9 to open the Actions panel. Let's enter the following code.

```
function buildboard ()
{
    _root.createEmptyMovieClip("board", 1);
    board._x = 0;
    board._y = 0;

    grid = new Array();

    bcnt = 0;
    for (var j = 4; j < 9; j++)
    {
        grid[j] = new Array();
        for (var i = 0; i < 10; i++)
        {
            var nm = "block_" + j + "_" + i;
            board.attachMovie("block", nm, bcnt);
            board[nm]._x = i * 32;
            board[nm]._y = j * 16;
```

```
                        var btype = (j) % 4 + 1
                        board[nm].gotoAndStop(btype);
                        grid[j][i] = btype;

                        bcnt++;
                    }
                }
            }
```

In this code, we're creating our first function of the game. This function is responsible for creating the grid of blocks at the top of the play area. Each block is an individual movie clip, and the entire block grid is created within another movie clip. This function is called at the beginning of game play when the player hits the Start Game button.

The first thing we're doing in this function is creating an empty movie clip with the instance name board. Within this movie clip we'll be attaching all the block movie clips, which make up the board. We're setting the x and y position of this movie clip to (0, 0), which is the upper-left corner of the screen. We're also creating a new array called grid. This will be used to keep track of our board. Finally, we're setting a variable called bcnt to 0. This will simply be incremented and used to specify the depth level of each block. No two movie clips are allowed on the same depth level.

After this we begin a loop to create our rows of blocks. Our outer loop, which is traversed with the j variable, corresponds to each vertical row of the game board. Notice that the loop starts at 4, and runs up to 8 (that's <9, which means the last row will be 8). This is because we want four rows of blank at the top of our board, before the five rows of blocks begin. Inside this loop the first thing we do is create a new array specified as grid[j]. In Actionscript this is how we have to create 2D arrays, which will allow us to address them as grid[j][i].

Our inner loop, using the i variable, specifies horizontal columns. We immediately begin by creating a temporary variable called nm, which will contain the name of the block movie clip we're attaching. The name will be formatted like so: block_j_i, so the first block will have an instance name block_4_0.

Once our movie clip name has been computed, we attach the movie clip from the library with the linkage name block into the board movie clip. Notice that we're attaching it at depth level bcnt. After this we set the screen position of the block, like so:

```
        board[nm]._x = i * 32;
        board[nm]._y = j * 16;
```

The block's horizontal x position will be a multiple of 32 (0, 32, 64, etc.) and its y vertical position will be a multiple of 16. This works because the block is 31 × 15 in size, so there will always be a 1-pixel boundary between each block.

We set the color of the block with these three lines of code:

```
var btype = (j % 4) + 1
board[nm].gotoAndStop(btype);
grid[j][i] = btype;
```

Since there are four colors of blocks, we will use the j (row) value to determine the color and ensure that each row is a different color. By saying (j % 4), we're using the modulus operator to make sure the value will always fall between 0 and 3. When j is 2, (j % 4) equals 2. When j is 3, (j % 4) equals 3. However, when j is 4, (j % 4) equals 0. The result loops around back to 0. That's what the modulus operator does; it causes a number to loop around and around. By adding 1 to the result, we ensure that btype will be a value of 1, 2, 3, or 4.

We then take btype and tell the block to gotoAndStop that frame. This will set the frame number of the block and thereby set the color. We're also storing the value of btype in our grid array for later use. Finally, we increment bcnt, and the loop repeats.

After this we have the code used to control the motion of the paddle. Enter the following code:

```
paddle.onEnterFrame = function()
{
    var xpos = _xmouse;
    if (xpos > (320 - (this._width / 2)))
        xpos = 320 - (this._width / 2);

    if (xpos < (this._width / 2))
        xpos = this._width / 2;

    this._x = xpos;
}
```

This code is attached to the onEnterFrame function of the paddle movie clip. This means this code is called every single frame. The code is very simple. We're taking the x position of the mouse cursor, with _xmouse, and assigning it to a temporary variable called xpos. Next, we're making sure that the xpos variable is never greater than 320 minus half the width of the paddle or less than half the width of the paddle.

This will ensure that the paddle does not move off the board. Since the right edge of the board is at 320, and the registration point of the paddle is in its center, then 320 minus half the width of the paddle is the farthest to the right it can move. Also, the left edge of the board is at 0, so if xpos is less than half the width of the paddle, again, it has moved off the board, this time to the left.

Once xpos has been properly constrained, this._x (the horizontal position of this, the paddle) is set to xpos. If we were to make the board a different width, then we would have to adjust the number 320. If we did plan on adjusting the board width, it would probably be a good idea to make a variable called boardWidth and set it to 320 and then use that in our paddle constraint code. For now, however, we're just going to use the number 320.

That's all there is to the paddle motion. The next thing we're going to do is create a function we will use to handle our fader movie clips. Remember, the faders are just a visual effect used to make the blocks disappear with some pizzazz. This code controls the creation of a fader, as well as the adjustment of score (because, when a fader is displayed, it means a block was hit so score should be increased). Enter this code next:

```
fadercnt = 0;
function makeFader(x, y)
{
    var nm = "fader" + fadercnt;
    board.attachMovie("fader", nm, fadercnt + 9999);
    board[nm]._x = x;
    board[nm]._y = y;
    score+=100;
    score_txt.text = score;
    fadercnt++;

    if (fadercnt == bcnt)
    {
        Mouse.show();
        lives_txt.text = "YOU WIN";
        delete ball.onEnterFrame;
    }
}
```

This function, makeFader, takes two parameters: x and y. These correspond to the screen position at which to attach an instance of the fader movie clip we created earlier. Taking the word "fader" and adding the variable fadercnt to it determines the name of the fader movie clip. This way each fader movie clip instance will have a different name, should several need to appear in rapid succession from a ricocheting ball.

The x and y positions are set to the x and y passed in, and the score is increased by 100 and displayed on screen. The fadercnt variable is incremented at this point.

We have one more if statement in here. We need to check to see if fadercnt is equal to bcnt. What does this mean? Well, in essence we're seeing if the game is over. Since bcnt will be equal to the total number of blocks on the board, and fadercnt increments each time one block is destroyed, when fadercnt is equal to bcnt, then this will be the last block. If this is the case, we show the mouse cursor (which will be hidden later, as we'll see) and set the text of the lives_txt text field to "YOU WIN." Last, we delete the onEnterFrame function of the ball movie clip to stop the ball from moving. We'll be looking at that function next.

Next, enter the following code. This code is fairly long and complex, as it is responsible for what essentially makes up all the game play. This code controls the motion of the ball as well as the destruction of blocks.

```
function ballAction()
{
    this._x += this.dx;
    this._y += this.dy;

    if (this._x < 0)
    {
        this._x = 0;
        this.dx *= -1;
    }
    if (this._x > 320)
    {
        this._x = 320;
        this.dx *= -1;
    }
    if (this._y < 0)
    {
        this._y = 0;
        this.dy *= -1;
    }
    if (this._y > 400)
    {
        // Lose a life
        lives--;
        lives_txt.text = lives;

        if (lives == 0)
        {
            Mouse.show();
            lives_txt.text = "GAME OVER";
            delete ball.onEnterFrame;
        }
        else
        {
            this._x = 160;
            this._y = 200;
            this.dx = 0;
            this.dy = 6;
        }
    }

    if (this._y < paddle._y && (this._y + this.dy) > paddle._y &&
(this._x + this.dx) > paddle._x - 41 && (this._x + this.dx) < paddle._x +
41)
    {
        this.dy = -6;
        this.dx = (this._x - paddle._x) / 5;
    }

    var grdx = Math.floor(this._x / 32);
    var grdy = Math.floor(this._y / 16);
    var ngrdx = Math.floor((this._x + this.dx) / 32);
    var ngrdy = Math.floor((this._y + this.dy) / 16);
```

```
if (grid[grdy][ngrdx] > 0)
{
    grid[grdy][ngrdx] = 0;
    var bnm = "block_" + grdy + "_" + ngrdx;
    board[bnm].removeMovieClip();
    makeFader(ngrdx * 32, grdy * 16);
    this.dx *= -1;
}

if (grid[ngrdy][grdx] > 0)
{
    grid[ngrdy][grdx] = 0;
    var bnm = "block_" + ngrdy + "_" + grdx;
    board[bnm].removeMovieClip();
    makeFader(grdx * 32, ngrdy * 16);
    this.dy *= -1;
}

if (grid[ngrdy][ngrdx] > 0)
{
    grid[ngrdy][ngrdx] = 0;
    var bnm = "block_" + ngrdy + "_" + ngrdx;
    board[bnm].removeMovieClip();
    makeFader(ngrdx * 32, ngrdy * 16);
    this.dy *= -1;
    this.dx *= -1;
}
}
```

This code is broken into three sections:

- Detecting collision between the ball and the walls. This also includes hitting the bottom wall, which effectively means the ball has fallen off the bottom of the screen and a life is lost.
- Detecting collision between the ball and the paddle.
- Detecting collision between the ball and the blocks.

We'll look at it in sections. Before we do, however, the first two lines of code perform one task:

```
this._x += this.dx;
this._y += this.dy;
```

These will increase the ball's _x and _y position by the values this.dx and this.dy. These values correspond to the ball's horizontal and vertical speed. This means that the ball will move left or right by this.dx and up or down by this.dy. If this.dx is a positive number, the ball will move to the right; if this.dx is a negative number, the ball will move to the left. The same applies to _y; a this.dy of less than zero will mean the ball is moving upward on screen, whereas a this.dy of greater than zero will mean the ball is moving downward on screen. We'll be looking at how these values are initially set a little later.

The next thing we do is detect collision with the walls. The left, right, and top walls are detected like so:

```
if (this._x < 0)
{
    this._x = 0;
    this.dx *= -1;
}
if (this._x > 320)
{
    this._x = 320;
    this.dx *= -1;
}
if (this._y < 0)
{
    this._y = 0;
    this.dy *= -1;
}
```

It's very simple. If the ball has moved left of the position 0, we move it back to 0 and then we flip the this.dx value. So, if the ball was moving left at 5 pixels per frame (this.dx would be equal to –5), upon collision with the left wall, we would place the ball's _x position at 0 and then flip this.dx so that it would become 5.

We do the same thing with the right wall, but now we're going to see if the ball's _x position has moved beyond 320. If so, we set it to 320 and flip this.dx. Finally, we see if the ball has hit the top of the screen, where this._y would be less than 0. If this is the case, we set this._y to 0 and then reverse the value of this.dy so that upward motion becomes downward motion.

Once these checks have been performed, we have a slightly more complex check to see if the ball has passed the bottom wall, which is really just the bottom of the screen.

```
if (this._y > 400)
{
    // Lose a life
    lives--;
    lives_txt.text = lives;

    if (lives == 0)
    {
        Mouse.show();
        lives_txt.text = "GAME OVER";
        delete ball.onEnterFrame;
    }
    else
    {
        this._x = 160;
        this._y = 200;
        this.dx = 0;
        this.dy = 6;
    }
}
```

Instead of doing a bounce and reversal of motion, all we need to do is check to see if the ball's _y has moved past 400, and if so, we subtract one life from the player and display that value in the lives_txt text field. Here we want to check to see if the player has used up all his lives, and if so, the game ends. We show the mouse cursor, display the words "GAME OVER" in the lives_txt text field, and then we stop the ball from moving by deleting its onEnterFrame event.

If the game has not ended, however, we merely need to move the ball to a valid position on screen and give it a new speed. We move it to screen position 160, 200 and set its this.dx to 0 (no horizontal motion) and this.dy to 6 (moving down toward the bottom of the screen at 6 pixels per frame).

Next, we detect collision with the paddle with the following long line of code:

```
if (this._y < paddle._y && (this._y + this.dy) >= paddle._y && (this._x
+ this.dx) > paddle._x - 41 && (this._x + this.dx) < paddle._x + 41)
    {
        this.dy = -6;
        this.dx = (this._x - paddle._x) / 5;
    }
```

This if statement checks a few conditions:

- Is the ball currently higher than the paddle? (this._y < paddle._y)
- Is the next position of the ball lower than or equal to the paddle? (this._y + this.dy) >= paddle._y
- Is the next position of the ball greater than the left edge of the paddle? (this._x + this.dx) > paddle._x − 41
- Is the next position of the ball less than the right edge of the paddle? (this._x + this.dx) < paddle._x + 41

If all of these conditions are met, the ball is about to collide with the paddle. We could use Flash's hitTest command, but that would not be accurate enough. If the ball is moving very fast, it is possible for it to be higher than the paddle one frame and lower than the paddle the next frame, never having actually had an opportunity for the hitTest command to evaluate as true.

If there is a collision between the ball and the paddle, the player has safely stopped the ball's descent, and accordingly we set the ball's dy value to −6, which is an upward velocity. The ball's dx value is adjusted based on where on the paddle the collision took place. Using this formula, (this._x - paddle._x) / 5, we will arrive at a dx value that causes the ball to move faster left or right depending upon how far left or right of the paddle's center the ball landed. Hit the paddle dead center, and the new dx value will be 0, which means the ball will move straight up.

Finally, we have the collision with the blocks to attend to. The first thing we do is determine what block the ball is currently in and what block the ball will next be in, with the following code:

```
var grdx = Math.floor(this._x / 32);
var grdy = Math.floor(this._y / 16);
var ngrdx = Math.floor((this._x + this.dx) / 32);
var ngrdy = Math.floor((this._y + this.dy) / 16);
```

By taking the ball's x position, dividing it by 32 (the width of each block), and then using the `Math.floor` function, we'll arrive at a number that corresponds to the horizontal grid position. `Math.floor` ensures that the number we compute will be rounded down to the nearest whole number. So, if `this._x / 32` produced 4.7, that would mean the ball was in horizontal grid 4. We do the same with `this._y` to determine the ball's vertical grid position. In this case, we divide by 16, because the block is 16 pixels in height.

Once we have values for `grdx` and `grdy`, we know the block at that position from the grid array, as `grid[grdy][grdx]`. Remember, `grdy` corresponds to rows, `grdx` corresponds to columns, and our `grid` array is indexed as rows ×columns.

We then compute two more variables: `ngrdx` and `ngrdy`. These are identical to `grdx` and `grdy`, except that these represent the *next* position of the ball by looking at the row and column at `this._x + this.dy` and `this._y + this.dy`.

Once we've computed these four variables, we check for block collision. This is simply a matter of checking our grid array. Let's look at the first one:

```
if (grid[grdy][ngrdx] > 0)
{
    grid[grdy][ngrdx] = 0;
    var bnm = "block_" + grdy + "_" + ngrdx;
    board[bnm].removeMovieClip();
    makeFader(ngrdx * 32, grdy * 16);
    this.dx *= -1;
}
```

We're checking to see if `grid` at our current row, next column is greater than 0. If that's the case, we're hitting a block from the left or right side and we must set the value of the `grid` array at that point to 0 and then remove the movie clip at that position. By setting it to 0, we're ensuring that no more collisions will register with that grid position. We're also making a call to the `makeFader` function and passing into it the position of the block that was removed. This will cause a white box to appear and fade out, as if the block has vanished, rather than simply disappearing in one frame. Last, we reverse the horizontal direction of the ball.

The last two checks behave almost exactly the same:

```
if (grid[ngrdy][grdx] > 0)
{
    grid[ngrdy][grdx] = 0;
    var bnm = "block_" + ngrdy + "_" + grdx;
    board[bnm].removeMovieClip();
    makeFader(grdx * 32, ngrdy * 16);
    this.dy *= -1;
}
```

```
if (grid[ngrdy][ngrdx] > 0)
{
    grid[ngrdy][ngrdx] = 0;
    var bnm = "block_" + ngrdy + "_" + ngrdx;
    board[bnm].removeMovieClip();
    makeFader(ngrdx * 32, ngrdy * 16);
    this.dy *= -1;
    this.dx *= -1;
}
```

The top check looks to see if we've hit the top or bottom of the block, and if so, reverses this.dy. Everything else it does the same as the first check. The last check handles the special case where the ball goes diagonally up and completely enters the block at one of its corners. In other words, in its current position the ball is not over any block, but in its next position it is completely within a block. In this case then we must reverse both its dx and dy values. Aside from that, everything else is still the same.

That's all there is to the ballAction function. The final function of code that we're going to write is the Start button code. This function is called when the player hits the Start button, and this is what gets everything going. Enter the following code next:

```
function startClick()
{
    buildboard();
    lives = 5;
    score = 0;
    score_txt.text = score;
    lives_txt.text = lives;

    ball.onEnterFrame = ballAction;
    ball._x = 160;
    ball._y = 200;
    ball.dx = 0;
    ball.dy = 6;

    Mouse.hide();

}
```

The first thing we do is call our buildboard function to create the blocks and fill in the grid array. Next, we set the variables lives and score to 5 and 0, respectively. Five lives would be a nice fair number to start with. We then display those values in their associated text fields on screen.

After this we set the value of the ball.onEnterFrame function to be the ballAction function that we just wrote. Now the ball will have a life of its own. We then set some initial values for the ball, which are the same values we saw earlier when a life was lost in ballAction. By setting the ball to 160,200 and setting its dy to 6, we cause the ball to be served to the player like in tennis. Finally, we hide the mouse cursor because we want the paddle to appear as if it is the mouse cursor. Without doing this, the mouse cursor appears very distractingly on screen.

We have one more line of code to enter now:

```
startButton.addEventListener("click", startClick);
```

This is how we add events to button components. We're using the addEventListener method to listen for the click event and assigning that event to call our startClick function.

That's it! Our game is ready to play. Make sure you save your work and press Ctrl-Enter to test the movie out. Press the Start Game button on screen, and good luck.

EXTENDING THE GAME

We could make several modifications to this game.

- How about adding more blocks? All that needs to be changed is the buildboard function.
- Perhaps try adding some randomness to the motion of the ball when it hits the walls, blocks, or paddle.
- For some more challenge, try adding a second ball. This is fundamentally simple to do. You just need to assign the ballAction function to more than one ball movie clip.
- We could add sound to this game, but we'll be looking at sound a little later in the book.

SUMMARY

In this chapter we've looked at:

- Motion: using horizontal and vertical velocity (dx and dy)
- Collision with walls and planes (the paddle is a moving plane)
- Collision with solid objects: the blocks
- Using arrays to represent physical on-screen displays, allowing for faster and simpler access to the state of the game

MOON FIGHTER

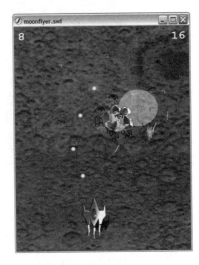

Moon fighter is our third game of the book, and in this one we're going to be using some of our previous ideas, as well as introducing the new concepts of background scrolling, scripted motion, and nested projectile collision. This game will be our most high-speed, action-intense game so far.

ABOUT THE GAME

In Moon Fighter you control a fighter ship that is rocketing along the surface of the moon, fighting wave after wave of enemy ships. The enemy ships will fly at you from the top of the screen, and your goal is very simple: shoot them, and they'll explode. The object is to destroy as many of them as you can in the allotted time period, while at the same time trying to avoid being hit (they're all kamikaze fighters), or your game is over.

Control is accomplished by moving the mouse left and right, and firing your cannon is simply a matter of pressing the left mouse button.

Holding down the button will fire a continuous stream of bullets—about three per second. Clicking the button rapidly, however, will allow you to fire many more bullets. Figure 5.1 shows a look at the game in play.

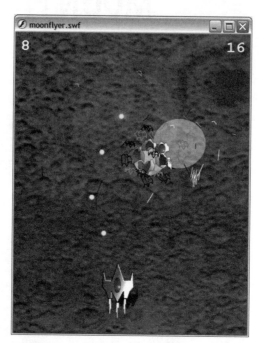

FIGURE 5.1   Moon Fighter in progress.

The enemy will attack in squadrons of three ships from the top of the screen. The enemy ships will move from the top to the bottom of the screen, and as they progress they'll move in a left-to-right wave pattern. This is based on a sine curve, but we'll get into that later. A new squadron of ships is sent at the player every second or so, which creates a nonstop, high-intensity experience. This style of game implies that the player will not be killing all the enemies, but just trying to kill as many as possible.

In the previous chapters, in order to get our feet wet, we looked at building things in great detail. Now that we're getting more advanced, we're going to focus less on the intricate steps such as:

- *In the Document Properties dialog box (opened with Ctrl-J), set the Width to 480, the Height to 400, and set the Frame Rate to 48 fps.*
- *Close the dialog box by clicking OK.*

And we'll be saying it more like this:

- *Set the width of the movie to 480, the height to 400, and the frame rate to 48.*

BUILDING THE GAME

Now we're going to build the game. The first thing to do is make sure that we have Macromedia Flash Professional 8 open.

1. Open a new Flash document.
2. Set the width of the new movie to 400, the height to 500, and the frame rate to 31 fps. The whole stage should look like Figure 5.2.

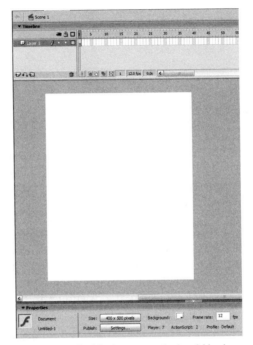

FIGURE 5.2   The blank stage as it should look.

3. Create a new dynamic text field in the upper-left corner of the screen and give it the instance name score_txt. You can use any font you want, but we used the standard _typewriter font. Set the point size to 26 and make sure the text is left-aligned. This text field will be used to display our score.
4. Create another new dynamic text field in the upper-right corner of the screen, and give it the instance name counter_txt. The font and point size should be the same as score_txt, although the text in this one should be right aligned.
5. Rename this layer and call it text. Everything should look like Figure 5.3.
6. Create a new layer beneath that and name it startbutton.
7. On that layer create a new button and make sure it has the text "START" on it. The simple one we created is shown in Figure 5.4.

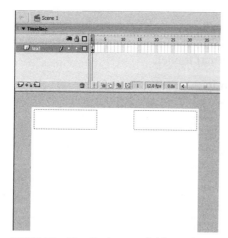

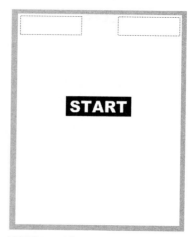

FIGURE 5.3 The display text fields on the stage.

FIGURE 5.4 The stage with the Start button.

8. Make sure the button has the instance name startButton.
9. To make things easier to see, set the background color of the movie to a dark gray. This will not be seen in the final game, but makes it easier for us to use at design time.
10. Create a ship movie clip. This is the main character—the ship player will be controlling. The best way to create this is to create an empty movie clip by selecting New Symbol from the Insert menu. In the New Symbol dialog box make sure its Behavior is set to Movie Clip and name it ship. Once you click OK, you'll be taken directly to editing this new movie clip. The ship that we created is shown in Figure 5.5.

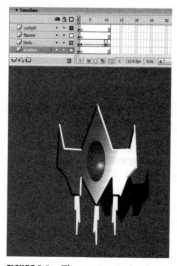

FIGURE 5.5 The ship movie clip.

11. Draw a similar ship directly on the stage. Make sure the nose tip of the ship is at the center registration point of the movie clip (where the small + is) and that the ship is facing upward. The center point is where bullets that you fire are going to originate. On the bottom-most layer of this movie clip, we drew a shadow of 50% alpha black so that in the main game the ship will appear to be hovering above the ground. Make sure this entire drawing is not grouped, because it needs to be able to do a shape tween animation (next step). The entire image should be around 60 pixels wide and 80 pixels high.
12. Notice that in Figure 5.5, the timeline of the ship is multiframed. This is because the ship contains its own death animation. A nice easy way to create a death animation is like so:
    a. Create a new keyframe on frame 2 with the F6 key (so that frame 2 is actually the first frame of the death animation).
    b. Create another keyframe on frame 10.
    c. On the frame 10 keyframe cut the image up and move the various parts around the stage at random, like in Figure 5.6.

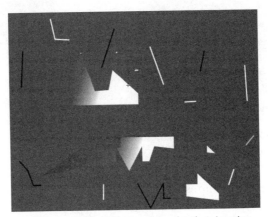

FIGURE 5.6   The final frame of the death animation.

    d. With the new frame 2 selected in the timeline, look in the Properties panel for the Tween drop-down box. Set Tween Type to a Shape Tween.
    e. Insert one more frame at frame 11. Make sure this one is blank. You can insert a blank frame by pressing F7 while the new frame is selected.
13. We need two code frames. Insert a new layer and call it code. In frame 1 insert the code stop();. In frame 11 create a new blank keyframe and insert the same code.
14. Go back to the main timeline, create a new layer called ship, and insert the newly created movie clip onto this layer by dragging it from the library. Place it nearer to the bottom of the screen, in the horizontal center.
15. Give it the instance name ship. This is an important step; otherwise the game will not work. The stage should now look like Figure 5.7.

16. From the main timeline, insert another new symbol (Insert menu, New Symbol). Set its Behavior to Movie Clip, and name it bob. Also, make sure the Export for Actionscript checkbox is checked and give it the Identifier name bob. This name is meant to demonstrate that our game could eventually support many different types of enemies. This enemy's name is bob. Click OK.

17. In the blank movie clip, start by drawing the enemy ship. It should be facing downward, like in Figure 5.8. It should be roughly the same dimensions as the player's ship. Our version is slightly shorter in height than the player's ship, but is exactly the same width: 61.

FIGURE 5.7   The stage with the new ship movie clip.

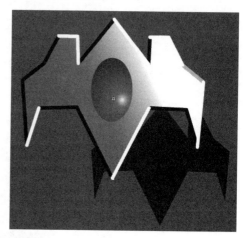

FIGURE 5.8   The enemy ship, bob.

18. This ship is going to behave similarly to the player's ship. Create an explosion animation by creating a new keyframe on frame 2 and another keyframe on frame 15. On frame 15 rip apart the drawing and then set the Tween Type of frame 2 to Shape. On a new layer below this draw a very small circle that starts on frame 2 and one on frame 15 that is roughly the same radius as the broken ship parts. Make this circle begin as 100% alpha white and be 0% alpha yellow by the end. This is the shockwave and fireball of the enemy explosion. It looks like Figure 5.9.

19. Add a layer to this movie clip and call it code. This movie clip is, like the ship movie clip, going to have two frames with code. In frame 1 insert the frame code stop();. In frame 2 insert the code this.removeMovieClip();. This causes the enemy ship to cease to exist once it has finished exploding.

That's it for the ships. Return to the main timeline. We're almost ready to begin coding, but we have two more things to create: the bullets and the background image.

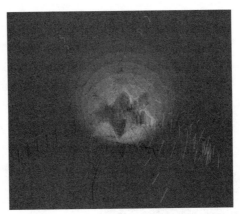

FIGURE 5.9   The final explosion animation of the enemy ship, seen with the onion skin turned on.

20. From the main timeline, insert a new movie clip (Insert menu, New Symbol). Name it `bullet` and make sure Export for Actionscript is checked. Give it the linkage identifier `bullet` and click OK.
21. In the new movie clip, draw a yellow or white circle that is 8 pixels by 8 pixels in size and is centered on the stage (the position would be –4, –4). The bullet should look like Figure 5.10.
22. That's it for the bullet. Go back to the main timeline.

We have one more movie clip to create: the background image. This is no normal background image, however; this is going to be a scrolling image. What does this mean? It means the image has to appear to scroll seamlessly for as long as required. No, we can't create a movie clip that is 9 million pixels high, and luckily we don't really need to do that. All we need is to create a movie clip that is twice the height of the screen.

23. Create a bitmap image in an external program. The image we used was created in a 3D graphics package and is simply a texture map image of the surface of the moon. This image should be 400 × 500, or exactly the same size as the stage. A good thing to do is to make sure the top and bottom of the image are approximately the same, so that when laid end to end, they would appear seamless. The image we used is shown in Figure 5.11.
24. Insert a new movie clip and name it `bgscroller`. Click OK. You will now be editing this movie clip.
25. From here, import the graphic you created or our graphic, which we have called `bgscroller.jpg` on the CD-ROM in the Chapter 5 folder. From the file menu, choose Import > Import to Stage.
26. Set the x and y position of this bitmap to 0, 0, like in Figure 5.12.

ON THE CD

FIGURE 5.10   The `bullet` movie clip, zoomed in 2000%.

FIGURE 5.11   Our image of the moon surface.

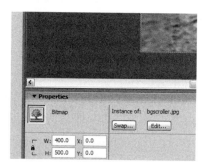

FIGURE 5.12   Positioning the moon image.

27. Once this has been done, make a copy of the bitmap by selecting it and holding down Alt while dragging the bitmap. Drag it up and to the left. The position doesn't matter because we're going to set that manually next.

28. Set the position of the second bitmap instance to an x of 0 and a y of −500. This image will now be flush aligned above the first bitmap. Now we have a moon surface that is exactly two screens, or 1000 pixels, in height.

29. Return to the main timeline.

30. Create a new layer at the bottom of all the other layers and call it `background`.

31. From the library, drag the `bgscroller` movie clip onto this layer and position it at exactly 0, 0. Give this movie clip the instance name `bgscroller`. The stage should now look like Figure 5.13. Notice that the background extends exactly two screens in height.

FIGURE 5.13   The final stage image with background scroller.

That's it for graphics. We've created all the elements, on stage and in the library, to make our game come to life. Now the game's ready to be coded.

CODING THE GAME

The code for Moon Flyer is a bit more complex than our previous games. The code for this game is divided into three distinct sections.

Setup: The area of the game where the game is initialized, scores are reset, and the player's ship is brought to life with an onEnterFrame function.

Create Projectile Function: This is the function responsible for handling the creation and handling of projectiles. In this game we use one type of projectile: the bullet.

Create Enemy Function: This is the function responsible for creating enemy instances, moving them, and detecting for collision between the enemy and the player ship.

Begin by creating a new layer in our main timeline and calling it Actions. This is the layer where we're going to be writing our code. Let's start with the setup function. Type the following code in the first frame of our new Actions layer. This code is the start of the setup function:

```
setup = function()
{

    firing = false;  // Is player firing?
```

```
fireRate = 10;   // Frame delay between shots
enemyTime = 0;   // Enemy creation timer
enemyRate = 30;  // Frame delay between enemy waves
score = 0;
score_txt.text = score;
counter = 20;    // Game time
counter_txt.text = counter;
```

We're simply initializing a few variables.

- The `firing` variable is a flag used to determine whether or not the player is firing.
- The `fireRate` variable is used to determine how frequently the gun will refire when the player is holding down the fire button (left mouse button). We want a certain amount of auto repeat, but we don't want to create a new bullet every single frame; otherwise the stream of bullets would practically look like a solid line. We want a delay of 10 frames so that, at our frame rate of 31 fps, a bullet will fire approximately three per second. We want the player to have to *work* for a faster fire rate by pressing the mouse button multiple times.
- `enemyTimer` is used to keep track of the amount of time since the last wave of enemies was created.
- `enemyRate` is used to define how often (in frames) a new wave of enemies will be created.
- `score` is self-explanatory, but below that we're placing the new score of 0 in the score_txt text field.
- `counter` is a variable that represents the number of seconds before game over. In this version of the game, game play is simply a race to see how many enemies can be killed before the timer runs out. After the counter variable is declared the counter_txt text field is being updated with the new time.

Enter the following code (this is still within the `setup` function):

```
ship.onMouseDown = function()
{
    firing = true;
    repeatTime = 0;
}

ship.onMouseUp = function()
{
    firing = false;
}
```

These two functions are the firing control functions, which are triggered when the player presses and releases the mouse button. In the `onMouseDown` (when the mouse is pressed) function we're setting the value of our `firing` flag to `True` and resetting the repeatTime to 0. When the mouse button is released, and on-MouseUp is triggered, we're setting the firing flag to False. On their own, these functions are pretty nonfunctional. The variables themselves are being used in the next section of code. Enter this:

```
ship.onEnterFrame = function()
{
    this.destx = _xmouse;

    var diffx = (this.destx - this._x)

    this._x += diffx * .15;

    if (firing && repeatTime == 0)
    {
        createProjectile("bullet", this._x,
this._y - 5, 0, -15);
    }
    repeatTime ++;
    repeatTime %= fireRate;

    if (enemyTime == 0)
    {
        var sx = Math.random() * 100 + 80;
        createEnemy("bob", sx, -30);
        createEnemy("bob", 400 - sx, -30);
        createEnemy("bob", 200, -30);
    }
    enemyTime ++;
    enemyTime %= 30;

}
```

This is the onEnterFrame code for the ship, which is going to run every frame. The first thing we're doing in this code is setting the value of the destx property to _xmouse, which is the current x position of the mouse cursor.

```
    this.destx = _xmouse;
```

The destx property is attached to this, which refers to the ship, since the onEnterFrame code is attached to the ship; the variable is essentially ship.destx. The destx variable refers to where we *want* the ship to be. Because we want motion to be smooth, we don't want the ship to instantly jump to the position of the mouse cursor. We want it to smoothly adjust its position so that it moves *toward* a desired position. This desired position is constantly being updated, and it is stored in destx.

Next, we create a temporary variable called diff that is used to store the difference in distance between the destx (desired position) and the actual _x position of ship.

```
var diffx = (this.destx - this._x)
```

If the ship was at position x of 40 and the mouse cursor (and therefore `destx`) was moved to position x of 60, `diffx` would be 20, which is 60 – 40. On the other hand, if the ship was at 100 and `destx` was 50, `diffx` would be –50, which is 50 – 100. In other words, it's a positive number if the ship wants to move right and a negative number if the ship wants to move left.

After this, we're simply adding that `diffx` to the _x position of the ship.

```
this._x += diffx * .15;
```

When we add `diffx`, however, we're multiplying it by 0.15, which essentially means, "move me 15% of the difference between my current position and my desired position." What would happen if we just did this:

```
this._x += diffx;
```

The ship would move instantly, in one frame, to the mouse cursor. This is not the smooth motion we want, so by introducing the 0.15 scale factor, we ensure that the ship will ease smoothly into place, each frame moving only 15% of the remaining distance. The remaining distance will constantly be changing as the ship moves, but still we will only move the ship 15% of what's left. This will cause our ship to slide very smoothly into place.

The next bit of code in our `onEnterFrame` function looks at firing bullets.

```
if (firing && repeatTime == 0)
{
    createProjectile("bullet", this._x,
this._y - 5, 0, -15);
    }
    repeatTime ++;
    repeatTime %= fireRate;
```

Here we're checking the status of the `firing` flag and the `repeatTime` variable. Remember that we set those in the `onMouseDown` and `onMouseUp` functions.

The principle is simple. If we're currently firing and the repeat timer is at 0, make a call to the `createProjectile` function (we'll be looking at that function shortly). The `createProjectile` function takes several parameters:

- The linkage name of the movie clip from the library to use as the new bullet instance. For fun, we could put anything in here that we have linked in our library (if we put the word "bob," our ship would be firing enemy ships out of its gun turret). This is so that in the future, we could support all sorts of different projectiles.
- The _x position and _y position at which to create this new bullet.
- The horizontal and vertical speed of this new bullet.

The one we're creating here starts at the _x position of the ship (which will correspond to the horizontal location of the nose of the ship). The _y position of the new bullet is at the _y position of the ship, minus 5. This means "start this bullet 5 pixels above the nose point of the ship." We start offset like this to create some initial momentum for the bullet, as well as to ensure that the bullet doesn't register a collision with the player's ship (and thus not allow the player to shoot himself).

The initial speed of the bullet has a horizontal value of 0, which means the bullet is not moving left or right at all, and a vertical value of −15, which means the bullet is moving up at a rate of 15 pixels per frame. If we didn't put a minus in front of the 15, the bullet would move down instead; negative number means up, positive number means down. The same applies to the horizontal speed; a negative number would cause the bullet to move left, and a positive number would cause the bullet to move right.

After this, we increment the `repeatTime` counter variable. We then perform a modulus (%) operation on this to make `repeatTime` loop back around to 0 when it reaches `fireRate`. This means that every 10 frames (as `fireRate` is 10) `repeatTime` will be equal to 0. At that point, if firing, the bullet will launch.

After this code, there is one more piece to the `onEnterFrame`:

```
if (enemyTime == 0)
{
    var sx = Math.random() * 100 + 80;
    createEnemy("bob", sx, -30);
    createEnemy("bob", 200, -30);
    createEnemy("bob", 400 - sx, -30);
}
enemyTime ++;
enemyTime %= enemyRate;
```

This is where enemies are created (yes, that's right, the ship is actually creating its own enemies). There's no special reason for placing it inside the ship's `onEnterFrame` other than the fact that the ship's `onEnterFrame` function is available for us to use. This behaves very much the same as the firing of bullets, where `enemyTime` is used to determine when enemies are launched at the players, which will happen every `enemyRate` frame. Whenever `enemyTime` is 0, we launch three enemies at the player by calling the `createEnemy` function three times at once.

The `createEnemy` function takes three parameters: movie clip linkage name, x position, and y position. The temporary variable `sx` is created, which will be set to a random number between 80 and 180 (`Math.random * 100` will create a number between 0 and 100, and adding 80 to this will make it be between 80 and 180). We create three enemy ships; one of them will have an _x position of `sx`, the next one will always have an _x position of 200 (dead center of screen), and the last one will have an _x position of 400 − `sx`, which is exactly opposite the first enemy ship. If the first enemy was 120 pixels from the left, the third enemy will be 120 pixels from the right. This will cause the enemy ships to always be launched in a nice, geometric formation, all of them equidistant from each other.

That's all the code in the ship's onEnterFrame function. Next, enter the following code (still within the setup function):

```
doCounter = function()
{
    counter--;
    counter_txt.text = counter;

    if (counter == 0)
    {
        delete ship.onEnterFrame;
        delete bgscroller.onEnterFrame;
        enemyLayer.removeMovieClip();
        projectileLayer.removeMovieClip();
        startButton._visible = true;
        clearInterval(countID);
    }
}

countID = setInterval(doCounter, 1000);
```

The goal of this function is to decrement the counter at a fixed rate, or interval. This function is called by Macromedia Flash Professional 8 using the setInterval function. The first line of the function decrements the counter variable, which we previously set to 20, and then displays that new value in the counter_txt text field.

After this, we handle the special case where counter is equal to zero, or in other words, time is up. When this happens, we kill the onEnterFrame function of the ship, kill the onEnterFrame function of the bgscroller (which we'll be looking at shortly), and delete the enemyLayer and projectileLayer movie clips (which we'll also be looking at shortly). We make the startButton visible again and then finally clear the interval countID, which is responsible for calling this, the doCounter function every second.

Below this, we create the interval using the setInterval function, which is very useful. To use it simply pass a function name and a value, in milliseconds, for how often you want that function to be called. setInterval will return an ID number for that particular interval (you can have many running at once).

```
countID = setInterval(doCounter, 1000);
```

Here we're telling setInterval to call doCounter every 1000 milliseconds, or 1 second. The resulting ID is stored in countID. Now our doCounter function is going to be called every second, and when it's done, the interval will remove itself from operation by issuing a clearInterval on countID.

After this, enter the following code, which is all still part of the setup function.

```
_root.createEmptyMovieClip("projectileLayer", 99);
projectileCount = 0;
```

```
_root.createEmptyMovieClip("enemyLayer", 98);
enemyCount = 0;

ship.swapDepths(100);
ship.gotoAndStop(1);
```

All of our bullets are going to be created within their own parent movie clip called projectileLayer and all of the enemies within their own movie clip called enemyLayer. So, here we're creating these two movie clips on the _root using the createEmptyMovieClip function. createEmptyMovieClip expects two things: an instance name and a depth level. Since no two movie clips can exist on the same depth level, the projectileLayer is going to be at depth level 99, and the enemyLayer is going to be at depth level 98. This means that technically, projectiles will be drawn on top of enemy ships.

Here two variables, projectileCount and enemyCount are both set to 0. These are used later in the creation of projectiles and enemies.

We're also moving the ship up to depth level 100 (higher than both the enemies and the bullets) and telling it to go to and stop on frame 1 of the ship animation. This means that if you died last round and your ship exploded, the ship will return to full integrity as we go back to the first, unexploded frame.

Last, enter the following code at the bottom of the setup function.

```
bgscroller.onEnterFrame = function()
{
    if (this._y >= 500)
    {
        this._y = 0;
    }
    this._y+=5;
}
}
```

This is an onEnterFrame function we're creating and attaching to the bgscroller movie clip. Remember that bgscroller is our moon surface background image. What we're doing is checking to see if the image has scrolled past a _y value of 500, and if so, moving it back to position 0. By moving it up 500 pixels, we're ensuring that the on-screen image doesn't change, since the background is a repeated bitmap, 500 pixels high. This code is critical for making our bgscroller appear to scroll indefinitely.

After this if statement, we move the bgscroller down by 5 pixels with

```
this._y+=5;
```

This is how we cause the scrolling motion to occur. If we change the number 5, we can make it scroll at a faster or slower rate. For the appearance of a much faster game, try a value of 15 or 25.

That's the end of the setup function. Next we're going to look at the create-Projectile function. Enter the following code after the end of the setup function:

```
createProjectile = function(type, x, y, dx, dy)
{
    var nm = "proj" + projectileCount;
    projectileLayer.attachMovie(type, nm, projectileCount);
    projectileLayer[nm]._x = x;
    projectileLayer[nm]._y = y;
    projectileLayer[nm].dx = dx;
    projectileLayer[nm].dy = dy;

    projectileLayer[nm].onEnterFrame = function()
    {
        this._x += this.dx;
        this._y += this.dy;

        if (this._y < 0) this.removeMovieClip();

        for (var i = 0; i < 10; i++)
        {
            var enm = "enemy" + i;
            if (this.hitTest(enemyLayer[enm]) &&
                enemyLayer[enm]._currentframe == 1)
            {
                enemyLayer[enm].play();
                score++;
                score_txt.text = score;
                this.removeMovieClip();
            }
        }
    }

    projectileCount ++;
    projectileCount %= 10;

}
```

As mentioned earlier, the createProjectile function takes five parameters: movie clip linkage ID, x position, y position, x speed dx, and y speed dy. The first six lines of code in this function are concerned with physically creating the new instance of our projectile.

```
var nm = "proj" + projectileCount;
projectileLayer.attachMovie(type, nm, projectileCount);
projectileLayer[nm]._x = x;
projectileLayer[nm]._y = y;
projectileLayer[nm].dx = dx;
projectileLayer[nm].dy = dy;
```

In a temporary variable, nm, we put the name of our new projectile. This is the text "proj" plus the value of the projectileCount variable, which was set to 0 in the

setup function. So, the very first projectile that is created will have the name
proj0.

Once nm is defined, we use the attachMovie function to attach an instance of
the movie clip defined in the type variable to the projectileLayer movie clip: the
empty movie clip we created in setup. The depth level at which we're creating this
new movie clip *within* projectileLayer is the value of projectileCount. So, proj0
would be at depth level 0, proj7 would be at depth level 7, and so on.

We set the _x and _y positions of the new movie clip projectileLayer[nm] to the
x and y values passed in. We also create two variables, dx and dy, attach them to
our new movie clip, and set them to the same dx and dy values that were passed in.

At this point our new bullet will be created to sit at its initial position (which
will be 5 pixels above the nose of the player's ship). After that we have the onEnter-
Frame function of the new movie clip.

```
projectileLayer[nm].onEnterFrame = function()
```

The first thing we do in this function is move the projectile along its dx and dy
values with:

```
this._x += this.dx;
this._y += this.dy;
```

We then check to see if the projectile has flown off the top of the screen (to
check if this._y is less than 0), and, if so, it's of no more consequence to our
game, so we can delete it by issuing this.removeMovieClip().

Next we make the projectile loop through each possible enemy and see if it is
currently colliding with that enemy.

```
for (var i = 0; i < 10; i++)
{
    var enm = "enemy" + i;
    if (this.hitTest(enemyLayer[enm]) &&
        enemyLayer[enm]._currentframe == 1)
    {
        enemyLayer[enm].play();
        score++;
        score_txt.text = score;
        this.removeMovieClip();
    }
}
```

This is nested projectile collision and is necessary to ensure that every projectile can hit every enemy. We simply loop from 0 to 9 and check if the projectile
has a valid hitTest on enemyLayer[enm]. When enemies are created in the create-
Enemy function, they're named similarly to the projectiles, with the text "enemy"
plus the value of a counter. Since enm will be "enemy" plus i, this new projectile
will be checking against enemy0, enemy1, enemy2 all the way up to enemy9, for a total
of 10 checks.

We're also checking to make sure the enemy is currently on frame 1 of its timeline by looking at its _currentframe property. This is because we only want hits to be valid when hitting enemies that aren't currently exploding.

Why are we only checking 10 enemies? What if 15 are on screen? Because we've limited the number of enemies that can be created to 10, so we don't have too many checks going on at one time. If there were 30 bullets and 30 enemies on screen, that would be 900 checks per frame, which is far too much for Flash 8 to handle at a realistic performance rate. Conversely, what if there were only three enemies on screen? Why are we checking all 10? Well, the _currentframe == 1 check will have a dual purpose. It will be false if the explosion is playing, but it will also be false if the enemy doesn't exist.

The hitTest method can work in one of two ways. The first way is to pass the name of a movie clip into it, and it will return true if this overlaps the movie clip in any way. When this occurs, it means the bullet is touching the enemy ship and is therefore killing that enemy. The other form of hitTest we'll be looking at is in the createEnemy function.

If the bullet is hitting the enemy, and the enemy is not currently exploding, we tell the enemy movie clip to begin its exploding animation with enemy-Layer[enm].play(). Then we increase the score by one, display that new score on screen, and finally tell the bullet to remove itself from existence with this.remove-MovieClip().

Whenever a movie clip no longer needs to exist, it's always a good idea to remove it with removeMovieClip, rather than simply making it invisible. Otherwise, the computer will still continue to execute its code, even though it can't be seen.

Finally, outside of the onEnterFrame definition, we're incrementing the variable projectileCount:

```
projectileCount ++;
projectileCount %= 10;
```

When projectileCount reaches 10, it will wrap back around to 0. This means there can only ever be 10 projectiles on screen at once, and any beyond 10 will start to overwrite the earlier ones. That's OK, because the game has been engineered so that it's basically impossible to have more than 10 on screen at once. The firing repeat rate is slow enough that there will only be a maximum of about three or four on screen at once if the player holds down the mouse button. If the firing repeat rate was increased, however, this 10 would have to be changed to a larger number. Be warned: increasing this number will exponentially increase the checks that the computer must perform, and exponentially decrease game performance.

That's it for the createProjectile function. Next is the createEnemy function. Enter this after the end of the createProjectile function:

```
createEnemy = function(type, x, y)
{
    var nm = "enemy" + enemyCount;
```

```
enemyLayer.attachMovie(type, nm, enemyCount);
enemyLayer[nm]._x = x;
enemyLayer[nm].xline = x;
enemyLayer[nm]._y = y;
enemyLayer[nm].dy = Math.random() * 3 + 10;
enemyLayer[nm].t = Math.random() * 6.28;

enemyLayer[nm].onEnterFrame = function()
{
    this._x = this.xline + Math.sin(this.t) * 100;
    this._y += this.dy;

    this.t += 0.1;

    if (this._currentframe == 1 &&
        ship.hitTest(this._x, this._y, true))
    {
        counter = 1;
        doCounter();
        ship.play();
    }

    if (this._y > 500) this.removeMovieClip();
}

enemyCount ++;
enemyCount %= 10;
}
```

This function is very similar in its construction to `createProjectile`, but the `onEnterFrame` function it attaches to the new enemy is very different. For starters, the function only takes three parameters: linkage name, x position, and y position. The horizontal and vertical speeds are determined by the function itself and are therefore not passed in. Let's look at the code.

```
var nm = "enemy" + enemyCount;
enemyLayer.attachMovie(type, nm, enemyCount);
enemyLayer[nm]._x = x;
enemyLayer[nm].xline = x;
enemyLayer[nm]._y = y;
enemyLayer[nm].dy = Math.random() * 3 + 10;
enemyLayer[nm].t = Math.random() * 6.28;
```

We're first storing, in a temporary variable `nm`, the name of the new enemy. Like the projectiles, this is a word ("enemy") plus the value of a counter (the `enemyCount` variable). In this case the enemies will be named `enemy0`, `enemy1`, `enemy2`, and so on. This new movie clip, with a `type` that's passed in, will be attached to the `enemyLayer` movie clip at depth level `enemyCount`.

The enemy's `_x` position is then set to the x that's passed in, and another property called `xline` is also set to the value x that's passed in. When the enemy moves down the screen, it will move in a wave pattern from left to right. The width of this wave (its amplitude) from furthest left to furthest right is 200 pixels. This motion is accomplished by moving from 100 pixels right of xline to 100 pixels left of xline, or xline + 100 to xline - 100, on and on. So, xline is exactly that: a straight line that moves down the screen, that the enemy is anchored to, and that moves back and forth.

We then set the _y value to the y that's passed in and set the dy (the vertical speed) to a random number from 3 to 13. The higher the number, the faster the enemy moves down the screen. Next we create a new property, t and set its value to a random number from 0 to 6.28. This value tells the enemy what part of the wave he's at—whether he's at the far left, far right, middle, or somewhere in between. If we don't make this a random number, all enemies appear on screen moving in the exact same way, and there's very little challenge for the player to avoid them.

This wave motion repeats over and over. We can think of the initial position (when t is 0) as the enemy perfectly positioned over its xline. As t increases (which it will be doing), the enemy moves right, arcs, and moves back left again. At the point where the enemy crosses back over xline, the value of t will be approximately 3.14, which is half of 6.28 and also happens to be the mathematical constant, pi. As t increases, the enemy will move left of xline and then arc back to cross xline again. At the point where it returns to xline, t will be 6.28, and the entire process will repeat. Look at Figure 5.14 to see this in action.

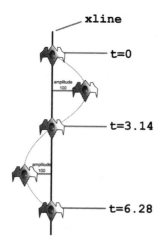

FIGURE 5.14 The motion of the enemy ship.

This is why we choose a random number for t, between 0 and 6.28, so that each enemy will initially be at a random point on its wave motion.

That's it for enemy property initialization. After this, we have the onEnter-Frame function of the newly created enemy.

```
enemyLayer[nm].onEnterFrame = function()
{
    this._x = this.xline + Math.sin(this.t) * 100;
```

```
    this._y += this.dy;

    this.t += 0.1;

    if (this._currentframe == 1 &&
        ship.hitTest(this._x, this._y, true))
    {
        counter = 1;
        doCounter();
        ship.play();
    }

    if (this._y > 500) this.removeMovieClip();
}
```

The first thing each enemy does each frame, is set its _x position to xline + Math.sin(this.t) * 100. This is the sine wave that we've been looking at. This causes the wave to be created as the position along the wave, this.t, is passed to the Math.sin function, and the result is multiplied by 100 to give a left-right oscillation from −100 to +100. When this is added to xline, it makes the wave exist on either side of xline, or from xline - 100 to xline + 100. This may all seem very complex, but it's a very rudimentary application of the trigonometric function sine.

After its _x position has been calculated and set, the enemy's _y position is incremented by this.dy, moving it down along the screen. Then, this.t is incremented by 0.1, moving the enemy along its wave. To make the enemy oscillate faster, change 0.1 to 0.2 or 0.3.

Next, we check to see if the enemy has collided with the player's ship. We first want to determine whether or not the enemy is already exploding (from being shot). It's only fair that an already shot enemy cannot still kill you. We use the second form of the hitTest method to check if the ship is touching the enemy. This form of hitTest takes a screen position x, y, and a flag. If the flag is true, hitTest returns true if the x, y coordinate is touching any solid part of the enemy movie clip. If the flag is false, solidity is not factored in, and true is returned if the x, y coordinate overlaps anywhere on the enemy's entire area defined by the furthest extents of its vector image. This is called its bounding box.

We use this form of hitTest so that things are a little more lenient on the player. Using the first form of movie clip to movie clip hitTest, it's far too difficult to avoid being hit. Using the second form, with an x and y point, we're really only going to register a collision if the player's nose tip touches the enemy's body anywhere solid. This means the enemy could technically pass through the player as long as he didn't touch the player's nose. This isn't 100% perfect, but at high speeds, the few missed collisions are hardly noticed. It actually creates a "phew!" effect as the player believes he has narrowly, and skilfully, avoided a near collision.

In the case of an actual collision, then we do three things:

```
    counter = 1;
    doCounter();
    ship.play();
```

We set the `counter` variable to 1 and then call `doCounter`. This will end the game. Looking at the `doCounter` function, we can see that it first decrements `counter` and then checks to see if it is 0. If so, it performs all the necessary steps to end the game. We're conveniently able to reuse `doCounter`. After that we tell the `ship` to play its animation, which will result in the player's ship exploding.

Finally, we check to see if the enemy has passed off the bottom of the screen:

```
if (this._y > 500) this.removeMovieClip();
```

If it has, the ship will remove itself from existence, thus ending all of its code execution and giving processor power back to the rest of the game. That's all the main code of the game. There's one more small piece of code to be entered after the end of the `createEnemy` function:

```
startButton.onRelease = function()
{
    this._visible = false;
    setup();
}
```

This code is attached to the Start button and will be executed when the player clicks on it. The first line hides the button, and the second line calls the `setup` function, which in turn starts the game.

That is all the code. Save your work and then try running the game by pressing Ctrl-Enter. You may want to resize the test window so that the edges line up perfectly with the 400 × 500 size of the stage. If you don't do this, the background scrolling effect won't look right, because you'll see it jump back up to the starting position when it loops. Figure 5.15 shows see what it looks like without resizing the display area.

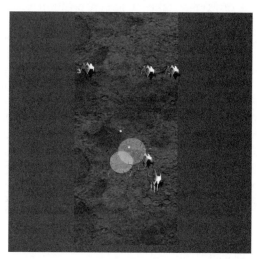

FIGURE 5.15   Running the game without resizing the display.

EXTENDING THE GAME

There are several ways that this game could be extended to develop it into a full-fledged action arcade title:

- Try adding a greater variety of enemy ships. Rather than just bob, create several and have them vary in their look and performance. You could even create a custom `onEnterFrame` function for each enemy type so that, while bob moves in a wave, others could move straight, faster, slower, and so on.
- Give enemies the ability to fire at you. This would require the enemy movie clip to make a call to `createProjectile` and require a change to `createProjectile` so that the projectile checks for collision with the player, which it currently doesn't do.
- Create several types of projectiles, perhaps missiles, or even laser beams, each with a different motion characteristic. How about a smart bomb that hones in on the nearest enemy or a bullet that moves, like bob, in a wave pattern?
- Create multiple levels. When the end of a level is reached, the next level could begin, with a different background image and so on. Perhaps give the player more than one life.
- Add sound (see the sound chapter for more information).

The possibilities are endless; creativity is the only limit.

SUMMARY

In this chapter we learned several key concepts:

- Creating multiple moving movie clips on the fly and giving them properties and behaviors.
- Detecting for collision using a nested loop (a loop within another loop). While we didn't actually have a loop physically within a loop, in the traditional sense, we did have a loop running on each bullet, and Flash was automatically looping through each bullet, every frame.
- Using the `Math.sin` function to create a wave motion.
- Smoothly scrolling a background image for an indefinite amount of time.
- The importance of deleting movie clips that are no longer needed.
- Creating movie clips within movie clips to ensure proper organization of graphics, as well as it being an easy way to instantly delete all of one type of movie clip. For example, delete all enemy ships at once by simply deleting the `enemyLayer`.
- Using the various forms of `hitTest` to perform intrinsic collision.

SOUND FOR GAMES

One of the most important aspects of game design, and one of the most often overlooked, is sound. Many game designers don't recognize sound's potential for enhancing the overall experience of a game. The addition of sound can elevate a game on several levels:

Professionalism: Players take games with good sound and/or music much more seriously.

Immersion: It's much easier for a player to become immersed in a game world that has a full sound aspect to it, rather than graphics and silence.

Feedback: An entire new layer of feedback can be presented to the player with the addition of sound. Players can be aware of things that are not visible, like a monster off screen, by simply hearing it.

When it comes to sound, designers tend to skip past this step altogether. After all, you can have a computer with no speakers attached, but you cannot have a computer without a monitor of some sort.

Just like visual design, the audio design in a game is an intricate process. Sound effects and music are finely tuned to match a specific style or genre. Are the sounds metallic and hard or are they spacey and light? The stylistic choices in sound are as important as the stylistic choices in design.

We're going to look at sound in two parts: sound effects and music. Sound effects have a more literal application in that they provide the audio we *expect* when playing a game. If we see a bomb explode, we expect to hear an explosion, if we see a racecar drive by, we expect to hear its engine.

Music, on the other hand, is much more interpretive. While sound effects are (often) more a matter of finding the sounds to match the visuals, music is an *artistic* choice made by the game designer or musician. Sound effects guide the player's perception of the *information* in a scene, but music guides the player's *emotional response* to a scene. Music is responsible for evoking a feeling that may not necessarily be natural to a particular time, place, or circumstance. We'll be looking at this in more detail in the music section.

 In case you're wondering, the author of this book is a professional game programmer but is also a lifelong musician (since the age of four) who has spent thousands of hours in front of a piano and a computer creating music for personal use and for games.

Sound Effects for Games

Sound effects in games are meant to provide the player with information about the state of the game in various forms. These forms are:

Game play events: These are the various events that take place during the game and are critical parts of the player's experience. These are the explosions, the monster growls, and the roaring engines. These sounds tend to mimic real life. In some cases, however, the sounds are not necessarily reality based but are still based on game events. For example, when the player grabs the power up, we may hear a synthesized sound effect. This is not a real-life sound, but it is an in-game event sound.

User interface: These are the sound effects that are designed to provide the player with an auditory feedback to interactions with the user interface, for example, clicking on a button or opening a menu. These sounds don't necessarily have a real-life counterpart; when a real-life person is choosing which inventory item to swap around, there won't be beeps and clicks as he moves a dagger from his backpack to his hand, but the user interface to do so in a game may be full of beeps and clicks.

There are several key steps to selecting a game play sound. First, you must make sure to find a good sound that accurately represents the game event you're trying to draw attention to. There are dozens of good online sound effects Web sites, as well as many sound effects libraries that can be bought and used in a royalty-free fashion. Two of the best of these sites are:

- *http://www.sound-effects-library.com/*
- *http://www.sounddogs.com/*

Often going into a local music store and looking for the sound effects libraries is all you have to do. Be aware to ensure that the usage license allows the use of these sounds in a royalty-free fashion; otherwise you may find that you owe someone a lot of money.

One of the best things Flash offers when it comes to sound is the ability to arbitrarily place these sounds in space, using the volume and pan functionality via the setVolume and setPan methods. We'll be looking at those shortly. For now, let's look at the basic creation and trigger of a sound.

Basic Sound Effect Trigger

When triggering a basic sound effect, we're looking at the act of importing a sound effect, setting it up for linkage in the library, and then using code to play that sound back at runtime.

1. Open up Macromedia Flash Professional 8 and start a new, blank movie.
2. From the File menu, choose Import > Import to Library.
3. In the dialog box that appears, navigate to and choose a sound effect. You can use your own or you can use the one we've provided on the CD-ROM, called myeffect.wav, in the Chapter 6 folder (see Figure 6.1). Be sure to copy the file from the CD-ROM to your hard drive before importing, as Flash can have problems when importing directly from a CD.

ON THE CD

FIGURE 6.1   Selecting a sound in the Import to Library dialog box.

4. Click Open.

Now the sound has been imported into the library of our new movie. It's almost ready to be coded to life, but we need to set up a few things first.

5. Open the library by pressing Ctrl-L or choosing Library from the Window menu. You should see the library appear as shown in Figure 6.2.
6. Right-click on the imported sound in the library, and choose Linkage from the pop-up menu.
7. In the Linkage Properties dialog box that appears, make sure that the Export for ActionScript checkbox is selected and type "myeffect" into the Identifier text box, like in Figure 6.3.
8. Click OK.

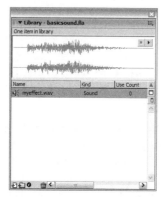

FIGURE 6.2 Viewing the library, which contains one imported sound.

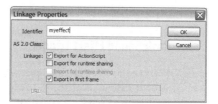

FIGURE 6.3 Editing the linkage properties for the imported sound.

Now that we've done that, this sound will be exported with the SWF file when it is created.

This is a good opportunity to look at setting the file output settings of our imported sound. Right-click on the sound in the library and select Properties. From within the box that appears, you can set the quality settings of the final exported file. The dialog box that appears looks like Figure 6.4.

At the bottom of the window you'll see the Compression drop-down menu. From here, you can choose one of several options:

ADPCM: This setting is best for short game sound effects, similar to the one that we just imported. This method of compression requires less CPU computation from the Flash Player, while maintaining a relatively small file size. The compression settings available are:

Sample Rate: This is the rate, in kilohertz, at which the sound will be resampled. The higher the number, the better the quality but the larger the file size. The available options are 5 kHz, 11 kHz, 22 kHz, and 44 kHz.

ADPCM bits: A digital sound is made up of a stream of distinct samples, which tend to oscillate up and down like a wave. Sounds stored in ADPCM format are stored by recording the *difference* between samples rather than the actual value of the sample. Since the difference from

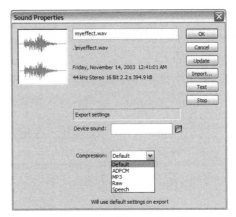

FIGURE 6.4   The Sound Properties dialog box.

one sample to the next tends to be very small, we only need a small number of bits to store that difference. This setting allows us to specify how many bits are used to store the differences. Play with this value to get a desired result. Valid values are 2, 3, 4, and 5 bits.

MP3: This uses the ever-popular MP3 compression formulas to store sounds in the SWF file. MP3 sounds take a bit more processor effort to play because of the complex nature of MP3 decoding and are therefore best used for longer sounds, such as soundtracks and music, which benefit most from the high compression ratio. The settings available are:

Bit Rate: This specifies the desired number of bits of data that we would like to have played in one second. This is measured in kilobits per second, or kbps. This method of compression specification is used because in an online Web environment, we want to base our compression on the available download bandwidth. The settings range from 8 kbps all the way up to 160 kbps. 8 kbps tends to be barely understandable, while 160 kbps is CD quality. The best thing to do is play with different settings until you arrive at a sound you're happy with. To save file size, it's possible to convert two-track stereo sounds to one-track mono, thus reducing the amount of data in the final SWF by 50%. The option to keep a sound in a stereo format is not available to you until you select a bit rate of 20 kbps or higher.

Raw: This format performs no compression on the sound and is therefore the best in quality and highest in file size. There is a sample rate option and a convert stereo to mono option. The higher the sample rate, the better the quality.

Speech: This uses a special form of MP3 compression that is specifically tuned to making human speech sound clearest while at the same time keeping file size at a minimum. There is also a sample rate option and a convert stereo to mono option. The higher the sample rate, the better the quality.

As you try different settings, remember to press the Test button to hear what each setting will sound like in the final SWF.

Go back to the main timeline, click on the first frame, and enter the following code:

```
mySoundObject = new Sound();
mySoundObject.attachSound("myeffect");
```

Here we're creating an instance of the Sound class and we're telling it to attach to itself the imported sound that we linked as myeffect in the library. The new sound object has several methods. The most important is the start method. Add this code below the previous two lines.

```
mySoundObject.start(0,1);
```

Test this movie with Ctrl-Enter; the sound will play once. The start method takes two parameters: offset and loop count. The offset is the number of seconds into the sound that you want it to begin playing. So, if you have a 10-second sound, and you pass a 5 in as the first parameter, the sound will begin playing at the 5-second mark; it will immediately start from the halfway point.

The second parameter is the loop count. This is how many times you want the sound to repeat. Putting a 0 or a 1 in here has the same effect; they both cause the sound to play once. If you put a 2 in as the loop count, the sound will play twice through before stopping.

Arguably, the second most important method is the stop method. It works very simply:

```
mySoundObject.stop();
```

ON THE CD

When that code is run it will cause the sound associated with mySoundObject to stop playing, no matter what it's currently doing. All of this code can be found in the file basicsound.fla in the Chapter 6 folder of the accompanying CD-ROM.

Macromedia Flash Professional 8 uses a 16-channel stereo sound buffer. This means you can have up to 16 full-stereo sounds playing at the same time (you can have hundreds of sound objects created) or 32 mono channels playing. If you have 16 stereo sounds playing and you try to play a 17th, nothing will happen. The sound simply will not start.

Volume and Pan Placement

One of the nice things we can do with our sounds in Flash is set their volume levels at real time using code and set their pan amount. Pan allows us to move a sound from one speaker to the other. This allows for the creation of some pretty advanced game stereo effects. If, for example, we wanted the sound of a monster approaching from the right, we could play a monster sound and pan it all the way to the right. The player would get the impression that a monster was off screen to the right.

Picking up from the example in the previous section, we have a single sound effect imported and linked, with a `Sound` object created in code called `mySound-Object`. Add the following code to the end of the previous code:

```
mySoundObject.setVolume(50);
mySoundObject.setPan(100);
```

When we run this movie, we'll hear the same sound effect, but this time it'll be quieter and it will appear to be panned all the way to the right.

The `setVolume` method takes one parameter: volume level. This is a number from 0 to 100, where 0 is essentially muted and 100 is full volume.

The `setPan` method takes one parameter as well: pan amount. This is a number from −100 to 100. When we pass in −100, the sound will be panned all the way to the left; passing in 100 will pan the sound all the way to the right. Passing in a 0 will cause the sound to be centered and split evenly between both speakers.

Add the following code after all the previous code:

```
_root.onMouseMove = function()
{
    mySoundObject.setPan(((_xmouse / 550) * 200) - 100);
    mySoundObject.setVolume((_ymouse / 400) * 100);
}
```

Also, make a change to the `Sound.start` method call so that the sound plays indefinitely, like so:

```
mySoundObject.start(0,9999);
```

This will cause the sound to play through 9,999 times. This isn't really infinite, but it's good enough. You'd be surprised at just how long it would take to play through the included sound effect almost 10,000 times: about 8 hours.

Run this movie and see what happens. When you move the mouse cursor around the stage area, the sound pans left to right depending on the horizontal x position of the mouse cursor, and the volume is increased and decreased depending on the vertical y position of the mouse cursor. This is a good tool to use to see just how a sound effect will sound in all different volume and pan combinations. All of this can be found in the file `basicsoundvolpan.fla` on the CD-ROM, in the Chapter 6 folder.

ON THE CD

We'll be looking more at the use of event sounds in the next chapter when we start getting into placing them in a game.

User Interface Sounds

Sounds that are employed in a user interface (UI) setting tend to be more symbolic in their nature, rather than literal. A soft glassy ding sound can be used to reinforce the user's selection of a particular menu option, not just for the *actual* physical dinging of a glass.

The stylistic choices made when matching UI sounds to their accompanying visuals are important. Are the visuals very ethereal and abstract? Then perhaps the sounds of heavy machinery and hydraulics should be bypassed in favor of spacier, airy sounds that use rich, pleasing tones. On the other hand, perhaps the visuals revolve around a post-apocalyptic machine world reminiscent of the film, *The Matrix*. In this case your sound decisions would best be along the lines of deep dark drones and the sound of heavy machinery. The stylistic choices of UI sounds are as interpretive as the visuals themselves.

The only real differentiation between game event sounds and UI sounds is the added option to embed the sounds directly onto the timeline of a button or animation. To create a button that automatically plays a certain sound when the user clicks on it, we would embed a sound specifically onto the Down frame in the timeline of that button. It's that easy. To make a sound play when the user rolls over a button, put a sound on the Over frame as well.

1. Create a standard button object on the stage. To begin with, simply draw a box on the stage, then select that box and press F8 to convert to symbol. Make sure that button is selected as the Behavior, like in Figure 6.5
2. Go into the timeline of the button by double-clicking on it or right-clicking on it and choosing Edit.
3. Import the sounds you would like to use for Over and Down frames by choosing Import > Import to Library from the File menu.
4. Inside the button rename the main layer from `Layer 1` to `Graphics` and create a new layer above it, called `Sound`. In the new `Sound` layer add three keyframes by selecting the first frame and pressing F6 twice. The end result should look like Figure 6.6.

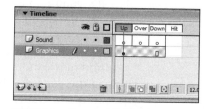

FIGURE 6.6 Creating the layers.

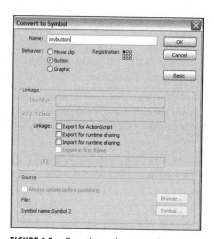

FIGURE 6.5 Creating a button object.

5. You can now place event sounds on the Up, Over, and Down frames. The sound on the Up frame will be triggered when the user moves the mouse cursor off of the button. The sound on the Over frame will be triggered when the user rolls onto the button, and the Down frame sound will be played when the user clicks on the button. Set the sounds on the frames as follows:

a. Go to the desired frame and select the frame in the timeline.

b. In the properties panel choose a sound from the Sound drop-down menu. All sounds in your library will be available for you to choose from (see Figure 6.7).

FIGURE 6.7   Setting a frame sound in the properties panel.

Once you've done that, the button will be sound enabled, and running the movie will show this. The other way to do UI event sounds is, of course, with the code from the previous section, but we'll be looking into that more in the next chapter.

MUSIC FOR GAMES

To understand the power of music, one doesn't need to look much farther than the Hollywood film industry. In movies music is an emotional cue card that we unconsciously follow, and it makes us feel and react in certain ways. We can see a completely static image, for example, a house on a hill, and if we hear soft romantic music we will feel contentment and well-being looking at it. On the other hand, if we were to hear some tense or scary music, we will look at this house with a sense of dread and foreboding and will feel fear when the camera starts to move toward it.

In games music plays a similar role, although at times music in games must also be used to drive the adrenaline of the player. To this end, there's usually a mix of something like driving techno (in modern Web games especially) to the fully realized cinematic scores of a digital Hollywood.

The act of creating music is more of an art form than merely a technical process of importing sounds and is thus harder to write about. Music must be created, obtained, or recorded in another application and then brought into Macromedia Flash Professional 8 as an MP3 or WAV file.

Music can be obtained in a fully complete, and looping, form from music Web sites such as Symphony Planet (*www.symphonyplanet.com*), or we can use music-creation packages such as Propellorhead Reason, or Acid Pro from Sony Pictures Digital Media Software and Services (previously from Sonic Foundry) to create full soundtracks or loop-based music. For more information on this, take a look at:

- *http://mediasoftware.sonypictures.com/products/acidfamily.asp*
- *http://www.propellerheads.se/*

In the next chapter we're going to look at taking and selecting music, putting it into a game, and using the sound code we've discussed in this chapter to make a game that has a complete soundtrack and set of sound effects.

SUMMARY

In this chapter we learned several key concepts:

- The different types and uses of sound effects in games
- Importing sounds and setting them up for linkage
- The sound compression settings
- Attaching sound at runtime with code
- Playing back and stopping sounds
- Modifying the volume and pan settings of a sound in real time
- Creating frame-based button sounds
- The purpose of music in games

SOUND HUNTER

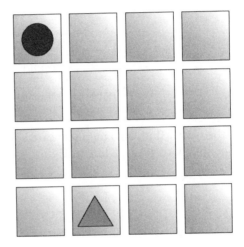

In the last chapter we looked at using sound in games and how we can best create sound effects and embed music. In this chapter we're going to take things one step further and create a game that is focused entirely on sound.

How do we do this? How do we create a game that revolves around sound rather than graphics? Well, typical Macromedia Flash 8 games tend to be stronger on graphics than sound, so we have our work cut out for us.

Well, what we're going to do is create a spin on the classic game *Memory Match*. In *Memory Match* the player is presented with a grid of cards. These cards are blank on one side and contain pictures on the other side. The picture sides start off facing down.

If there are 16 cards, there are a total of eight pictures, and each picture exists on two cards. The player must flip over two at a time in order to find matches. When they reveal two cards that do not match, the cards are flipped back over and the player must use his memory to *remember* where the cards are and then proceed. This mismatch is illustrated in Figure 7.1.

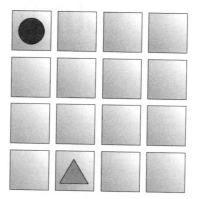

FIGURE 7.1   Mismatched cards.

If the player finds two identical cards, then those cards are removed from the board and play continues, like in Figure 7.2 and Figure 7.3.

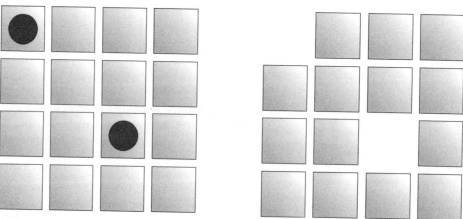

FIGURE 7.2   Matched cards.

FIGURE 7.3   The matched cards are removed.

Usually, the game is played with two people and the players compete to get the most number of matches. The player with the most number of matches at the end is the winner.

That's typical *Memory Match*. In our game, however, we're not going to be matching pictures. We're going to be matching *sounds*. The idea is that the game is played identically, with a grid of cards, but when you click on a card, you don't see a picture—you hear a sound. The object is to match up all the sounds and clear the board.

CREATING THE GAME

The 18 sounds we've chosen consist of many things. The sounds are:

- Arcade sound
- Bell ding
- Brushing teeth
- Car horn
- Car start
- Chicken cluck
- Coins poured
- Dog bark
- Garbage disposal
- Ping-pong ball
- Pouring coffee
- Punch grunt
- Sawing wood
- Swirly sound
- Sword whip
- Telephone ring
- Toilet flush
- Zipper

These are fairly random sounds taken from real life. The idea is to use sounds that are very distinct from one another, so that the matching is easy. For example, to use 18 variations of foghorn sound would probably make the game impossible to play.

ON THE CD

We're going to create this game by building upon an already-existing FLA file. From the Chapter 7 folder on the CD-ROM, open up the file soundHunterSounds.fla. This contains no graphics, movie clips, or code. All we have is a library full of our 18 sounds, imported and linked to save you time. The linkage names of the sounds are s0, s1, s2, and so on up to s17. Look at Figure 7.4 to see this library.

1. On the stage draw a box that is 80 pixels wide and 60 pixels high. Make sure it's white with a black outline.
2. Select the entire box and Press F8 to convert to symbol. Make sure its behavior is set to Button and give it the name inbut.
3. Press OK
4. Double-click on the newly created button, and once inside, copy the first frame twice by clicking in the frame and pressing F6 two times.
5. On the second frame change the color of the box to Orange.
6. On the third frame change the color of the box to Blue.
7. Return to the main timeline.

Now we have created the button that will be used to trigger the events. Next, we must create the movie clip we'll be attaching at runtime to create our on-screen grid.

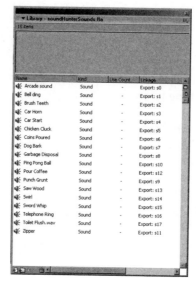

FIGURE 7.4 The library of sounds in soundHunterSounds.fla.

8. With the button selected, press F8.
9. This time make sure that the behavior is set to Movie Clip and name it card.
10. Select the Export for ActionScript checkbox and in the identifier text field name it card.
11. Press OK.

Now the movie clip on stage is simply a movie clip that contains one instance of the button, inbut. We must now go into the movie clip and give the button an instance name so we can attach code to it.

12. Double-click on the newly created movie clip.
13. Once inside, select the button and give it an instance name of inbut from the properties panel.
14. Return to the main timeline.

Now we can safely delete this movie clip from the stage because it is linked in the library and ready to be used. The stage should once again be completely blank. The library should be the same as when we started except that now it also contains a movie clip called card set up for linkage as card and a button called inbut.

THE CODE

The game is ready to be coded. On the main timeline click on frame 1 of the Actions layer and if it's not open already, open the Actions window by pressing F9.

Enter the following code:

```
numsounds = 18;
selone = -1;
```

This will create two variables that are used later on. Next, start the creation of the `build` function, like so:

```
function build ()
{
```

This function is going to be used to physically create the board on screen, as well as create sound objects and attach code to the buttons. Inside this function, add the following code:

```
for (var i = 0; i < (numsounds * 2); i++)
{
```

This is our main creation loop. Notice that we're creating exactly twice as many cards as there are sounds. Next, add the following code:

```
nm = "crd" + i;
_root.attachMovie("card", nm, i);
_root[nm]._x = (i % 6) * 82 + 44;
_root[nm]._y = Math.floor(i / 6) * 62 + 34;
```

Here we're attaching the cards to the stage and placing them in their appropriate position in the grid. Each card is called `"crd"` + i, and that name is stored in `nm`. We have `crd0`, `crd1`, `crd2`, and so on, up to `crd17`. We're calling the `attachMovie` function to place an instance of `card` on the stage and giving it the instance name stored in `nm` at depth level `i`. We then set the card's _x and _y positions based on the formulas:

_x is (i % 6) * 82, and then 44 is added to move it off of the left edge of the screen. The _x position of the card will be a multiple of 82, based on the value of i % 6. Using the modulus operator (%) i % 6 will always return a number that is either 0, 1, 2, 3, 4, or 5. Once it reaches 6, i % 6 will return 0, and the cycle will repeat. This way, we will get six cards per row.

The _y position of the card is calculated by taking the value of `i`, dividing it by 6, and using `Math.floor` on that result. This means the first six cards will be on row 0, the next six cards will be on row 1, and so on. The row number is then multiplied by 62, and 34 is added to move it down from the top of the screen.

In the end, we'll have a grid on screen of 6 × 6 cards, each column being 82 pixels wide, and each row being 62 pixels high. Since the cards are 80 × 60, there will be a 2-pixel border between all the cards. Look at Figure 7.5 to see the final grid.

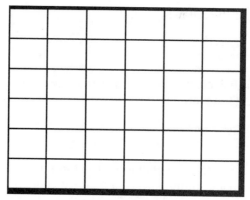

FIGURE 7.5   The game grid of cards.

Enter the following code next:

```
snd = "s" + (i % numsounds);
_root[nm].s = new Sound(_root[nm]);
_root[nm].s.attachSound(snd);
_root[nm].myid = (i % numsounds);
```

This code gives every card its own instance of the Sound class, and the sound that it attaches is derived from "s" + (i % numsounds). This means the first 18 cards will contain sounds s0, s1, s2, s3, up to s17, and the second 18 cards will also contain s0, s1, s2, s3, up to s17. There isn't much randomness to this, but don't worry—we'll be shuffling the cards soon.

Once the new instance of the Sound class, s, is created on the card movie clip, the sound ID name stored in the string snd is used and that ID is attached to the Sound class, using attachSound. Each card is then given a variable called myid, which is simply the number of the sound attached to it. This is used later.

Next, enter the following code:

```
_root[nm].inbut.onRelease = function()
{

    this._parent.s.start(0,0);
```

This is where we start to attach code to the button inside the card. This button, inbut, is given an onRelease function, which will be triggered when the user clicks and releases the mouse button on it. The first thing we do is tell the sound to play by calling the start method of the Sound class. Remember that the Sound class s is attached to the card movie clip, and not to the button. Since this onRelease function is attached to the button, we must tell the sound to play by calling this._parent, rather than simply this.

When a card is first clicked, we mark it as selected by doing a very simple adjustment to its _xscale and _yscale. When the player selects a card, we set its _xscale and _yscale to 80, which gives the effect of making the card appear to have a black border around it, making it appear selected, as shown in Figure 7.6.

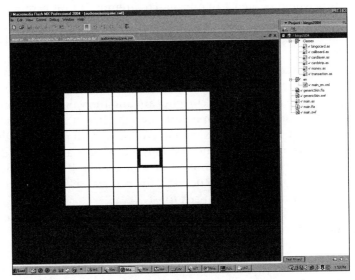

FIGURE 7.6   Selected card effect performed with _xscale and _yscale.

As a result, we can determine if a card is already selected by simply checking its _xscale value. That's the first thing we do. Enter the following code:

```
if (this._parent._xscale == 100)
{
    if (selone == -1)
    {
        selone = this._parent;
        this._parent._xscale = this._parent._yscale = 80;
    }
    else
    {
        if (this._parent.myid == selone.myid)
        {
            selone._visible = false;
            this._parent._visible = false;
            selone = -1;
        }
        else
        {
            selone._xscale = selone._yscale = 100;
            selone = -1;
        }
    }
}
```

We first make sure the card is not already selected. If it's not, then we check the value of the selone variable. This is used to determine whether or not we have a card already selected. When selone is −1, we have no other card selected, and this would be step 1 of our match attempt. In this case we simply set selone to be the value of the card movie clip (it now becomes a reference to the movie clip) and we then set the _xscale and _yscale of the selected card to 80, making it shrink by 20%.

If selone is not equal to −1, we know this is the second step in the match attempt and the player is now trying to see if he's found his match. By comparing the value of myid in the current card and the value of myid in the currently selected card (in selone), we can determine whether or not they contain the same sound.

If the myid variables match, we make both cards invisible and set selone back to −1. The match was successful, so both cards are removed from the board. If, on the other hand, the sounds do not match (this._parent.myid is not equal to selone.myid), we simply deselect the original selection by resetting its scale to 100, and then we set selone back to −1.

That's it for the build function. Finish off the rest of the function by closing all opened curly braces, like so:

```
            }
        }
    }
```

Here's the build function in its entirety:

```
function build()
{
    for (var i = 0; i < (numsounds * 2); i++)
    {
        nm = "crd" + i;
        _root.attachMovie("card", nm, i);
        _root[nm]._x = (i % 6) * 82 + 44;
        _root[nm]._y = Math.floor(i / 6) * 62 + 34;

        snd = "s" + (i % numsounds);
        _root[nm].s = new Sound(_root[nm]);
        _root[nm].s.attachSound(snd);
        _root[nm].myid = (i % numsounds);

        _root[nm].inbut.onRelease = function()
        {

            this._parent.s.start(0,0);

            if (this._parent._xscale == 100)
            {
                if (selone == -1)
                {
                    selone = this._parent;
                    this._parent._xscale =
```

```
                                this._parent._yscale = 80;
                    }
                    else
                    {
                        if (this._parent.myid == selone.myid)
                        {
                            selone._visible = false;
                            this._parent._visible = false;
                            selone = -1;
                        }
                        else
                        {
                            selone._xscale=selone._yscale=100;
                            selone = -1;
                        }
                    }
                }
            }
        }
    }
```

Now that the `build` function is done, enter the following code and try running the movie:

```
build();
```

It plays correctly, but the match for any card is exactly three cards above or below it. They've been created in this exact layout, with their sound IDs in the grid below:

s0	s1	s2	s3	s4	s5
s6	s7	s8	s9	s10	s11
s12	s13	s14	s15	s16	s17
s0	s1	s2	s3	s4	s5
s6	s7	s8	s9	s10	s11
s12	s13	s14	s15	s16	s17

This is problematic, of course, because there's not much challenge when all the cards are in the exact same position every game. We need to create a function to shuffle the cards into new, random positions. We'll call our new function `shuffle`. Delete the call to `build()` for now and enter the following code below the last line of our `build` function.

```
shuffle = function()
{
```

This is our function definition. The `shuffle` procedure works on a very simple principle. Pick any two cards and swap their positions and then repeat that process several hundred times. This will cause all the cards to eventually be moved to random locations around the board.

To that end, enter the following code:

```
for (var i = 0; i < 200; i++)
{
```

This is how many times we're going to do a random card swap: 200 times. This is enough that, on average, every card will have been swapped about five times, causing the board to be very randomly shuffled. Enter the following code:

```
var c1 = Math.floor(Math.random() * numcards * 2);
var c2 = Math.floor(Math.random() * numcards * 2);
```

Here we're simply choosing two random numbers: c1 and c2. These refer to the cards we're going to swap. c1 will be a random number between 0 and 35, and so will c2. We can take these values and use them to determine which two cards we're going to swap. Enter the following:

```
var tx = _root["crd" + c1]._x;
var ty = _root["crd" + c1]._y;
```

The first thing to do is store the position of card c1 in two temporary variables: tx and ty. In order to do the swap, we have to remember where the first card used to be, because we'll be overwriting that position with:

```
_root["crd" + c1]._x = _root["crd" + c2]._x;
_root["crd" + c1]._y = _root["crd" + c2]._y;
```

Card 1, defined as "crd" + c1 will now be moved to be above card 2, defined as "crd" + c2. Once this has happened, we can now move card 2 to the location that card 1 used to occupy, which was stored in tx and ty. Add the following.

```
        _root["crd" + c2]._x = tx;
        _root["crd" + c2]._y = ty;
    }
}
```

That's the end of the shuffle function. Now add the following two lines of code:

```
build();
shuffle();
```

And that's the entire game. We must call shuffle after calling build, because we can only shuffle once our card movie clips have been created. Try the game out. The final game can also be found in the Chapter 7 folder, using the files audiomemorygame. swf and audiomemorygame.fla.

One of the interesting things about this game is the way our brains handle the information. Generally, *Memory Match* relies upon a visual picture and imprint of the drawing on the card. In Sound Hunter, we don't have the visual aid. We have to use our auditory memory. Some people are better at it than others. For example, visual artists tend to do very well at *Memory Match*, and accordingly it would make sense that musicians would do very well at Sound Hunter; but that has not been studied. Ultimately it just shows you whether you're a visual person or an auditory person.

SUMMARY

In this chapter we looked at using the sound object to create a simple *Memory Match* game. We looked at:

- Dynamically attaching sound objects at runtime
- Creating code to play those sounds
- Randomly shuffling objects on screen using a random swap procedure

SAVING DATA

Imagine this: a player is on level 19 of your game, he's defeated two of the five super bosses, he has a large inventory of items, and has brought his character's vital stats up to an all-time high. Oh, and he also has 8,352 gold pieces, which is enough to make him moderately rich in this game universe.

If this were a professional game in a box, bought at the store, the player would come to expect no less than the ability to press a Save button and save all of his progress into a safe and sound file on the hard drive so he could continue his adventures another day. The ability to save your game, or save the map you've designed or any other number of types of saves, is a standard and expected feature of professional games.

Enter the Macromedia Flash Player (the software to play SWF files, not a person). Now we have an operating-system independent player that draws graphics, plays sound, and gives the user almost infinite control over the interface. What the Macromedia Flash Player doesn't give us, however, is full random access to the user's hard drive and thus the ability to arbitrarily save any information we want.

What's the reason for this? Security. Since SWF files tend to be downloaded off the Web and played on a large number of machines transparently to the user (think of all the Flash banner ads you've seen), presenting the developer with unhindered access to the user's hard drive presents a real opportunity for malicious developers. All one would need to do would be to write an SWF that created a malicious VBS (Visual Basic Script) file on the hard drive. That script could be executed at a later date by some other process (or if the Flash player was as open as professional development systems, it could, itself, execute the VBS file).

So Macromedia has taken away the ability to arbitrarily write files and then maliciously execute these files. Does this mean that all hope is lost for our players who are about to enter the most difficult dungeon in the game?

No, all hope is not lost, because Macromedia has given us the `SharedObject` class. This was introduced in Macromedia Flash MX, and it's still available to us today, in Flash 8.

THE `SharedObject` SOL FILE

The `SharedObject` is a class that allows us to create files on the user's hard drive that adhere to the `SharedObject` file format. These files, which have an extension of SOL, can contain any type of data that we create within our movie. These basic types of data include:

- Arrays
- Numbers
- Strings
- Booleans
- Objects, which are made up of any of the above data types

This means that though we can't just create arbitrary files, which could be potentially malicious scripts, we can create files that will suit our purposes: data storage files. SOL files aren't stored anywhere on the user's hard drive, however. They're stored in a very specific location, thereby increasing their security even further. Typically, the Macromedia Flash Player will create any new SOL files in a hidden directory off of the user's main hard drive. Here's a path to the SOL files from drive C: `C:\Documents and Settings\UserName\Application Data\Macromedia\Flash Player`.

Where you see the word `UserName`, it is usually substituted with the actual name of the logged in user, or perhaps if you have no one specific user account, it will be the administrator account. For the author of this book, SOL files are stored at `C:\Documents and Settings\Glen Rhodes\Application Data\Macromedia\Flash Player`.

In Figure 8.1 we can see the full path to the `SharedObject` root.

 You may have trouble finding the `Application Data` folder because by default it is a hidden folder. You must first disable hidden folders by opening up an Explorer window and choosing Tools > Folder Options. Choose the View tab, and then finally make sure Show Hidden Files and Folders is selected, like in Figure 8.2.

FIGURE 8.1   The root path
of SharedObject storage.

Within this SharedObject root folder, you'll see a small or large list of subfolders, depending on how many sites you have visited that have created SharedObjects on your hard drive. Each subfolder is named according to the Web site it came from (see Figure 8.3).

FIGURE 8.2   How to see hidden
folders.

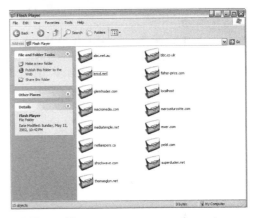

FIGURE 8.3   The SharedObject storage root
folder.

Notice that there is a folder called localhost. This is where SharedObjects are stored when the user runs an SWF file locally, instead of from the Web. From within each directory, things are usually even further subdivided based on the *name* of the SWF file. So, for example, if we look inside the glenrhodes.com folder, we see what's in Figure 8.4.

Notice that there's a directory called resizeable2.swf. Within this folder are all the SOL files created by the file resizeable2.swf from glenrhodes.com. There are, however, some SOL files directly in the root of the glenrhodes.com folder. When creating SharedObjects, we'll soon see that it's possible to specify the location to which they're written within the domain's folder, and that it's possible to have

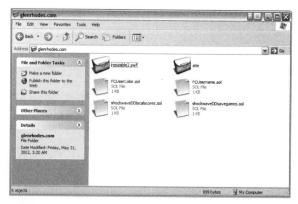

FIGURE 8.4 The contents of the `glenrhodes.com` folder on the author's hard drive.

the SOL files written to the root location, or in other words, the top level of the `glenrhodes.com` folder. We cannot write them any higher up, however.

`SharedObjects`, or SOL files, can almost be thought of as cookies. It's possible to have them written to the user's hard drive without his knowledge, as long as the user has initially consented to giving your Web site permission to create `SharedObjects` in the first place. By default, the Macromedia Flash Player allows any Web site to create `SharedObjects`, up to a maximum of 100 k in size. Once the `SharedObject` surpasses this size, it will present the user with a warning box asking him to allow the `SharedObject` to be saved. At this time the user can modify the maximum size from unlimited down to none. Be warned that at this point the user can completely deny your Web site write access. Figure 8.5 shows this dialog box.

FIGURE 8.5 The `SharedObject` size limit selection box.

If the player chooses a new maximum file size that happens to be less than the file size currently in use by the SWF, the user will be warned that the `SharedObjects` are about to be deleted. The user can also at this point click on the Never Ask Again checkbox, in which case he'll never be prompted for file size warnings; if the size exceeds the set maximum, the set maximum will be increased.

The best thing to do is try to ensure that your game never needs to use more than 100 k of data for a save file. Then the user will never have to worry about file size settings, warnings, permissions, and so on. Web users today tend to get very nervous when they're presented with warning boxes telling them that the application they're running is trying to access their local hard drive, even though SharedObjects are *very* secure. The only malicious thing that could be done with SharedObjects would be to create an SOL file that fills up the user's hard drive. This could happen if the user selected Unlimited file size at a malicious site. Generally, users should only select Unlimited if they trust the site.

THE SharedObject CLASS

ON THE CD

Now that we've looked at the intricacies of how the files associated with Shared-Objects are stored on the user's hard drive, we're going to look at the code required to create these SharedObjects, or SOL files. All of this example code can be found on the CD-ROM in the Chapter 8 folder.

The SharedObject class has a surprisingly small number of methods and parameters. The methods are:

SharedObject.clear(): This is the method we call if we want to destroy a SharedObject that we have created on the user's hard drive in the past. This removes all the data from the SharedObject and then deletes it from the disk.

SharedObject.flush(): We call the flush method to immediately write all the data in a SharedObject to the hard drive. Generally, we build our Shared-Object at runtime, and then when we're happy with it, we write it to the disk with SharedObject.flush().

SharedObject.getLocal(): This is the function we use to load, or initially create, the SOL file.

SharedObject.getSize(): This returns the current size, in bytes, of a SharedObject.

The SharedObject has only one property: SharedObject.data. It is into this property that we put all of the data that we want to save to the disk. The data property is essentially an object into which we can assign any number of properties, and all of these properties are saved with the SharedObject SOL file.

Under normal operational circumstances, saving data to the user's hard drive should present no problem at all, but we do have to allow for the occasional circumstance in which the user has, in the past, set up their Flash Player to reject SharedObjects.

Let's create an example in which we save data associated with a game. Start by creating a new, blank movie. Into the first frame, enter the following code:

```
setPlayerInfo = function()
{
    player = new Object;
    player.health = 45;
    player.strength = 98;
    player.pname = "Ralph";
    player.inventory = new Array("Sword", "Knife", "Healing Potion",
"Rune", "Empty Quiver", "Rations");
```

```
        player.currentLevel = 3;
    }
```

This represents an in-game example of the kind of data we might need to store. Here we have a player named Ralph with a health level of 45 and a strength level of 98 and he's carrying a sword, a knife, a healing potion, a rune, an empty quiver, and some rations. To represent all this data, we store it in a generic object called player, which is created when we call this setPlayerInfo function.

The player's health and strength are stored as numeric variables on the player object. The player's name is stored in the string variable pname, and his entire inventory is stored in an array called inventory.

Now that we've got the player object defined, let's look at saving it. Enter the following code next:

```
savePlayer = function()
{
    playerSO = SharedObject.getLocal("playerInfo");
    playerSO.data.playerDat = player;
    playerSO.flush();
}
```

This will create a new SharedObject SOL file on the hard drive. The file will be called playerInfo.sol. We store the reference to this active SharedObject in the variable playerSO. Using the letters SO is common when referring to SharedObjects. Now, any references to, or actions we want to perform on, this SharedObject will be through the playerSO variable.

Once the SharedObject is opened and created, we create a new property on the data object of playerSO. This property is called playerDat, and we set it to be the value of the player object. This will save the entire body of the player object, including the structure, the array, and all variable names and data.

The last thing we do in that function is call the flush method to force the SharedObject file to be saved to the hard disk.

Finally, we have one more function to define.

```
loadPlayer = function()
{
    playerSO = SharedObject.getLocal("playerInfo");
    player = new Object();
    player.health = playerSO.data.playerDat.health;
    player.strength = playerSO.data.playerDat.strength;
    player.pname = playerSO.data.playerDat.pname;
    player.inventory = new Array();
    for (var i = 0;
        i < playerSO.data.playerDat.inventory.length;
        i++)
    {
        player.inventory[i] =
        playerSO.data.playerDat.inventory[i];
    }
```

```
        player.currentLevel = playerSO.data.playerDat.currentLevel;
}
```

This performs the opposite function to `savePlayer`. This opens the `playerInfo` `SharedObject` but then stores the value of its `data.playerDat` properties into the local object `player`. In this case we're creating all the properties in our `player` object, as if we were creating them from scratch, like in the `setPlayerInfo` function. For this reason, we cannot simply say:

```
player = playerSO.data.playerDat;
```

This would cause `player` to merely be a reference to the `playerDat` object on `playerSO.data`. If the `playerSO` were to be closed or overwritten, then `player` would cease to point at anything.

Let's test out the functionality so far. Add the following two lines of code:

```
setPlayerInfo();
savePlayer();
```

First we call the `setPlayerInfo` function, which creates our initial `player` object and fills it up with data about the player. Then we call the `savePlayer` function, which will save the player to disk.

Save this movie and call it `datasave.fla`. Run the movie at this time. Nothing much will appear to happen. Once the blank stage has appeared, close it again. We can go into our SOL file root and look for the `playerInfo.sol` file to confirm that everything has been created. To find this file, you'll have to go into the `local-host` folder off of the `SharedObject` root. Once inside there, you'll have to locate the directory structure within that the Flash Player has created to emulate the directory structure that your `datasave.fla` is sitting in.

For example, if your `datasave.fla` was sitting in the folder `c:\myFlashFiles`, then the location of the `playerInfo.sol` file will be `C:\Documents and Settings\UserName\Application Data\Macromedia\Flash Player\localhost\myFlashFiles\datasave.swf\`.

Remember that the `datasave.swf` in this path is actually a folder, not a file. Once in the right location, you should see `playerInfo.sol`. This file is a binary format file, so viewing it in a text viewer will yield mostly garbage. However, when viewed in a raw hex viewer, the contents look something like Figure 8.6.

```
00000000h: 00 BF 00 00 00 DA 54 43 53 4F 00 04 00 00 00 00 ; .¿...ÚTCSO......
00000010h: 00 0A 70 6C 61 79 65 72 49 6E 66 6F 00 00 00 00 ; ..playerInfo....
00000020h: 00 09 70 6C 61 79 65 72 44 61 74 03 00 06 68 65 ; ..playerDat...he
00000030h: 61 6C 74 68 00 40 46 80 00 00 00 00 00 00 08 73 ; alth.@F€.......s
00000040h: 74 72 65 6E 67 74 68 00 40 58 80 00 00 00 00 00 ; trength.@X€.....
00000050h: 00 05 70 6E 61 6D 65 02 00 05 52 61 6C 70 68 00 ; ..pname...Ralph.
00000060h: 09 69 6E 76 65 6E 74 6F 72 79 08 00 00 00 06 00 ; .inventory......
00000070h: 01 30 02 00 05 53 77 6F 72 64 00 01 31 02 00 05 ; .0...Sword..1...
00000080h: 4B 6E 69 66 65 00 01 32 02 00 0E 48 65 61 6C 69 ; Knife..2...Heali
00000090h: 6E 67 20 50 6F 74 69 6F 6E 00 01 33 02 00 04 52 ; ng Potion..3...R
000000a0h: 75 6E 65 00 01 34 02 00 0C 45 6D 70 74 79 20 51 ; une..4...Empty Q
000000b0h: 75 69 76 65 72 00 01 35 02 00 07 52 61 74 69 6F ; uiver..5...Ratio
000000c0h: 6E 73 00 00 09 00 0C 63 75 72 72 65 6E 74 4C 65 ; ns.....currentLe
000000d0h: 76 65 6C 00 40 08 00 00 00 00 00 00 00 09 00 ; vel.@.........
```

FIGURE 8.6   The raw data of the `playerInfo.sol` file.

All numbers are stored as ASCII characters, so you can't see the actual values of the health and strength properties. You don't really need to know what all of this means, but you can see that all the variable names are contained within, thus indicating that our data was indeed saved.

Now that we've got things successfully saving, let's make a small change to our FLA file to get things loading. Go and comment out our last two lines of code, like so:

```
//setPlayerInfo();
//savePlayer();
```

Below them, enter the following code:

```
loadPlayer();
trace ("Player Name: " + player.pname);
trace ("Player Health: " + player.health);
trace ("Player Strength: " + player.strength);
trace ("Player Inventory: " + player.inventory);
trace ("Player Current Level: " + player.currentLevel);
```

This code simply calls the loadPlayer function to get the information from the SharedObject into the new player object. Below that we have five trace statements, designed to display the values of the new player object. When this is run, we should see the following in the output window:

```
Player Name: Ralph
Player Health: 45
Player Strength: 98
Player Inventory: Sword,Knife,Healing Potion,Rune,Empty Quiver,Rations
Player Current Level: 3
```

Notice that our player has all of his information back, even though we made no calls this time to the setPlayerInfo function. This means we successfully loaded all of his statistics from the SOL file through the SharedObject.

UPLOADING AND DOWNLOADING FILES TO AND FROM THE SERVER

One of the coolest introductions to Flash 8 is the ability to upload and download files directly from Flash, via a file post, using the new FileReference class. Traditionally, if we wanted to do this in Flash, we would create a separate Web page that contained a file submission form field, which would then upload the file to the server and pass a message back to Flash via JavaScript.

In Flash 8 Macromedia has introduced the ability to trigger a file upload process directly from Flash, so we can easily pull up a dialog box, present the user with a choice of files on his hard drive, and then submit one or more files to the server.

This seems like a massive security breach, doesn't it? Well, luckily, Macromedia was thinking about security when they added this feature. There are a few important rules that apply when making use of the `FileReference` class:

- You cannot preset the default upload or download location that the `FileReference` class will use to get or store its files. The default location shown in the dialog boxes is the most recently browsed folder or, if that location cannot be determined, the desktop.
- You cannot read from or write to the transferred file. The API takes care of this process, but you are not allowed to do anything more than get a *reference* to a file in the `FileReference` instance. In other words, the actual local file path is never, ever exposed to the Flash application. Only the file name is exposed.
- The Flash application that initiated the upload or download cannot access the uploaded or downloaded file on the hard drive. This is what makes the `FileReference` class fully secure and prevents malicious software from being downloaded and executed on the user's machine.

Uploading

At its core, the `FileReference` class is the container in which we specify a single file to upload, while the `FileReferenceList` class is used to specify multiple files to upload, and the `FileReferenceList` represents a group of `FileReference` objects.

To open a file browser window using the `FileReference` class, use the following code:

```
import flash.net.FileReference;
var fileRef = new FileReference();
fileRef.browse();
```

This code will create a new instance of the `FileReference` class and then tell it to open a File Upload dialog box, as shown in Figure 8.7.

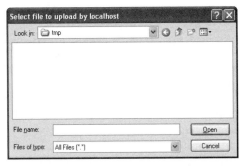

FIGURE 8.7   The default `FileReference` File Upload dialog box.

To upload the selected file, we need to watch out for an event called `onSelect`, which is fired when the user hits the OK button on the dialog box. The code is as follows:

```
import flash.net.FileReference;

var listener:Object = new Object();
listener.onSelect = function(file:FileReference):Void
{
    if(!file.upload("http://somesite.com/upscript.php"))
    {
        trace("Upload dialog failed to open.");
    }
}

var fileRef:FileReference = new FileReference();
fileRef.addListener(listener);
fileRef.browse();
```

The server script we call must be configured to accept file uploads. When a file has been selected for upload, we have access to the following properties about it:

creationDate: A `Date` object that traces to Thu Nov 10 17:00:59 GMT-0500 2005

modificationDate: A `Date` object that traces to Fri Nov 11 13:34:03 GMT-0500 2005

size 153310: The file size in bytes

type .jpg: The extension of the file

name myPicture.jpg: The file name

Downloading

Downloading a file with the `FileReference` class is similar to the upload, but the user will be prompted to select a location to save the file to, rather than a location from which to upload a file. Consider the following example code.

```
import flash.net.FileReference;
var fileRef = new FileReference();
var url:String = "http://www.somesite.com/some_file.pdf";
fileRef.download(url, "some_file.pdf");
```

Here we would prompt the user with a File dialog box that would suggest saving the file under the name `some_file.pdf`. The user would have the option of changing the filename if he wanted to. Once he had selected the filename and location and clicked Save, the file download would begin.

We can monitor the progress of a loading file by using the `onProgress` event, which returns a reference to the `FileReference` object, as well as the number of bytes loaded and the total number of bytes.

```
var listener:Object = new Object();

listener.onProgress = function(file:FileReference,
                              bytesLoaded:Number,
                              bytesTotal:Number):Void
{
    trace(file.name + " has loaded " + bytesLoaded + " out of " +
bytesTotal);
}

var fileRef = new FileReference();
fileRef.addListener(listener);
var url:String = "http://www.somesite.com/some_file.pdf";
fileRef.download(url, "some_file.pdf")
```

That's it for our basic overview. That's just a start at looking at the `FileReference` object. For further details, refer to the help system in Flash.

SUMMARY

That's all there is to the `SharedObject` for our purposes. We'll be looking at using it in more detail throughout the remainder of this book in real game practical examples. The concepts we learned were:

- How Macromedia Flash Professional 8 stores `SharedObjects` on the hard disk
- The compatible data formats for storing in a `SharedObject`
- How to create `SharedObjects` through code
- How to set the data in a stored `SharedObject` through the `data` property
- How to retrieve that data at a later time
- How to upload and download files using the `FileReference` class

OPTIMIZATION FOR GAMES

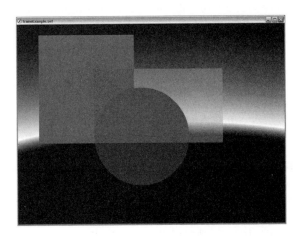

When it comes to games, nothing is more important than the performance and playability of the game. When elements of the game become so complex that the visual performance appears to choke, sputter, and slow down, the player will quickly get tired of the experience and most likely erase your site from the history list.

The art of how to stop this from happening is in knowing how to create the most optimized game possible. If we look at it, *optimize* is a derivative of the word *optimal*, which essentially means "perfect." So how do we go about making a *perfectly* performing game?

What kind of things would cause such degradations in performance? Well, in Macromedia Flash Professional 8, it is due to graphics issues 95% of the time. The problems to look out for are:

- Graphics with a high vector count
- Graphics with large and complicated gradients
- Graphics with over-usage of alpha transparency
- Overly excessive areas of animation and motion
- Inefficiently written code

The first thing to do is remember the user. The user doesn't and shouldn't have to understand concepts like optimization, frame rates, vector count, and alpha. A user doesn't forgive a moment or two of uncontrollable performance in favor of a terrific multi-layered-alpha-gradient misty waterfall background. The user doesn't see why such *background* things should interfere with his *foreground* action: the game he's playing. Imagine driving down the road in real life. Would you expect the beautiful sunset in the distance to cause your car to jitter and skip, becoming uncontrollable? Of course not. These are optional background elements of life and as such should be nonimpacting on game play experience. If, however, there was a large obstacle such as a boulder, and hitting it caused you to stop in your tracks, then this is an intentional slow down. This is part of the game play: the foreground experience.

The problem with the complex background image is simple: it is not optimized. It has not been designed with the game in mind. Remembering this is very important. Game graphics cannot be arbitrarily and haphazardly designed. They must be usable and must not interfere with the main focus of what the game is.

The paint job on your car should not cause your car to have problems running.

One of your greatest assets is an artist who understands these concepts and knows how to best implement good optimization. For example, that complex background with the waterfall could probably be easily rendered out as a single bitmap image. Since the Flash Player renders bitmaps out much faster than vectors, the experience will be much smoother—much more optimized.

The idea is to take as much workload off of the Flash Player at runtime and return that workload back into game performance. If we have a gradient alpha background with a bird flying in front of it, that gradient alpha must be *calculated* and *rendered* constantly as the bird flies across it. This is a lot of work for the Flash Player. If, on the other hand, we took that final gradient alpha image and rendered it out to a flat bitmap, then at runtime the Flash Player would have no calculating to do. It would merely have to show the bitmap, as is.

Let's look at the specifics of what makes Macromedia Flash Professional 8 work the way it works.

THE FRAME

We know that Macromedia Flash Professional 8 works in frames. We've seen that throughout the book so far. Let's take a look at what exactly goes on in the rendering of a frame. Let's assume we have a frame with a gradient sunset background on the bottom layer, a red square on the next layer, a blue circle on the next layer, and a 50% alpha green rectangle on the top layer. Take a look at Figure 9.1 to see the final frame.

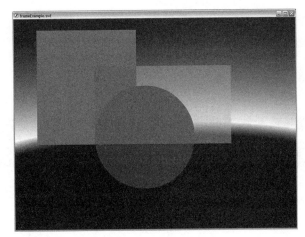

FIGURE 9.1   The final frame.

From the bottom layer up, layers are rendered. All rendering takes place in an off-screen area, very quickly, before the finished image is copied into the visible region of the Flash Player. This off-screen area is known as an off-screen *buffer*. The Flash Player will not advance to the next frame until the entire frame has been rendered in the buffer. Take a look at Figure 9.2 to see an example.

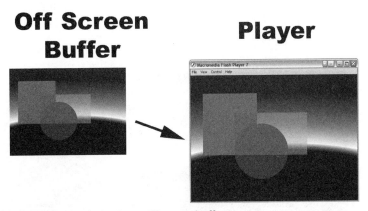

FIGURE 9.2   Rendering in an off-screen buffer.

1. The gradient sunset is drawn. Even though this graphic is mostly covered by other shapes, it still must be drawn in its entirety before the rendering engine can determine what portions of it will be overwritten. This can be seen in Figure 9.3.
2. The red square is drawn as shown in Figure 9.4, taking up a good portion of area that has already been drawn. Anything that was underneath the red square was *unnecessarily* drawn.

FIGURE 9.3   The sunset layer. The lowest layer rendered.

FIGURE 9.4   The red square. The second layer.

3. The blue circle is then drawn on top of the other two graphics, like in Figure 9.5. Again, any area that is covered by the blue circle is now painted over and lost. All of the pixels directly under the blue square never needed to be drawn, but they were anyway.

4. The green 50% alpha rectangle is drawn on top of everything, like Figure 9.6. In this case, before Flash can draw any pixels, it must *read* the pixels underneath it, then carefully combine the colors to create the appearance of semitransparency. This means the 50% alpha rectangle requires *two* graphic operations per pixel, while the solid graphics only require one. This makes semitransparent vectors approximately twice as slow as solid vectors.

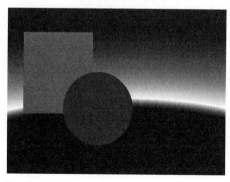

FIGURE 9.5   The blue circle. The third layer.

FIGURE 9.6   The 50% alpha rectangle. The top layer.

5. The image is complete. The rendered frame is transferred into the Flash Player window and becomes visible to the player. This repeats several times per second, up to the requested frame rate.

If this frame took half a second to draw, then, even if we requested 30 frames per second as our frame rate, it would still draw *no faster* than 2 frames per second (once every half a second). Remember, the frame rate we specify in Macromedia Flash Professional 8 is only a *maximum* speed limit. If the rendering engine simply cannot draw entire frames in enough time to meet our requested frame rate, our movie will not run at the desired frame rate. This is one of the critical signs that optimization is necessary.

Invalidation

In order for the Flash Player to be a viable platform for large moving graphics, it must be extremely optimized in the way it renders its graphics in the off-screen buffer. To that end, the Flash player will do whatever it can to ensure that it only redraws things that have *changed* from frame to frame.

When a movie clip or graphic on the screen changes in any way from one frame to the next, the area around that movie clip is said to have been *invalidated*. For example, if a movie clip moves 10 pixels to the left (either with code or keyframe animation), the region where the movie clip sits is now flagged as "invalid" and must be rerendered.

Take for example the images in Figures 9.7 and 9.8. The first image represents frame 1 and the second image is frame 2. The snowman is a movie clip, and so is the tree that it's standing in front of. The only thing that has changed is the snowman's position.

FIGURE 9.7   Frame 1: the snowman in his original position.

FIGURE 9.8   Frame 2: the snowman in his new position.

Looking at Figure 9.9, we can see the regions that have become invalidated because their contents now need to be redrawn. The left region needs to be refilled with the background image of the ground, sky, the tree, and the right region, which used to be background image, now needs to be filled with the snowman.

Now here's the problem, and this is one of the critical keys to understanding optimization. How does the Flash Player know *what* to draw in that left snowman silhouette? Remember, that region was overwritten in the last buffer once the

FIGURE 9.9   The effective regions of invalidation.

original snowman was drawn on top of it. The right silhouette is easy: the Flash Player just has to draw the snowman, but what happens with the left region of invalidation? The Flash Player must logically draw in the area of the background that was previously hidden.

Here's the problem: in order to do that, the Flash Player must rerender the *entire* tree. Since the few branches that the snowman covered were *lost* in the buffer, the Flash Player must recalculate them and draw them. In order to do that, it must do the entire tree. That's right; in order to move a snowman that is relatively small, the Flash Player must rerender the snowman *and* the tree. It's the areas that have changed that must be redrawn, and the areas that change can be bigger than the movie clip that moved; the effects are far reaching.

Consider our previous example with the sunset/square/circle/rectangle. If we were to move the square around, the Flash Player would have to be constantly rerendering the circle, rectangle, and background. This would represent a near-worst case scenario. For relatively little movement, we're taxing the rendering engine.

Does this mean we avoid moving things on screen? No, of course not. It *does* mean we have to be smart about the way we create our games and movies to begin with. Looking back at our original image, we could have done a few things to make the rendering more efficient.

- We could convert the entire background image (all four layers) into one bitmap image. As long as we don't want to move any of the individual components around, making the background into a flat bitmap will greatly reduce the amount of work the Flash Player must perform to draw it. In our original vector version, for every pixel on the user's screen, the Flash Player will have performed several low-level calculations. In a bitmap version, the Flash Player's efforts will be a 1:1 ratio between original image and render: exactly one pixel calculation per pixel of render output.

- We could move the elements so that they don't all overlap each other. This way we reduce redundant rendering and make the regions of invalidation easier and cleaner. Instead of invalidating essentially the entire screen, keeping things spread apart will ensure that no more than one or two of the movie clips will be invalidated at once. This will speed up our rendering time and consequently keep us closer to our target frame rate.

We've talked briefly about them, so now let's look at each of the graphic pitfalls and culprits in detail and see how we can work to optimize things and make our game run as smoothly and efficiently as possible.

Vector Complexity

This may seem obvious, but it is not as well known as we might think. The bottom line is this: the more vector points there are that go into a movie clip, the more processor time the Flash Player must take to render that movie clip.

This means that as the designer is creating graphics, he or she should be asked to make their images with as few points as possible. Instead, make efficient use of the lines and curves. Take, for example, the image in Figure 9.10. This image shows a line that has been drawn in segments, and we can see all of the separate vector points that make it up. There are eight points in the line. Now, eight is not actually a lot to worry about, but we're illustrating a point here.

Perhaps the artist was using a pen tool and didn't clean up the line. Whatever the reason, the line probably should have been drawn something like Figure 9.11. In this image the line takes on the exact same shape, but it has a much smoother look and only takes up three vector points. We've increased this line's efficiency by over 200% and made it look better in the process.

FIGURE 9.10   The unoptimized line.

FIGURE 9.11   The optimized line.

The optimization becomes more obvious when we look at the hand-drawn house in Figure 9.12. This is a house that is made up of very simple lines and shapes, yet because of its unoptimized, hand-drawn nature, it is littered with hundreds of unnecessary vector points.

FIGURE 9.12 The unoptimized house.

What can we do to save this house? Well, there are a few options. First, we could let Macromedia Flash Professional 8 perform its own graphic optimization by making use of the Optimize tool. To do this, we select the entire image and then choose Modify > Shape > Optimize, or press Ctrl-Alt-Shift-C. When we do this, there will be a dialog box presenting us with several options, like in Figure 9.13.

Once we've chosen our optimization settings and pressed OK, Macromedia Flash Professional 8 will perform a series of calculations to reduce the number of vectors used to construct the image. When done, it will report to us the number of curves in the original image and the number of curves in the new, optimized version, like in Figure 9.14.

FIGURE 9.13 The Optimize Curves Tool dialog box.

FIGURE 9.14 The Optimize Curves tool results.

It's important to play with the different settings, because sometimes they can turn out perfectly, and other times they can turn out less than ideal, like in Figure 9.15.

The other approach is the manual approach. Similar to the way we traced over our original unoptimized line, we can also trace over all the elements in the house to create a fully optimized version. By manually going in with the Line tool and drawing single lines to span large curves, and then bending them to fit, we've created a line version of our house that fits directly over top of our old house (see Figure 9.16).

FIGURE 9.15   The over-optimized (albeit stylish) house.

FIGURE 9.16   The unoptimized house compared to the manually optimized house.

When we hide the old house and make our new house's lines into thick, black lines, we can see the new look, as shown in Figure 9.17.

The best proof of this optimization is when we run the Optimize Curves tool again. Look at Figure 9.18 to see the results.

We have truly drawn the most efficient house possible, and as a result, Macromedia Flash Professional 8 cannot optimize it any further. The total number of curves being used now is 77. That has dropped from our original image with 487 curves.

The difference between vector points and curves is that curves are the actual lines, while vector points are the anchors that form the beginning and end of a curve. There are two vector points per curve, although sometimes several curves will share the same vector point. For this reason, it's more useful to measure our graphics in curves rather than vector points.

FIGURE 9.17   The final, manually optimized house.

FIGURE 9.18   Attempting to optimize curves on the manually optimized house.

GRADIENTS

When the Flash Player has to solid fill an object, it's generally pretty easy for it to look up the color and then fire those pixels to the buffer. However, when the Flash Player encounters a gradient, everything changes. With gradients, we're not just talking about simple, flat colors; we're talking about fills that have as much complexity and math behind them as vector curves do.

The key things to remember with gradients are:

Keep them simple: Try to use a gradient with two or three colors maximum. The fewer colors used, the easier and faster the calculations performed by the Flash Player.

Keep them small: Try to avoid creating huge full-screen gradients. Try to keep gradients to small movie clips or objects. The larger the surface area of the gradient, the more likelihood that it will be invalidated by some other action and require a full rerender.

Render as a bitmap: You can take the workload off the Flash Player if you simply take that gradient and render it in another program such as Adobe Photoshop as a bitmap image. There are no calculations required to show a bitmap (it's as simple as drawing a solid color), so it will add much back to your game's performance.

Use linear gradients: Because of the difference in formula, linear gradients are slightly faster to render than radial gradients.

Generally speaking, if you can get away with using two colors rather than a gradient, it's better to use the two colors. In Figure 9.19 the image on the left uses two simple shapes to give the appearance of light and shadow. The image on the right, however, uses a radial gradient. The image on the right will render much faster.

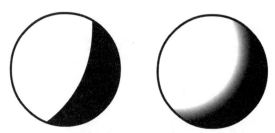

FIGURE 9.19 Shadows with and without gradients.

Unfortunately, there are no absolute rules. It's up to the artist to use some common sense and have a good understanding of gradients to know where they are necessary, where they aren't, and where they can be substituted for either bitmaps or simple shapes.

BITMAPS

We've talked a little bit about bitmaps, but let's look at what they really are. A bitmap is a way of representing an image wherein the details for the image are stored as colored dots, called pixels, in a large grid. Figure 9.20 shows a bitmap of a gradient in a square, blown up several hundred times normal magnitude. You can see the pixels individually, as large squares of color.

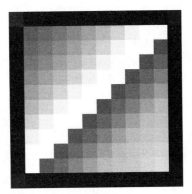

FIGURE 9.20 A bitmap image.

As a rule of thumb, if a vector image has more curves in it than it physically has pixels on the screen, then it's probably best to convert it into a bitmap. In other words, let's say you have a vector image on screen that takes up 20 × 20 pixels. That's a total of 400 pixels in area. Let's also say this image is a very complicated vector red rose, with all the intricacies of the petals. Finally, let's say this vector image is made up of 1200 curves.

Congratulations, you have successfully created an image with more detail than can *possibly be seen.* Assuming, of course, that there's no zooming into the rose, it's probably best to take this rose and use a bitmap equivalent of it instead. You could either take a screenshot and crop it in another program or export from Macromedia Flash Professional 8 directly using File > Export > Export Image. Once you've done this and then re-imported the rose as a regular 20 × 20 bitmap, you can put them next to each other to compare. Sure, if you zoom in, you'll see the pixelization of the bitmap, but if you keep them both at 100% zoom (as the movie would be playing on the Web), there should be no noticeable difference. After all, they're both taking up exactly 400 pixels. It's just that the bitmap is not wasting any time with excessive calculations.

Take for example the image in Figure 9.21. These two teleportation pads look identical, but they're not. One of them is a bitmap and one of them is a vector. This image shows them both at 100%, as would be seen in the game at runtime. This is a fairly complex image with several gradients and many curves.

Can you tell which one is which? The answer is no, of course, because they're identical. One is just a bitmap representation of the screen rendering of the vector. In other words, in the end, it's *all about pixels*, because final renderings *are* pixels on the screen. The only difference between these two teleportation pads is that one of them will render much faster than the other. However, if we zoom in, we see the effect of the pixels, like in Figure 9.22.

We've said that bitmaps don't require any calculations to render into the buffer. That's only true if the bitmap is not rotated and is at 100% scale. As soon as we zoom, rotate, or skew the bitmap, we should consider not using the bitmap. Bitmaps are lightning fast to render when drawn at 100% their initial state, but as soon as we make a modification to the zoom or rotation, we introduce several more calculations that must be applied to each pixel, thus making bitmaps the slower option.

FIGURE 9.21   One is bitmap, one is vector. Can you tell?

FIGURE 9.22   Zooming in shows the difference.

ALPHAS

Another performance killer is the use of colors that aren't at 100% alpha. These are colors that we're asking the Flash Player to "please draw the background through these." We see a semitransparent image and it looks totally natural to us, but this requires quite a bit of processing to create.

1. The area below the non-100% alpha is finished rendering.
2. The Flash Player must then read the pixels in the buffer, beneath the non-100% alpha image.
3. On a pixel-by-pixel basis, the Flash Player must then compare the under-image, with the non-100% alpha image and carefully combine the colors of each individual pixel.
4. For each pixel, the final result will be the color that is *actually* drawn to the buffer.

The _alpha is a processor-expensive property. Yes, it looks fantastic, but it also takes twice as much work to render as a regular 100% solid image. For this reason, the Flash Player will treat objects with an _alpha of 100% very differently than objects with an _alpha of less than 100%. A completely opaque object will be sent through a completely different (and faster) rendering channel.

QUALITY

One of the best ways to reduce processor load, and increase the performance of a game is to change the Macromedia Flash Professional 8 _quality property. Quality is used to determine how the Flash Player renders things at runtime. When the quality is at its highest, all lines and edges are antialiased four times and bitmaps are smoothed. Antialiasing is a technique whereby the edges of objects are smoothed with their backgrounds to remove the staircase edges.

Four-times antialiasing produces great smooth edges but requires a lot of work. Antialiased edges are essentially like thin strips of non-100% alpha graphics.

Setting the quality to medium, however, means that antialiasing is only done two times and results in a slightly less smooth image but renders the antialiasing almost twice as fast.

Setting the quality to low means there will be no antialiasing at all, so edges will be very jagged. This can wreak havoc on a vector image but has no noticeable difference on a bitmap image. If we have a bitmap image in our game, and we have antialiasing turned off, it doesn't matter; because our bitmap may have already been antialiased in another software package, and that antialiasing is saved in the image file.

There is some very simple code to set the quality of the rendering engine at runtime. We could do something like set to low quality when there's a lot of movement and then set it back to high quality when the movement stops. The code is:

```
_quality = "LOW";
_quality = "MEDIUM";
_quality = "HIGH";
```

Alternatively, at runtime the user can right-click on the stage and choose the quality from the context menu that appears. Try playing the game Mars Racer, from Chapter 14, at different quality settings. Notice the difference in performance from one mode to the other.

BITMAP CACHING

With the arrival of Macromedia Flash Professional 8, we have been given a way to control how Flash uses the vector rendering engine in such a way that we ensure Flash does not waste time redundantly rendering vectors over and over again. Prior to Macromedia Flash Professional 8, Flash would render an image with vectors by calculating and drawing the vectors that make it up every single frame if things were changing on the stage.

This meant that if we had a vector image that consisted of 20,000 vectors, Flash would go through the painstaking effort of rendering those 20,000 vectors every frame. That's an optimization nightmare, but the tradeoff seemed to be to simplify the images and make them look less than what the artist intended.

Enter the bitmap cache. Macromedia had a brilliant idea. They said, rather than recompute the vector image every frame, why not compute it *once* and then make a bitmap snapshot of that rendered image and store that in memory. This rationale is based on the fact that bitmaps can be rendered and drawn *much faster* than vectors can. Suddenly, our 20,000-vector image is drawn only once, and then the movie clip that encompasses it is *cached* as a bitmap. Any further use of that movie clip results in the bitmap cache being used rather than the vector data being replotted.

That is, until you rotate or scale the cached movie clip. Once you do that, the vector-rendering engine is alerted that you have changed the mathematical nature and orientation of the image, so it must be recomputed to have a new and accurate representation in its bitmap cache.

If all we're doing, however, is moving a movie clip around the screen by changing its _x and _y properties, bitmap caching will make our movie clip blaze with optimized glory. So, how do we tell Flash to turn on bitmap caching for a movie clip? Simple. It's one line of code:

```
myMovie_mc.cacheAsBitmap = true;
```

This would take a movie clip called myMovie_mc and tell Macromedia Flash Professional 8 that once the vectors in the movie clip are calculated, we should only ever be looking at the nicely saved and stored bitmap cache of the rendered movie clip.

You can also turn on the bitmap caching property from the Properties panel in the Flash IDE directly. It's in the Movie Clip Properties dialog box, opened with Ctrl-F3. Look for the checkbox that says Use runtime bitmap caching.

Starting in Chapter 11, we're going to look into the whole Macromedia Flash Professional 8 bitmap system with much more detail and get an idea of some of the most amazing uses for it and watch as Flash takes a step in the direction of the most powerful bitmap-based systems such as Nintendo, Sega, and any of the classic PC games from the bitmap golden age.

CODE

One of the biggest killers of game performance is badly written code. We're going to look closely at that in the next chapter, when we develop our optimized game. A single function, called many times during a frame can make or break the performance of a game. A function that is called 1000 times per frame, with each call using a millisecond, will cause the game to slow down to one frame per second.

If that one function was made more efficient, we could get it back to a position where it's feasible to use without reducing the number of times it's called. However, sometimes the best solution is to just reduce the number of calls to these frequently called functions.

SUMMARY

In this chapter we've looked at the various facets of optimization, including:

- How the frame is rendered
- Region invalidation
- Creating optimized graphics including vector images, bitmaps, gradients, and alphas
- Changing the quality of a movie playback to get the optimum performance
- Using the new bitmap caching capabilities of Flash 8
- How code affects performance

THE OPTIMIZED GAME: AA BOMB

We should endeavor to make all games as optimized as possible, so the game in this chapter really doesn't perform much differently than other games in this book because they're all very optimized.

What we are going to do, however, is look at a few cheats that we can apply to improve performance significantly. While the next chapter will focus on the true power of bitmaps and the `BitmapData` class in Flash Professional 8, this chapter will focus on ways to optimize and improve a traditional, vector-based game.

THE GAME

This game is called AA Bomb, and it takes place in London during World War II. You control three antiaircraft guns in London while the German Luftwaffe is bombing the city. Flying through the air are hundreds of bomber planes. Your goal is to shoot down as many as you can before all of your antiaircraft guns are destroyed. See the game in action in Figure 10.1.

FIGURE 10.1   AA Bomb in action.

As they fly, the bombers will drop bombs, and you must shoot the bombs, or, if they hit the ground near an antiaircraft gun, that gun will be destroyed. You must also try to shoot down the planes, and each plane takes a total of five hits before it falls flaming to the ground. Each hit causes the plane to take on slightly more damage, with more and more flames shooting from it until it falls from the sky.

All three antiaircraft guns fire at the same position on screen: the mouse cursor. Moving the mouse around causes the barrels of the guns to aim at the cursor, and pressing and holding the left mouse button causes the guns to fire. As you fire, bullets will fly up into the night, streaking across the sky and either flying off screen or hitting an aircraft or bomb. Every time you shoot down an enemy aircraft, the kill count will increase. The basic goal is to shoot down as many as you can before your antiaircraft guns are destroyed. Seems like a bit of a futile game—knowing that the game ends only when you die—but this is war. The main goal is simply to get the highest score.

The enemy is kind enough to drop all their bombs with parachutes so that you have a chance to shoot them down before they hit the ground. Let's take a look at the individual pieces of the game, and see how things work.

EXPLORING THE GAME

ON THE CD

The FLA for this game is in the Chapter 10 folder on the CD-ROM, and it's called `optimized.fla`. Open it up in Macromedia Flash Professional 8 now. You'll see the stage as it appears in Figure 10.2.

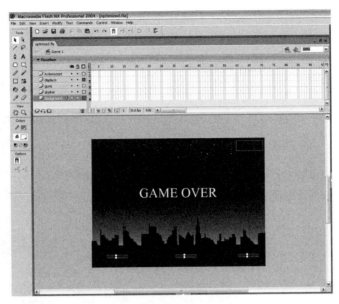

FIGURE 10.2   The AA Bomb game stage.

Like we did in previous chapters, we're going to go through this game a piece at a time and look at and learn what we've got in the FLA, rather than build it from the ground up, tutorial-style.

Our stage consists of five layers to begin with. From the bottom up, they are:

- background
- skyline
- guns
- displays
- Actionscript
- background

The background layer is simply a gradient with some stars at the top. The gradient transitions from yellow at the bottom, to orange to black and blue. This is meant to be the flames of the burning city below, fading up into the night sky. This layer can be seen in Figure 10.3.

This layer is where we provide our first bit of optimization. The background is one large bitmap that fits nicely on the stage. We could have left this as simply a vector gradient–filled box, with several small vectors for the stars, but let's do a bit of a comparison and see why we didn't:

- **Vector version:**
  - One gradient box, four vectors (one per corner), plus the additional math required for rendering the gradient every time areas of it are invalidated

- 15 Stars of 4 vectors each = 60 vectors
- Calculating the entire image
- Transferring to screen
- **Bitmap version:**
  - Transferring to screen

FIGURE 10.3   The background bitmap.

We can see that "transferring to screen" is inevitable, but when we use the bitmap the vector-based calculations are not required. Consider that the vector version must perform these calculations *every* frame (whenever an area is invalidated, which happens constantly, as the planes and bombs are moving). The bitmap version, however, must perform *no* calculations, but merely blast the pixels to screen, which is one of the fastest operations a computer can perform.

So this is our first layer and our first big optimization.

skyline

The skyline, as seen in Figure 10.4, is a vector shape of a silhouette of London under siege. The skyline is all contained within a movie clip with the instance name, `skyline`. At runtime this movie clip is placed on top of everything else so that falling bombs and planes appear to fall *behind* the buildings and thus into the city.

FIGURE 10.4   The `skyline` layer.

This is a vector shape, but because it is a silhouette, it lacks any detail other than edge curves and vectors, of which there are 177 in the entire movie clip. This gives the player the sense of a detailed and ruined city without requiring the high number of vectors required to draw such a detailed image.

guns

This layer contains three antiaircraft guns. These are three instances of the same movie clip, called cannon, and they have instance names cannon1, cannon2, and cannon3. They're all placed at a _y value of 360, and _x values of 75, 275, and 475.

An individual gun is simply two horizontal black bars, 66 pixels long and 3 pixels thick, placed about 8 pixels apart. These bars are the two barrels of the cannon, and they are lined up with the registration point such that they fall vertically on either side of it and are far right aligned with it, like in Figure 10.5.

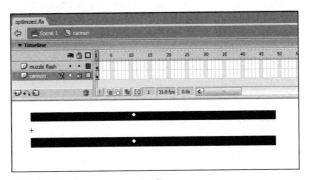

FIGURE 10.5   A cannon movie clip.

This is the default layout of the cannon at 0 degrees rotation. Remember, when you move the mouse around the screen, each gun turns to point at the mouse cursor. For this reason, we must make sure our pivot point is in the right position on the movie clip, and in this case that pivot point is the *base* of the cannon. Zero degrees of rotation always points to the right.

Approximately halfway up the length of each barrel is another movie clip. This movie clip has no image on frame 1, so it doesn't show up as anything but a small white circle at design time. At runtime, however, when we tell this movie clip to play, we get a bright muzzle flash. These have the instance names muzzleFlash1 and muzzleFlash2. These are added to create a more dramatic effect when the guns are fired. The muzzle flash is a three-frame movie clip; frame 1 is blank, frame 2 is a small flame, and frame 3 is a large flame. Figure 10.6 shows this muzzle flash on frame 3 for the right barrel.

When these guns are fired, they alternate barrels after each shot. The only purpose for this effect is realism; real antiaircraft guns of the era usually consisted of two or more barrels that fired in succession.

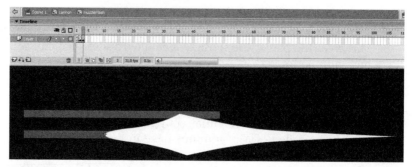

FIGURE 10.6   The muzzle flash.

displays

This layer simply contains a movie clip (instance name gameOver) that contains text that reads "Game Over." This movie clip is initially hidden at runtime and is only displayed when all of the player's guns have been destroyed.

This layer also contains a text field in the upper-right corner to display the total number of planes shot down. This text field has the instance name kills_txt and contains nothing at runtime.

Actionscript

The last layer is the layer upon which all of our Actionscript code is written. We'll be getting to that in the next section of the chapter.

Linked Movie Clips

The library of this game also contains several movie clips that are not initially on the stage but attached at runtime. They are the bombs, bullets, and planes. Looking in the library, let's take a look at each of these.

Bombs

The bomb is set up in the library to export with the linkage ID name of bomb. On frame 1 of the movie clip, the bomb is simply a black silhouette shape of a bomb and a parachute, and it's aligned to an orientation of 0 degrees, which means it is pointing to the right, like in Figure 10.7.

Its registration point is right in the body of the bomb, which means that's where the bomb pivots from as it falls. This is consistent with the way this kind of thing behaves in real life. This silhouette sports 34 vector curves.

On frames 2 to 15 we have an explosion, which is simply a fading white alpha gradient, like in Figure 10.8. When the bomb hits the ground, we tell this animation to play. There's a bright flash of the light from the explosion, and then it fades out quickly.

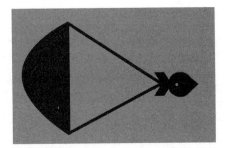

FIGURE 10.7   The bomb.

FIGURE 10.8   The bomb's explosion.

On the final frame of the animation, there is one line of code:

```
this.removeMovieClip();
```

This removes the bomb movie clip from the game because the bomb has exploded at this point and it no longer requires the computer's attention.

Bullets

The bullet movie clip is in the library embedded with the linkage name `bullet`. This is the movie clip that is placed on the stage at runtime when the player fires the antiaircraft guns. The bullets streak up from the barrels of the guns and into the sky, where they eventually fly off screen.

The bullet movie clip is two frames long: frame 1 is the bullet coming from the left barrel, and frame 2 is the bullet coming from the right barrel. They're offset enough from center such that they align perfectly with one of the two barrels. Each bullet instance that is created during game play is set to show either frame 1 or frame 2, depending on which barrel the gun is firing from. Figure 10.9 shows these two frames.

Notice that the bullets are long and thin to imply motion. Once these are moved across the screen, the stretched look translates into looking like a moving streak of light across the sky.

Surrounding each bullet is a large invisible circle, meant to increase the surface area that the bullet takes up to make collision detection between bullets and planes a little less difficult. Figure 10.10 shows an outline mode image of the bullet and its surrounding invisible circle. This invisible circle is simply a circle with a color of alpha zero. This means it is still used in collision detection and `hitTest`, without being visible to the player.

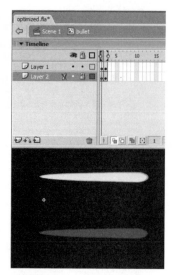

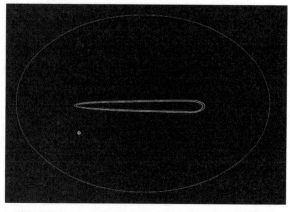

FIGURE 10.10 The bullet movie clip with its invisible hit region.

FIGURE 10.9 The bullet movie clip.

Planes

The last linked movie clip is the plane. This movie clip is set up for linkage in the library with the linkage ID `plane`. This movie clip is six frames long, and each frame shows the plane getting more and more damaged. Frame 1 is the plane intact, with no damage, as shown in Figure 10.11.

The plane is simply a silhouette, with four white circles on the surface to simulate landing lights, taillights, wing lights, and a cockpit beacon. The vector image has no outline applied to it, as that would not be necessary and would just increase the workload on the rendering engine. The other five frames represent the five stages of damage, leading ultimately to a flaming plane that we plummet to the ground with code. Figure 10.12 shows the plane in its most damaged state.

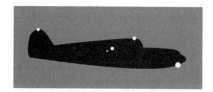

FIGURE 10.12 Frame 6 of the plane, fully damaged.

FIGURE 10.11 Frame 1 of the plane, undamaged.

Each of the flames seen in Figure 10.12 are instances of the same five-frame flame animation. When these are all played together, and the plane is animated across the screen or falling to the ground, the effect is a very believable image of a plane being shot down.

That's all the graphics in the game. There are very few graphics used, and all of them are very simple in one way or another. Either they're silhouettes, making them simply outlines, or they're bitmaps, thus reducing their rendering times.

Now that we've covered all the graphics in the game, let's look at the Action-script code required to bring it to life.

EXPLORING THE CODE

The code for this game revolves around the creation of movie clip objects at run-time as the game play proceeds. The logic of movie clip creation is something like this:

- Every 1000 milliseconds the game generates a plane at the right edge of the screen, at a random height and traveling at a random speed. When a plane leaves the screen space, it is removed from existence.
- For every plane, each frame there's a 1 in 150 chance that it will drop a bomb. Since our movie is running at 31 frames per second, this means that on average, every 5 seconds a plane will drop a bomb. When a bomb hits the ground, it will explode. If the explosion occurs near enough that the explosion animation intersects with any of the guns, that gun will be destroyed.
- As the player moves the mouse, the guns will aim at the mouse cursor on screen.
- When the player is pressing and holding the left mouse button, the guns will fire, generating bullets that follow the angle of the cannon and there-fore fly toward the mouse cursor. When a bullet leaves the screen space, it is removed from existence.
- When a bullet passes over a bomb, that bomb movie clip is removed from existence.
- When a bullet passes over a plane, the plane is damaged. If the plane is damaged five times or more, it is considered incapacitated and will fall to the ground.

Let's start looking at the code on the Actionscript layer. The first thing we'll see is this:

```
_root.createEmptyMovieClip("bullets", 10);
bCount = 0;

_root.createEmptyMovieClip("planes", 11);
pCount = 0;

_root.createEmptyMovieClip("bombs", 12);
bmCount = 0;
```

What we're doing here is creating three empty movie clips. These will be the movie clips that will house either our bullets, planes, or bombs. By encapsulating these items within their own movie clips, we greatly reduce the workload on `hitTest` so that one `hitTest` with the `bullets` movie clip is all that's required to see if a bullet is striking an object, rather than doing a `hitTest` with every bullet.

We also have three variables, `bCount`, `pCount`, and `bmCount`. These variables are used to keep track of the individual instances of the bullets, planes, and bombs as they're created. Next, we have:

```
cannonEnterFrame = function()
{
```

This is the control function for the cannon. This function will be applied to each cannon later. Continuing on, we have:

```
var diffx = _root._xmouse - this._x;
var diffy = _root._ymouse - this._y;

this.ang = Math.atan2(diffy, diffx);

if (this.ang > 0)
{
    diffy = 0;
    this.ang = Math.atan2(diffy, diffx);
}

    this._rotation = this.ang * (180 / Math.PI);
```

This is the essential code to cause the cannon to rotate toward the mouse cursor. This is based on the radial motion code we discussed in Chapter 9. We look at the distance between the mouse cursor's x position and the cannon's _x position and storing it in `diffx`. We then do the same thing for _y and store it in `diffy`.

We then use the `Math.atan2` function to determine the angle formed between the cannon and the mouse cursor.

Then we check to see if the angle is greater than zero. If it is, that means the cannon is pointing down into the ground. This can only happen if `diffy` is a positive number greater than 0, and thus the mouse cursor is lower than the cannon base. We cannot allow this to happen, so we manually reset `diffy` to 0, and re-compute `this.ang`. By doing this we ensure that the angle will never drop below the ground.

Finally, we set the _rotation of the cannon movie clip to be the value angle, converted to degrees. Next we have:

```
if (bombs.hitTest(this._x, this._y, true))
{
    this.alive = false;
    numAlive--;

    if (numAlive == 0)
    {
        gameOver._visible = true;
```

```
        }

        delete this.onEnterFrame;
    }
}
```

Here we're checking to see if the _x, _y position of this cannon is touching anything solid on the bombs movie clip. This will most likely only happen when a bomb is exploding because at that point its surface area is greatly increased because of the size of the explosion.

This is a nice fast way of determining whether or not a bomb has exploded near enough to a cannon to destroy it. If it has, we set the alive flag of the cannon to false and decrement the numAlive variable. We'll see these set later, but each cannon by default has an alive value of true, and the numAlive variable is set to 3 to begin with.

If numAlive is 0, all the cannons have been destroyed and the game is over, so we show the gameOver movie clip. We then also kill the onEnterFrame function of the cannon so that it no longer continues to track the mouse cursor. The entire cannonEnterFrame function is listed here:

```
cannonEnterFrame = function()
{
    var diffx = _root._xmouse - this._x;
    var diffy = _root._ymouse - this._y;

    this.ang = Math.atan2(diffy, diffx);

    if (this.ang > 0)
    {
        diffy = 0;
        this.ang = Math.atan2(diffy, diffx);
    }

    this._rotation = this.ang * (180 / Math.PI);

    if (bombs.hitTest(this._x, this._y, true))
    {
        this.alive = false;
        numAlive--;

        if (numAlive == 0)
        {
            gameOver._visible = true;
        }

        delete this.onEnterFrame;
    }
}
```

After this, we have:

```
dofires = function()
{
    if (cannon1.alive) fireBullet(cannon1);
    if (cannon2.alive) fireBullet(cannon2);
    if (cannon3.alive) fireBullet(cannon3);
    AAShot.start(0,0);
}
```

When this function is called, the three cannons will fire. A cannon will only fire, however, if its `alive` flag is set to `true` and therefore it hasn't been destroyed. The other thing we do here is play the `AAShot` sound. This is the echoing sound of antiaircraft fire. After this code, we have:

```
_root.onMouseDown = function()
{
    dofires();
    bfire = setInterval(dofires, 170);
}
```

This is how we make the game respond to the mouse by starting to fire. First, we make an immediate call to `dofires`, and then we use `setInterval` to cause a repeated call to `dofires` every 170 milliseconds. This will cause each gun to fire a bullet approximately 6 times per second. This happens when the player presses down on the mouse button. The mouse release, on the other hand, clears the interval call to `dofires`, like so:

```
_root.onMouseUp = function()
{
    clearInterval(bfire);
}
```

After this, we have the following code:

```
fireBullet = function(who)
{
```

This is the `fireBullet` function that is called from `dofires`. The `who` that's passed in is a reference to the cannon firing this bullet. The first thing we do is create an instance of the linked movie clip `bullet` and attach it to the `bullets` empty movie clip that we created earlier on the `_root`. The instance is named `"bullet"` + `bCount`, which means the first bullet of the game will be `bullet0`, then `bullet1`, and so on. The depth level for each new bullet is also determined by `bCount`.

```
var nm = "bullet" + bCount;
bullets.attachMovie("bullet", nm, bCount);
```

Then we move the bullet so that it is lined up with the end of the gun barrel, as that's where we want it to appear. We use the radial equation of converting angle and distance to an x and a y offset. The angle in this case is the angle of the cannon firing the shot, and the distance is 40, which means we'll be placing this bullet 40 pixels from the base of the cannon, along the cannon's angle.

```
bullets[nm]._x = who._x + Math.cos(who.ang) * 40;
bullets[nm]._y = who._y + Math.sin(who.ang) * 40;
```

Next we have:

```
bullets[nm]._rotation = who._rotation;

bullets[nm].dx = Math.cos(who.ang) * 11;
bullets[nm].dy = Math.sin(who.ang) * 11;
```

Here we set the _rotation of the bullet to match the _rotation of the cannon and give the bullet some velocity: dx and dy. The speed of each bullet is 11, which means the bullet will move along the angle of the cannon 11 pixels per frame. Since "11 pixels at any angle" doesn't really make sense, we instead determine dx and dy, which is the amount to move along the x axis and the amount to move along the y axis, in order to simulate the bullet's movement of 11 pixels at any angle.

Next we have:

```
bullets[nm].gotoAndStop((bCount % 2) + 1);
who["muzzleFlash" + ((bCount % 2) + 1)].play();
```

We then use bCount % 2 to determine which barrel we'll be shooting from. bCount % 2 will return either 0 or 1, depending on the value of bCount. When bCount is 0, bCount % 2 will be 0. When bCount is 1, bCount % 2 will be 1. As we increase bCount, however, when bCount is 2, bCount % 2 will be 0, and when bCount is 3, bCount % 2 will be 1, and so on. So we tell the bullet to go to a frame indicating left or right barrel (remember, frame 1 is a left-barrel bullet and frame 2 is a right-barrel bullet. Once we've done this, we tell the appropriate muzzle flash in the cannon to play.

Next we have:

```
bullets[nm].onEnterFrame = function()
{
    this._x += this.dx;
    this._y += this.dy;

    if (this._x < -100 || this._x > 650
        || this._y < -100)
    {
        this.removeMovieClip();
    }
}
```

This is the onEnterFrame function for the new bullet, and it's responsible for controlling its motion. It's a very simple motion and so all we do is add dx and dy to _x and _y each frame. We do one more check to see if the bullet has left the screen by either going 100 pixels off the left or right side of the screen, or 100 pixels off the top of the screen. We have a little bit of overlap (100 pixels) so that the bullet doesn't vanish as *soon* as it hits the screen edge, but rather once it's far enough off screen that it cannot be sent anymore. If the bullet has flown off screen, we remove it from existence so that no more computation of it is necessary.

Finally, we have:

```
        bCount++;
    }
```

Here we simply increment the bCount variable so that the next bullet created has a unique name and is on a unique depth level inside of the master bullets movie clip. The entire fireBullet function is listed here:

```
fireBullet = function(who)
{
    var nm = "bullet" + bCount;
    bullets.attachMovie("bullet", nm, bCount);
    bullets[nm]._x = who._x + Math.cos(who.ang) * 40;
    bullets[nm]._y = who._y + Math.sin(who.ang) * 40;

    bullets[nm]._rotation = who._rotation;

    bullets[nm].dx = Math.cos(who.ang) * 11;
    bullets[nm].dy = Math.sin(who.ang) * 11;

    bullets[nm].gotoAndStop((bCount % 2) + 1);
    who["muzzleFlash" + ((bCount % 2) + 1)].play();

    bullets[nm].onEnterFrame = function()
    {
        this._x += this.dx;
        this._y += this.dy;

        if (this._x < -100 || this._x > 650
            || this._y < -100)
        {
            this.removeMovieClip();
        }

    }

    bCount++;
}
```

After this, we have a function that is very similar to fireBullet, but instead of firing bullets it fires planes onto the screen. This is the launchPlane function:

```
launchPlane = function()
{
```

```
var nm = "plane" + pCount;
planes.attachMovie("plane", nm, pCount);
planes[nm]._x = 600;
planes[nm]._y = Math.random() * 200 + 20;
```

The first thing we do is create the new `plane` movie clip, with the instance names of `plane0`, `plane1`, `plane2`, and so on, based on `pCount`. These `plane` movie clip instances are created in the `planes` movie clip, which we created earlier on the `_root`, and we attach the `plane` movie clip from the library.

We then set the `_x` position to 600, which is off the right side of the screen, and set the `_y` position to a random number between 20 and 220. This means the planes will come in from the right side of the screen at varying heights.

Next, we have:

```
planes[nm].dx = -(Math.random() * 3 + 3);
planes[nm].dy = 0;

planes[nm]._yscale = -100;
```

We set the horizontal speed of the plane (`dx`) to a random number between −3 and −6. This means it will be traveling to the left on screen at a random speed. We also set the `dy` (vertical) speed to 0, which means the plane is not falling or rising, but flying perfectly level.

We set the `_yscale` of the plane to −100. We need to do this to flip the plane vertically so it doesn't appear to fly to the left upside down. Remember that we drew our plane at a 0 degree angle, which was upright, to the right. When the plane travels left, our rotation code (below) will rotate the plane around to the left, but as a result the plane will be upside down. Figure 10.13 shows this principle. The plane flying to the right is upright, so the plane flying left is upside down, because we're using true radial motion. So we must flip the `_yscale` to cause the plane to be upright again.

FIGURE 10.13   The `plane` movie clip's orientation at different angles.

In real aviation this is what happens in a plane when the pilot "pulls up" and reverses direction 180 degrees. When he does this, the plane will be upside down and he must then "roll" the plane to become upright again. Our reversal of _yscale is essentially this rolling upright action. Next we have:

```
planes[nm].gotoAndStop(1);
planes[nm].hit = 0;
```

This ensures that the plane is stopped on its undamaged frame and that its hit count is 0. Next we have the onEnterFrame function for the plane.

```
planes[nm].onEnterFrame = function()
{
    this._x += this.dx;
    this._y += this.dy;

    this._rotation = Math.atan2(this.dy, this.dx) *
                          (180 / Math.PI);
```

This is where we set the _rotation of the plane based on the value of its speed. We need to constantly recompute this because when a plane is hit and begins to fall, its dy will increase, so its angle will increase as it falls toward the ground. Next we have:

```
if (this._x < -100 || this._y > 500)
{
    this.removeMovieClip();
}
```

If the plane has flown off screen left or fallen to the ground, remove it. Next:

```
if (bullets.hitTest(this._x, this._y, true) &&
    this.hit < 5)
{
    this.hit++;
    this.gotoAndStop(this.hit + 1);
}
```

If the plane is touching a solid area in the bullets movie clip (being hit by a bullet) and its hit value is less than 5 (it's not already destroyed), increase the hit value and go to the appropriate damage frame. After this we have:

```
if (this.hit == 5)
{
    kills++;
    kills_txt.text = kills;
    this.hit = 6;
}

if (this.hit == 6)
{
```

```
        this.dy += 0.1;
    }
```

If `hit` is 5, we increase the player's `kills` and display that score in the `kills_txt` text field. We then set `hit` to 6, which means dead. In the next `if` statement, if `hit` is 6, we increase the plane's `dy` value. This will happen every frame until the plane is off the bottom of the screen. Because of our dynamically calculated plane `_rotation`, it will always arc down toward the curve, which is what real planes do. Last, we have:

```
if (Math.random() * 150 < 1 && this.hit < 5)
    dropBomb(this._x, this._y + 5, this.dx / 3);


    }

    pCount++;
}
```

This is where we have our 1 in 150 chance of dropping a bomb. If `Math.random()` * `150` is less than 1 and the plane is currently not destroyed, it will call the `dropBomb` function, which takes an x position and y position and an x speed. The bomb is launched to go exactly one-third of the speed of the plane because the parachute is assumed to have had a slowing effect. The y position used is the plane's `_y` plus 5, which is five pixels below the plane, so it appears that the bomb was dropped from underneath the plane.

At the end of this `launchPlane` function, we increment `pCount`. That's it for the `launchPlane` function. Here's the whole function:

```
launchPlane = function()
{
    var nm = "plane" + pCount;
    planes.attachMovie("plane", nm, pCount);
    planes[nm]._x = 600;
    planes[nm]._y = Math.random() * 200 + 20;

    planes[nm].dx = -(Math.random() * 3 + 3);
    planes[nm].dy = 0;

    planes[nm]._xscale = 70;
    planes[nm]._yscale = -70;

    planes[nm].gotoAndStop(1);
    planes[nm].hit = 0;

    planes[nm].onEnterFrame = function()
    {
        this._x += this.dx;
        this._y += this.dy;

        this._rotation = Math.atan2(this.dy, this.dx)
```

```
                                   * (180 / Math.PI);

            if (this._x < -100 || this._y > 500)
            {
                this.removeMovieClip();
            }

            if (bullets.hitTest(this._x, this._y, true) &&
                this.hit < 5)
            {
                this.hit++;
                this.gotoAndStop(this.hit + 1);
            }
            if (this.hit == 5)
            {
                kills++;
                kills_txt.text = kills;
                this.hit = 6;
            }
            if (this.hit == 6)
            {
                this.dy += 0.1;
            }

            if (Math.random() * 150 < 1 && this.hit < 5)
                dropBomb(this._x, this._y + 5, this.dx / 3);

        }

        pCount++;
    }
```

We have another line of code after this:

```
planeLauncher = setInterval(launchPlane, 1000);
```

This begins the process of launching a plane every 1000 milliseconds, or every second. Because the planes travel at differing speeds, they will not be evenly spaced on screen, which creates a more realistic invasion effect.

Our last big function is the `dropBomb` function, and like `fireBullet` and `launch-Plane`, it revolves around the creation of movie clips and the functions associated with them. The `dropBomb` function creates an instance of a bomb on screen and then causes it to fall and explode on impact with the ground.

The function begins like so:

```
dropBomb = function(x, y, dx)
{
    var nm = "bomb" + bmCount;
    bombs.attachMovie("bomb", nm, bmCount);
    bombs[nm]._x = x;
    bombs[nm]._y = y;
```

```
bombs[nm].dx = dx;
bombs[nm].dy = 0;
bombs[nm].gotoAndStop(1);
```

This function takes three parameters: x, y and dx. This is the location on screen that we'd like to create the bomb and the horizontal speed we want it to have when it's created. We don't pass in a vertical speed, dy, because these bombs are dropped from a plane and are vertically stationary until gravity begins to pull them down.

We create an instance of the linked movie clip bomb and give it an instance name based on "bomb" + bmCount, which will be bomb0, bomb1, bomb2, and so on. We attach this instance to the bombs movie clip that we created earlier on the _root.

When the bomb is created, we set its _x and _y position to the x and y passed in, and we set its dx to the dx passed in. We set its dy value to 0.

We then tell the bomb to stop on frame 1 of its timeline, which is the frame with the bomb and parachute silhouette. If we didn't tell it to do this, the bomb would explode upon creation. Next we have the onEnterFrame function for the bomb.

```
bombs[nm].onEnterFrame = function()
    {
        this._x += this.dx;
        this._y += this.dy;

        this._rotation = Math.atan2(this.dy, this.dx)
                        * (180 / Math.PI);

        if (this._x < -100)
        {
            this.removeMovieClip();
        }
```

Here, like with the planes, we move the bomb along its dx/dy path. We also set the _rotation of the bomb dynamically based on the angle created by its path. This will cause the bomb to point downward steeper and steeper as it falls. We also check to see if the bomb has moved off screen to the left because its momentum carried it there. If so, it's out of the game space, so we just remove it to reduce CPU load. Next we have:

```
if (bullets.hitTest(this._x, this._y, true))
{
    this.removeMovieClip();
}
```

This will cause the bomb to be destroyed if a bullet has hit it. We're checking to see if the x and y position of the bomb is touching a solid area on the bullets movie clip. This means that the best way to kill a bomb is to shoot its registration point, which is the tip of the bomb. After this, we have:

```
if (this._y > 350)
{
    this.play();
    this._rotation = 0;
    delete this.onEnterFrame;
}
```

This will check to see if the bomb has hit the ground. If it has, we cause the bomb to explode by playing its animation, and we set its _rotation to 0, because we don't want the explosion animation itself, which is narrow and tall, to be rotated. We also kill the onEnterFrame function of the bomb so that it will not continue to "fall" with gravity. Remember also, on the last frame of the bomb explosion, there's code to remove the bomb movie clip itself from existence.

Last in this function, we have:

```
    this.dy += 0.05;
    this.dx *= .99;
}

bmCount++;
}
```

This increases the bomb's vertical speed (dy) by 0.05 each frame, which will cause the bomb to accelerate toward the ground. We also multiply the horizontal speed of the bomb by 0.99 every frame. This will cause the bomb to lose its horizontal momentum after it's released. We can assume that the parachute is slowing the bomb down.

We then increment bmCount at the end of the dropBomb function. Here's the dropBomb function in its entirety.

```
dropBomb = function(x, y, dx)
{
    var nm = "bomb" + bmCount;
    bombs.attachMovie("bomb", nm, bmCount);
    bombs[nm]._x = x;
    bombs[nm]._y = y;

    bombs[nm].dx = dx;
    bombs[nm].dy = 0;

    bombs[nm].gotoAndStop(1);

    bombs[nm].onEnterFrame = function()
    {
        this._x += this.dx;
        this._y += this.dy;

        this._rotation = Math.atan2(this.dy, this.dx)
                    * (180 / Math.PI);
```

```
        if (this._x < -100)
        {
            this.removeMovieClip();
        }

        if (bullets.hitTest(this._x, this._y, true))
        {
            this.removeMovieClip();
        }

        if (this._y > 350)
        {
            this.play();
            this._rotation = 0;
            delete this.onEnterFrame;
        }

        this.dy += 0.05;
        this.dx *= .99;

    }

    bmCount++;
}
```

That's it for the major functions. The remaining code that we have on our Ac-tionscript layer is responsible for assigning functions and setting initial values for variables.

```
cannon1.onEnterFrame = cannonEnterFrame;
cannon2.onEnterFrame = cannonEnterFrame;
cannon3.onEnterFrame = cannonEnterFrame;

cannon1.alive = true;
cannon2.alive = true;
cannon3.alive = true;
numAlive = 3;

kills = 0;
kills_txt.text = kills;

skyline.swapDepths(15);
gameOver.swapDepths(20);
gameOver._visible = false;

AAShot = new Sound(cannon1);
AAShot.attachSound("AAShot");
```

We set each cannon's onEnterFrame function to be cannonEnterFrame, and then we set the alive variable in each cannon to true. We set the numAlive variable to 3 to indicate that all cannons are operational.

We then set the `kills` variable to 0, and display that in the `kills_txt` text field. We move the `skyline` movie clip to depth level 15, which ensures that it will always be drawn on top of every element in the game. The `bullets` are at depth 10, the `planes` are at depth 11, and the `bombs` are at depth 12. This means all of these objects will appear to fall into the city or, in the case of the `bullets`, emerge from within the city.

We also move the `gameOver` movie clip to level 20, so it appears on top of everything, and we make it invisible so it's only shown at the end of the game. Finally, we create a new `Sound` object, and link it to the `AAShot` sound effect from the library. This is the sound of the guns firing.

That's the entire game. You can run this and see what kind of score you can achieve. The game itself is `optimized.swf`, and it's found in the Chapter 10 folder on the CD-ROM.

SUMMARY

In this chapter we looked at:

- Creating a game with optimized graphics based on silhouettes and other simple shapes
- Using a bitmap as a background to speed up performance
- Aligning a movie clip to point at the mouse cursor
- Creating multiple instances of many objects dynamically for a high-intensity game experience
- Dynamically calculating angles based on the horizontal and vertical speed of an object
- Using simple `hitTest` on entire encapsulating movie clips in order to quickly determine if collision has taken place

BITMAPS, THE BITMAP DATA OBJECT, AND BITMAP ART

A s we saw in Chapter 9, one of the best ways to optimize the performance of a game in Flash 8 is to make use of bitmaps rather than vectors to display our game graphics. As a general rule, computers just do bitmaps faster because computers are bit driven and all computer memory is essentially one large bitmap. Remember, bitmap refers to a map of bits and doesn't necessarily have to refer to anything visual.

For example, a sound file, once loaded into memory, is a series of bits in sequence that define the sound—in essence a long map of bits—a bitmap. Also, once your operating system is loaded into memory, it too occupies a fixed number of bits (albeit a large number of them) and is also therefore a bitmap.

Generally, a long series of bits is grouped together in units known as bytes, with 8 bits per byte. Take a look at Figure 11.1 and see how the byte data of a raw sound file and that of a bitmap image look quite similar, because remember, it's all just a stream of bits.

FIGURE 11.1 (Top) A series of bytes from a sound file and (bottom) an image file. There are no fundamental differences.

For that reason, we say *bitmapped image* when referring to a graphic that is represented by a long series of bits. This expression has been reduced to *bitmap*, though remember, it's technically misleading because *bitmap* genuinely refers to any series of bits in a row, no matter what their content represents. A bitmap is in fact a bit map (note the space between the two words).

The most important thing to remember with bitmap images is that they are *fast*. When dealing with bitmaps, we're speaking the same language the computer speaks, at a fundamental level. When moving, copying, manipulating, and drawing bitmaps, the processor has a series of built-in functions that allow it to do this manipulation at blazing speeds. This is why working with bitmapped graphics will always be faster than working with purely vector-based images.

We've seen that when we use vectors to represent our images, Flash takes those vectors and renders them into an off-screen buffer, which is itself a large bitmap. That's the first step in the process: mathematically plotting and rendering the vector images, bringing them from a theoretical description of curves and colors, and turning them into a digital plot of pixels. That step can be hugely time-consuming, depending on the complexity of our vector images. Once they have been converted into their representative bitmap, getting them on screen is a matter of quickly copying the series of bits from the off-screen buffer into video memory, making them appear on screen.

So, now that Flash has done all this work calculating and converting these vectors into reality, what does it do next frame? Well, if the vectors are moving, it will do *all* that work again to ultimately arrive at the same result.

Seems like a bit of a waste doesn't it—to perform several thousand mathematical calculations, only to do it all over again when nothing has changed about the vector image itself? It has merely moved on screen, but it is no different. Why not take that single image that we rendered and reuse its bitmap representation to move it around, rather than its vector source, over and over. Seems logical, but it was impossible until Flash 8.

Now we're able to use the `cacheAsBitmap` property to force Flash 8 to use the bitmap representation of a vector image as the on-screen source, rather than doing the math over and over.

Simply setting the `cacheAsBitmap` property to `true` on a movie clip will cause Flash to always use the cached, rendered image of that movie clip, rather than constantly rerendering it every frame. It's done like this:

```
myClip_mc.cacheAsBitmap = true;
```

Bitmap theory goes a lot further with Flash 8 now thanks to `cacheAsBitmap` and the powerful new `BitmapData` class. Let's look at some of the fundamental concepts of bitmaps in games and how we can use them in association with the `BitmapData` class to make fast and powerful bitmap-driven games.

TILES AND TILE PAGES

When creating bitmap-based games in Flash 8, the strongest weapon we have at our disposal is the `BitmapData` class. We can copy, paste, move, position, repeat, tile, and otherwise manipulate bitmaps in any number of ways to create entire screens full of blazingly fast graphics. One of the best ways we can demonstrate this is with a traditional tile-based side-scroller game such as *Super Mario Brothers*.

It is called a tile-based side-scroller because there are two distinct traits that all these games possess:

Tile-Based: All game screens are made up of a series of repeating tiles taken from a master tile set.

Side-Scroller: The game screen scrolls (horizontally and vertically) as the player moves through the game world.

From our demo game in the next chapter, we're using the following master tile set.

Notice that it consists of a series of square tiles, each of which is 32×32 pixels in size. This master tile set is all that is required to create a rich and interesting level. In essence, a level consists of a series of tile numbers arranged in a grid, each corresponding to a tile from the tile set. So, for example, using the tile set from Figure 11.2, we would look at each tile as numbered from 0 up, where the first tile, tile 0, is the one in the upper-left corner of the tile set, tile 1 is the next one over to the right, followed by tiles 2, 3, 4, and so on.

It turns out that computers are faster if we keep our math to numbers like 2, 4, 8, 16. . ., so what we do here is imagine there are 16 tiles per row, even though the image created by our talented artist only uses 7 per row for this level. This means our tiles are actually numbered as shown in Figure 11.3.

FIGURE 11.2 An example tile set.

FIGURE 11.3 The tile set, showing the tile numbers..

So, the second row down, far left tile (the treasure) is tile number 16. This means we can easily have 16 tiles across and 16 tiles down, giving us 256 different tiles, which is a nice large amount for a game.

Thus, in game, a level is represented as something like this:

```
0,0,0,0,0,0,0,0,0,0,0,0,0,65,51,22,66,0,0,0,0,16,0,0,0,0,0,0,0,0,0,0,0,0,0,
0,0,0,0,0,0,38,17,0,0,0,0,0,0,0,0,0,0,0,0,0,0,0,0,0,0,0,0,0,0,0,0,0,0,0,0,
0,0,0,0,0,0,0,0,0,0,0,0,0,0,0,0,0,0,0,0,0,0,0,16,0,0,32,0,0,16,0,0,67,64,0,
32,0,0,0,0,0,0,0,0,22,0,0,0,0,0,0,0,0,0,0,0,0,0,0,49,22,0,0,0,0,0,0,0,0,0,
0,0,0,0,0,0,0,0,0,0,0,0,0,0,0,0,0,0,0,0,0,0,0,0,0,0,0,0,0,0,0,0,0,0,0,0,0,
0,0,0,0,0,0,0,0,0,0,0,0,0,64,0,0,0,0,0,1,0,21,38,0,0,0,0,32,0,0,0,0,0,0,0,
0,0,0,0,0,21,50,0,0,0,0,0,0,0,0,0,0,0,0,0,0,0,0,0,0,0,0,0,0,0,0,0,0,0,0,0,
0,0,0,0,0,0,0,0,0,0,0,0,0,0,0,0,0,0,32,0,0,0,0,1,0,2,3,0,0,0,0,0,64,0,0,0,0,
38,0,0,0,0,0,16,0,0,0,1,0,0,0,0,0,0,0,0,0,0,17,20,18,19,18,22,0,0,0,0,0,0,0,
0,0,0,0,0,0,0,0,0,0,0,0,0,0,0,0,0,0,0,0,0,0,0,0,0,0,0,0,0,0,0,0,0,0,1,0,0,
0,0,17,34,18,35,37,20,0,0,0,0,64,1,0,0,0,0,0,0,0,0,32,0,0,0,0,21,38,
```

That's just a taste. It goes on and on and on. What a game engine would do is build a huge bitmap that is the level put together from our tile set, using that tile data. It reads, from left to right, each number in the tile data and copies the corresponding tile into the position on screen that corresponds to the position in the tile data. The first tile, 0, is copied into the upper-left corner of the world, position 0 horizontally, 0 vertically (from now on, written as x, y). The next tile over, also 0, is then copied into position 32, 0. The next tile goes to 64, 0, then 96, 0 and so on.

The example tile data is taken from the game in the next chapter, in which the world is 90 tiles wide and 75 tiles tall. Based on the width of our screen bitmap, we can fit 15 tiles horizontally and 11 tiles vertically on one screen. This means an entire level is 6 screens wide and nearly 7 screens tall. This allows for a nice big level.

In the tile data, once the 90th item is reached, we move to the second row of tiles and begin building the second row. Once all this is done, we will be left with a huge image, which will be (90 × 32) wide and (75 × 32) high, or 2880 × 2400 pixels. That is our world.

THE BitmapData CLASS

In Flash Professional 8, we use the new `BitmapData` class to handle all of our bitmap work including pixel manipulation, copying, scrolling, and display. Let's take a look at how we begin. The first thing we want to do is make sure we've used the import statement to tell Flash how to use the different constructs that will be required to do everything we need to do with the `BitmapData`.

```
import flash.display.*;
import flash.geom.*;
```

Within `flash.display`, we have all of the different pieces associated with the `BitmapData` class. The `flash.geom` definitions tell Flash how to use the various geometry classes required by the `BitmapData` class. These are `rectangle` and `point`.

Once we've got these in place, we can immediately begin by defining a large `BitmapData` object.

```
var gameboard:BitmapData = new BitmapData(2880, 2400, true, 0x000000);
```

This creates a huge blank `BitmapData` object that is 2880 × 2400 in size. The third parameter tells the constructor that we want this `BitmapData` object to have alpha associated with it (allowing for transparency) and that we want it to initially be filled with `0x00000000`. That is the color definition for black with an alpha value of zero.

You may be used to seeing `0xRRGGBB`, but now with 32-bit alpha in our `Bitmap-Data` objects, we're defining color as `0xAARRGGBB`, where `AA` represents the alpha value, from `00` to `FF`, where `00` is transparent and `FF` is solid. So, if we wanted to fill our bitmap initially with solid black, we'd use `0xFF000000`, or if we didn't want to use any alpha at all, we'd pass in false for the third parameter, and then the fourth parameter would only require a traditional `0xRRGGBB` color value.

Now our `BitmapData` object is ready to have things copied into it. If we wanted to use a tile set as our source image, we would need to create a second `BitmapData` object. Lets say, for example, that we had a bitmap image in the library and we set it up so that it had a linkage identifier and was set to export as `texturepage`. We would create a new `BitmapData` object that contains all of its pixels like so:

```
var texturePage:BitmapData = BitmapData.loadBitmap("texturepage");
```

This would grab the bitmap image from the library and load it into a new `BitmapData` object, and we'd have that all ready to go as the variable `texturePage`.

Now, building our world image is simply a matter of copying pixels from `texturePage` to `gameBoard`. Here's how we do that:

```
srcx = tileNum % 16;
srcy = Math.floor(tileNum / 16);
var tRect:Rectangle = new Rectangle(srcx * tileWidth,
                                    srcy * tileHeight,
                                    tileWidth, tileHeight);
var destPt:Point = new Point(j * tileWidth,
                             i * tileHeight);
gameboard.copyPixels(texturePage, tRect, destPt);
```

We use the `copyPixels` method of the `BitmapData` class. We specify two geometric objects.

The source rectangle: A rectangular area specifying what pixels from the source we would like to copy.

The destination point: A point on the target specifying where we'd like to place the pixels we're copying.

First we take `tileNum`, which corresponds to the exact tile number in our tile set page, from 0 to 1, 2, 3, 4, 5. . . . Once we've determined what tile we want to use as our source, we have to do a quick calculation to determine where that tile physically sits on the tile page. We calculate `srcx` and `srcy`, which will be an x and y position, in *tilespace*. This means we're looking at the number of tiles across and number of tiles down at which a particular `tileNum` occurs. For example, `tileNum` 10 would have a `srcx` of 10 and a `srcy` of 0 for the 10th tile across, first row down.

So, if `tileWidth` and `tileHeight` are both 32, and `srcx` and `srcy` refer to a specific tile, simply multiplying `srcx` by `tileWidth` and multiplying `srcy` by `tileHeight` will give us the pixel coordinates of the tile we want to copy.

To see how the source tiles map onto our game world, take a look at Figure 11.4.

Let's look at an example. Imagine we want to copy tile 35 to the screen. The first thing we do is calculate `srcx` and `srcy`.

```
srcx = 37 % 16;
srcy = Math.floor(37 / 16);
```

When we use the modulus operator, the `%`, we are given the remainder after dividing the left number by the right number. So, if we take 35 and divide it by 16, we get a remainder of 5, because 37/16 = 2, remainder 5. Thus, our `srcx` is 5, or the fifth tile over. If we take 37/16 and take the `Math.floor` of it, we simply round the result down and remove the decimal, which results in 2. Our `srcy` is 2.

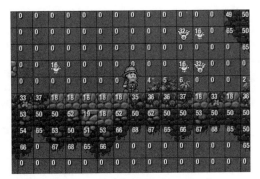

FIGURE 11.4 How the tiles are copied and positioned in game space.

Now we have srcx = 5 and srcy = 2: fifth tile across, second tile down. Next we take those two numbers and multiply them by 32 and get a rectangle that starts at x of 160, and y of 64 and is 32 × 32 in size. This rectangle would be literally defined as:

```
var tRect:Rectangle = new Rectangle(160, 64, 32, 32);
```

Our destination point is calculated in a very similar way. Since, while putting together our background image, we will be looping through the entire level data, we will be going row after row, column by column. If we loop with variables i and j, we could do it like so:

```
for (var i = 0; i < 75; i++)
{
    for (j = 0; j < 90; j++)
    {
```

That's 75 rows of 90 tiles across. Using these two values, the destination point is easily calculated and constructed at:

```
var destPt:Point = new Point(j * tileWidth,
                             i * tileHeight);
```

Once we've got the source rectangle, and the destination point calculated, we simply tell the gameboard BitmapData object to grab these pixels and copy them across from the texturePage, like so.

```
gameboard.copyPixels(texturePage, tRect, destPt);
```

Since the gameboard supports alpha values and the source image we used for our tile page also has alpha values (it's taken from a PNG), all our tiles will have holes in them where we want, to be able to see through to the background nicely.

BACKGROUNDS AND BUFFERS

Once we've got our entire world image ready to go for the current level, we're only part of the way to making the *screen* image the player sees while playing the game. The player only sees a small window into this huge 2880 × 2400 image, so we really only need to take a piece of it and copy it across. We simply need a screen-sized square that is centered around a hypothetical position in the board where the player is currently positioned. This is another simple `copyPixels` call, but with one small twist.

If we simply make a call to `copyPixels` every frame, we're going to have a problem with trails being left behind as the gameboard moves. This is caused by the zero alpha pixels not being changed from frame to frame, but pixels with nonzero values being placed in those spaces every frame. The result is a little strange looking, as shown in Figure 11.5.

How do we fix this? Very simply, we need to overwrite the screen space every frame with something else before we copy the chunk of gameboard over. What should we use to wipe the slate clean? We could use solid black, but what if we used another bitmap image? Something like a far distant, slightly blurry background? What if we panned this slightly, based on the player's position? What would we end up with? A really nice, high-depth, distant parallax background, as shown in Figure 11.6.

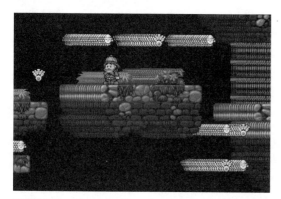

FIGURE 11.5 The trail effect of not erasing the buffer each frame.

FIGURE 11.6 The background in place.

We're accomplishing two tasks at once. Our distant background is both our desired image and our eraser. What's the process to make this happen? It's simple.

First, near the top of our program, we have to create another `BitmapData` object. This will be our game screen, and this is what will ultimately be displayed to the user. This is the canvas upon which we build each frame of our game environment, sometimes referred to as a *buffer*. Our game screen is 480 × 320 in size:

```
var gameScreen:BitmapData = new BitmapData(480, 320,
                                           false, 0);
```

This time we don't need to see through it, because the distant background will be part of the image itself, so we pass in `false` for alpha transparency. We then have to tell Flash that we'd like this `gameScreen` bitmap to appear on the stage. Without doing this, all of our bitmaps will be strictly in memory and will have no visual manifestation.

```
_root.createEmptyMovieClip("outScreen", 0);
outScreen.attachBitmap(gameScreen, 0);
```

We create a movie clip called `outScreen` and then use the `attachBitmap` method to attach the `gameScreen` `BitmapData` object to the movie clip.

The `attachBitmap` method takes a source `BitmapData` object and then a depth number, which corresponds to the depth at which the `BitmapData` object will be drawn, just like the depth passed in with the traditional movie clip methods `attach-Movie` and `createEmptyMovieClip`.

Once we've got this all set up, any pixels we write to the `gameScreen` `BitmapData` object will appear physically on the stage.

Now, our background image, the image we're using as our eraser, is loaded into a `BitmapData` object like so:

```
var worldBack:BitmapData = BitmapData.loadBitmap("worldback");
```

This, very similar to our tile page, would take a bitmap image called `worldback` from the library and copy its pixels into the `BitmapData` object `worldBack`.

Now let's assume that the position of our world is calculated by the character's position minus a certain amount to keep the world centered on the character. Let's also assume that the position of the `gameboard` has been calculated for us and is stored in variables `offx` and `offy`. Here's the code to build our finished game screen:

```
var tRect:Rectangle = new Rectangle(offx, offy, 480, 320);
var wRect:Rectangle = new Rectangle(0, 0, 480, 320);
var destPt:Point = new Point(0, 0);

gameScreen.copyPixels(worldBack, wRect, destPt);
gameScreen.copyPixels(gameboard, tRect, destPt);
```

We create two rectangles. Both are the size of the screen. The `tRect` rectangle refers to the pixels from `gameboard` that we'd like to copy, and `wRect` refers to the far background, our eraser. The `destPt` point is simply 0, 0, because we will always be copying our finished image into the upper-left corner of the game screen.

We then make two calls to `copyPixels`. First, we take the `worldBack` distant background and then we take the pixels associated with our player's position in the `gameboard`. We must perform the `copyPixels` in that order: `worldBack` first, followed by `gameboard`. Just like that, our world springs to life, as shown in Figure 11.7.

In the next section we're going to be led on a fascinating journey into the world of creating game art and specifically, creating artwork that is custom suited to working within the context of a bitmap image–based tile game. This section is contributed by the graphic artist Chris Hildenbrand.

FIGURE 11.7   The game from Chapter 12.

CREATING A LOOK AND FEEL FOR THE GAME

Contribution by Chris Hildenbrand

Great games might be able to do without good graphics—examples like *Tetris®* or more recently *N* come to mind—but generally a good game is enhanced by good graphics. They should match the game, blend in with the game play without overpowering it, and basically increase fun factor.

For the creative director at a flash-games company the task of making flash games get this edge is an everyday challenge. Where do you start? There are two common scenarios: (a) the game is in the early development stages, the idea of the game play is born, and an early design doc has being drafted or (b) the game is done or nearly done and now it's time to replace the placeholder art.

In either case sit back and think before rushing out and opening the graphic program. What are the main elements of the game? What restrictions will the game encounter (e.g., screen size, downloadable file size, speed issues [Flash 8 still is not C++ when it comes to full-screen effects or huge particle storms])? How much time do I have to do all the art?

Once you have worked out the basics—which might not take more than a 5-minute coffee break—think about the games you like. Which style of graphics do you like in your games? This might not necessarily be a style you will be able to produce, as most commercial games have been created by a whole army of artists and coders, but it gives you an idea of how others did it—successfully. Studying the screenshots is very helpful when you try to determine the layout of your game's interfaces, score and progress bars, or even the color scheme you could use in your own game.

Certain game genres have their specific feel. You could probably pick a racing game from a shooter by looking at a credits page or the effects used in the logo.

One of the key aspects of good game graphics is consistency. Your game should look like one piece from the moment the first preloader appears to the game-over screen. With game development sometimes taking months or even years, it's hard to keep a consistent look.

It is helpful to take one screen, either as a screen grab if the game is already in progress or made from scratch, that includes all the essential elements that will make the game fun. Creating this mock-up screen serves several purposes:

- It helps to reveal problems with the design at an early stage. (Does the playable character stand out enough from the background? Is the score bar too big or too small? Is the font I chose still readable when sized to the requirements of the game screen?)
- It functions as a reference for the other artwork later on or other artists involved in the project.
- It helps communicate the game idea to others in an easier way than the design document could.
- It helps make a change in a test-area without having to touch the game. (How will the player sprite look with an orange helmet instead of green? Will it look OK to move the score to the bottom rather then the top?)
- Keep your work in progress files and update them as you go. It can be a huge timesaver if you are thinking about major additions or changes to your game to quickly try them out in the graphic program first.

To make these changes as quickly as possible, use graphic tools that allow layering and keep the elements on separate layers for easy alterations.

When you have not worked on a project for a while and need to add more art to it, take the old screens and work with them. It will show very quickly if the new elements do not match the old.

Sometimes it might be inevitable that you go back to the mock and change the whole look because the style of the game changed or your skill level has increased as you did the art.

It's a painful task, but a rounded and polished game will make it worthwhile it in the end.

Pixel Art versus Vector Art

Flash is capable of using vector as well bitmap art. Does that mean one is better than the other? No, it's just a matter of using the advantages of each format to make the best use of both for your game.

Vector art is very flexible and allows scaling, rotating, and all the messing around you can think of while keeping perfect display quality.

Pixel art gets messy, and the display quality might end up being poor when you make these kinds of alterations to your pixel art inside Flash.

If you need to be able to zoom into elements of the game and use a lot of scaling but still want it to look great, you should consider vectors.

Vector art can be created with less effort and offers a lot of reusability of shapes and forms. This makes it easy to deform existing elements and rearrange them to form new objects for your game.

Bitmaps are more cumbersome to work with. Reusing elements is limited because as soon as you start to rotate smaller elements they lose their sharp edge because of the graphics program antialiasing (smoothing of edges by using neighboring colors) or lose their detail because of lack of antialiasing.

 Mix and match. If you are familiar with tools used to create either style or have access to them, it's well worth trying to create certain elements in vectors and then export them into your bitmap program (or even do a quick and dirty copy and paste if the programs allow it). There will be more on this topic in following paragraph.

On the other hand, vector art has a huge impact on the performance of your game effects such as gradients, complex transparencies, and objects consisting of a lot of nodes, which can slow down your game dramatically. In this area bitmaps truly shine. They allow faster display and take a much smaller toll on your performance. If performance is an issue for your game, bitmaps are the way to go.

It all comes down to your game and your capabilities to create art. You might feel more comfortable with bitmaps or you might do everything in vector art because you just like the style better. Go for it! Just keep in mind the principles discussed in this chapter and the new powers that Flash 8 has to handle bitmap images.

The following examples use both tools and might give you some ideas on how to improve your workflow or simply inspire you to try something new.

Going into Detail 1: A Main Character

The term *character* might be misleading, as the main object in your game might be anything from a spaceship to a dune buggy to a classic hero. Whatever you choose, it should be the center of your design. The rest of the game graphics have to fit in with your choice of style for the main character.

If you enjoy sketching, this is where it starts, and most of the time it's time well spent. Get a pile of paper and a pencil and sit down and draw. One the one hand, it's a nice break from working in front of the computer screen (and let's face it, you probably spend too much time staring at it), and on the other hand, it's not as restricted as the computer work. You can go wild and do things that might not even work in the game but spark some new ideas.

For those who prefer to stay digital and would not want to miss their undo function, a good start might be a blank canvas about twice or three times the size of the character in the game. The larger canvas allows for a faster and less restricted workflow. Instead of putting one pixel next to the other, you can use a pencil tool and roughly sketch without the need to be 100% accurate.

Start out with a rough doodle that shows the proportions of your character and gives you a general idea of the shapes. Add a second layer on top of the first one and work out some details, loosely at first and more detailed as you move along.

The snow-wolf example had to stay within a size of 200 pixels by 160 pixels with no color restrictions (see Figures 11.8 to 11.10).

FIGURE 11.8   The initial snow-wolf sketch.

FIGURE 11.9   Snow-wolf sketch after clean up.

FIGURE 11.10   Snow-wolf sketch after flat coloring.

You can still see the initial drawing through the more detailed line art. It's also a good start to use basic shapes like circles and tubes to arrange the elements that form the character later on.

Once you are happy with the sketch, it is reduced to the final size. By enhancing the contrast and altering the tone-curve, you reduce the sketch to two colors (black and white) and then manually clean it up to remove stray pixels.

Coloring the main shapes with the fill tool allows quick color composition. The black outline is then used as a color mask and copied to a separate layer placed above the others with additional layers for highlights and shadows added below (see Figures 11.11 to 11.13).

FIGURE 11.11   Snow-wolf with highlights added.

FIGURE 11.12   Snow-wolf with shadows added.

FIGURE 11.13   Snow-wolf with fine details added.

By selecting the colored areas as a mask, you can easily start shading without running into the background. You want to keep the background clean to allow transparency once the art is displayed inside the game.

As a final touch, highlights and shadows were added using an antialiased pen with varying degrees of softness on separate layers. Figures 11.14 to 11.17 show the different effects of this technique.

Optimizing your character is essential to keep the amount of work and the number of files down. Depending on the game, its engine, and the use of the resources, it sometimes makes sense to break up a character into different objects. Let's take these sprites from the flash shooter *HeliAttack3* as an example, as shown in Figure 11.18.

FIGURE 11.16   Example 3.

FIGURE 11.15   Example 2.

FIGURE 11.14   Example 1.

FIGURE 11.17   Example 4.

The player movement had to be elaborate, allowing the use of over 30 different weapons while running, crouching, jumping, and climbing. The download size restricted the use of graphics, and the focus had to be on keeping the file size within limits.

Being a 2D side-scrolling game, *HeliAttack3* artwork only needed to be done in one direction and was then flipped in Flash for movement in the opposite direction. In order to make this shortcut not too visible, the highlights and shadows where toned down a bit with the sun coming down on the player in a near 180 degree angle.

Even though Flash is able to rotate bitmaps, the player's main body was tilted in several images to ensure a decent display quality while looking up or down, as shown in Figure 11.19.

FIGURE 11.19   Looking up or down in *HeliAttack3*.

FIGURE 11.18   Character from *HeliAttack3*.

Also, the torso was separated from the arms and the legs. This way legs could be animated separately using just an eight-frame cycle. The standing position was used as a base and the animations were painted in layers above it. This way it was easy to create the next step by working on top of the shape of the previous step. Later the animation was fine tuned and then exported to 1-bit transparent PNGs, as shown in Figure 11.20.

FIGURE 11.20   The torso animation in *HeliAttack3*.

On top of those two elements, the arms and weapons are displayed with animations for reloading as well as separate objects for empty shells and bullets. For these fast-moving elements (following the mouse's position in the game) no rotations were created but were left to Flash to handle. This can be seen in Figure 11.21.

FIGURE 11.21   The handheld elements in *HeliAttack3*.

While the graphics for most of the game elements were pixeled, the interface images were created using vectors to determine the look and coloring of the health indicator in the game. This can be seen in Figures 11.22 and 11.23.

FIGURE 11.22   The vector-based health indicator in *HeliAttack3*.

FIGURE 11.23   The health indicator in *HeliAttack3*.

The initial character portrait was created from circles and then deformed and fitted with outlines to allow more contrast between elements when resized to the smaller in-game dimensions.

The main advantage of using vectors for these images was the ability to reuse a lot of the shapes in the next image of the sequence. For example, the helmet stayed the same throughout the five images—only the rotation and position was changed, and wear and tear as blood splatters were added later in the bitmap program.

To show you this way of combining vector and bitmap elements in detail let's look at another sample. The task at hand was the creation of some character art for dialogue screens.

In order to find some inspiration and create a look that is natural, it's helpful to search on the Internet for reference photos. In this case it was a young male face for the game's hero. The photo was reduced to a quick hand-drawn sketch highlighting the main features and proportions, as shown in Figure 11.24.

The sketch was brought into the vector program as the bottom layer, and vector shapes were created on top to give the illustration a clean, inked look, as seen in Figure 11.25. It also allows quick alterations; for example, the eyes were enlarged to give the character a younger, more boyish look. Color and basic shading were added in the vector program for easier editing and corrections, as shown in Figure 11.26.

The vector shape was then copied into the bitmap tool as a new object and scaled down to the right size. The edges were manually cleaned up to allow 1-bit transparency (Figure 11.27) and give the portrait enough contrast when being displayed on the matching background.

FIGURE 11.24   The initial hand-drawn sketch.

FIGURE 11.25   The vector inking.

FIGURE 11.26   Character sketch with color and basic shading added.

FIGURE 11.27   Character sketch with the edges cleaned up and transparency added.

Use a color least likely to appear in the art (e.g., magenta) for the transparent color. It also needs to stand out enough to spot stray pixels.

The portrait shape was masked and new layers added on top. Highlights and shadows were painted on using an airbrush tool, as shown in Figure 11.28. Different layers using different transparency settings make it easy to fine-tune lighting and contrast. The character used in game appears in Figure 11.29 and Figure 11.30. We can see other examples of characters in Figure 11.31.

FIGURE 11.28 Character sketch with highlights and shadows added.

FIGURE 11.29 The final character.

FIGURE 11.30 The character in the game with background.

FIGURE 11.31 Examples of other characters.

Going into Detail 2: The Level Graphics

Most likely your game will consist of more than just a major character. Another essential element is the look of the level. Let's start with a sample background for a nice sunny outdoor scene, as shown in Figure 11.32.

Starting with an empty canvas, I set up a multicolor gradient fill ranging from dark blue to light blue to white to light brown and finally black. I used the fill on the background, which is the lowest layer. This gradient was to be the foundation of the sky I wanted to achieve.

On a new layer the basic shapes of the clouds were sprayed using a 50% transparency setting for the layer, as shown in Figure 11.33. Using a soft airbrush tool made the shapes nice and airy.

FIGURE 11.32 The starting of the outdoor scene.

FIGURE 11.33 Background with basic clouds added.

More detailed highlights were added on the next layer. This time the transparency was set to 70% to stand out more, like in Figure 11.34. Different shapes of clouds created a more believable, wind torn look. Look for a reference photo if you are unsure about the look you are trying to create.

After the lighter parts were done, the shadows were added on a separate layer (using a very high level of transparency). This can be seen in Figure 11.35.

Using a color other than black for shadows gives you a softer and in most cases more natural look.

Finally, a layer for the details was added (80% transparency), and more contrast and some details were sprayed on top, as shown in Figure 11.36.

The same layering technique was applied to great the background for the sample game from Chapter 12. In this case it was a warm and colorful jungle mood we were after (Figure 11.37). It started with a light yellow to dark green gradient with some light spring green in the middle of the gradient. In the layer on top, the shading was applied with a broad airbrush tool and refined with a smaller size afterward. The idea is not to create too much detail, as the focus should remain on the player and the level in the front of the jungle. I kept it slightly blurry with soft edges and only little highlights on top.

FIGURE 11.34   Background with more detailed clouds added.

FIGURE 11.35   Background with some shading added.

FIGURE 11.37   The Jungle Adventure background.

FIGURE 11.36   The final details layer of the background added.

Finally, the light effects of light coming through openings in the tree tops was added by simply drawing a horizontal line with a wide and very soft airbrush in a separate layer. This object was rotated nearly 90 degrees to a vertical orientation and then duplicated, flipped, and rotated a little for the other beams.

The last touch was a soft eraser (with 80% transparency, antialiasing, and 100 softness) to create a more irregular look for the beams by erasing random bits and pieces. If you want to add more detail to your background like in this example, it might be helpful to mix vectors and bitmaps again, as shown in Figure 11.38.

FIGURE 11.38   A more detailed background image.

The background in Figure 11.38 was created just like the earlier examples. The refinery was added by starting with the most distant layer, which could still be airbrushed because of the blurred effect caused by the setting sunlight. The shapes of the refinery were more intricate and needed to have clean and straight technical edges. Achieving this by hand can be a slow and painstaking process. To save time I created the silhouette using black vector shapes—basic squares, circles, and lines of varying thickness. All this was copied and pasted into the existing sky background as a new layer. This layer was used as a mask, and I could easily apply the shading and highlights on top of the black shape without fear of painting into the sky.

The background in Figures 11.39 to 11.41 that was used in *HeliAttack3* takes this mixing all the way. Various layers of vector objects were combined with light beams and effect layers.

FIGURE 11.39   The final background image.

FIGURE 11.40   Underneath this technical mess lie simple vector shapes.

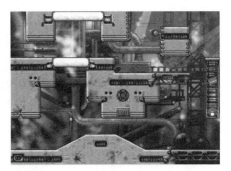

FIGURE 11.41 Adding the foreground tiles creates an atmospheric feel.

Creating Tile Graphics

Creating tiles for platforms, borders, or backgrounds is another time-consuming task in the game design process.

Lets start with something common—the almighty grass tile. Starting with an empty canvas (e.g., 32 × 32 pixels), you choose your background color—in this case a nice dark green—and fill the whole tile. Changing to a lighter tone close to the background green and using a soft pen tool, you apply the pattern, in this case a slightly wind-torn medium-length grass (see Figure 11.42).

FIGURE 11.42 The basic tile background.

The main hurdle when doing tiles is that they have to match seamlessly to each other and in many cases at each of the four sides. Some graphic programs provide functions to help with the creation of tiles. The smaller the tiles are, the less help these tools tend to be.

An easy way to test and work on your tile is to create a canvas three times the size of the tile and fill it with nine tiles (three rows by three columns) and work on the center piece (put it in a layer and mask it to keep from painting outside your tile). Every few steps replace the outside tiles with duplicates of the one you are working on to see how seamlessly they match.

To add variations I took the same tile and started painting longer shapes on top, using a slightly different green. This will stand out and appear to be longer and wilder grass. Again I had to make sure it would tile seamlessly. The final grass tile can be seen in Figure 11.43.

When using tiles, make sure you have enough transition and variation tiles to avoid repeating patterns and harsh borders.

Platform tiles in most cases are less of a worry, as most of them only have to seamlessly connect to two sides. Let's look at the jungle game. The tile set used for the game can be seen in Figure 11.44.

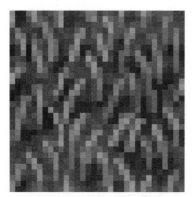

FIGURE 11.43   The final grass tile.

FIGURE 11.44   The tile set used in the jungle games.

There are two basic blocks. First is the platform block that allows the player to walk and second is the background pattern block in darker brown to add visual variation to the game. Most of the other blocks derive from one of these.

I started with a blank 32 × 32 pixel canvas and gave it a warm darkish brown color. Using a pen tool with a round tip and medium antialiasing setting, I drew the basic shapes of the rocks—making sure the shape on the right edge would correspond with the left edge. I added highlight and shadow and fine-tuned the tiling. The final result can be seen in Figure 11.45.

Once I had the first block done and knew it would tile well, I duplicated it to a new image and painted over the center section to create a variation and at same time make sure it would still tile well with the first block. This variation can be seen in Figure 11.46.

Keeping the 2 pixels on either side mostly untouched, I could create a new and different-looking center and match it to the sides.

FIGURE 11.45   The main game block.

FIGURE 11.46   A variation on the final main block tile.

Figure 11.47 shows another mock screen from *HeliAttack3*, testing the tiles of the jungle level. The game uses three layers: the bitmap in the background that stays stationary (using the least amount of detail and appearing a little blurred), the darker foliage of a slower moving parallax layer, and the foreground tiles that act as platforms and in part as decoration (e.g., the smaller bushes growing on the branches). Overall, it remains easy to recognize which areas are accessible to the player because of consistent coloring, harsher highlights, and more detail of the foreground items.

FIGURE 11.47   A full mock-up example from *HeliAttack3*.

About Chris Hildenbrand

Chris "DayDream" Hildenbrand started working on pixel art with his first computer—a Commodore c64—using a joystick and Paint Magic. A few years later, the Commodore Amiga 2000, with its proper mouse control, animations, and a 32-color palette, allowed him to begin work on professional games. This led to his own development studio, which then began releasing games for the Amiga, Atari ST, and PC.

Moving into Web and packaging design in the 1990s, it took the introduction of Macromedia Flash 3 and the possibility to create online games accessible to everyone surfing the Web to get him back into game development. He has been working as a freelance artist on various online, console, and mobile phone games for clients such as Disney, Warner Brothers, Cartoon Network, MTV, and Jamdat as well as producing his own titles, teaming up with independent coders. The most successful recent launch was *HeliAttack3*, with over 142 million game plays in the first 90 days of its release.

CONCLUSION AND SUMMARY

In the next chapter we're going to look at how to take the basic world we've created and turn it into a complete game. This will involve the addition of characters, physics, and collision rules so that the tiles are more than just graphics, but have some physical interactivity to them.

Using the concepts covered in this chapter for creating full-screen graphics and images and using the `BitmapData` object, we're now able to create very, very fast and optimized games in Flash without having to suffer any of the traditional slow-downs associated with vector-rendering inefficiency. We have seen the following:

- How the concept of a bitmap applies to anything that contains a series of bits and isn't merely a concept used to convey images, even though that is what it has become universally known for.
- How games can be built up of screens full of regular, repeating, square-shaped graphics known as tiles. Using tiles, large game worlds can be built with minimal overhead.
- How to use the `BitmapData` class to copy rectangular areas of pixels from tile pages to create larger images.
- How screens are built up in a virtual buffer and then displayed on screen by continually copying background and foreground sections across and then attaching the end result to a movie clip, thus making it visible.
- How to create stunning game characters, backgrounds, and tiles that work specifically within the context of bitmap image–based games.

JUNGLE ADVENTURE

In the last chapter we looked at how to use the `BitmapData` class to do some pretty powerful things with bitmap images in Flash and how to create a tile-based level-rendering engine using bitmap tiles and static backgrounds. Now we're going to take it one step further and make a full game with it.

The game will be called Jungle Adventure and it will follow the exploits of a daring adventurer-explorer, as limited as those adventures may be. We're going to have one basic level, designed with our level editor, and the game will consist of solid tiles, climbable tiles, background tiles, and collectable tiles. The tiles will appear as:

Solid tiles: Blocks, bricks and walls
Climbable tiles: Ladders
Background tiles: Bushes, flowers, and hanging vines
Collectable tiles: Gold treasures

The background tiles are not to be confused with the far background, which will scroll in the distance, in parallax. By background tiles, we simply mean that the player will be able to pass in front of them without any physical interaction. These are strictly decorative tiles. Solid tiles are just that—solid. We cannot pass through them, but we can stand on top of them. Climbable tiles (ladders) will be such that when you are in front of one, you can press the up arrow key to climb up and press the down arrow key to climb down. The collectable tiles simply disappear when you pass over them, as if you have picked them up.

This chapter is divided into two sections. First, we will look at creating a level editor, which is a prerequisite to the game, because we will initially require a level to make our game work. The level editor and the game share much of the same code base, specifically as it applies to rendering of the map. The level editor does not, however, have any physics or character animation functionality.

Take a look at the game now, to get a quick feel for how it plays. The game can be found in the Chapter 12 folder on the CD-ROM, under the filename `tilegame.swf`. Give it a quick run. Run left and right with the left and right arrow keys. Press the spacebar to jump and press up and down to climb and descend the ladders. The game should look something like Figure 12.1.

FIGURE 12.1 The game Jungle Adventure in action.

THE LEVEL EDITOR

From the Chapter 12 folder, open the file `tilegameedit.fla` in Macromedia Flash Professional 8. This is the level editor, and when opened, it should look something like Figure 12.2.

The level editor is pretty straightforward. Press Ctrl-Enter to run it and take a look at it in action (Figure 12.3).

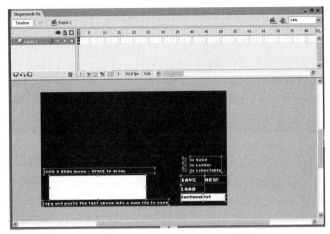

FIGURE 12.2   The level editor in Flash.

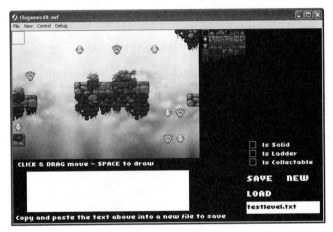

FIGURE 12.3   The level editor in action.

The layout of the level editor is divided into four areas:

- The upper-left corner is the map, and this is where you place your tiles. The map can be panned by clicking and dragging or by pressing the arrow keys to scroll. You place tiles down by hitting the spacebar. This is all rendered via our `BitmapData` method discussed in the previous chapter.
- The upper-right corner contains the tile selector. Click on a tile and you will see it enlarged directly below. Next to this enlarged view are three option boxes. Use these to set the properties of the selected tile. For example, the bricks have their Is Solid option set, while the ladders have their Is Ladder option set. Note that any tile type with the Is Collectable

option set will disappear if you run over it. The greenery has no options set, because it is purely visual and has no interactivity.

- The lower-right area of the screen contains the level loading and saving boxes, as well as a space for the name of the file you would like to load.
- When you hit the Save button, the area in the lower-left corner of the screen is filled with text. This is the data for the level, and this text must be copied and pasted into a text editor and saved by hand for it to be used in a game. One such file is included: the sample level called `testlevel.txt`. We have to manually create and save these files because Flash doesn't have the ability to write directly to an arbitrary file on the hard disk.

Run the level editor for a few minutes. Get familiar with it. Scroll around and select some tile types from the tile selector. Place them in the map by pressing and holding the space bar. If you hold the space bar, you will be able to drag-draw your selected tile.

To begin with, let's look at the movie clips on stage. The interface is very simple and does not require too much explanation or study, but we'll work quickly, to go over everything.

The Save, Load, and New Buttons and File Name Text Field

In the lower-right corner of the stage, as shown in Figure 12.4, are three buttons, with the text Save, Load, and New. If you double-click inside them, you will see that they all have a hit area defined on their Hit frame that is slightly larger than their text, so that they're easy to click on. They have the instance names `save_btn`, `load_btn`, and `new_btn`. That is all the attention they require at this point.

FIGURE 12.4   The `save_btn`, `load_btn`, `new_btn`, and `filename_txt`.

Directly below those three buttons is a single text field that has been set to type Input Text, and has the instance name `filename_txt`. This text field is used when the Load button is pressed to specify what file should be loaded off the hard drive. It is set to `testlevel.txt` by default.

The Is Solid, Is Ladder, and Is Collectable Option Boxes

These are three simple boxes that are used to indicate the status of parameters for each tile in the tile set. They are very, very, simple. The text is simply painted onto the stage as a graphic, and the three option boxes are instances of the same movie clip with the name `checkbox`. The three boxes have the instance names `solid_cb`, `ladder_cb`, and `collect_cb`.

The option box, or `checkbox`, movie clip is simply two frames. In frame 1, the box is black with a white outline, and in frame 2 the box is filled solid white. There is also one simple line of code on frame 1 to stop the `checkbox` movie clip from playing and rapidly flickering between frame 1 and frame 2. That code is:

```
stop();
```

Figure 12.5 shows the inside of the option box.

FIGURE 12.5   The option box movie clip, `checkbox`.

The Output Text Field

In the lower-left corner of the stage is a single text field with the instance name `out_txt`. This is the text field into which the complete level data is placed when the Save button is pressed. Once done, the level data must be copied and pasted into a regular text editor such as Notepad and saved as a file. This is how the demo level `testlevel.txt` was created.

Items in the Library

In the library there is an item that is set with the export linkage name `chooserbox`. This is the box that is used to indicate where the cursor is in the world editor. This will represent where the next tile will be placed if the space bar is pressed. This movie clip is attached to the stage at runtime.

Take a look at the movie clip in the library and double-click on it. The `chooserbox` is simply a 32 × 32 box, that has a 20-frame animation. The animation is a color pulse from yellow to blue, meant to ensure that the box is visible over all different colors of background (see Figure 12.6).

In the library we also have two more items that are set to export with linkage names. These are named `texturepage` and `worldback`. They are bitmap images, and one is the tile set for the level and the other is the background image that displays behind everything.

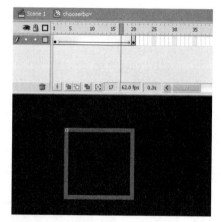

FIGURE 12.6 The chooserbox movie clip.

The Code

Now that we've seen all of the assets that make up the level editor, it's time to look at the code that makes it tick. Take a look at frame 1 of the Actions layer. We have the following code:

```
import flash.display.*;
import flash.geom.*;

var grid:Array = new Array();

var gameboard:BitmapData = new BitmapData(2880, 2400,
                                          true, 0x000000);
var worldBack:BitmapData = BitmapData.loadBitmap("worldback");
var bigBack:BitmapData = new BitmapData(2880, 320,
                                        false, 0);
```

Here we're telling Flash that we're going to be using the classes associated with flash.display and flash.geom, the former being for all our BitmapData code and the latter for all our rectangle and point code.

After that, we create a new array called grid. This will hold the data for our level. Then we create three BitmapData objects. The first one is the gameboard, as discussed in the previous chapter. This is one large image that will be made up of the arrangements of tiles that define our level. The second BitmapData object contains the image associated with the far background. This is simply a green blurred image meant to approximate a distant jungle.

The third BitmapData object will be used as a special BitmapData object to make our background image more interesting. Rather than having one solid, unmoving screen, we're going to "wallpaper" the background image three times in a row, creating one large, wide image. This will allow our background image to pan ever so slightly with the foreground to create a really strong 3D parallax effect.

The next code we have is this:

```
for (var i = 0; i < 3; i++)
{
    var tRect:Rectangle = new Rectangle(0, 0, 731, 320);
    var destPt:Point = new Point(i * 731, 0);
    bigBack.copyPixels(worldBack, tRect, destPt);
}

var texturePage:BitmapData = BitmapData.loadBitmap("texturepage");
var gameScreen:BitmapData = new BitmapData(480, 320,
                                           false, 0);

_root.createEmptyMovieClip("outScreen", 0);
outScreen.attachBitmap(gameScreen, 0, true, false);
outScreen.attachMovie("chooserbox", "cbox", 2);
```

Right away, the first thing we do is copy the large background image three times into the bigBack BitmapData object. Since the background is 731 pixels wide, we place each copy 731 pixels apart, creating one large seamless image. Remember that tRect refers to the rectangle defining the source image (in this case the entire background bitmap) and the destPt refers to the position in our destination where we'd like to place that copy.

Next we create our texturePage BitmapData object, which consists of the image in the library set to export as texturepage. This is our image of the tiles, as shown in Figure 12.7, and will be used for all our tile-drawing operations.

FIGURE 12.7   The tiles in the texturepage bitmap.

Next we create a movie clip called outScreen. This is the movie clip that will hold our world, and it is the gateway into the otherwise virtual world of Bitmap-Data objects. We attach the BitmapData object gameScreen and an instance of our chooserbox movie clip, as this will be needed for our level-building interactions.

Let's look at more code.

```
outScreen.onPress = function()
{
    dragging = true;
    startmousex = _xmouse + offx;
    startmousey = _ymouse + offy;
}

outScreen.onRelease =
outScreen.onReleaseOutside = function()
{
    gameselx = Math.floor((this._xmouse + offx) / 32);
    gamesely = Math.floor((this._ymouse + offy) / 32);

    repaintTile(gameselx, gamesely);
    dragging = false;
}


var dragging:Boolean = false;
```

This code handles the clicking and dragging of the world, used to move it around and to determine where our chooserbox appears. The first part handles what happens when the user presses down on the mouse button. We set a flag called dragging to true and then make note of the starting position of the mouse, which is a measurement of the screen coordinates of the mouse, plus a virtual off- set called offx and offy.

The second function is responsible for what happens when the mouse is released. First, we set the variables gameselx and gamesely to the tile that the mouse is currently over the top of. This will be where our chooserbox appears later. Then, we repaint the tile at that spot and set the dragging variable to false. The repaint- Tile function is responsible for redrawing a specific tile in the gameboard at any given x and y coordinate (in tile space, not pixels). We then set dragging to false and initialize dragging outside the function as well, also setting it to false by default.

Next we have:

```
_root.createEmptyMovieClip("tilechooser", 1);
tilechooser.attachBitmap(texturePage, 0, true, true);
tilechooser._xscale = 50;
tilechooser._yscale = 50;
tilechooser._x = 490;
tilechooser.attachMovie("chooserbox", "cbox", 2);


var selTileBitmap:BitmapData = new BitmapData(32, 32,
                                             false, 0);
_root.createEmptyMovieClip("selectedTile_mc", 2);
selectedTile_mc._xscale = 300;
selectedTile_mc._yscale = 300;
```

```
selectedTile_mc.attachBitmap(selTileBitmap, 0,
                             true, false);
selectedTile_mc._x = 490;
selectedTile_mc._y = 266;
```

Here we're creating two movie clips. One is a movie clip that contains an image of the `texturePage` BitmapData object. This is to be our tile selector, and the scale is set to 50% so that the tile selector appears smaller on screen and therefore allows us to fit 256 tiles if we need to (in 16 rows of 16 tiles). We also attach an instance of the `chooserbox` movie clip, with the instance name `cbox`, to be used for its second purpose: indicating what tile we have selected in the tile chooser. This movie clip is placed at 490, 0.

Next, we create a single `BitmapData` object called `selTileBitmap` that is 32 × 32 pixels in size. This will contain an image of the currently selected tile. This is also embedded in a movie clip, which is called `selectedTile_mc`. The scale on this movie clip is set to 300%, so that the selected tile is drawn, three times normal size, down at position 490, 266. This just gives us a nice zoomed-in view of the currently selected tile.

Next, we have the following code:

```
tilechooser.onRelease = function()
{

    selx = Math.floor(this._xmouse / 32);
    sely = Math.floor(this._ymouse / 32);

    this.cbox._x = selx * 32;
    this.cbox._y = sely * 32;

    var tRect:Rectangle = new Rectangle(selx * 32,
                                        sely * 32,
                                        32, 32);

    var destPt:Point = new Point(0, 0);
    selTileBitmap.fillRect(new Rectangle(0, 0, 32, 32),
                                         0);
    selTileBitmap.copyPixels(texturePage, tRect, destPt);
    selectedTile = sely * 16 + selx

    if (solid_array[selectedTile] == 1)
        solid_cb.gotoAndStop(2);
    else
        solid_cb.gotoAndStop(1);

    if (ladder_array[selectedTile] == 1)
        ladder_cb.gotoAndStop(2);
    else
        ladder_cb.gotoAndStop(1);

    if (collect_array[selectedTile] == 1)
        collect_cb.gotoAndStop(2);
```

```
        else
            collect_cb.gotoAndStop(1);

    }

    var selx:Number = 0;
    var sely:Number = 0;
    var selectedTile:Number = 0;
```

This code handles the selection of a tile from the tile chooser. When the mouse is pressed down on the `tilechooser` movie clip, the first thing we do is determine the x and y (in tile space) of the selected tile. This is done by simply taking the mouse position relative to `tilechooser`, dividing it by 32, and rounding it down. We then place the `cbox` movie clip at the position of the selected tile so it is highlighted.

We then create a new rectangle, `tRect`, which encompasses the selected tile in its entirety. Next we blank out the `selTileBitmap` by filling it with color 0 (black) and then copying the pixels from the currently selected tile over the top. This will cause the currently selected tile to appear, zoomed in, beneath the tile chooser, as shown in Figure 12.8.

FIGURE 12.8 The tile chooser and
the selected tile zoomed below.

We then fill the variable `selectedTile` with the value of the currently selected tile, based on the system where the first row is tile numbers 0 to 15, the second row is 16 to 31, the third row is 32 to 47, and so on. The equation is `sely * 16 + selx`.

The last three pieces of code in that function are responsible for looking at the arrays `solid_array`, `ladder_array`, and `collect_array` to determine if the tile we just selected has any of those flags set. If so, the appropriate option box is sent to frame 2 (the selected frame); otherwise, it is sent to frame 1, the unselected frame. This means that as we select different tiles from the tile chooser, the options boxes will change to reflect the state of those tiles.

We then create our three variables, `selx`, `sely`, and `selectedTile`.

Next we have:

```
var solid_array:Array = new Array();
var ladder_array:Array = new Array();
var collect_array:Array = new Array();

for (var i = 0; i < 256; i++)
{
    solid_array[i] = 0;
    ladder_array[i] = 0;
    collect_array[i] = 0;
}

solid_cb.onPress = function()
{
    if (this._currentframe == 1)
    {
        this.gotoAndStop(2);
        solid_array[selectedTile] = 1;
    }
    else
    {
        this.gotoAndStop(1);
        solid_array[selectedTile] = 0;
    }
}

ladder_cb.onPress = function()
{
    if (this._currentframe == 1)
    {
        this.gotoAndStop(2);
        ladder_array[selectedTile] = 1;
    }
    else
    {
        this.gotoAndStop(1);
        ladder_array[selectedTile] = 0;
    }
}

collect_cb.onPress = function()
{
    if (this._currentframe == 1)
    {
        this.gotoAndStop(2);
        collect_array[selectedTile] = 1;
    }
    else
    {
        this.gotoAndStop(1);
        collect_array[selectedTile] = 0;
    }
}
```

This handles the setting of the flags for each tile. It is, in essence, the same code in triplicate. We'll look at just the solid_array to understand how it is done with the ladder_array and the collect_array. First, we create our new array. Since we can have a maximum of 256 tiles, we set the value of 256 elements of these arrays to 0. This means that by default all tiles have no attributes, meaning they're all nonsolid.

We then have code to handle clicks on the three option boxes. When an option box is pressed, we check to see the current frame that it is resting on. If it's on frame 1, it's currently unselected, so we tell it to gotoAndStop(2) and to jump to frame 2 and then we set the value in the appropriate array to 1. Since the index we're using is selectedTile, the tile we have selected will be updated. The opposite occurs if the current frame was frame 2 to begin with, in which case it was already selected, so we deselect it and then set its value to 0.

All of this code is applied evenly to the three arrays via the three option boxes. Now we have enough code to handle all our tile selection and option-setting needs.

The code continues like so:

```
for (var i = 0; i < 75; i++)
{
    grid[i] = new Array();
    for (j = 0; j < 90; j++)
    {
        grid[i][j] = 0;
    }
}

function newBoard()
{
    var gameboard:BitmapData = new BitmapData(2880,
                                              2400, true,
                                              0x000000);
    for (var i = 0; i < 75; i++)
    {
        grid[i] = new Array();
        for (j = 0; j < 90; j++)
        {
            grid[i][j] = 0;
        }
    }
    repaintGrid();
}
```

Here we populate our grid array with 75 arrays of 90 elements. This in essence creates a 2D array that we can use like so: grid[row][column]. We initially set everything to 0, which means tile 0. Tile 0 therefore should always be clear, unfilled, and transparent. We also have a function, newBoard, that creates a new gameboard BitmapData object, blanks out the grid, and then makes a call to the function repaintGrid.

This newBoard function is called when the user hits the New button on screen. After this, we have the following code:

```
function repaintGrid()
{
    for (var i = 0; i < 75; i++)
    {
        for (j = 0; j < 90; j++)
        {
            if (grid[i][j] > 0)
            {
                srcx = grid[i][j] % 16;
                srcy = Math.floor(grid[i][j] / 16);

                var tRect:Rectangle = new Rectangle(srcx *
                                        32, srcy * 32, 32, 32);
                var destPt:Point = new Point(j * 32,
                                              i * 32);
                gameboard.copyPixels(texturePage, tRect,
                                     destPt);
            }
        }
    }
}

function repaintTile(j, i)
{
    srcx = grid[i][j] % 16;
    srcy = Math.floor(grid[i][j] / 16);

    var tRect:Rectangle = new Rectangle(srcx * 32,
                                        srcy * 32, 32, 32);
    var destPt:Point = new Point(j * 32, i * 32);
    gameboard.copyPixels(texturePage, tRect, destPt);
}
```

The repaintGrid function is the function equivalent to the core concept in the previous chapter. This is the function that builds our big gameboard image, from the level data, and the tile set BitmapData object. We loop through every element in the grid array, and if anything is greater than zero (because zero is passed over and never drawn—treated as blank), we take the value at that grid coordinate and determine the matching tile number, which will be contained in grid[i][j]. With this value, we can determine the exact rectangle that defines the source tile image in the texturePage, and we can proceed to copy the tile from that location, to the position defined by j*32, i*32 in our gameboard. Once this entire function has completed, our gameboard will be filled completely with the big picture of the entire level.

The repaintTile function is similar to the repaintGrid function, except that all it does is repaint one tile on the map, rather than the entire map. This function is called when the user draws a tile on the gameboard by moving the mouse and pressing the space bar. This allows us to only update a single tile, rather than re-drawing hundreds of tiles just because one tile changed.

After this, we have the following code:

```
var offx:Number = 0;
var offy:Number = 0;
var gameselx:Number = 0;
var gamesely:Number = 0;

rootonEnterFrame = function()
{
    if (offx < 0) offx = 0;
    if (offy < 0) offy = 0;
    if (offx > 2400) offx = 2400;
    if (offy > 2080) offy = 2080;

    outScreen.cbox._x = (gameselx * 32) - offx;
    outScreen.cbox._y = (gamesely * 32) - offy;
    if (outScreen.cbox._x < -32 ||
        outScreen.cbox._y < -32 ||
        outScreen.cbox._x > (480-32) ||
        outScreen.cbox._y > (320-32))
    {
        outScreen.cbox._visible = false;
    }
    else
        outScreen.cbox._visible = true;

    var tRect:Rectangle = new Rectangle(offx, offy,
                                        480, 320);
    var wRect:Rectangle = new Rectangle(offx / 5, 0,
                                        480, 320);
    var destPt:Point = new Point(0, 0);

    gameScreen.copyPixels(bigBack, wRect, destPt);
    gameScreen.copyPixels(gameboard, tRect, destPt);

    if (Key.isDown(Key.RIGHT))
    {
        offx += 5;
    }
    else if (Key.isDown(Key.LEFT))
    {
        offx -= 5;
    }

    if (Key.isDown(Key.DOWN))
    {
        offy += 5;
    }
    else if (Key.isDown(Key.UP))
    {
        offy -= 5;
```

```
        }

        if (dragging)
        {
            offx = startmousex - _xmouse;
            offy = startmousey - _ymouse;
        }

        if (Key.isDown(Key.SPACE))
        {
            outScreen.onRelease();
            grid[gamesely][gameselx] = sely * 16 + selx;
            repaintTile(gameselx, gamesely);
        }
    }

    _root.onEnterFrame = rootonEnterFrame;
```

This code is responsible for handling the events of the level editor every frame. This includes rendering our level image every frame and handling the key presses.

The first thing we do is define offx and offy. These two variables are used to determine what pixel in our gameboard BitmapData object is going to define the upper-left corner of the outScreen movie clip. This is how we pan through the world. We change the values of offx and offy, and the window into the world moves and our game world pans. The gameselx and gamesely variables, as we've seen before, are used to define which tile in the game world we currently have selected.

The rootonEnterFrame function will be run every frame. The first thing we do is make sure that offx and offy have not been extended too far and do not allow us to see beyond the bounds of the 2880 × 2400 level.

We then move the cbox movie clip (our tile selection box), based on the values of offx and offy. This ensures that the cbox movie clip, which is independent of the gameboard, will appear to move with it, nonetheless. We then have a few lines of code to ensure that the selection box is not visible if its bounds are such that it is outside of the rectangular area that defines the 480 × 320 window into the gameboard. If we don't do this, the cbox moves over the top of things that it shouldn't, such as the tile chooser and the Save, New, and Load buttons.

After that, we have our three magic lines of code that make much of this engine fly. This is the code (taken from above):

```
    var tRect:Rectangle = new Rectangle(offx, offy,
                                        480, 320);
    var wRect:Rectangle = new Rectangle(offx / 5, 0,
                                        480, 320);
    var destPt:Point = new Point(0, 0);

    gameScreen.copyPixels(bigBack, wRect, destPt);
    gameScreen.copyPixels(gameboard, tRect, destPt);
```

Here we're going to use the magic discussed in the previous chapter. We're copying the bigBack into the gameScreen and then copying the section of gameboard over the top, thus creating our overall finished frame. Notice that something is new in the wRect calculation. We've got our x coordinate as offx / 5, rather than 0, as we did in the previous chapter. This will cause our background image to pan slowly in the background as we drag the world around with the mouse. This will enhance the 3D effect.

After that we have code to handle the pressing of the left, right, up, and down arrow keys, which can be used as a simple form of panning.

Then we check to see the value of the dragging variable. If it is true (and we are currently in the process of dragging the gameboard), we calculate offx and offy as the value of startmousex and startmousey, minus the current position of the mouse cursor. Recall that the startmousex and startmousey variables were set up above, when the mouse button was pressed and dragging was initiated.

After that, we handle the pressing of the spacebar, which calls the outScreen. onRelease function, thereby moving the selection box to the position under the mouse cursor as well as setting the new tile at that location and redrawing the tile by calling repaintTile. This is, in essence, how we *draw* our level.

Last, we tell Flash to run the code every frame by setting the onEnterFrame function of the _root to the rootonEnterFrame function.

Next, we have the following code:

```
save_btn.onRelease = function()
{
    saveLevel();
}

load_btn.onRelease = function()
{
    loadLevel(filename_txt.text);
}

new_btn.onRelease = function()
{
    newBoard();
}
```

This code very simply gives functionality to our three buttons: Save, Load, and New. If the save_btn is pressed, we call the function saveLevel (to follow shortly). If load_btn is pressed, we call the function loadLevel and pass into it the value of the text contained in the filename_txt text field. If the new_btn is pressed, we call the newBoard function, which was defined earlier.

Next, we have:

```
function saveLevel()
{
    exp = "";
    for (var i = 0; i < 75; i++)
```

```
    {
        for (j = 0; j < 90; j++)
        {
            exp += grid[i][j] + ",";
        }
    }
    out_txt.text = "&ldat=" + exp;
    out_txt.text += "&sol=" + solid_array;
    out_txt.text += "&lad=" + ladder_array;
    out_txt.text += "&col=" + collect_array;
}
```

This is the saveLevel function, which simply steps through the entire contents of the grid array and exports them as one long, comma-delimited string. That data is sent to the out_txt text field, along with the values of the solid_array, ladder_array, and collect_array, to define the attributes for each tile type. Because we'll be loading these into a LoadVars object, we save our data as if it is ampersand delimited name=value pairs, where you have:

```
varname1=value&varname2=value&varname3=value.
```

The LoadVars object will automatically break those into variables when the data is loaded back in later. In this case our variables are named ldat, sol, lad, and col, for Level Data, Solid, Ladder, and Collectable.

Finally, we have the following code:

```
function loadLevel(fname)
{
    my_lv = new LoadVars();
    my_lv.onLoad = function()
    {

        var dats = this.ldat.split(",");

        var cnt = 0;
        for (var i = 0; i < 75; i++)
        {
            grid[i] = new Array();
            for (j = 0; j < 90; j++)
            {
                grid[i][j] = dats[cnt++];
            }
        }

        solid_array = this.sol.split(",");
        ladder_array = this.lad.split(",");
        collect_array = this.col.split(",");

        repaintGrid();

    }
```

```
          my_lv.load(fname);

      }
      loadLevel(filename_txt.text);
```

This is the reverse of the saveLevel function. This function takes a filename and then loads the file associated with that name. The LoadVars object will automatically break it into its variable names, so once the onLoad event is triggered, we can be sure there already is a variable called ldat ready for us to break into an array, which we do with

```
      var dats = this.ldat.split(",");
```

We then step through each element in that array, and place it into the grid array. We then grab the values of sol, lad, and col and place those into the solid_ array, ladder_array, and collect_array.

Then we make a call to repaintGrid to make the level we've just loaded appear on screen.

The final line of code in our program automatically loads the level name that is already waiting in the filename_txt text field. In this case that means the level editor automatically loads testlevel.txt when it runs. Give it a try!

Here is the entire level-editor code for review.

```
      import flash.display.*;
      import flash.geom.*;

      var grid:Array = new Array();

      var gameboard:BitmapData = new BitmapData(2880, 2400,
                                                  true, 0x000000);
      var worldBack:BitmapData = BitmapData.loadBitmap("worldback");
      var bigBack:BitmapData = new BitmapData(2880, 320,
                                                  false, 0);

      for (var i = 0; i < 3; i++)
      {
          var tRect:Rectangle = new Rectangle(0, 0, 731, 320);
          var destPt:Point = new Point(i * 731, 0);
          bigBack.copyPixels(worldBack, tRect, destPt);
      }

      var texturePage:BitmapData = BitmapData.loadBitmap("texturepage");
      var gameScreen:BitmapData = new BitmapData(480, 320,
                                                  false, 0);

      _root.createEmptyMovieClip("outScreen", 0);
      outScreen.attachBitmap(gameScreen, 0, true, false);
      outScreen.attachMovie("chooserbox", "cbox", 2);

      outScreen.onPress = function()
```

```
{
    dragging = true;
    startmousex = _xmouse + offx;
    startmousey = _ymouse + offy;
}

outScreen.onRelease =
outScreen.onReleaseOutside = function()
{
    gameselx = Math.floor((this._xmouse + offx) / 32);
    gamesely = Math.floor((this._ymouse + offy) / 32);

    repaintTile(gameselx, gamesely);
    dragging = false;
}

var dragging:Boolean = false;

_root.createEmptyMovieClip("tilechooser", 1);
tilechooser.attachBitmap(texturePage, 0, true, true);
tilechooser._xscale = 50;
tilechooser._yscale = 50;
tilechooser._x = 490;
tilechooser.attachMovie("chooserbox", "cbox", 2);


var selTileBitmap:BitmapData = new BitmapData(32, 32,
                                             false, 0);
_root.createEmptyMovieClip("selectedTile_mc", 2);
selectedTile_mc._xscale = 300;
selectedTile_mc._yscale = 300;
selectedTile_mc.attachBitmap(selTileBitmap, 0,
                             true, false);
selectedTile_mc._x = 490;
selectedTile_mc._y = 266;

tilechooser.onRelease = function()
{

    selx = Math.floor(this._xmouse / 32);
    sely = Math.floor(this._ymouse / 32);

    this.cbox._x = selx * 32;
    this.cbox._y = sely * 32;

    var tRect:Rectangle = new Rectangle(selx * 32,
                                        sely * 32,
                                        32, 32);
    var destPt:Point = new Point(0, 0);
    selTileBitmap.fillRect(new Rectangle(0, 0, 32, 32),
                           0);
    selTileBitmap.copyPixels(texturePage, tRect, destPt);
    selectedTile = sely * 16 + selx
```

```
        if (solid_array[selectedTile] == 1)
            solid_cb.gotoAndStop(2);
        else
            solid_cb.gotoAndStop(1);

        if (ladder_array[selectedTile] == 1)
            ladder_cb.gotoAndStop(2);
        else
            ladder_cb.gotoAndStop(1);

        if (collect_array[selectedTile] == 1)
            collect_cb.gotoAndStop(2);
        else
            collect_cb.gotoAndStop(1);

    }

    var selx:Number = 0;
    var sely:Number = 0;
    var selectedTile:Number = 0;

    var solid_array:Array = new Array();
    var ladder_array:Array = new Array();
    var collect_array:Array = new Array();

    for (var i = 0; i < 256; i++)
    {
        solid_array[i] = 0;
        ladder_array[i] = 0;
        collect_array[i] = 0;
    }

    solid_cb.onPress = function()
    {
        if (this._currentframe == 1)
        {
            this.gotoAndStop(2);
            solid_array[selectedTile] = 1;
        }
        else
        {
            this.gotoAndStop(1);
            solid_array[selectedTile] = 0;
        }
    }

    ladder_cb.onPress = function()
    {
        if (this._currentframe == 1)
        {
            this.gotoAndStop(2);
            ladder_array[selectedTile] = 1;
        }
```

```
        else
    {
        this.gotoAndStop(1);
        ladder_array[selectedTile] = 0;
    }
}

collect_cb.onPress = function()
{
    if (this._currentframe == 1)
    {
        this.gotoAndStop(2);
        collect_array[selectedTile] = 1;
    }
    else
    {
        this.gotoAndStop(1);
        collect_array[selectedTile] = 0;
    }
}

for (var i = 0; i < 75; i++)
{
    grid[i] = new Array();
    for (j = 0; j < 90; j++)
    {
        grid[i][j] = 0;
    }
}

function newBoard()
{
    var gameboard:BitmapData = new BitmapData(2880,
                                              2400, true,
                                              0x000000);
    for (var i = 0; i < 75; i++)
    {
        grid[i] = new Array();
        for (j = 0; j < 90; j++)
        {
            grid[i][j] = 0;
        }
    }
    repaintGrid();
}

function repaintGrid()
{
    for (var i = 0; i < 75; i++)
    {
        for (j = 0; j < 90; j++)
        {
            if (grid[i][j] > 0)
            {
```

```
                        srcx = grid[i][j] % 16;
                        srcy = Math.floor(grid[i][j] / 16);

                        var tRect:Rectangle = new Rectangle(srcx *
                                          32, srcy * 32, 32, 32);
                        var destPt:Point = new Point(j * 32,
                                                       i * 32);
                        gameboard.copyPixels(texturePage, tRect,
                                             destPt);
                    }
                }
            }
        }

        function repaintTile(j, i)
        {
            srcx = grid[i][j] % 16;
            srcy = Math.floor(grid[i][j] / 16);

            var tRect:Rectangle = new Rectangle(srcx * 32,
                                        srcy * 32, 32, 32);
            var destPt:Point = new Point(j * 32, i * 32);
            gameboard.copyPixels(texturePage, tRect, destPt);
        }

        var offx:Number = 0;
        var offy:Number = 0;
        var gameselx:Number = 0;
        var gamesely:Number = 0;

        rootonEnterFrame = function()
        {
            if (offx < 0) offx = 0;
            if (offy < 0) offy = 0;
            if (offx > 2400) offx = 2400;
            if (offy > 2080) offy = 2080;

            outScreen.cbox._x = (gameselx * 32) - offx;
            outScreen.cbox._y = (gamesely * 32) - offy;
            if (outScreen.cbox._x < -32 ||
                outScreen.cbox._y < -32 ||
                outScreen.cbox._x > (480-32) ||
                outScreen.cbox._y > (320-32))
            {
                outScreen.cbox._visible = false;
            }
            else
                outScreen.cbox._visible = true;

            var tRect:Rectangle = new Rectangle(offx, offy,
                                            480, 320);
            var wRect:Rectangle = new Rectangle(offx / 5, 0,
                                            480, 320);
            var destPt:Point = new Point(0, 0);
```

```
    gameScreen.copyPixels(bigBack, wRect, destPt);
    gameScreen.copyPixels(gameboard, tRect, destPt);

    if (Key.isDown(Key.RIGHT))
    {
        offx += 5;
    }
    else if (Key.isDown(Key.LEFT))
    {
        offx -= 5;
    }

    if (Key.isDown(Key.DOWN))
    {
        offy += 5;
    }
    else if (Key.isDown(Key.UP))
    {
        offy -= 5;
    }

    if (dragging)
    {
        offx = startmousex - _xmouse;
        offy = startmousey - _ymouse;
    }

    if (Key.isDown(Key.SPACE))
    {
        outScreen.onRelease();
        grid[gamesely][gameselx] = sely * 16 + selx;
        repaintTile(gameselx, gamesely);
    }
}

_root.onEnterFrame = rootonEnterFrame;

save_btn.onRelease = function()
{
    saveLevel();
}

load_btn.onRelease = function()
{
    loadLevel(filename_txt.text);
}

new_btn.onRelease = function()
{
    newBoard();
}
```

```
function saveLevel()
{
    exp = "";
    for (var i = 0; i < 75; i++)
    {
        for (j = 0; j < 90; j++)
        {
            exp += grid[i][j] + ",";
        }
    }
    out_txt.text = "&ldat=" + exp;
    out_txt.text += "&sol=" + solid_array;
    out_txt.text += "&lad=" + ladder_array;
    out_txt.text += "&col=" + collect_array;
}

function loadLevel(fname)
{
    my_lv = new LoadVars();
    my_lv.onLoad = function()
    {

        var dats = this.ldat.split(",");

        var cnt = 0;
        for (var i = 0; i < 75; i++)
        {
            grid[i] = new Array();
            for (j = 0; j < 90; j++)
            {
                grid[i][j] = dats[cnt++];
            }
        }

        solid_array = this.sol.split(",");
        ladder_array = this.lad.split(",");
        collect_array = this.col.split(",");

        repaintGrid();

    }
    my_lv.load(fname);

}
loadLevel(filename_txt.text);
```

That's the entire level editor. With that, we can create big and exciting levels. Now, onto the game!

THE GAME

Much of the core of the game runs on the same engine as the level editor, specifically where it applies to the rendering of the world. The difference is that while in the level editor the world is in a small window in the upper-left corner of the stage, in the game the world takes up the entire stage, because it is scaled up exactly 200%. This allows us to have a maximum enjoyable game experience.

Open up the file `tilegame.fla`. This time, taking a look at the stage reveals that there is absolutely nothing there to begin with. We have a completely empty stage that is 960 × 640 in size and set to have a frame rate of 62 fps, with the default export settings for Flash 8.

Open up the library to take a quick look at what we have. The library can be seen in Figure 12.9.

FIGURE 12.9   The library from `tilegame.fla`.

We can see that just like in the level editor, we have the `worldback` and `texturepage` bitmaps set to export at runtime. We don't have any of the interface buttons in the library (Save, Load, or New) and we don't have the `chooserbox`, because these are all elements specific to the level editor.

However, press Ctrl-Enter right away and see things come to life, as shown in Figure 12.10 and Figure 12.11.

One other important asset that can be found in the library is a movie clip called `playerSprite`, with the export name `playerrun`. This is the player, and is a multiframed animation that consists of a run cycle and a climbing pose. The `playerSprite` movie clip can be seen in Figure 12.12.

This movie clip is attached to the game world at runtime, in much the same way that the `chooserbox` was attached to the level-editor world. It is a movie clip that is placed over the top of the `gameScreen` `BitmapData` object that contains the rendered frame of the world.

FIGURE 12.10   The game in progress. Climbing a ladder.

FIGURE 12.11   The game in progress.

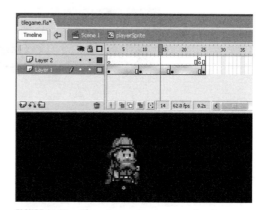

FIGURE 12.12   The `playerSprite` movie clip.

Let's begin by looking at the code, which is attached to frame 1, of the only layer in the movie. First we have:

```
import flash.display.*;
import flash.geom.*;

var grid:Array = new Array();

var tileWidth:Number = 32;
var tileHeight:Number = 32;

function repaintGrid()
{
    for (var i = 0; i < 75; i++)
    {
        for (j = 0; j < 90; j++)
        {
```

```
        if (grid[i][j] > 0)
        {
            var srcx:Number = grid[i][j] % 16;
            var srcy:Number = Math.floor(grid[i][j] /
                                                  16);

            var tRect:Rectangle = new Rectangle(srcx *
                                                 tileWidth,
                                      srcy * tileHeight,
                                                 tileWidth,
                                                 tileHeight);
            var destPt:Point = new Point(j * tileWidth,
                                          i * tileHeight);
            gameboard.copyPixels(texturePage,
                                  tRect, destPt);
        }
    }
  }
 }
}
```

We begin as with the level editor by importing the classes associated with the flash.display and flash.geom packages. We define the grid array and then define two variables, tileWidth and tileHeight, both as 32. These are used in all computations involving tile placement and collision detection.

We then jump straight to our repaintGrid function, which is identical to the earlier function, except instead of having 32s hardcoded, we're using tileWidth and tileHeight. Other than that, it's an identical function, taking the grid array and completely populating the gameboard BitmapData object.

Next, we have the following code:

```
var gameboard:BitmapData = new BitmapData(2880, 2400,
                                           true, 0);
var worldBack:BitmapData = BitmapData.loadBitmap("worldback");

var bigBack:BitmapData = new BitmapData(2880, 320,
                                         false, 0);
for (var i:Number = 0; i < 3; i++)
{
var tRect:Rectangle = new Rectangle(0, 0, 731, 320);
var destPt:Point = new Point(i * 731, 0);
bigBack.copyPixels(worldBack, tRect, destPt);
}

var texturePage:BitmapData = BitmapData.loadBitmap("texturepage");
var gameScreen:BitmapData = new BitmapData(480, 320,
                                            false, 0);

_root.createEmptyMovieClip("outScreen", 0);
outScreen._xscale = 200;
outScreen._yscale = 200;
outScreen.attachBitmap(gameScreen, 0);
outScreen.attachMovie("playerrun", "player", 1);
```

Here we create our big `gameboard` `BitmapData` object and our `worldBack` `Bitmap-Data` object, loaded from the `worldback` bitmap image in the library. We then create our large `bigBack` `BitmapData` object to contain the tiled background image.

Once these are created, we proceed to fill the `bigBack` `BitmapData` object with three side-by-side copies of the `worldBack` image to create our large tiling, distant parallax background image.

Once we've created this, we load the tile set from the library by pulling `texturepage` into its own `BitmapData` object, `texturePage`.

Finally, we create the movie clip, `outScreen`, that will hold our world—the portal into our `BitmapData` universe—by attaching the `gameScreen` `BitmapData` object to it. We set the scale of `outScreen` to 200% so that it takes up the full 960 × 640 stage. We also attach an instance of the `playerrun` embedded movie clip, with the instance name `player`. This will be our game character soon.

Next, we have the following code:

```
var charx:Number = 32;
var chary:Number = 40;
var dx:Number = 0;
var dy:Number = 0;
var climbing:Boolean = false;
var jumpdisabled:Boolean = false;
var onGround:Boolean = false;
```

Here we're setting up a series of variables necessary to run the game engine:

- `charx` and `chary` refer to the player's position, in world space. This means the player could be at `charx` of 0 up to 2880.
- `dx` and `dy` refer to the player horizontal and vertical speed. `dx` specifies how fast the player is running, left or right. If `dx` is negative, he's running to the left; if it's positive, he's running to the right. If `dy` is negative, he's moving up; if `dy` is positive, he's moving down.
- `climbing` is set when the player is in the process of climbing a ladder. It is needed for some logic checks.
- `jumpdisabled` is used later to prevent the character from rejumping once he's jumped; otherwise, he can bounce along like a rabbit without the player ever letting go of the space bar.
- `onGround` simply keeps track of whether or not the player is airborne or is standing on firm ground.

Next, we have our main game loop. We'll look at it in sections:

```
rootonEnterFrame = function()
{

    if (charx < 0)
    {
        charx = 0;
        dx = 0;
    }
```

```
        if (chary < 0)
        {
            chary = 0;
            dy = 0;
        }

        offx = charx - 240;
        offy = chary - 160;

        if (offx < 0)
        {
            offx = 0;
        }
        if (offy < 0)
        {
            offy = 0;
        }
```

Here we set the values of the offx and offy variables, which are used to determine what section of gameboard to show on screen. These were also used in the level editor, but here we're setting them based on the position of the character. We want the game world to always be centered on the character. We also do a few quick checks to ensure that the game world will never pan past the left or top of the map.

Next we have:

```
    outScreen.player._x = charx - offx;
    outScreen.player._y = chary - offy;

    var tRect:Rectangle = new Rectangle(offx, offy,
                                        480, 320);
    var wRect:Rectangle = new Rectangle(offx / 5, 0,
                                        480, 320);
    var destPt:Point = new Point(0, 0);

    gameScreen.copyPixels(bigBack, wRect, destPt);
    gameScreen.copyPixels(gameboard, tRect, destPt);

    charx += dx;
    chary += dy;

    if (Key.isDown(Key.RIGHT) && dx < 5)
    {
        dx+=.5;
        outScreen.player._xscale = 100;
        outScreen.player.play();
    }
    else if (Key.isDown(Key.LEFT) && dx > -5)
    {
        dx-=.5;
        outScreen.player._xscale = -100;
        outScreen.player.play();
```

```
        }
        else
        {
            if (Math.abs(dx) < 1)
            {
                if(!climbing)
                    outScreen.player.gotoAndStop(1);
                else
                    outScreen.player.gotoAndStop(25);
            }
        }

        dx *= .90;
```

The first thing we do is make sure the `player` movie clip, which is the image of the main character, is positioned properly on screen, by taking the `charx` and `chary` and subtracting the value of `offx` and `offy`. This translates the movie clip from a game-world space into screen pixel space.

Once that's done, we proceed with our now-famous world rendering of painting the background and then overlaying the section of `gameboard` that we're over.

We then move the character by changing the `charx` and `chary` values by `dx` and `dy`, respectively. This is how the physics of motion is simulated.

We then check to see if the left or right arrow keys are being pressed. If so, we adjust the value of `dx` to create an accelerating effect, to either the right or left. As `dx` changes over time, the amount that we move the player (which *is* `dx`), will also increase or decrease. This will create the motion we're after.

If neither of the arrow keys is being pressed, we assume the player is standing still. We check to make sure he has no horizontal motion by making sure `dx` is less than 1, or greater than –1. If the character's not climbing a ladder, we go to his regular standing frame, which is legs together, standing on the spot, as shown in Figure 12.13.

If, on the other hand, he is motionless but standing on a ladder, because `climbing` is `true`, we go to his climbing frame, as shown in Figure 12.14.

FIGURE 12.13   Standing on the spot.

FIGURE 12.14   The climbing frame.

We have one final line of code in this listing: dx *= .90. This slowly applies a 10% decay to the value of dx every frame. This will cause the character to gradually slow to a stop, should the player not press either the left or the right arrow keys.

Next, we have the following code:

```
var cgridx:Number = Math.floor(charx / tileWidth);
var cgridy:Number = Math.floor(chary / tileHeight);
var nextx:Number = Math.floor((charx + dx) /
                               tileWidth);
var nexty:Number = Math.floor((chary + dy) /
                               tileHeight);

onGround = false;

if (solid_array[grid[nexty][cgridx]] == 1)
{
    if (dy > 0)
    {
        chary = (nexty * tileHeight) - 1;
        var cgridy:Number = Math.floor(chary /
                               tileHeight);
        dy = 0;
        onGround = true;
    }
    else if (dy < 0)
    {
        chary = (nexty * tileHeight) +
                (tileHeight + 1);
        var cgridy:Number = Math.floor(chary /
                               tileHeight);
        dy = 0;
    }
}
else
{
    if (ladder_array[grid[cgridy][cgridx]] == 1 &&
        dy >= 0)
    {
        dy = 0;
        if (chary%tileHeight < 5 &&
                !Key.isDown(Key.DOWN))
            chary = ((cgridy-1) * tileHeight) +
                    tileHeight-1;
        onGround = true;
    }
}
```

This is the heart of our collision code. It is with this code that the world becomes "solid." Here we cause the player to interact with the tiles, to give the game the interactivity required to call it a game.

The first thing we do is create four important variables. cgridx and cgridy represent the *current* position of the player in tile space. This is the exact tile he is currently standing on. nextx and nexty represent the *next* tile he will potentially be standing on, if we calculate his current position, plus either dx or dy.

We then set the value of the onGround variable to false, as an assumption, until we know otherwise.

Next, we look to see if the next tile the player will be on, in the vertical direction, is solid or not. We're looking at the solidity of the tile at grid[nexty][cgridx]. This is the tile value of his *current* x position, but his *next* y position. In other words, straight up or down from the current position. We can take the value of that tile and use it as an index directly into the solid_array to know if this next vertical tile is solid or not.

So, if the character is about to jump or fall into a solid tile, we check to see what direction he's going. If dy is greater than zero, he's falling and his feet are hitting the ground, so we do a quick adjustment to firmly plant him atop the solid tile (rather than what could potentially be a pixel or two *into* the tile, depending on how fast he's falling). We then recalculate his cgridy in case we've moved him into a tile he wasn't in before. We then set his dy speed to zero; there's no point in continuing to fall, so stop all vertical motion. Finally, we set the value of onGround to true, because the character is, after all, standing on the ground.

If, however, the character's vertical speed is less than zero, he is actually hitting a solid tile above him—in essence, hitting his head. We do a similar adjustment, this time placing the character firmly *below* the tile he's colliding with, and then recalculating his cgridy variable. Then we set his dy to zero again, because he can no longer be moving up, but we do not set onGround to true.

The else statement is in the case where the character's not hitting a solid tile in the upward or downward directions. We have to do a quick check here to see if he's on a ladder yet still falling. It may be that he jumped into a ladder from the side. In this case, we have to cease all falling motion because it is assumed that the character will have grabbed the ladder.

We do one strange little check:

```
if (chary%tileHeight < 5 &&
        !Key.isDown(Key.DOWN))
    chary = ((cgridy-1) * tileHeight) +
            tileHeight-1;
```

This is a special case used to check if the character is on a ladder, yet *really close* to the top of the ladder (within 5 pixels), and if the player's not pressing the down arrow key. In this case, rather than making the character stay on the ladder, we simply pop him up one tile and position him firmly atop the ladder. The reason for this is that it got a little frustrating getting really, really close to the top of the ladder, then pressing the left or right arrow keys to step onto a platform, yet still hitting the wall. Intuition tells us the character should be able to just lift his knee an inch and he'll be on the platform above. The game logic, however, was failing to understand this and was not letting us step off the ladder onto the platform above it. Figure 12.15 shows this issue in action. We have disabled that line of code to see the problem. Notice that the character's foot is only one pixel into the ladder below, but as far as he's concerned, he's still colliding with the tile to the right and cannot move.

FIGURE 12.15 Being stuck at the top of the ladder.

The single line of code fixes this problem by gently helping the player to the tile above if he's almost there.

After that check, we set the value of onGround to true, because the character is on a ground of sorts. The main purpose of onGround, as we'll see, is to stop gravity from pulling the character down.

After that, we have the following code:

```
var cgridy:Number = Math.floor(chary / tileHeight);
var nexty:Number = Math.floor((chary + dy) /
                                tileHeight);

if (ladder_array[grid[cgridy][cgridx]] != 1)
    climbing = false;

if (Key.isDown(Key.UP) &&
    ladder_array[grid[cgridy][cgridx]] == 1)
{
    dy = 0;
    if (solid_array[grid[Math.floor((chary - 3) /
        tileHeight)][cgridx]] != 1)
            chary-=3;

    if (chary%tileHeight < 5)
        chary = ((cgridy-1) * tileHeight) +
                tileHeight-1;
    dx = 0;
    climbing = true;
}
if (Key.isDown(Key.DOWN) &&
    ladder_array[grid[cgridy][cgridx]] == 1)
{
```

```
        dy = 0;
        if (solid_array[grid[Math.floor((chary + 3) /
                tileHeight)][cgridx]] != 1)
                    chary+=3;
        dx = 0;
        climbing = true;
    }
```

First, we recompute `cgridy` and `nexty` because the code before may have changed the value of `chary`, and upcoming checks require an accurate value for `cgridy` and `nexty`. Then we check to see if the character is standing on a ladder. If he isn't, we set the value of `climbing` to `false`.

Next, we check to see if the player is pressing the up arrow or the down arrow. If he's pressing the up arrow key, and the grid square the character is on is a ladder and the tile above him is not a solid tile (he can't climb into a rock), we move him up by three pixels. Then we do that same magic check as before to make sure he's not almost into a new blank tile. We also set his horizontal motion, `dx`, to zero, because we don't want him to be climbing while still appearing to slide to the left or right. We then set the value of the `climbing` variable to `true`.

Pressing the down arrow key is treated in a similar way. We want to make sure the character's not trying to descend *into* a floor, which might be at the bottom of the ladder. If not, we move the character 3 pixels down. We then set `dx` to zero, and set the value of `climbing` to `true`.

That is all the code associated with climbing ladders. Next we have:

```
    var cgridy:Number = Math.floor(chary / tileHeight);
    var nexty:Number = Math.floor((chary + dy) /
                            tileHeight);
    var nextx:Number = Math.floor((charx + dx) /
                            tileWidth);

    if (solid_array[grid[cgridy][nextx]] == 1)
    {
        if (dx > 0)
        {
            charx = (nextx * tileWidth) - 1;
        }
        else if (dx < 0)
        {
            charx = (nextx * tileWidth) +
                    (tileWidth + 1);
        }

        dx = 0;
    }
```

Once again, we recompute the values of `cgridy` and `nexty`, in case they have been adjusted. We also recompute the value of `nextx`, because if `dx` was set to 0 on the ladder, `nextx` might now be a different tile.

This is the code we use to see if the character is running into a solid tile, horizontally. This occurs if he's running along and simply runs into a wall or a block. We check to see if the tile he'll next be in, at `grid[cgridy][nextx]`, is solid. If it is, we check to see which direction he's running. If he's running to the right (`dx > 0`), we stop him and set his position so that he is flush against the left edge of the wall but not inside it.

Similarly, if he is running to the left and hits a wall in that direction, we also stop him and move him so he's flush with the right side of the wall. We then set `dx` to zero, because he is no longer moving.

Next we have this code:

```
if (collect_array[grid[cgridy][cgridx]] == 1)
{
    grid[cgridy][cgridx] = 0;
    var tRect:Rectangle = new Rectangle(0, 0,
                              tileWidth, tileHeight);
    var destPt:Point = new Point(cgridx * tileWidth,
                              cgridy * tileHeight);
    gameboard.copyPixels(texturePage, tRect, destPt);
}
if (collect_array[grid[cgridy-1][cgridx]] == 1)
{
    grid[cgridy-1][cgridx] = 0;
    var tRect:Rectangle = new Rectangle(0, 0,
                              tileWidth, tileHeight);
    var destPt:Point = new Point(cgridx * tileWidth,
                              (cgridy-1) * tileHeight);
    gameboard.copyPixels(texturePage, tRect, destPt);
}
```

This is where we check to see if the tile the character is on, or the tile directly above him, contains any collectable items. We check two tiles because the character is technically taller than a single tile, so we need to check the tile encompassing his lower and upper body. If the type of tile at his position has a `collect_array` value of 1, we set the type of the tile to 0 and then use some regular tile copying code to copy the tile from position zero in the tile set onto the `gameboard`, thus erasing the collectable tile from existence.

Next, we have this code:

```
if (onGround == false)
{
    dy += .2;
    if (dy > 5) dy = 5;
}

if (dy < 0) outScreen.player.gotoAndStop(9);

if (Key.isDown(Key.SPACE))
{
    if (!jumpdisabled)
```

```
        {
            if (onGround)
            {
                dy = -5;
                jumpdisabled = true;
            }
        }
    }
    else
    {
        jumpdisabled = false;
    }
}
```

This is the end of the main game loop. Here we handle the jumping and vertical momentum. The first part says, if the character's not standing on the ground, increase the value of dy by 0.2. This is gravity. It means that if the character's not on the ground, make him fall. He will continue to accelerate downward until his falling speed reaches 5, at which point he will never pass that speed. This can be thought of as his terminal velocity.

If dy is less than zero, the character is on an upward trajectory, which means we want to show frame 9 of the player animation, which is simply a frame with the legs apart and the arm outstretched—a classic jumping pose. If dy is less than zero, he's jumping up.

Last, we check to see if the player is hitting the space bar. If he is, and the value of jumpdisabled is not true and the character is on the ground, we set his dy to −5, giving him a nice upward velocity, and set jumpdisabled to true.

The idea here is this: if the space bar is being held down and jumpdisabled is true, it means the player simply hasn't released the space bar since his last jump, and we don't want him to be able to jump again; the character will appear to be hopping like a rabbit on the spot if the player holds the space bar down. Of course, we still don't want him to be able to jump if onGround is not true, because that means a character could jump, and before he even begins falling back down to earth, the player could release the space bar and jump again from midair. They call that flying, not jumping.

If the space bar is *not* being pressed, however, we can safely set jumpdisabled to false. That's all there is to the jumping code.

Next we have:

```
function loadLevel(fname)
{
    var my_lv:LoadVars = new LoadVars();
    my_lv.onLoad = function()
    {

        var dats = this.ldat.split(",");
```

```
    var cnt = 0;
    for (var i = 0; i < 75; i++)
    {
        grid[i] = new Array();
        for (j = 0; j < 90; j++)
        {
            grid[i][j] = dats[cnt++];
        }
    }

    solid_array = this.sol.split(",");
    ladder_array = this.lad.split(",");
    collect_array = this.col.split(",");

    repaintGrid();
    _root.onEnterFrame = rootonEnterFrame;


    }
    my_lv.load(fname);

}

loadLevel("testlevel.txt");
```

We've seen this before, in the level editor. This is exactly the same. We load the level, break up the variables, parse them into their appropriate arrays, paint the grid, and begin the game. We also load testlevel.txt by default.

Here is the complete code listing:

```
import flash.display.*;
import flash.geom.*;

var grid:Array = new Array();

var tileWidth:Number = 32;
var tileHeight:Number = 32;

function repaintGrid()
{
    for (var i = 0; i < 75; i++)
    {
        for (j = 0; j < 90; j++)
        {
            if (grid[i][j] > 0)
            {
                var srcx:Number = grid[i][j] % 16;
                var srcy:Number = Math.floor(grid[i][j] /
                                                    16);

                var tRect:Rectangle = new Rectangle(srcx *
                                                    tileWidth,
                                        srcy * tileHeight,
```

```
                                                        tileWidth,
                                                        tileHeight);
                        var destPt:Point = new Point(j * tileWidth,
                                                     i * tileHeight);
                        gameboard.copyPixels(texturePage,
                                             tRect, destPt);
                    }
                }
            }
        }

        var gameboard:BitmapData = new BitmapData(2880, 2400,
                                                  true, 0);
        var worldBack:BitmapData = BitmapData.loadBitmap("worldback");

        var bigBack:BitmapData = new BitmapData(2880, 320,
                                                false, 0);
        for (var i:Number = 0; i < 3; i++)
        {
        var tRect:Rectangle = new Rectangle(0, 0, 731, 320);
        var destPt:Point = new Point(i * 731, 0);
        bigBack.copyPixels(worldBack, tRect, destPt);
        }

        var texturePage:BitmapData = BitmapData.loadBitmap("texturepage");
        var gameScreen:BitmapData = new BitmapData(480, 320,
                                                   false, 0);

        _root.createEmptyMovieClip("outScreen", 0);
        outScreen._xscale = 200;
        outScreen._yscale = 200;
        outScreen.attachBitmap(gameScreen, 0);
        outScreen.attachMovie("playerrun", "player", 1);

        var charx:Number = 32;
        var chary:Number = 40;
        var dx:Number = 0;
        var dy:Number = 0;
        var climbing:Boolean = false;
        var jumpdisabled:Boolean = false;
        var onGround:Boolean = false;


        rootonEnterFrame = function()
        {

            if (charx < 0)
            {
                charx = 0;
                dx = 0;
            }
            if (chary < 0)
            {
```

```
        chary = 0;
        dy = 0;
}

offx = charx - 240;
offy = chary - 160;

if (offx < 0)
{
    offx = 0;
}
if (offy < 0)
{
    offy = 0;
}

outScreen.player._x = charx - offx;
outScreen.player._y = chary - offy;

var tRect:Rectangle = new Rectangle(offx, offy,
                                    480, 320);
var wRect:Rectangle = new Rectangle(offx / 5, 0,
                                    480, 320);
var destPt:Point = new Point(0, 0);

gameScreen.copyPixels(bigBack, wRect, destPt);
gameScreen.copyPixels(gameboard, tRect, destPt);

charx += dx;
chary += dy;

if (Key.isDown(Key.RIGHT) && dx < 5)
{
    dx+=.5;
    outScreen.player._xscale = 100;
    outScreen.player.play();
}
else if (Key.isDown(Key.LEFT) && dx > -5)
{
    dx-=.5;
    outScreen.player._xscale = -100;
    outScreen.player.play();
}
else
{
    if (Math.abs(dx) < 1)
    {
        if(!climbing)
            outScreen.player.gotoAndStop(1);
        else
            outScreen.player.gotoAndStop(25);
    }
}
```

```
    dx *= .90;


    var cgridx:Number = Math.floor(charx / tileWidth);
    var cgridy:Number = Math.floor(chary / tileHeight);
    var nextx:Number = Math.floor((charx + dx) /
                                       tileWidth);
    var nexty:Number = Math.floor((chary + dy) /
                                       tileHeight);
    onGround = false;

    if (solid_array[grid[nexty][cgridx]] == 1)
    {
        if (dy > 0)
        {
            chary = (nexty * tileHeight) - 1;
            var cgridy:Number = Math.floor(chary /
                                        tileHeight);
            dy = 0;
            onGround = true;
        }
        else if (dy < 0)
        {
            chary = (nexty * tileHeight) +
                    (tileHeight + 1);
            var cgridy:Number = Math.floor(chary /
                                        tileHeight);
            dy = 0;
        }
    }
    else
    {
        if (ladder_array[grid[cgridy][cgridx]] == 1 &&
            dy >= 0)
        {
            dy = 0;
            if (chary%tileHeight < 5 &&
                    !Key.isDown(Key.DOWN))
                chary = ((cgridy-1) * tileHeight) +
                        tileHeight-1;
            onGround = true;
        }
    }

    var cgridy:Number = Math.floor(chary / tileHeight);
    var nexty:Number = Math.floor((chary + dy) /
                                       tileHeight);

    if (ladder_array[grid[cgridy][cgridx]] != 1)
        climbing = false;

    if (Key.isDown(Key.UP) &&
        ladder_array[grid[cgridy][cgridx]] == 1)
```

```
    {
        dy = 0;
        if (solid_array[grid[Math.floor((chary - 3) /
            tileHeight)][cgridx]] != 1)
                chary-=3;

        if (chary%tileHeight < 5)
            chary = ((cgridy-1) * tileHeight) +
                    tileHeight-1;
        dx = 0;
        climbing = true;
    }
    if (Key.isDown(Key.DOWN) &&
        ladder_array[grid[cgridy][cgridx]] == 1)
    {
        dy = 0;
        if (solid_array[grid[Math.floor((chary + 3) /
                tileHeight)][cgridx]] != 1)
                    chary+=3;
        dx = 0;
        climbing = true;
    }

var cgridy:Number = Math.floor(chary / tileHeight);
var nexty:Number = Math.floor((chary + dy) /
                                    tileHeight);
var nextx:Number = Math.floor((charx + dx) /
                                    tileWidth);

if (solid_array[grid[cgridy][nextx]] == 1)
{
    if (dx > 0)
    {
        charx = (nextx * tileWidth) - 1;
    }
    else if (dx < 0)
    {
        charx = (nextx * tileWidth) +
                    (tileWidth + 1);
    }

    dx = 0;
}

    if (collect_array[grid[cgridy][cgridx]] == 1)
    {
        grid[cgridy][cgridx] = 0;
        var tRect:Rectangle = new Rectangle(0, 0,
                                    tileWidth, tileHeight);
        var destPt:Point = new Point(cgridx * tileWidth,
                                    cgridy * tileHeight);
        gameboard.copyPixels(texturePage, tRect, destPt);
    }
```

```
if (collect_array[grid[cgridy-1][cgridx]] == 1)
{
    grid[cgridy-1][cgridx] = 0;
    var tRect:Rectangle = new Rectangle(0, 0,
                               tileWidth, tileHeight);
    var destPt:Point = new Point(cgridx * tileWidth,
                               (cgridy-1) * tileHeight);
    gameboard.copyPixels(texturePage, tRect, destPt);
}

if (onGround == false)
{
    dy += .2;
    if (dy > 5) dy = 5;
}

if (dy < 0) outScreen.player.gotoAndStop(9);

if (Key.isDown(Key.SPACE))
{
    if (!jumpdisabled)
    {
        if (onGround)
        {
            dy = -5;
            jumpdisabled = true;
        }
    }
}
else
{
    jumpdisabled = false;
}
}

function loadLevel(fname)
{
    var my_lv:LoadVars = new LoadVars();
    my_lv.onLoad = function()
    {

        var dats = this.ldat.split(",");

        var cnt = 0;
        for (var i = 0; i < 75; i++)
        {
            grid[i] = new Array();
            for (j = 0; j < 90; j++)
            {
                grid[i][j] = dats[cnt++];
            }
        }
```

```
            solid_array = this.sol.split(",");
            ladder_array = this.lad.split(",");
            collect_array = this.col.split(",");

            repaintGrid();
            _root.onEnterFrame = rootonEnterFrame;


        }
        my_lv.load(fname);

    }

    loadLevel("testlevel.txt");
```

That's all the code we have for the game engine as it stands. Congratulations on making it this far. This is the beginning of a game engine that can be turned into something much bigger, if done right.

Where can we take it from here? The rest is up to you. Here are some suggestions:

- Add some sound effects
- Add some enemies
- Add an end-game or a beginning-game with a title screen, level selection, and so on
- Make the items count for some point value

SUMMARY

In this chapter we covered:

- Taking the concepts from the previous chapter and applying them to a full game engine
- Creating a level editor to build level maps
- Using the data from those level maps to render the world image
- Using a tiled background image to make the background wider and give it some horizontal pan
- Using the level data to drive collision logic
- Climbing, jumping, falling, and colliding with the physical world

13

PHYSICS FOR GAMES

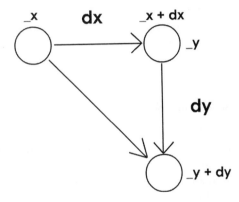

One of the things that differentiates mediocre, simple games from really advanced games these days is their use of physics. Sure, a game can be programmed with the most incredible graphics, Hollywood sounds, and 835 levels of action, but how real does it feel to the player? The better a game emulates the physics of real life, the more the player will be able to get into it and believe in it—to suspend his disbelief. We touched upon this concept earlier when we looked at the importance of realistic control.

Most people cringe at the thought of physics, and associate with it the memory of grueling hours in front of a high-school textbook. Yes, physics can get very intense and very involved. Luckily, the physics that we'll be looking at, and indeed the physics used in many games, is very, very simple.

THE PHYSICS OF MOTION

The physics that we'll be looking at essentially aims to deconstruct motion and emulate it with numbers. We'll be looking at five kinds of motion:

- Normal rectangular motion
- Bounce
- Gravity
- Wind
- Circular, or rotational, motion

We also have another force that acts upon all these motions at any time, and that force is known as *friction*.

The first four types of motion are all related to simply creating forces that act upon the horizontal (_x) position and the vertical (_y) position. The fifth type of motion uses a slightly different method to represent the motion variables (rotation and speed), but in the end that too gets converted to x and y.

Normal Rectangular Motion

We've already looked at this. In Chapter 4 we took our first look at the "normal" type of motion. Normal rectangular motion is simply defined as the rate at which an object moves along an axis or several axes.

This means we can move an object normally along one axis (x) by simply modifying the x position of that object over time. In the case of Macromedia Flash Professional 8, our time interval is measured in frames, so this motion would be measured as how much an object's _x position is changed each frame. This amount is referred to as dx.

Figure 13.1 shows what we're talking about. The object we're going to be talking about is a ball. A ball at position _x in one frame will be at position _x + dx in the next frame, so dx is the amount by which we're moving the ball. The actual value that dx holds is irrelevant to this discussion, but it should be noted that the smaller the value of dx, the less the ball will move each frame, and therefore the slower its motion will appear.

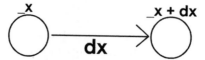

FIGURE 13.1   Moving the ball along one horizontal axis.

This is motion along one axis, almost like a train on a track. When we're talking about the computer monitor, however, we're talking about a two-dimensional surface, so there will be another axis: the vertical axis y. Motion in the case of the y-axis is expressed using another variable, identical in purpose to dx, called dy. The dy variable is the amount that we want the object to move vertically each frame. Take a look at Figure 13.2.

In the case of Figure 13.2, we're looking again at motion along one axis only, except it's a different axis this time. It's more of a rocket ship than a train.

In general, these two forces (dx and dy) act on the same object in the same frame (an object doesn't tend to move down for a frame then right for a frame). To accommodate the desire for diagonal motion along a dx, dy path, we need to do the very simple task of combining the motions, like in Figure 13.3.

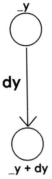
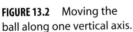
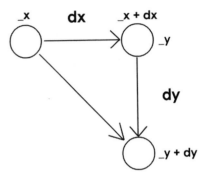

FIGURE 13.2   Moving the ball along one vertical axis.

FIGURE 13.3   Moving along two axes.

In the case of Figure 13.3, we're moving along two axes, x and y. This means that every frame we add dx to _x and we add dy to _y. In the end, the ball will appear to move diagonally, like the diagonal line in Figure 13.3. In Macromedia Flash Professional 8 we would express this with the following code:

```
ball.dx = 2;
ball.dy = 2;

ball.onEnterFrame = function()
{
    this._x += this.dx;
    this._y += this.dy;
}
```

When this code is placed on the main timeline of a movie that has a movie clip on the timeline with the instance name ball, the ball will spring to life with basic, normal motion. It will move 2 pixels to the right and 2 pixels down, each frame. This can be seen in normal.fla on the CD-ROM in the Chapter 13 source files. Run it to see basic normal motion.

ON THE CD

If the value of dx is a negative number, the ball will move to the left instead of the right, because _x would be decreasing each frame. Similarly, if the value of dy is a negative number, the ball will move up instead of down.

Bounce

We looked at bounce a little bit in Chapter 4 as well, when the ball bounced off the walls and off of the blocks. Essentially, bounce is just an extension of the previous motion. In the case of bounce, however, we make a modification to dx and dy based on certain conditions being satisfied (namely, collision with walls and floors detected).

Much like normal motion, we treat the bounce separately on the x and y axes. Let's look at the simplest example: while moving the ball along the _x axis, by dx, we encounter the right wall, which is at _x position 500. What should happen to dx in this case? It should reverse, so that movement to the right becomes movement to the left. However, the faster the ball was moving right, then the faster the ball should rebound to the left. To do this, our post-bounce dx should be somehow related to our pre-bounce dx. The easiest way to do this? Multiply dx by −1.

If we move like this every frame:

```
this._x += this.dx;
```

then we must check for collision with the right wall, like so:

```
if (this._x > 400)
```

How does this work? Well, since the right wall is nothing more than an imaginary vertical line, all we need to do is see if the ball has crossed that line. Also, because we're only concerned with the horizontal bounce right now, we don't need to bring _y into the equation. We're just looking to see if _x has crossed the x = 400 position. Figure 13.4 shows this in practice. The ball travels toward the wall, and each time we check to see if it has crossed 400. In the final position, it has crossed over 400, and our if statement will evaluate to true.

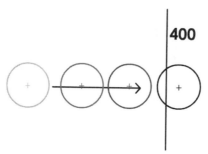

FIGURE 13.4   Collision with the right wall.

Remember that our comparison check will be relative to the registration point of the movie clip in question. In the case of the ball, the registration point is in the dead center of the movie clip. In Figure 13.4 you can see the registration point as the small + symbol in the middle of the ball. Only in the ball's final position has this registration point crossed 400. There's a small problem with this: the ball's leading edge will appear to pass through the wall; it does not collide until the registration point hits. This doesn't make the ball look very solid. How do we overcome this?

Well, first, let's look at the dimensions of the ball. It's made up of a `_width` and a `_height`. The distance from the registration point to the right edge is exactly `_width / 2`. Therefore, what we want to do is check not to see if `_x` has passed 400, but instead see if `_x + _width / 2` has passed 400. This way, the image in Figure 13.5 will properly cause a collision.

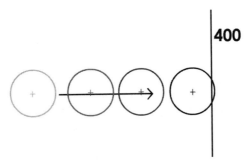

FIGURE 13.5   Correcting for registration point offset.

How does this change our `if` statement? Very simply:

```
if (this._x > 400)
```

becomes

```
if (this._x + this._width / 2 > 400)
```

So we've got the `if` statement settled. What exactly do we *do* once it evaluates `true`? The first thing will be to move the ball *back* into a legal region. Remember, since we're checking to see if it has passed 400, technically we're checking to see if it's *in* the wall a small bit. It's OK however, because this illegal positioning will never be seen. It is all corrected before this frame loop has even finished executing (remember, this collision check happens immediately after the normal motion of `this._x += this.dx`). So we move the ball back into the legal region like so:

```
this._x = 400 - this._width / 2;
```

This will ensure that the ball moves back to the position exactly flush with the wall. This is the furthest position a ball can occupy without triggering the `if` statement. This is illustrated in Figure 13.6.

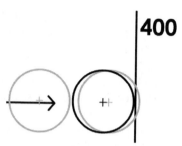

FIGURE 13.6 Moving the ball back into the valid region.

The next thing to do is to reverse the ball's motion, or in other words,

```
this.dx *= -1;
```

So, moving to the right at dx of 3, the ball will hit the wall and then begin moving to the left at a dx of –3. This will cause the ball to continue moving left, as its dx will now be permanently changed. This entire code would be:

```
this._x += this.dx;
this._y += this.dy;

if (this._x + this._width / 2 > 400)
{
    this._x = 400 - this._width / 2;
    this.dx *= -1;
}
```

How about collision with the left wall? It's very similar. This time we're simply checking to see if the registration point, minus half the width of the ball, has passed the left edge. If so, we move it back into the valid region and reverse dx yet again. Assuming that our left wall is at position 10, our code for this looks like so:

```
if (this._x - this._width / 2 < 10)
{
    this._x = 10 + this._width / 2;
    this.dx *= -1;
}
```

That's identical to our previous code, but reversed. These two blocks of code would successfully have the ball bouncing back and forth from left to right forever. However, add any dy into the mix and the ball would eventually fly off the top or the bottom of the screen, never to be seen again. What does this mean? We have to do collision with the *ceiling* and *floor* as well. In respect to our gravity-free world, the ceiling and floor are both basically just two more walls; turn your monitor sideways and you wouldn't be able to tell the difference.

What does this mean for our bounce code? Well, it means everything is identical to the horizontal code, except that we substitute _y for _x and _height for _width. Sounds simple, right? It is. Let's look at the floor collision.

```
if (this._y + this._height / 2 > 300)
{
    this._y = 300 - this._height / 2;
    this.dy *= -1;
}
```

Our floor in this example is at _y 300, so we're checking to see if the bottom of the ball has crossed over the 300 level, and if so, move it so the bottom of the ball is just touching the 300 level and reverse the dy value; what was moving down is now moving up.

Finally, we have a ceiling at _y position 10, which we will hit like so:

```
if (this._y - this._height / 2 < 10)
{
    this._y = 10 + this._height / 2;
    this.dy *= -1;
}
```

All of these blocks of code are finally run together in one nice onEnterFrame, like so:

```
ball.dx = 2;
ball.dy = 2;

ball.onEnterFrame = function()
{
    this._x += this.dx;
    this._y += this.dy;

    if (this._x + this._width / 2 > 400)
    {
        this._x = 400 - this._width / 2;
        this.dx *= -1;
    }

    if (this._x - this._width / 2 < 10)
    {
        this._x = 10 + this._width / 2;
        this.dx *= -1;
    }

    if (this._y + this._height / 2 > 300)
    {
        this._y = 300 - this._height / 2;
        this.dy *= -1;
    }
```

```
if (this._y - this._height / 2 < 10)
{
    this._y = 10 + this._height / 2;
    this.dy *= -1;
}
}
```

ON THE CD

All of this can be found in the file bounce.fla in the Chapter 13 source files on the CD-ROM. When we run this code, the ball will move around the screen, bouncing off the walls as it hits them. Since there's no gravity yet, perhaps it's best to think of this as the top-down view of an air hockey table. You might want to try starting with higher dx and dy values so the ball moves faster around the table.

We mentioned earlier in this chapter another force that can act upon all these motions, and that is *friction*. Friction is essentially a force that acts to decay the motion of an object over time. In the case of our ball, the most friction would probably be encountered when it hits the wall. How do we translate this into code? Well, recall that we're reversing the motion like so:

```
this.dx *= -1;
```

The answer is right there in that piece of code. This will reverse the velocity by 100%, and therefore no momentum will be lost. However, we could do the following:

```
this.dx *= -.9;
```

This would reverse the motion, but only by 90%, so a dx of 10 will be reversed to be –9. The next collision will be –90% of that, or 8.1, then –7.29, then 6.561, and so on, until it would eventually reach near zero. Because it's always a percentage, it's possible for it to never reach zero. In this case, we normally put a check in place to see if the velocity has dropped below a fixed amount, say 0.001, and then we simply set it to 0. We've put this together in the sample file bouncedecay.fla in the Chapter 13 files on the CD-ROM. We used –80% as our bounce amount. Watching this for a few moments, it's possible to see the decrease in velocity pretty quickly.

ON THE CD

What would happen if we used a value greater than 1? For example,

```
this.dx *= -1.1;
```

This means, reverse my speed and increase it by 10%. This is going to speed up the ball at each hit, and eventually the ball will be flying around too fast to see. This can be seen in bounceenergize.fla.

Finally, it's possible for us to decay the motion of the object regardless of when it bounces. Looking back at the original example where our collisions maintained 100% velocity on each bounce, we can add the following two lines of code, just below the line this._y += this.dy;

```
this.dx *= 0.99;
this.dy *= 0.99;
```

This creates a very realistic decay of motion as the ball moves around, gener-ally slowing down as it goes, until it finally glides to rest. This can be seen in the file bouncemotiondecay.fla.

Gravity

If our previous example were thought of as a top-down view of an air hockey table, then its motion makes perfect sense. If, however, our y-axis were to truly represent the vertical plane, the only way our previous motion would be possible would be in a space ship far away from any source of gravity.

The truth of the matter is that real life on Earth includes gravity. Gravity is so normal to us that we expect it as part of normal motion. Even images of astro-nauts on the moon make sense because they include a sense of familiarity in the gravity. Sure, the gravity is lower, but things follow the same basic "up is up" and "down is down" rules. We can go as far as to say, it's gravity that lets us naturally comprehend the concept of up and down. Some people get their lefts and rights confused, because they have no distinct difference, but up and down will never be confused—gravity tells them apart.

What, at its core, is gravity? Well, there are several scientific theories about gravity. The commonly accepted theory is that gravity is the result of space and time being curved around solid objects. This means very little to us, but it essen-tially means that objects will always attract each other as they fall into each other's space and time. When you drop a golf ball to the ground, the ball always falls down. However, because all objects have a gravitational force (their indenta-tion in the space-time fabric) the ball does indeed attract the Earth toward it as well. Does the Earth move? No, not really. The difference in gravitational force between the planet and a golf ball is so astronomical that the only gravitational force we'll ever see is the Earth acting upon the ball and all other objects in the world. It's possible to have an object with so much gravity that light itself cannot get up enough speed to leave its surface. When this happens, the object appears completely black; in astronomy this is known as a black hole. It's not really a hole; it's just a body (usually an ancient star) with such density that one teaspoon full of its matter would weigh 100 million tons.

In the context of our games, how complex do we have to make our gravity? Does every object have to have a mild gravitational pull on every other object? No. We're going to take the more traditional approach to gravity. We're going to look at gravity the way we have come to understand it through real-life experi-ence. For us, the definition of gravity is this: Gravity is a constant force acting to accelerate the downward velocity of an object over time.

Let's look an example. We have a ball moving down at 4 pixels per frame, or dy = 4. It starts out at position 0. It moves down by 4, and then next frame, dy increases to 8, so the ball moves down 8 pixels, and so on. Look at Figure 13.7. At the left side we see the ball. The ball follows a downwardly accelerated motion as gravity picks it up and pulls it faster and faster. Look at the _y position of the ball. It starts out at 0, then it moves down to 4, then to 12, 24, and after five frames it has reached a _y of 40.

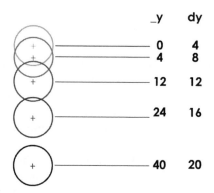

_y	dy
0	4
4	8
12	12
24	16
40	20

FIGURE 13.7   The downward motion of gravity.

What do we notice about the position change? It's not constant. Constant would be 0, 4, 8, 12, 16—moving 4 per frame. Our ball in the above example is *accelerating* downward. The right column of numbers in Figure 13.7 shows the dy value at each frame. In frame 1 the ball has a dy of 4; in frame 2 it increases to 8, then to 12, then to 16, 20, and so on. Notice something about the change in dy? It *is* a constant amount of change; it's increasing by 4 each frame.

That's what gravity is! It's acceleration in the *motion* of an object, and the *motion* of an object in turn changes the *position* of an object. So, gravity doesn't directly affect the position of any object; gravity only acts upon the motion of an object. It's that motion that in turn is responsible for pulling the object in the direction that gravity is coming from. Just look at a helicopter. Gravity is at work, but the position doesn't necessarily change, because the rotors are spinning fast enough to cause enough of an upward thrust to perfectly counter the effects of gravity. Gravity is accelerating the helicopter downward, and the rotors are therefore *accelerating* the helicopter upward. When these two accelerations match, the object remains in balanced equilibrium. Remember that we're talking about acceleration here, not actual motion; we're talking about the *changes* of motion.

In our code we've looked at the motion variables dx and dy. These are used to change the position of an object over time. That means gravity is simply the change in dy over time. In terms of code, what does this all boil down to? It's deceptively simple.

```
this.dy += 3;
```

That's all there is to it. In this case we're saying, increase the value of dy by 3 every frame. In our previous bounce examples, we set dx and dy to specific values and then left them (unless of course we account for friction). In this case, we're *increasing* dy by a fixed amount every frame. This can be thought of as *change in dy*.

Add that single line of code to the end of the onEnterFrame we've been making, just after the last bounce check, like so:

```
if (this._y - this._height / 2 < 10)
{
    this._y = 10 + this._height / 2;
    this.dy *= -1;
}

this.dy += 3;
}
```

Since no object is able to completely preserve 100% of its velocity on a bounce off the ground, it's best to change the ground bounce code to this:

```
if (this._y + this._height / 2 > 300)
{
    this._y = 300 - this._height / 2;
    this.dy *= -.9;
}
```

These changes can also be found in gravity.fla, in the Chapter 13 files on the CD-ROM.

Now the ball will bounce back up with 90% of its collision velocity. Remember that as an object accelerates downward, its dy will increase. Accordingly, when it strikes the ground and reverses the value of its dy, it will bounce upward with an equally large recoil. In other words, the harder it hits the ground, the harder it will bounce up. If by the time the ball hits the ground, its dy has increased to 20, then it will hit the ground and bounce up at –20, or if we use the 90% bounce ratio, it will bounce up at –18. However, immediately, gravity will begin to *increase* dy, so –18 will become –15, –12, –9, –6, –3, and 0. As it's doing this, its upward motion will slow down until, for the frame when it has dy of 0, it will not move vertically at all. After this, dy will increase to a positive number and the ball will again begin falling. This is the arc of our bounce. Figure 13.8 shows this in action. Each ball represents one frame. Note that the dx (horizontal speed) is a constant, and it not influenced by the bouncing motion in any way. The rate of gravity is also a constant. The only thing changing is dy and of course the physical position of the ball, being acted upon by dx and dy.

Wind

Guess what wind is? If you guessed that it is simply a change in dx, you were right. It's eloquently simple. While we increased dy to cause a downward acceleration toward the floor, we will increase (or decrease) dx to cause acceleration toward the *wall*; it's just gravity on the x-axis!

dx = 2
gravity = 4

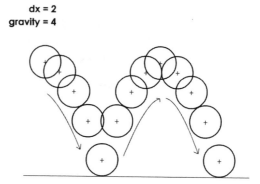

FIGURE 13.8 The arc of the bouncing ball.

Add the following code after the gravity line:

```
this.dx += 1;
```

That number 1 can be changed to anything, and the larger the number, the stronger the wind. This will cause the ball to be blown into the right wall. Alternatively, you can do this:

```
this.dx += -1;
```

This causes the ball to be blown to the left. The code should also be changed so that the horizontal collision reflects the dx of the ball back by 90% again. The whole thing should look like so:

```
ball.onEnterFrame = function()
{
    this._x += this.dx;
    this._y += this.dy;

    if (this._x + this._width / 2 > 400)
    {
        this._x = 400 - this._width / 2;
        this.dx *= -.9;
    }

    if (this._x - this._width / 2 < 10)
    {
        this._x = 10 + this._width / 2;
        this.dx *= -.9;
    }

    if (this._y + this._height / 2 > 300)
    {
        this._y = 300 - this._height / 2;
        this.dy *= -.9;
    }
```

```
if (this._y - this._height / 2 < 10)
{
    this._y = 10 + this._height / 2;
    this.dy *= -1;
}

this.dy += 3;
this.dx += 1;
}
```

ON THE CD

This can be found in `wind.fla` in the Chapter 13 files on the CD-ROM.

Normally, wind has a vertical component to it as well, since wind doesn't always run perfectly parallel to the horizon. If you want, you can introduce this component after the gravity line, with another change in `this.dy`. Alternatively, we could use radial wind, where the wind is coming from a particular angle at a particular speed.

To do this, however, we have to understand how we can take angle and speed and somehow convert that into a usable `xWind` and `yWind`. We're talking about converting angle and velocity into their horizontal and vertical components. We're talking about *radial motion*.

Radial Motion

Take a look at Figure 13.9. We can see the usual "ball moving from one position to another" image, almost like Figure 13.3. There's one small difference in Figure 13.9. Though we're talking about the exact same motion (from one position to the next), the way in which that motion is defined is very different.

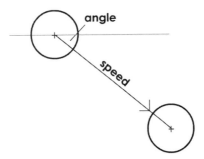

FIGURE 13.9   Radial motion.

Rather than look at the motion as a fixed `dx` and `dy`, we're looking at the motion as the two values angle and speed. Both systems of motion use two values. They both have the same end result of simply moving an object from one location to another, but they have a few key differences.

- With radial motion, it's possible to perform a constant change of angle, causing the ball to roll around in a circle.

- With radial motion, we can increase the value of speed, without changing angle, causing the ball to accelerate faster, in any direction, rather than just on the x or y axis.
- With radial motion, we can act independently of rectangular coordinate systems. Rather than looking at it as moving up/down/left/right, we look at it as moving at an angle, angle + 90, angle + 180, and angle + 270. This means we have a four-directional coordinate system that doesn't have to be lined up with the four directions of x, y screen coordination. This is great for things like top-down driving games, where we want to turn a car and drive straight at any angle, even if the road doesn't happen to be lined up with a screen axis.

In Figure 13.10 you'll see how radial motion and rectangular motion (dx and dy) are related to each other. Ultimately, as we're working in screen space where we have to conform to pixels, we must convert back from our radial coordinate system (sometimes called a polar coordinate system) to good old dx and dy.

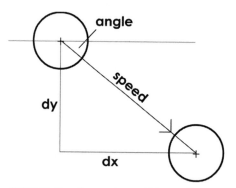

FIGURE 13.10   Comparing radial coordinates to rectangular coordinates.

The magic is, yet again, very simple. One line of code calculates dx and one line of code calculates dy. They look like this:

```
this.dx = Math.cos(this.angle) * this.speed;
this.dy = Math.sin(this.angle) * this.speed;
```

The formula is almost identical for dx and dy. The only difference is that dx uses Math.cos and dy uses Math.sin. If we had an angle of 0 and a speed of 10, we would expect the ball to move 10 pixels to the right each frame. That means we would expect dx to be 10 and dy to be 0. Let's look at the formula and see if this works out.

The initial angle is 0. Math.cos(0) equates to 1, and Math.sin(0) equates to 0. That means

```
this.dx = 1 * this.speed;
this.dy = 0 * this.speed;
```

If we put in speed, we get

```
this.dx = 1 * 10;
this.dy = 0 * 10;
```

which equates to

```
this.dx = 10;
this.dy = 0;
```

which is exactly what we expected. If we change the angle, dx and dy will change. Let's look at the angle 0.6.

```
Math.cos(0.6) is 0.82534
Math.sin(0.6) is 0.56464
```

So,

```
this.dx = 0.82534 * this.speed;
this.dy = 0.56464 * this.speed;
```

Which means

```
this.dx = 0.82534 * 10;
this.dy = 0.56464 * 10;
```

Therefore,

```
this.dx = 8.2534;
this.dy = 5.6464;
```

This means that in order to move a total speed of 10 at an angle of 0.6 radians (about 34.377 degrees), the ball must move 8.2534 pixels along _x and 5.6464 pixels along _y.

Remember that all the trigonometric math functions in Actionscript take radians, not degrees (even though the _rotation property of movie clips is measured in degrees). Moving between degrees and radians is similar to converting from miles to kilometers and vice versa.

1 degree = 0.01745329252 radians.

Alternatively, one full circle of 360 degrees is equal to 6.283185 radians (which happens to be 2 × PI). This means that one full circle is not an even number of radians. It's often difficult for people to get over that concept. We seem to expect a full circle to have an even number of degrees and even number of radians, but why should it? When something weighs an even 1000 pounds, why should it also weigh an even number of kilograms?

To convert from degrees to radians, multiply the degree value by 180/`Math.PI`.

radians = degrees * (180/`Math.PI`)

To get from radians to degrees, multiply by `Math.PI` / 180.

degrees = radians * (`Math.PI`/180)

Note that this also means that `dx` and `dy` are now *computed* each frame and that applying any change to them via gravity or wind will be pointless as those changes will be erased when `dx` and `dy` are freshly computed next frame. Let's look at the code to put this into action.

```
ball.angle = 0;
ball.speed = 5;

ball.onEnterFrame = function()
{
    this.dx = Math.cos(this.angle) * this.speed;
    this.dy = Math.sin(this.angle) * this.speed;

    this._x += this.dx;
    this._y += this.dy;

    this.angle += 0.1;
}
```

At the start of the frame we compute `dx` and `dy`, and then, as in all our previous examples, we add `dx` and `dy` to `_x` and `_y`. After this, we increase `angle` by 0.1. This will cause the ball to move around in a circle, like a car on a track viewed from above. The above code is found in `radial.fla` in the Chapter 13 files on the CD-ROM.

ON THE CD

Alternatively, we could start `angle` at any particular value and change speed to 0. Then, we could increase speed every frame, which would cause the ball to accelerate away into the distance at the angle we specified. See this in the following code (found in `radialzoomaway.fla`):

```
ball.angle = .6;
ball.speed = 10;

ball.onEnterFrame = function()
{
this.dx = Math.cos(this.angle) * this.speed;
this.dy = Math.sin(this.angle) * this.speed;

this._x += this.dx;
this._y += this.dy;

this.speed += 1;
}
```

Later on in the book, in the sample optimized game (Chapter 10), we'll be looking at using this radial motion in the control of a vehicle moving around in a curved manner. For now, let's look back at our wind code and see how we can create radial wind that blows from any angle.

Our original code had us adding a fixed value to dx to produce the wind. Now, we're going to compute separate windDX and windDY values to make the wind blow the way wind really blows. First, beneath the definition of the dx and dy of the ball, we need to define the values of the wind angle and speed, like so:

```
ball.dx = 15;
ball.dy = 15;

windAngle = 0;
windSpeed = 3;
```

As we discussed earlier, using an angle of 0 means our wind will only blow to the right, which is exactly what our previous example wind did, without the use of radial math. If we can get this to mimic the original, then we're in good shape for now. At the end, after the gravity code, we must make our code look like this:

```
this.dy += 3;

var windDX = Math.cos(windAngle) * windSpeed;
var windDY = Math.sin(windAngle) * windSpeed;

this.dx += windDX;
this.dy += windDY;

}
```

Notice that the original line this.dx += 1 is gone. Notice too that dy is being acted upon *twice*, once from gravity and then again from the vertical component of the wind. This is correct.

If we run this now, it should behave exactly like our old wind.fla, except that the wind is a little stronger (our previous example used wind with a speed of 1; this wind has a speed of 3). This can be found in radialwind.fla.

Try changing the wind angle and wind speed to

```
windAngle = -1.8;
windSpeed = 2;
```

Now our wind is blowing at −1.8 radians, or about −103 degrees. Since −90 degrees would be straight up, −103 degrees is almost straight up, but also slightly to the left. This means gravity will have less effect, as the ball is being elevated by wind, and it will gradually come to rest on the left wall.

What happens if we add this line of code to the end:

```
windAngle+=0.03;
```

This means the angle of wind will be constantly changing, and the wind will, over time, blow from every direction. This will play havoc on the ball, as its forces are constantly shifting. Try setting the initial windSpeed to 4 (so it's 1 stronger than gravity). When the winds begin to blow upward, the ball will elevate and move toward the ceiling. This can be seen in radialwindmoving.fla in the Chapter 13 files on the CD-ROM.

ON THE CD

SUMMARY

This concludes our game physics chapter, but it by no means represents the end of our use of physics in this book. On the contrary, now we really get going. The topics covered here have included all of the major physics concepts required for games. In the next chapter we're going to take everything from this chapter and apply it in a really fun game. We've covered:

- The forces of motion in game physics including:
  1. Normal rectangular motion
  2. Bounce
  3. Gravity
  4. Wind
  5. Radial forces
  6. Friction

- How to integrate many of these concepts into a cohesive whole

MARS RACER

In the previous chapter we learned all about the major physics used in games including gravity and rotational motion. In this chapter we're going to take all of that stuff and bring it together into a very cool game.

OVERVIEW

Let's start off by applying a few things we've learned so far to this game. Here are the things we'd like to include:

- Plot and story
- Good control
- Good physics
- Challenge
- Sound

This looks like the recipe for quite a good game. Let's look at each of these components individually. If you want to look at the game right away, you can start off by running the SWF file, `marsracer.swf`, in the Chapter 14 source files on the CD-ROM.

Plot and Story

The year is 2136 and the Earth has become so overpopulated that the human race has had no choice but to look elsewhere for a habitat. They have turned their attention to the planet Mars, which is nothing but one large red desert.

*Scientists believe, however, that it would be possible to "terraform" Mars—to turn its harsh, cold and lifeless atmosphere into an Earth-like atmosphere capable of supporting life. The answer lies in **water**. With enough water in the sky, scientists could increase the greenhouse gases in the atmosphere, thus raising the ambient temperature of the planet. Once this is done, the rains would begin to fall, and the planet could support liquid water, which would flow across the surface, forming rivers and oceans. From here, scientists could introduce bacteria and simple plants to begin the process of converting the carbon dioxide–rich environment into an oxygen-rich environment.*

Once this is done, they would have created a new Earth.

Now it all comes down to you. In order to get this water into the Martian atmosphere, you must drive your four-wheel-drive all-terrain vehicle across the surface of the planet and find the pockets of frozen water near the ground. You must scoop them up one at a time and watch as the planet slowly transforms into a life-giving world.

Watch out, though! Mars is littered with deep canyons, rocks, and hills. Also, there appear to be giant bones of an ancient race of creatures, recently discovered, strewn across the surface.

Can you help give life to Mars?

That's the story of Mars Racer. In principle, the story is to serve as a motivation for continuing to drive across the surface of the planet and getting as far as you can. The object is to drive along from left to right, collecting all the suspended frozen water droplets, as shown in Figure 14.1, until Mars has been completely transformed into a planet capable of supporting human life. As you collect water drops, you'll see the water meter at the right side of the screen gradually fill up. When it is completely full, you've won the game, and the planet has been completely transformed. Every time you pick up a water droplet, you are given an extra life.

In the beginning, the planet will look red, barren, and dead, like Figure 14.2. By the end of the game, once you've collected enough water drops to fill the water meter entirely, Mars will be green and full of life, and the sky will be blue, like Figure 14.3.

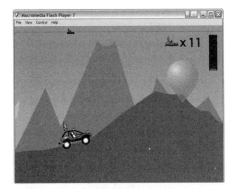

FIGURE 14.1   Mars Racer in play.

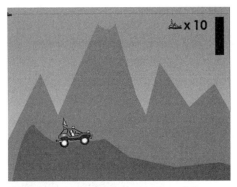

FIGURE 14.2   Mars at the beginning of the game, with no water collected.

FIGURE 14.3   Mars, completely terraformed.

Good Control

The vehicle moves along the surface of the planet, following the contours of the hills and the objects it encounters. Movement is accomplished by simply pressing the arrow key in the direction you want to go—left or right.

The vehicle is equipped with a hydraulic launching system that allows it to jump into the air. This is accomplished by pressing the Control key. The only stipulation when jumping is that at least one wheel must be touching the ground in order to jump. Jumping is caused by the hydraulic extension of the wheels and them pushing off the ground, so if no wheel is touching the ground, there can be no jump.

One of the other important aspects of the control in Mars Racer is the use of the terrain to aid you in your travel. By using hills and ridges, you can achieve enough speed to launch yourself farther than if you just drove and jumped off the edge. The game follows completely realistic physical laws, with some slight modifications for playability reasons, but we'll look at that in the next section. If you fall off a cliff and disappear off the bottom of the screen, then a life has been used up, and you are returned to the beginning of the level.

As with most action games, there is a small learning curve while you get used to the controls. After a little while, you'll be racing along and sailing off ramps, over hills and canyons, and across giant monster bones.

Good Physics

The physics of this game is one of the areas where it shines the most. The vehicle smoothly follows the terrain, which is one giant movie clip, and maintains its own independent momentum. So, if you drive quickly up a hill, the vehicle will drive up that hill, but if the hill drops off suddenly, the vehicle will still continue on its upward path, through the air, eventually tilting forward and down, until the front wheel hits the ground, and the vehicle bounces out and the rear wheels hit the ground. This motion is illustrated in Figure 14.4.

FIGURE 14.4   The physics of driving fast up a hill.

The distance of the jump does, of course, depend on the speed of the vehicle when entering the hill. For example, if the vehicle reached the crest of the hill with very little speed, it would simply round the top and drive down the other side, like in Figure 14.5.

FIGURE 14.5   The physics of driving slowly up a hill.

The vehicle uses an independent suspension system. The wheels move independently of the chassis, while the chassis is responsible for holding the wheels a fixed distance apart. It's a relationship known as inverse kinematics, where one moving element affects the motion of another moving element, while the second element also has an inverse effect on the motion of the first element.

The independent suspension means that the wheels will appear to reach down when the vehicle is airborne, and they will appear to compress into the vehicle when it lands. In Figure 14.6 the front wheel can be seen to be reaching down, while the back wheel has landed and the shocks have compressed, driving the wheel up into the chassis.

In principle, the vehicle can be thought of as two balls that move along the ground in parallel to each other like in Figure 14.7. These two balls are the wheels, and they follow the physical rules of a ball: they roll down hills, bounce off objects, and fall with gravity. The only thing we don't do here is have them bounce off the ground when they hit. We want the weight of the vehicle to prevent this bounce.

FIGURE 14.6   Independent suspension in landing.

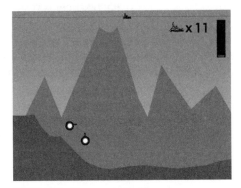

FIGURE 14.7   The two wheels.

The wheels are the critical part of the physics of this game. The other part is the chassis of the car. The chassis sits so that its rotation is angled exactly along the line connecting the two wheels and it is positioned exactly halfway between the two wheels, as shown in Figure 14.8.

However, when one of the "balls" gains more speed than the other, then the tendency will be for the wheels to pull apart. This happens, for example, when one wheel drops off a cliff, and the other one has not yet reached the edge. In this case the chassis of the vehicle is responsible for keeping the wheels a fixed distance from each other. It will pull both wheels back toward each other along the angle of its rotation. This will have the end (and desirable) result of causing this precariously balanced vehicle to slowly fall off the edge of the cliff, as would happen in real life. Figure 14.9 shows this happening.

FIGURE 14.8 The position of the chassis relative to the wheels.

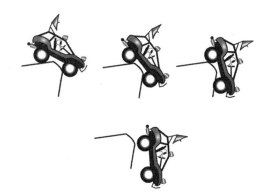

FIGURE 14.9 The wheels want to move apart as one starts to fall and the other doesn't. The chassis holds them together so the entire vehicle falls off the edge.

So, each wheel is responsible for independently moving itself, while the chassis keeps it all together. The nice thing about these physics is that they're very simple and straightforward to implement, with a relatively small amount of code required to handle them, and this code works for all cases of regular terrain consisting of hills, bumps, ramps, and canyons. This means that if you position the vehicle on a slight incline, it will gradually roll down that incline, picking up speed as it goes. If it reaches the bottom and there's a hill on the other side, it will start rolling up that hill until it loses speed and rolls back down. This will repeat until the vehicle comes to rest in between the two hills.

Challenge

With this game, we try to strike the right balance of ease and challenge—of playability and difficulty. This means that, for the most part, we can drive along the surface of Mars by simply holding down the arrow key and watching the physics engine perform. Occasionally, however, we reach a jump that just doesn't quite allow us to clear a canyon without using the jump button. Or perhaps, we find a jump that takes us high into the air but brings us down right next to a boulder, which we then crash into and bounce off of, and then roll backward down a hill and into a canyon.

We can never quite predict what a level will hold, because the computer randomly generates each level at runtime. That's right, there is no level design associated with this game, only a series of formulas used to create the terrain and place objects including boulders, bones, water drops, and the finish line.

This means that each time we play the game, we're presented with a unique set of challenges and we never know what we'll get.

As the game progresses and we collect more and more water droplets, the background image will gradually change color from Mars-like to Earth-like. The distant background image (the mountains and sky) will be stationary, while the foreground terrain scrolls beneath the vehicle. This is known as parallax scrolling, and it creates the illusion of great depth and distance between the foreground and the background.

Sound

The final aspect of this game is the sound. We have music and sound effects for all elements in the game. The events that have specific sound effects are:

- General sound of engine idling.
- Motor revving sound when vehicle pulls away or changes direction.
- "Boing" sound when vehicle jumps.
- Falling whistle sound when vehicle falls into a canyon.
- Smash/crash sound when vehicle hits a boulder or other solid object.
- Fast country music. This music is a hoedown style of country music and is meant to create a familiar tie between Earth pickup-truck races through the dirt.

ELEMENTS OF THE GAME

This is our biggest and most complex game so far. As a result, we're going to focus less on the piece-by-piece building of the graphics and objects and instead open our source FLA file and go through it, understand the different elements, and then look at the code in detail.

ON THE CD

In Macromedia Flash Professional 8 open up the marsracer.fla source file from the Chapter 14 folder on the CD-ROM. The stage should look something like what's in Figure 14.10.

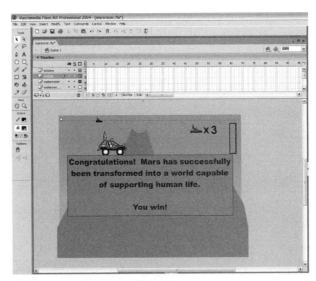

FIGURE 14.10   The stage of Mars Racer.

From the very bottom layer up, let's look at the individual graphics and movie clips that make up this game. All the layers can be seen in Figure 14.11.

FIGURE 14.11   The layers of Mars Racer.

The Sky

The bottom layer of our movie's stage contains a single movie clip called back-groundSky, which has an instance name sky (see Figure 14.12). This movie clip serves two distinct purposes:

- To provide a static background image to the foreground action while the game is being played.
- To have a color transform applied to it over time, as the player collects more water. Gradually, the color transform will take the brown mountains and pink sky and transform it into gray mountains with blue sky.

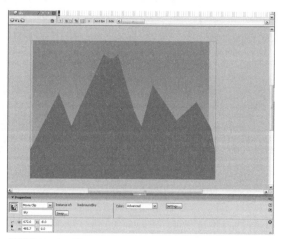

FIGURE 14.12   The sky movie clip.

The movie clip consists of two layers: a background gradient for the sky and a vector shape for the mountains. This background remains motionless while the action passes in front of it, creating the parallax effect mentioned earlier. This makes the mountains truly look far away.

The Ground

The next layer up, above the background sky, is the ground. This is the terrain upon which the player will be driving. We mentioned earlier that the terrain is generated randomly at runtime, and because of this, the ground movie clip is empty on this layer. We simply have an instance of the empty movie clip, ground; its instance name is also ground. When we say that this movie clip is empty, it means we have created a new movie clip, placed it on the stage, but have drawn nothing inside it.

The position of this initial movie clip does not matter, but in our file, it's sitting in the upper-left corner of the stage. When the game runs, the terrain is generated *inside* this movie clip as a series of lines and curves using the Macromedia Flash Professional 8 draw API. More on that when we get to the code.

The Wheels

On this layer we have two instances of the wheel movie clip, with the instance names wheel0 and wheel1. The wheel movie clip consists of two elements: the tire and the suspension strut. The strut is simply a black line that is behind the wheel and has entwined around it a red zig-zag line. The red line is meant to be the spring that is wrapped around the strut. The wheels on the stage (800% magnification) can be seen in Figure 14.13.

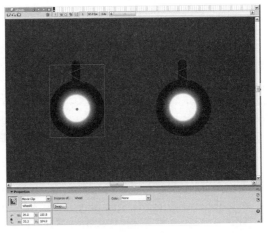

FIGURE 14.13   The wheel movie clips on stage.

Initially, these wheels are oriented so that the suspension struts point straight up. When the game is playing, the wheels will be rotated so that the struts always point up into the chassis of the vehicle. When the wheels extend, this will cause the struts to appear connected to the vehicle's axle.

The Chassis

The chassis, or body of the car, is on the next layer above the wheels. The chassis can be seen in Figure 14.14 and is meant to, on the whole, resemble a dune buggy or some other sort of off-road vehicle we would find on Earth.

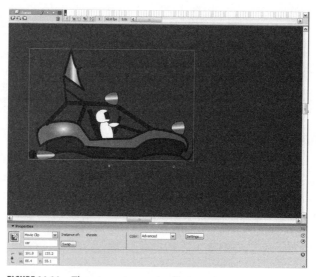

FIGURE 14.14   The chassis movie clip on stage.

The chassis on stage is an instance of the movie clip called chassis, and the instance name is car. Graphically, the contents of the chassis are nonfunctional and are merely meant to give the vehicle its look. They could be changed completely, and the game would still work. The graphics that make up the chassis are as follows:

- The body and metal roll cage.
- Lights on the front and top of the body.
- A super satellite/water scooper 2000 mounted on top of the roll cage.
- A muffler at the bottom rear of the body.
- A smoke animation that plays continuously at the back of the muffler. This smoke animation is simply a black ball that moves back and up and fades to 0% alpha. This animation is a movie clip inside the chassis movie clip, and the smoke animation is *not* on the timeline of the chassis itself.

- A driver in a space suit, seated at the steering wheel. This is our hero—who we are pretending to be.

The Miniature Cars

On the next layer are two instances of the `chassis` movie clip and one full stage-width horizontal red line, as shown in Figure 14.15.

FIGURE 14.15   The two mini cars and red line.

One of the cars has an instance name `minicar` and is an instance of a movie clip named `minicar`. The `chassis` movie clip is contained *within* `minicar`.

The other car has no instance name and is an instance *of* the `chassis` movie clip. They serve two completely different purposes:

The `minicar` instance: The `minicar` movie clip is moved along the red line on screen based upon how far along the level the player has progressed. This is used as a progress meter to see how far it is until the end of the level. Inside `minicar` the `chassis` movie clip has had a color transform applied to it, making it completely black.

The other instance: This instance is larger and is at the right side of the screen. It has no instance name. It is simply placed next to the score to indicate lives remaining, like in Figure 14.16.

The Water Meter

The next two levels are used to make up the water meter. This meter is simply a blue box inside a black box. The blue box gradually increases in height as the player collects water droplets, until the black box is completely filled and the game is won.

FIGURE 14.16   The lives-remaining car.

The bottom layer, called `watermeterBack`, is the black box that is the container for the blue box on the next layer. The next layer is called `watermeter` and contains one instance of the movie clip `waterMeter`. The instance name is also `waterMeter`. The whole water meter, with both layers, can be seen in Figure 14.17.

FIGURE 14.17   The water meter.

The blue box `waterMeter` is exactly 100 pixels in height so that we can adjust its size by simply changing its `_yscale` value. The registration point of this movie clip is at the very bottom of the blue box, which ensures that as we increase its `_yscale`, it will grow from the bottom of the black box, upward. This is how we create the illusion of the water meter filling up.

The Score Text

The next layer up contains the text used to display the score. The text consists of two pieces: a broken-apart "x" graphic, which means "multiplied-by," and a dynamic text field with the instance name `lives_txt`. This can be seen in Figure 14.18.

The dynamic text field `lives_txt` is always updated to display the number of lives the player has remaining. In the game, the "x" appears next to the smaller instance of the chassis, which ultimately communicates to the player that he has a certain number of lives left.

The End Clip

The next layer contains a movie clip that consists of two frames. Frame 1 contains the message:

```
Congratulations! Mars has successfully
been transformed into a world capable
of supporting human life.

You win!
```

Frame 2 contains the text:

```
Game Over
```

The movie clip is named `endClip` and has an instance name of `endClip`. It is centered on the stage and is only brought into play at the end of the game, either when the player loses by running out of lives or wins by completely filling the water meter and transforming Mars into a life-supporting planet. The `endClip` movie clip appears as in Figure 14.19.

FIGURE 14.18   The score text.

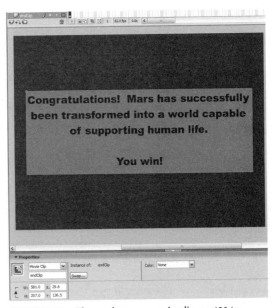

FIGURE 14.19   The end game movie clip, `endClip`.

The Actions Layer

The top layer in this movie is the layer called Actions. This is the layer upon which we will be entering all of our Actionscript. We won't go into any further detail on this until the section on code.

The Sounds

That's it for movie clips on stage. Next we have several sounds, which are embedded in the library and set up for linkage with linkage names (see Chapter 6 for more information on importing and setting up sounds and linkages).

The sounds we're using are set up with different compression settings to best take advantage of the type of sound, and they're linked with the following names:

enginerev: The sound played when the user accelerates from a stationary position or changes direction. Compressed ADPCM, 11 kHz, 2 bit. This is a low-pitched, hoarse sound so it doesn't require much detail to be maintained.

engineloop: The general sound of the vehicle's engine running. Plays constantly. Compressed ADPCM, 22 kHz, 2 bit. This is also low pitched and doesn't have much detail. Less detail means we can user a lower bit level.

bounce: The sound made when the user presses the jump button and the vehicle is able to jump (at least one wheel being on the ground). ADPCM, 22 kHz, 4 bit. Higher pitched, more detail.

fall: The sound made when the vehicle falls into a canyon and a life is lost. ADPCM, 22 kHz, 3 bit.

crash: The sound made when the vehicle hits a straight vertical object like a boulder or a cliff face. ADPCM, 22 kHz, 2 bit.

song: This sound is a music loop called song.wav found in the Chapter 14 folder on the CD-ROM. It's a country hoedown type of song with banjo, guitar, bass, and drums. MP3, 48 kbps. As this is longer, and it's music, it lends itself better to MP3 compression.

ON THE CD

At runtime we create several sound objects and attach to them these linked sounds.

Embedded Movie Clips

There are two movie clips embedded in the library that aren't on the stage at design time. These are the movie clips used to create water droplets on the terrain and obstacles such as boulders and bones on the terrain.

The water droplet is a one-frame movie clip called waterDrop, with the linkage name waterDrop. It simply consists of an upside-down teardrop shape, meant to represent the frozen water and is placed throughout the terrain when the terrain is rendered.

The boulders and bones are part of a six-frame movie clip called trackObjects, with the linkage name trackObjects. Each frame contains a different obstacle, from boulders, to large bones, to a Finish sign, placed at the end of each level.

That's all of the objects used to create this game. All that we have left to look at now is the code.

CODE FOR THE GAME

The code for this game is ultimately the heart of the experience. The code is broken down into several sections:

- Random level generator function
- Vehicle control function: wheels
- Main game loop function
- Color initialization and control function (for background image morph)
- Vehicle control function: chassis
- Sound definitions
- Game start

There are also several other support functions such as a score display updater and a key handler. We'll be looking at the code in the order that it appears in the game, from top to bottom.

makeRandomTerrain

The first function we're going to look at is the makeRandomTerrain function. This is responsible for using the draw API to create a random terrain surface over which the player will drive the vehicle. This function places objects such as boulders and monster bones, as well as water drops and the finish line. Here's the code:

```
ground.cacheAsBitmap = true;

makeRandomTerrain = function()
{
    var basey = 250;
    var x = 0;
    var ang = 0;
    var hei = basey - 220;
    var pit = 0;
    var lastpit = 0;
    var boulderCount = 0;
```

At the top we use the cacheAsBitmap flag to tell Flash to use a bitmap cache of our background world. This will take advantage of the new bitmap strengths of Flash 8 and will make things run significantly faster. After that, is the initialization of the function:

- The basey variable is used to define the baseline upon which the terrain is built. This ends up being near the very bottom of the screen. This is the lowest point that the terrain will drop to, with the exception of canyons, which drop completely off screen.

- The x variable is used to keep track of where we are in our drawing.
- The ang variable is used to keep track of the current angle of the hill. This angle is used to create the up and down motions of the hills.
- The hei variable is a maximum height for the terrain. This is near the top of the screen.
- The pit variable is used as a counter to keep track of the creation of pits, or canyons. This variable is used to define how wide a particular pit will be.
- lastpit is used in the same operation. This variable will be used to ensure that pits don't appear to close together.
- boulderCount is used in the creation of boulders and bones. It's used as a counter to create the movie clips, and it's incremented when a new item is placed on the map.

Next, we have:

```
ground.clear();
ground.moveTo(0,basey);
ground.beginFill(0x915039);

ground.createEmptyMovieClip("objs", 1);

_root.waterMC.removeMovieClip();
_root.createEmptyMovieClip("waterMC",
                          _root.getNextHighestDepth());
waterMC._y = 295;

var steps = 0;
```

This clears anything created with the draw API in the ground movie clip, and then it moves the position of the drawing cursor to 0 horizontally (farthest left point on the level) and at the base of the map as defined by basey. We then call the beginFill method of the draw API, which tells the draw API that anything we draw from now forward should be used to define a solid shape until the endFill method is called later on. We're not using the draw API's lineStyle method because, in the interest of optimization, our terrain has no outlines—only solid color.

After this, we create an instance of a movie clip called objs inside the ground movie clip. We also create a new instance of a movie clip called waterMC, on the _root timeline, using the getNextHighestDepth function to determine the next highest unoccupied depth layer. We then set the vertical (_y) position of this empty movie clip to 295. This is the base of where we will want the terrain to be placed (to come later), and we want this to be lined up with the terrain, so we must place it at 295 (where the terrain will be placed later). We're creating a new waterMC movie clip outside of ground because we want to use waterMC for some hitTesting later on.

The last line of code sets up a counter called steps, whose function we'll see shortly. Next, we have:

```
while (x < 15100)
{
    var wid = Math.random() * 100 + 50;

    hei += Math.sin(ang) * wid;
    ang += (Math.random() * 2) - 1;
```

This is the start of a large loop within `makeRandomTerrain`, which is responsible for creating the physical terrain. Our levels have a maximum width of 15,100 pixels. The levels are created through a series of segments, each attached to the next. A segment can be between 50 and 150 pixels wide. Look at Figure 14.20 to see how the segments are placed next to each other. The figure shows how the `wid` variable is used to create segments of varying width. Notice that some segments are straight, while others are curved. This is handled by the rendering engine.

Each segment can be at any angle. Figure 14.21 shows how the angle is used to create the slopes. A segment with an angle of 45 degrees, and a `wid` of 50 means it's sloping down at 45 degrees and is 50 pixels wide and `Math.sin(ang) * wid` pixels high, which is about 35 pixels in our example. In Figure 14.21 we can see how the `ang` variable is used to create the slopes. We use a series of angles, rather than just random x and y values because we want the hills to follow natural hill-like curves, which tend to flow up and down.

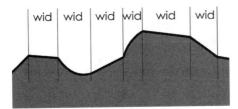

FIGURE 14.20   Terrain generation 1: the `wid` variable.

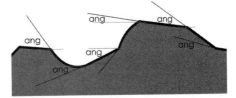

FIGURE 14.21   Terrain generation 2: the `ang` variable.

Once we have calculated this width and stored it in `wid`, we modify the `hei` variable based on that width, multiplied by the `Math.sin` value of the angle of the hill. This uses straightforward radial motion, which we looked at in the previous chapter. After this segment has been created, we modify the `ang` variable by increasing or decreasing it by up to 1 or –1. This means that anything between 0 and 1 will increase the angle (slope further down), and anything between 0 and –1 will decrease the angle (slope further up). This causes the hills to gradually rise and fall.

Next we have:

```
if (pit > 0)
{
    hei = basey + 300;
    pit--;
```

```
}
else if (hei < -100)
{
    hei = -100;
    ang = .1;
}
else if (hei > basey - 100)
{
    hei = basey - 100;
    ang = -.1;
}
```

This is responsible for controlling the vertical endpoint of the current segment. First, if `pit > 0`, that means we're drawing a pit, so always make the height 300 off the bottom of the screen, which is out of sight enough to create the appearance of a canyon or pit. The `pit` variable, when greater than 0, will be decremented each iteration with the `pit--` line of code. This means that when a pit commences, the `pit` variable is set to a random number between 2 and 5, and this determines how wide the pit will be.

Otherwise, in the second `if` statement, if the `hei` value has somehow surpassed –100, then we set it back to –100 and change `ang` to 0.1. When the `hei` variable is less than –100, the current segment is too high (heading off the top of the screen), so we force it to halt its ascent and change its `ang` to 0.1, which will make it be angled down slightly. This has the effect of creating bumpy plateaus at the top of the screen from time to time that give the player a moment to drive without worry. Figure 14.22 shows this high plateau.

Conversely, the third `if` statement checks to see if the hill has reached the ground level and follows the same simple rules, stopping the descent of the hill and giving the new hill a slightly upward slope. Figure 14.23 shows how this bumpy plateau is created at the bottom of the screen.

FIGURE 14.22   Bumpy plateau at `hei` of –100.

FIGURE 14.23   Bumpy plateau at `hei` of basey –100.

It may seem that some of these numbers (−100, `basey − 100, waterMC._y = 295`) are fairly arbitrary and nonintuitive. Most of these have been arrived at through trial and error; see what looks good and natural on screen and you're seeing the end results of several hours of tweaking.

The next section of code we have is as follows:

```
if (lastpit > 0) lastpit--;

if (Math.random() < 0.033 && pit == 0 && x > 700
    && lastpit == 0)
{
    // begin a pit
    pit = Math.floor(Math.random() * 3) + 3;
    lastpit = pit + 5;

    // Create a small ramp
    hei = ohei - 40;
}
```

This code is responsible for the generation of pits, or canyons. The first thing we do is decrement the `lastpit` variable if it's greater than 0. This variable is set when a pit is created and is used to ensure that there is an "island" of at least 5 segments between two pits.

If `Math.random` is less than 0.66 (a 1 in 30 chance), `pit == 0` (currently not in the middle of drawing a pit), `x > 700` (we don't want to draw a pit for at least 700 pixels from the start of the level, giving the player a chance to gain speed) and `lastpit == 0` (we haven't *just* finished drawing a pit), then we will start drawing a new pit. The first thing we do is set the pit variable to a number between 3 and 5, calculated as a random number between 0, 1, or 2, with 3 added at the end, meaning each pit can be either 3, 4, or 5 segments wide. Remember, however, that the segments themselves are of a variable and random width, so overall, pits can have a wide range of widths.

We then set the `lastpit` variable to `pit + 5`. Since `lastpit` and `pit` will be decremented each frame, and `lastpit` must be 0 for a new pit to commence, there will always be a buffer of five segments during which no pit can be created after the last one is finished drawing.

Finally, we use `hei = ohei -40` to create a small ramp at the beginning of each pit. This ramp will have a height of 40 pixels and can be used by the player to get just a little bit of extra jump going into a canyon.

The next code we have is:

```
// Choose between a flat ground segment or a
// curved segment
if (Math.random() > .5)
{
    x+=wid;
    ground.lineTo(x, hei);
}
```

```
else
{
    ground.curveTo(x + wid / 2, hei + (ang * 10),
                   x + wid, hei);
    x += wid;
}
```

This code is responsible for drawing our segment line. First, we randomly choose 50/50 between drawing a straight line and drawing a curved line. The only difference between the two lines is ultimately the way the vehicle drives over them. The `lineTo` method takes two parameters: an x and a y location. A straight line is simply drawn from the current line position, to (x, hei). This is done after x is incremented by `wid`. Remember, since we have no `lineStyle` defined, we're not actually drawing anything at this point. We're merely defining edges of a solid shape (the whole terrain) that will not appear until we end off with `endFill` later.

The other side of our random outcome draws our line as a curve using `curveTo`, rather than a straight edge. The `curveTo` function takes four parameters: `controlx`, `controly`, x and y. The x and y variables tell the draw API where you want the line to end up, but the `controlx` and `controly` position acts like a magnet that pulls the line toward it as it draws. The effect is a line with a bulge, or curve, in it. In our case, the `controlx` is at x + wid / 2, which is the x position exactly halfway along the current segment.

The `controly` value is a little less logical and a little more trial and error. This takes the `hei` variable and adds to it the value of ang * 10. Since `ang` will be a positive number on the way down and a negative number on the way up, the curves bulge upward on the uphill swing and curve downward on the downhill swing.

We increment x *after* the call to `curveTo` because in the call to `curveTo` we're calculating by adding `wid` to x during the calculation.

Look at Figure 14.24. Notice that on the left side of the hill (ang <0) the curved segments bulge upward, but on the right side of the hill (ang >0) the curved segments bulge downward. This may not necessarily be a realistic situation, but it's a nice rule that the terrain renderer can follow to create some varied surfaces.

FIGURE 14.24   The curved terrain segments.

Now on to the following code:

```
if (Math.random() < .1 && ang > -.1 &&
    x > 500 && x < 14000)
{
    var nm = "bldr" + boulderCount;
    ground.objs.attachMovie("trackObjects",
                            nm, boulderCount);
    ground.objs[nm]._x = x;
    ground.objs[nm]._y = hei + 10;
    ground.objs[nm].gotoAndStop(Math.floor(Math.random()
                            * 4) + 1);
    boulderCount++;
}

if ((steps % 25) == 20)
{
    var nm = "drop" + waterMC.getNextHighestDepth();
    waterMC.attachMovie("waterDrop", nm,
                        waterMC.getNextHighestDepth());
    waterMC[nm]._x = x;
    waterMC[nm]._y = hei + 2;
}
```

This code is responsible for creating boulders and bones and water droplets throughout the level. The first `if` statement creates boulders and bones. First we have a random statement that is used to check if `Math.random` is less than 0.1—a 1 in 10 chance. We also check to see if `ang > -.1` because we don't want objects to be created on a very steep upward hill; this is impossible to jump over. Finally we make sure that `x > 500` and `x < 14000` so that there will be no objects created at the far left edge of the map or the far right edge. If all of these conditions are satisfied, we create the object.

Each object is given the instance name bldr plus a number. This number represents the current counter of the objects. So, the first object will be `bldr0`, the next will be `bldr1`, and so on. We then attach to `grounds.objs` an instance of the `trackObjects` movie clip from the library, with that new instance name. We set the new object's _x position to the x position of our current segment, and then we set its _y position to the y position of the current segment, plus 10 (`hei + 10`). Finally, the new movie clip is told to go to a random frame between 1, 2, 3, or 4. This will cause one of four different objects to be placed on the terrain.

The second `if` statement is responsible for creating the water drops, which are spread evenly throughout each level. The `if` statement itself ensures that a water droplet will be placed every 25 segments, with `if ((steps % 25) == 20)`. This means the first water drop will be placed at segment 20, and then drops will be placed every 25 segments beyond that, using the modulus operator. If so, we create a new water drop inside the `waterMC` movie clip that we created on `ground` earlier. The drops are named `drop0`, `drop1`, `drop2`, and so on, and an instance of the `waterDrop` movie clip is placed on the terrain with each instance.

The new water drop is placed similarly to the boulder objects, but we don't need to issue a gotoAndStop, because the water drop is only one frame in length. We're also placing its _y position at hei + 2 so that it's always just above the terrain.

We're almost done our loop iterator. We have just a few more lines of code:

```
    steps++;
    ohei = hei;
}
```

We increment the steps variable to keep track of how many segments we've drawn so far, and then we set the value of the ohei variable to hei. This can be thought of as the old height—the height of the last segment. This was used in the computation to draw the small ramp before the pit.

That's the end of the main terrain renderer loop, but we're not finished drawing our terrain just yet. We still need to close off our fill with endFill and do a few other small things. Look at the following code, which comes next:

```
    var nm = "finisher";
    ground.objs.attachMovie("trackObjects", nm, boulderCount);
    ground.objs[nm]._x = x - 600;
    ground.objs[nm]._y = hei + 10;
    ground.objs[nm].gotoAndStop(6);

    ground.lineTo(x, basey + 400);
    ground.lineTo(0, basey + 400);
    ground.endFill();

    lastGet = 0;
}
```

The first thing we do here is similar to the way the other trackObjects were created: create an instance of the trackObject and call it finisher. This is the finishing line of the level, and it's placed 600 pixels before the very last x position of terrain—the edge of the map. We then tell finisher to gotoAndStop frame 6, which is the frame with the finish line, like in Figure 14.25.

FIGURE 14.25 The finisher object.

Next, we draw a line from the end of the last segment down to 400 pixels below the ground and then all the way back to the beginning of the map, 400 pixels down as well. This creates the right edge and bottom of the solid terrain object. Once we've brought the drawing cursor back to this point, we simply have to call ground.endFill, and our terrain will be complete and solid.

The last thing we do is set the lastGet variable to 0. This will be seen later, but this essentially is used to keep track of the last water droplet you picked up.

That's it for the makeRandomTerrain function. Here it is in its entirety for review.

```
makeRandomTerrain = function()
{
    var basey = 250;
    var x = 0;
    var ang = 0;
    var hei = basey - 220;
    var pit = 0;
    var lastpit = 0;
    var boulderCount = 0;

    ground.clear();
    ground.moveTo(x,basey);
    ground.beginFill(0x915039);

    ground.createEmptyMovieClip("objs", 1);

    _root.waterMC.removeMovieClip();
    _root.createEmptyMovieClip("waterMC",
                            _root.getNextHighestDepth());
    waterMC._y = 295;

    var steps = 0;

    while (x < 15100)
    {
        var wid = Math.random() * 100 + 50;

        hei += Math.sin(ang) * wid;
        ang += (Math.random() * 2) - 1;

        if (pit > 0)
        {
            hei = basey + 300;
            pit--;
        }
        else if (hei < -100)
        {
            hei = -100;
            ang = .1;
        }
        else if (hei > basey - 100)
        {
```

```
    hei = basey - 100;
    ang = -.1;
}

if (lastpit > 0) lastpit--;

if (Math.random() < 0.033 && pit == 0 && x > 700
    && lastpit == 0)
{
    // begin a pit
    pit = Math.floor(Math.random() * 3) + 3;
    lastpit = pit + 5;

    // Create a small ramp
    hei = ohei - 40;
}

// Choose between a flat ground segment or a
// curved segment
if (random(10) > 5)
{
    x+=wid;
    ground.lineTo(x, hei);
}
else
{
    ground.curveTo(x + wid / 2, hei + (ang * 10),
                   x + wid, hei);
    x += wid;
}

if (Math.random() < .1 && ang > -.1 && x > 500
    && x < 14000)
{
    var nm = "bldr" + boulderCount;
    ground.objs.attachMovie("trackObjects",
                            nm, boulderCount);
    ground.objs[nm]._x = x;
    ground.objs[nm]._y = hei + 10;
    ground.objs[nm].gotoAndStop(Math.floor(Math.random()
                               * 4) + 1);
    boulderCount++;
}

if ((steps % 25) == 20)
{
    var nm = "drop" + waterMC.getNextHighestDepth();
    waterMC.attachMovie("waterDrop", nm,
                        waterMC.getNextHighestDepth());
    waterMC[nm]._x = x;
    waterMC[nm]._y = hei + 2;
}
```

```
        steps++;
        ohei = hei;
    }

    var nm = "finisher";
    ground.objs.attachMovie("trackObjects", nm, boulderCount);
    ground.objs[nm]._x = x - 600;
    ground.objs[nm]._y = hei + 10;
    ground.objs[nm].gotoAndStop(6);

    ground.lineTo(x, basey + 400);
    ground.lineTo(0, basey + 400);
    ground.endFill();

    lastGet = 0;
}
```

showLives

The next function is a very short and simple function; responsible for displaying on screen the number of lives the player has.

```
function showlives()
{
lives_txt.text = lives;
}
```

When showlives is called, the value of the lives variable will be displayed in the lives_txt text field.

wheelControl

The wheelControl function is responsible for moving the wheels along the terrain and controlling their general physics and collision. The wheelControl function is used twice, assigned to each wheel's onEnterFrame event. Let's begin looking at the code.

```
function wheelControl()
{
```

First we define the function. Simple enough.

```
    this._y += this.dy;
    accelerating = false;
```

Immediately, we're applying the vertical motion to the wheel, by moving its _y along by its dy value, which could be negative (moving up) or positive (falling down). The value of dy is set by a number of things, which we'll be seeing. The accelerating variable is a flag used to determine whether or not the player is pressing the arrow keys and thus accelerating the vehicle in any one direction. We'll be looking at this soon.

Next, we have:

```
if (Key.isDown(Key.RIGHT) && oneOnGround)
{
    this.dx += 0.3;
    mydir = 1;
    accelerating = true;
}
if (Key.isDown(Key.LEFT) && oneOnGround)
{
    this.dx -= 0.3;
    mydir = -1;
    accelerating = true;
}
```

This code is responsible for accepting the user input. First we check to see if the player is pressing the right arrow key. If so, and if at least one wheel is on the ground (oneOnGround, which we'll be looking at later), we increase the wheel's dx by 0.3, set the value of the mydir variable to 1, and set the value of the accelerating variable to true. By increasing dx, rather than simply moving _x, we create a motion by which the vehicle gradually speeds up from being motionless.

Alternatively, if the player is pressing the left arrow key, we do things very similarly, but we decrease dx by 0.3 and set mydir to –1. The variable mydir is used later for a few different things, including determining which way to flip the graphic of the chassis to indicate vehicle direction. This code is followed by:

```
if (accelerating && Math.abs(this.dx) < 2)
{
    enginerev.start(0,0);
}
```

This is how we create the initial sound of the engine revving (as opposed to the constant sound of the engine idling). If the player is accelerating by pressing a directional key, we can assume his "foot is on the gas." Also, if the value of dx is less than 2, or greater than –2, we know the vehicle is most likely moving from stationary or in the process of changing direction. In either case, this is when the most pressure is on the engine to gain speed, so it's here that we choose to play the enginerev sound.

After this, we have:

```
if (oneOnGround) this.dx *= 0.98;
this.dy += 0.5;
```

This applies natural forces to the wheel. The first line applies some friction or degradation of horizontal velocity (dx) by maintaining only 98% of the velocity, as long as at least one of the wheels is touching the ground. This also means that if the player stops holding down any arrow keys, the vehicle will eventually roll to a stop.

The second line is gravity. We naturally apply a constant positive force on the dy variable, meaning that no matter what happens, the vehicle will fall back to the ground, or when touching the ground already, will stay there.

Next, we have a very important if block: the code responsible for controlling the arbitrary collision with the terrain. We begin it like so:

```
if (ground.hitTest(this._x, this._y, true))
{
```

We first check to make sure that the wheel is touching the terrain. We don't want to bother checking for collision if the wheel is not even touching the terrain. If the wheel does seem to be touching the terrain, then we need to figure out just how deep into the terrain it is.

Consider the situation in Figure 14.26. We have a single wheel moving along the terrain horizontally, and at some point the terrain begins to slope up. At this point, the horizontally moving wheel will move in front of the solid part of the terrain, or from the player's perspective, into the ground. When this happens, we have to make sure the wheel is moved *up* to the first valid position that isn't in the terrain. To do this, we must do a series of hitTest commands, starting at the current position of the wheel and moving up one pixel at a time until hitTest returns false. At this point, we have found the surface point of the terrain, and this is where the wheel must be placed. Figure 14.26 is exaggerated for illustration purposes, but this constant readjustment of the wheel's _y value, based on a line of hitTests occurs every frame, resulting in a wheel that moves like the one in Figure 14.27—smoothly over each bump.

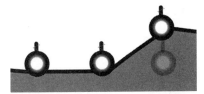

FIGURE 14.26   A single wheel moving *into* the terrain.

FIGURE 14.27   The wheel tracing the contour of the terrain.

Back to the code: when the wheel is successfully touching the ground, we start an upward climb, checking the hitTest at each position:

```
var ty = this._y;
var cnt = 0;
while (ground.hitTest(this._x, ty, true))
{
    ty--;
    cnt++;
}
```

We create a temporary variable called `ty`, which holds the current `_y` position of the wheel. We also create a temporary variable called `cnt` and set it to 0. Then, we perform a `while` loop, checking for a collision at the point (`this.x`, `ty`) on the terrain. If there is a collision, we decrease `ty` to check the next pixel up. We also increment `cnt`, because we'll need it in a few moments.

When the `while` loop finally ends, and `hitTest` fails, we'll be left with a y value in `ty` that shows us where we can safely place the wheel and a `cnt`, which will be the number of the slope that this climb consists of. On average, when we're going up small slopes, `cnt` will usually be less than 5. The purpose of `cnt` is to determine if we've got a really high climb in front of us. Usually this would happen when the wheel hits a wall. In fact, next we have this:

```
if (cnt > 70)
{
    // Hit a Wall
    wheel0.dx *= -1;
    wheel1.dx *= -1;
    ground._x -= this.dx;
    crash.start(0,0);
}
```

We've decided that 70 is the magic number. Anything 70 and below will be considered just a very, very steep hill. However, anything above 70 is considered too steep to climb and is instead treated like a wall.

When this is the case, then we say the wheel has hit a wall and we reverse the direction of *both* wheels and move the background map slightly to ensure that the wheel doesn't get "trapped" in the background (a wheel that is constantly reversing its `dy` value because this code keeps triggering). We also play the `crash` sound effect at this point.

The `else` condition to this is, of course, when the wheel has hit a slope:

```
else
{
    this._y = ty;

    if (cnt < 5) cnt = 0;
    this.dy += -cnt / 3;

    this.onGround = true;
}
```

The first thing we do is set the `_y` value of the wheel to the value of `ty`: the top of the terrain. Next, we check to see if `cnt` is less than 5. If so, we set it to 0, because we don't want it to have an effect on the next line of code: the line of code that adjusts the wheel's `dy` value based on the value of `cnt`. This gives the wheel some vertical velocity based on the amount it has climbed, the end effect being that when the wheel reaches the top of the slope, it has enough velocity to continue to climb and soar through the air. We simply increase `dy` by `-cnt / 3`.

This is a carefully arrived at number that seems to best translate into the most realistic preservation of upward momentum. Try different values here to see how it makes a difference to how the vehicle flies off the edge of ramps.

The last thing we do in this block is to set the value of the onGround flag for that wheel to true. This is used later to determine when one wheel, or both wheels, are touching the ground.

Next we have an else block for the first if statement, where ground.hitTest checked to see if the wheel was touching the ground at all. This else block is simply:

```
    }
    else
        this.onGround = false;
```

We set the value of the onGround flag to false because the wheel is not on the ground.

The final lines of code in the wheelControl function are as follows:

```
    if (this.dy > 15)
        this.dy = 15;
    if (this.dy < -15)
        this.dy = -15;
}
```

These simply apply caps to the maximum vertical speed the wheel can have. This can be thought of as terminal velocity and is necessary to prevent the vehicle from flying off screen for hundreds of feet when it gets a good launch off of a steep slope. Conversely, we don't want the wheel to fall so fast that it drives itself so deep into the ground that it goes more than 70 pixels down, causing the wall collision code to trigger (at which point the wheel would be stuck in the ground).

That's it for wheelControl below the end of the function; we do a few small things to bring it to life:

```
    wheel1.dx = 0;
    wheel1.dy = 0;
    wheel1.onEnterFrame = wheelControl;

    wheel0.dx = 0;
    wheel0.dy = 0;
    wheel0.onEnterFrame = wheelControl;

    _quality = "MEDIUM";
```

This simply sets the initial dx and dy values of both wheels to 0 (unmoving) and then sets the onEnterFrame function of both wheels to wheelControl. We set our movie _quality to "MEDIUM" here because the draw API rendering engine seems to have difficulty rendering such a large movie clip (the terrain) at high quality; it causes a rendering glitch. Take a look at Figure 14.28 to see this rendering bug when _quality is left at default—"HIGH".

FIGURE 14.28 The rendering glitch at high quality.

On its own, the wheelControl function will allow the wheels to drift apart; this is the motion of the wheels without the inversely kinematical effect of the rigid chassis holding them in place. We'll be looking at that in a little while. Here's the wheelControl function in its entirety:

```
function wheelControl()
{

    this._y += this.dy;

    accelerating = false;

    if (Key.isDown(Key.RIGHT) && oneOnGround)
    {
        this.dx += 0.3;
        mydir = 1;
        accelerating = true;
    }
    if (Key.isDown(Key.LEFT) && oneOnGround)
    {
        this.dx -= 0.3;
        mydir = -1;
        accelerating = true;
    }

    if (accelerating && Math.abs(this.dx) < 2)
    {
        enginerev.start(0,0);
    }

    if (oneOnGround) this.dx *= 0.98;
    this.dy += 0.5;

    if (ground.hitTest(this._x, this._y, true))
    {
        var ty = this._y;
        var cnt = 0;
        while (ground.hitTest(this._x, ty, true))
```

```
        {
            ty--;
            cnt++;
        }

        if (cnt > 70)
        {
            // Hit a Wall
            wheel0.dx *= -1;
            wheel1.dx *= -1;
            ground._x -= this.dx;
            crash.start(0,0);
        }
        else
        {
            if (cnt < 5) cnt = 0;
            this._y = ty;
            this.dy += -cnt / 3;
            this.onGround = true;
        }
    }
    else
        this.onGround = false;

    if (this.dy > 15)
        this.dy = 15;
    if (this.dy < -15)
        this.dy = -15;

}
ground.onEnterFrame
```

This is the code that is attached to the onEnterFrame function of the ground movie clip, which contains the terrain rendering. This handles things like player death, and the player finishing a level. We begin as usual:

```
ground.onEnterFrame = function()
{
```

The first thing we do after this is:

```
this._x -= wheel1.dx;
waterMC._x = this._x;

minicar._x = (-this._x / this._width) * 640;
```

One of the fundamental principles at work in this game is the fact that the vehicle itself doesn't move; the ground movie clip actually moves backward underneath the wheels, which are only moving up and down with the terrain. As such, here we move the terrain left by the value of wheel1.dx. Since both wheels are always moving in unison at the same dx value, we only need to use one of them as a reference. This is exactly how we create the horizontal motion associated with the wheels moving along the terrain surface. After this, we must move the waterMC to match the same location as the ground. We want the water drops, which are supposed to be on the ground, to move with the ground.

Last, we move the minicar horizontally to the position that best indicates the progress through the level. The formula (-this._x / this._width) * 640 will yield a number between 0 and 640, which is the width of the screen.

Next, we have:

```
if (this._x > 0)
{
    this._x = 0;
    wheel1.dx = 0;
    wheel0.dx = 0;
}
```

This simply stops all wheel motion and moves the ground to _x of 0 if the _x value of ground has become greater than 0. This stops the player from driving off the left edge of the map; you can't go left of the starting line.

The next code we have deals with the player falling into a canyon or pit.

```
if (wheel1._y > 600)
{

    if (lives == 0)
    {
        endClip._visible = true;
        endClip.gotoAndStop(2);
        delete wheel0.onEnterFrame;
        delete wheel1.onEnterFrame;
        delete this.onEnterFrame;
        delete car.onEnterFrame;
        return (false);
    }

    // Fall to Death in a Pit
    wheel1._y = 100;
    wheel1.dx = 0;
    wheel1.dy = 0;

    wheel0._y = 100;
    wheel0.dx = 0;
    wheel0.dy = 0;

    this._x = 0;
    fall.start(0,0);

    lives--;

    showlives();

}
```

This works very simply. If the _y value of wheel1 (and thus, the vehicle in general) has moved greater than 600, then the wheel has fallen well off the bottom of the screen and into a pit. If so, we first check to make sure that the player isn't out of lives. If he is, we show the endClip with the words Game Over, disable all of the onEnterFrame functions associated with the game, and then abort the function early with return (false).

Otherwise, we assume the player is just losing a life. In this case, we move both wheels back on screen, 100 pixels from the top of the screen, reset the dx and dy values of both wheels, and then move the terrain back to its starting position at _x of 0. We then play the fall sound effect, decrease the player's lives by one, and then update the lives display on screen by calling showLives.

Last, we have this code:

```
if (-this._x > this.objs.finisher._x)
{
    // Pass the Finish line
    wheel1._y = 100;
    wheel1.dx = 0;
    wheel1.dy = 0;

    wheel0._y = 100;
    wheel0.dx = 0;
    wheel0.dy = 0;

    this._x = 0;
    makeRandomTerrain();
}
}
```

This code is to check and see if the player has crossed the finish line by passing the _x value of the finisher movie clip. If this has happened, we move both wheels back to a _y value of 100, and set all dx and dy values to 0. We also move the terrain back to position 0 and generate a new random level by calling make-RandomTerrain. This takes the player to the next, never-before-seen level.

Here's the ground.onEnterFrame in its entirety:

```
ground.onEnterFrame = function()
{
    this._x -= wheel1.dx;
    waterMC._x = this._x;

    minicar._x = (-this._x / this._width) * 640;

    if (this._x > 0)
    {
        this._x = 0;
        wheel1.dx = 0;
        wheel0.dx = 0;
    }
```

```
if (wheel1._y > 600)
{

    if (lives == 0)
    {
        endClip._visible = true;
        endClip.gotoAndStop(2);
        delete wheel0.onEnterFrame;
        delete wheel1.onEnterFrame;
        delete this.onEnterFrame;
        delete car.onEnterFrame;
        return (false);
    }

    // Fall to Death in a Pit
    wheel1._y = 100;
    wheel1.dx = 0;
    wheel1.dy = 0;

    wheel0._y = 100;
    wheel0.dx = 0;
    wheel0.dy = 0;

    this._x = 0;
    fall.start(0,0);

    lives--;

    showlives();

}

if (-this._x > this.objs.finisher._x)
{
    // Pass the Finish line
    wheel1._y = 100;
    wheel1.dx = 0;
    wheel1.dy = 0;

    wheel0._y = 100;
    wheel0.dx = 0;
    wheel0.dy = 0;

    this._x = 0;
    makeRandomTerrain();
}
}
```

After this, but before the next function, a few initializations take place:

```
ground._x = 0;
ground._y = 295;
```

```
ground.c = new Color(ground);
ground.t = new Object();
ground.t.ra = 100;
ground.t.ga = 100;
ground.t.ba = 100;
ground.t.rb = 0;
ground.t.gb = 0;
ground.t.bb = 0;

sky.c = new Color(sky);
sky.t = new Object();
sky.t.ra = 100;
sky.t.ga = 100;
sky.t.ba = 100;
sky.t.rb = 0;
sky.t.gb = 0;
sky.t.bb = 0;
```

First, we move the ground to its proper starting position of x = 0 and y = 295. This value of 295 is a good position that ensures that the ground terrain is roughly centered vertically on screen.

After this, we create two Color objects and two color transform objects. These are used to subtly adjust the sky and ground colors as the player collects more water drops, breathing life into Mars. Initially, we declare all the color values as neutral, by setting the red, green, and blue percentages to 100 (ra, ga, and ba), and the red, green, and blue offsets to 0 (rb, gb, and bb).

For more information about the use of the Color class, refer to the integrated Actionscript dictionary included with Macromedia Flash Professional 8.

setWetLevel

This function takes a value between 0 and 1 and uses that value to adjust the color objects according to our specifications. Essentially, a value of 0 is completely dead Mars, and a value of 1 is completely transformed Mars. The function looks like so:

```
function setWetLevel(lvl)
{
    ground.t.ra = 100 - (66 * lvl);
    ground.t.gb = 66 * lvl;
    ground.t.bb = 12 * lvl;

    sky.t.ra = 100 - (66 * lvl);
    sky.t.rb = 66 * lvl;
    sky.t.gb = 56 * lvl;
    sky.t.bb = 132 * lvl;

    ground.c.setTransform(ground.t);
    sky.c.setTransform(sky.t);

    waterMeter._yscale = lvl * 100;
}
```

The numbers within the function are responsible for adjusting the transforms and therefore the colors of the sky and ground. The first thing we do is calculate the ra, gb, and bb values for the ground.t color transform object. In its final state, we want the transformed Mars to have an ra of 33 (red value in the ground is reduced by 66%), increase the green offset, gb, by 66, and increase the blue offset, bb, by 12.

For the sky, it's similar. We want ra to eventually be 33, rb to be 66, gb to be 56, and bb to be 132; we want the sky to be very blue.

We then apply these color transforms to the ground and the sky via their Color objects, contained in c, and then we update the waterMeter._yscale variable based on the water level passed in.

That's it for the setWetLevel function.

myOnKeyDown

This function is responsible for handling the pressing of the Control key to jump.

```
function myOnKeyDown()
{
    if (Key.isDown(Key.CONTROL) && oneOnGround)
    {
        bounce.start(0,0);
        if (mydir == -1)
        {
            wheel0.dy = -11;
            wheel1.dy = -10;
        }
        else
        {
            wheel0.dy = -10;
            wheel1.dy = -11;
        }
    }
}

var myListener = new Object();
myListener.onKeyDown = myOnKeyDown;
Key.addListener(myListener);
```

When the key is pressed, we first make sure that at least one wheel is on the ground by checking the oneOnGround variable (which we'll see created later). We then play the bounce sound effect and then finally check the value of mydir. If mydir is –1, then the vehicle is facing left, so we make the left wheel have a bit more jump strength than the right wheel. If mydir is 1, the vehicle is facing right, so we give the right wheel a little more jump strength. The idea is that the vehicle's front wheel jumps a little higher than its back wheel.

We then create a new listener object, myListener, and set it's onKeyDown function to myOnKeyDown. Finally, we tell the Key object to listen to our listener by calling the Key.addListener function.

We're almost there. We just have one more main function for this game to be complete.

car.onEnterFrame

This is the code attached to the chassis of the vehicle, and this is where our inverse kinematics comes in to play. We start the function like so:

```
car.onEnterFrame = function()
{
```

And then we move on to:

```
var midy = (wheel1._y + wheel0._y) / 2;

this._x = 189.1;
this._y = midy;
```

Here we're setting the _y value of the chassis to be at the point exactly half way between the two wheels. We're hard-coding the _x value to be 189.1. Since the ground moves horizontally, and the vehicle doesn't move, there is no reason to have the _x position to anything but a fixed position. This is the position at which the vehicle looks best.

Next we check for vehicle rotation:

```
var diffx = (wheel1._x - wheel0._x);
var diffy = (wheel1._y - wheel0._y);

var ang = Math.atan2(diffy, diffx);

this._rotation = 180 * (ang / Math.PI);
wheel0._rotation = this._rotation + 40;
wheel1._rotation = this._rotation - 40;
```

By looking at the difference in x and y between the two wheels, we can get values for `diffx` and `diffy`. The `Math.atan2` function works by taking two distances and determining the angle formed between them. This will give us an angle in radians. We simply have to convert that angle to degrees with `180 * (ang / Math.PI)` and set the chassis' `_rotation` to that.

We then take that `_rotation`, and set the `_rotation` of the wheels to `this._rotation + 40` and `this._rotation - 40`. This is done so that the suspension struts point up into the vehicle.

After this, we have:

```
allOnGround = wheel0.onGround & wheel1.onGround;
oneOnGround = wheel0.onGround | wheel1.onGround;
```

This creates two boolean variables: `allOnGround` and `oneOnGround`. The `allOnGround` variable will be true only if both wheels are touching the ground, and the `oneOnGround` variable will be true if either wheel is touching the ground. We're using the logical and (&) operator and the logical or (|) operator.

Next we have:

```
if (allOnGround && !accelerating && (ang < -.1 || ang > .1))
{
    // Natural roll downhill
    wheel0.dx += ang / 2;
    wheel1.dx += ang / 2;
}
```

This will cause the vehicle to roll down a hill if the player is not accelerating; all wheels are on the ground, and the angle is steep enough to cause the roll (less than −0.1 or greater than 0.1). The roll is accomplished by increasing each wheel's dx value. As the dx value increases, the physics will cause the wheels to be pulled down, and they'll appear to roll down the hill at an ever-quickening pace—just like real life.

Next, we perform the inverse kinematics on the wheels, bringing them back into the body of the chassis.

```
if (ang < -1.4) ang = -1.4;
if (ang > 1.4) ang = 1.4;

var dist = Math.sqrt((diffx * diffx) + (diffy * diffy));

if (dist > 61 || dist < 58)
{
    wheel0._x = this._x - Math.cos(ang) * 30;
    wheel0._y = this._y - Math.sin(ang) * 30;

    wheel1._x = this._x + Math.cos(ang) * 30;
    wheel1._y = this._y + Math.sin(ang) * 30;
}
```

First we check to see if the angle of the chassis is greater than 1.4 or less than −1.4. This is to stop the vehicle from going completely vertical. Next, we compute the distance between the two wheels using Math.sqrt((diffx * diffx) + (diffy * diffy)), which is the Pythagoras distance equation, where distance = $\sqrt{(a^2 + b^2)}$.

Then we check to see if dist is greater than 61 or less than 58. These are our tolerances for the wheels to move laterally, as the suspension is assumed to have some leeway. If the wheels have moved too far apart or too close together, we *move* them back to position, exactly 30 pixels on either side of the chassis' center point. We use a basic radial equation to take the sin and cos of ang (which is the angle of the chassis) and multiply them by 30 to get the new positions for the left and right wheels.

Next, we have:

```
this._xscale = mydir * 153.8;
```

This sets the _xscale of the chassis to be either 153.8 or −153.8, depending on the direction of mydir. We're not using 100 because, through trial and error, it was decided that 153.8% made the chassis seem to fit best on the wheels.

The last block of code in this function is responsible for detecting and grabbing the water drops.

```
if (waterMC.hitTest(this._x, this._y, true))
{
    for (var i = lastGet;
            i < waterMC.getNextHighestDepth();
            i++)
    {
        if (waterMC["drop" + i].hitTest(this._x,
                                        this._y, true))
        {
            waterMC["drop" + i].removeMovieClip();
            lastGet = i + 1;
            gWetLevel += 0.02;
            setWetLevel(gWetLevel);
            lives++;
            showlives();

            if (gWetLevel >= 1)
            {
                endClip._visible = true;
                endClip.gotoAndStop(1);
                delete wheel0.onEnterFrame;
                delete wheel1.onEnterFrame;
                delete ground.onEnterFrame;
                delete this.onEnterFrame;

            }

            break;
        }
    }
}
```

First we check to see if the chassis has triggered a collision with the waterMC, by seeing if the chassis' _x and _y position are touching any solid area of the waterMC. This means it's technically possible to appear to touch water without triggering the hitTest, but it's close enough. In the case of a collision, we loop through all the water drops, starting at the last one you picked up (so we don't check the beginning water drops over again), and see if that's the drop the chassis is touching.

If it is, we remove the water drop from existence with removeMovieClip, and then we set lastGet so the next check will start at the next water drop. We then increase the value of the gWetLevel variable by 0.02, and call setWetLevel with that variable. We'll be looking at the creation of gWetLevel in a moment. We then increase the player's lives by one, rewarding him with an extra life, and then we update the lives display on screen by calling showLives.

When gWetLevel has reached 1, the player has successfully collected enough water and has won the game; Mars is completely transformed. We then display the endClip and show the congratulations screen, which is frame 1. We stop all running onEnterFrames so that the game will stop running.

Finally, we have a break line, which is run when the player successfully picks up a water drop. We don't need to keep checking for collision when they've grabbed a water drop; it's not possible to grab more than one at a time because they're spaced too far apart on the map, so there's no point in looping through (and wasting processor time) all the remaining water drops.

The `car.onEnterFrame` in its entirety looks like this:

```
car.onEnterFrame = function()
{
    var midy = (wheel1._y + wheel0._y) / 2;

    this._x = 189.1;
    this._y = midy;

    var diffx = (wheel1._x - wheel0._x);
    var diffy = (wheel1._y - wheel0._y);

    var ang = Math.atan2(diffy, diffx);

    this._rotation = 180 * (ang / Math.PI);
    wheel0._rotation = this._rotation + 40;
    wheel1._rotation = this._rotation - 40;

    allOnGround = wheel0.onGround & wheel1.onGround;
    oneOnGround = wheel0.onGround | wheel1.onGround;

    if (allOnGround && !accelerating && (ang < -.1 || ang > .1))
    {
        // Natural roll downhill
        wheel0.dx += ang / 2;
        wheel1.dx += ang / 2;
    }

    if (ang < -1.4) ang = -1.4;
    if (ang > 1.4) ang = 1.4;

    var dist = Math.sqrt((diffx * diffx) + (diffy * diffy));

    if (dist > 61 || dist < 58)
    {
        wheel0._x = this._x - Math.cos(ang) * 30;
        wheel0._y = this._y - Math.sin(ang) * 30;

        wheel1._x = this._x + Math.cos(ang) * 30;
        wheel1._y = this._y + Math.sin(ang) * 30;
    }

    this._xscale = mydir * 153.8;

    if (waterMC.hitTest(this._x, this._y, true))
    {
```

```
        for (var i = lastGet;
             i < waterMC.getNextHighestDepth(); i++)
        {
                if (waterMC["drop" + i].hitTest(this._x,
                                        this._y, true))
                {
                waterMC["drop" + i].removeMovieClip();
                lastGet = i + 1;
                gWetLevel += 0.02;
                setWetLevel(gWetLevel);
                lives++;
                showlives();

                if (gWetLevel >= 1)
                {
                    endClip._visible = true;
                    endClip.gotoAndStop(1);
                    delete wheel0.onEnterFrame;
                    delete wheel1.onEnterFrame;
                    delete ground.onEnterFrame;
                    delete this.onEnterFrame;
                }

                break;
            }
        }
    }
}
```

The last few lines of code in the game are responsible for creating the sound objects:

```
mainsong = new Sound();
mainsong.attachSound("song");
mainsong.setVolume(50);
mainsong.start(0, 99999);

crash = new Sound();
crash.attachSound("crash");

fall = new Sound();
fall.attachSound("fall");

bounce = new Sound();
bounce.attachSound("bounce");

enginerev = new Sound(car);
enginerev.attachSound("enginerev");

engineloop = new Sound(car);
engineloop.attachSound("engineloop");
engineloop.start(0,99999);
engineloop.setVolume(50);
```

We create sound objects for all of our game sounds. We create the `mainsong` sound object and begin it playing and set it to loop 99,999 times, which means it will essentially play forever. The other sound effects are simple event sounds and they're defined as normal sounds.

The `engineloop` sound, which is the sound of the idling engine, is defined here and is attached to the `car` movie clip (the chassis). It too is set to loop forever, but its volume is set to 50 because we want a subtle background idle.

Finally, the last few lines of code:

```
gWetLevel = 0;
makeRandomTerrain();
setWetLevel(gWetLevel);
lives = 10;
showlives();

endClip._visible = false;
endClip.stop();
```

We initialize `gWetLevel` to 0, create a new random terrain, set the colors for the current `gWetLevel`, set the initial number of `lives` to 10 and show the lives on screen. We also hide the `endClip` and stop it from playing, as it's a two-frame animation that would continuously loop if we didn't stop it.

That's the entire game. Now that you understand how it works, run through it, play it, and watch the mayhem ensue.

SUMMARY

In this chapter we created a fun game based around a robust physics engine. We learned:

- How to apply the elements of good control and physics
- How to create a random terrain using the draw API
- How to create a physics engine that includes arbitrary collision with a movie clip surface using a strip of hitTests
- How to apply vehicular physics using independent suspension
- How to create a simple inverse kinematics effect
- How to use the `Color` object to create some interesting real-time color transition effects
- How to create a fun, exciting game that's challenging and rewarding

15

CREATING STANDALONE GAMES

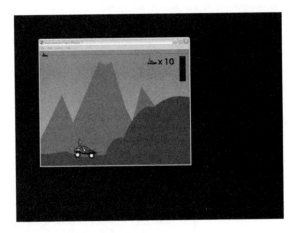

The thing that ultimately separates a "professional game" from a "Flash game" is the method by which it is delivered. Just take a look at the perception surrounding the delivery method of the two different types of game:

- Macromedia Flash Professional 8 Game:
  1. Played in a Web browser.
  2. Limited to the screen size of the browser.
  3. If played at a large screen size, will inevitably perform slowly.
  4. Must be online to download and play the game every time.
- A professional game:
  1. Played directly by clicking on a desktop shortcut or item in the system menus.
  2. Can play full-screen, covering every inch of screen real estate.
  3. Performs fast and smooth, no matter what the resolution.
  4. Can be played at any time, regardless of the state of the Internet connection.

A professional game is something that would be developed in C/C++ using one of the different types of technologies including DirectX. Ultimately, a game written using a native system platform (like DirectX) will be faster and more powerful.

Let's look at two cases in which it would be better if our Macromedia Flash Professional 8 game was a professional game and available for download.

CASE 1: FULL SCREEN

Imagine the following situation. You've just finished your best Macromedia Flash Professional 8 game of all time and you're happy with how it performs. It fits nicely inside a 640 × 480 window. You decide to play it full screen by maximizing the player window, or by pressing Ctrl-F when playing in the standalone player (which is what will happen when we double-click directly on an SWF file on a computer with the Macromedia Flash Professional 8 development environment installed).

Let's use Mars Racer from Chapter 14 as an example. Run this game by directly double-clicking on the file `marsracer.swf`, which can be found in the Chapter 15 folder on the CD-ROM. This game runs in a 640 × 480 window, by default, as shown in Figure 15.1.

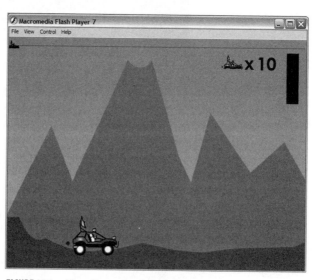

FIGURE 15.1   Mars Racer, by default in a 640 × 480 window.

As soon as you switch to full screen (by pressing Ctrl-F), weird things begin to happen. First, the draw API begins to have difficulty rendering the terrain, and glitches occur like those shown in Figure 15.2.

FIGURE 15.2   Mars Racer full screen; glitches seen in the terrain rendering, making the terrain appear inverted.

Also, the performance of the game decreases substantially. Now, we can switch to Low quality mode by right-clicking on the movie as it plays and selecting Low from the Quality menu in the pop-up menu that appears, as shown in Figure 15.3. When we do this, the terrain glitches disappear.

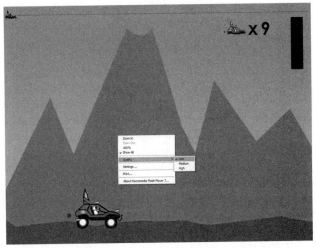

FIGURE 15.3   Mars Racer full screen; setting quality to Low.

However, unless you're using an extremely powerful computer, the game will still slow down noticeably and to the extent that the quality of the game play will be degraded.

What is causing this? Well, on a computer that has its screen resolution set at 1024 × 768, for example, maximizing the movie window, or resizing to full screen with Ctrl-F, will cause our 640 × 480 resolution game to be *rendered* at 1024 × 768. Macromedia Flash Professional 8 doesn't actually *change* the settings of the video card like a professional game would.

Let's look at the numbers. When running at 640 × 480 (which is in a small window), Macromedia Flash Professional 8 is responsible for drawing 640 × 480, or 307,200 pixels. In a 1024 × 768 screen, it looks like Figure 15.4.

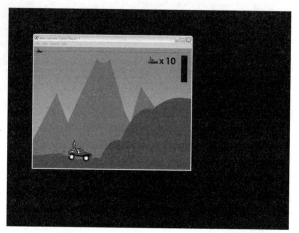

FIGURE 15.4   Mars Racer in its default window, at 640 × 480 on a 1024 × 768 screen.

As soon as we press Ctrl-F, or simply maximize the window, we cause the game to change to a window size of 1024 × 768, or 786,432 pixels total. This is an increase by a factor 2.56 times as many pixels and therefore 2.56 times as much workload. Yes, it looks nice to have the game stretch from edge to edge, but for such a nicety we have to pay a hefty price in game performance—a price that may not be possible to pay on computers that are only just able to play the game fast enough in a 640 × 480 window.

What would a professional game do differently? Well, the professional game would make use of a few C/C++ video routines and it would *change* the video card itself to 640 × 480. Imagine what happens when the actual resolution of the monitor is 640 × 480; the game will appear full-screen yet will still be smoothly using the original designed resolution, as the natural 640 × 480 *window* size will be sufficient enough to fill the *screen* from edge to edge.

We're essentially talking about performing a trick; it's like we're zooming the monitor down to the size of the Macromedia Flash Professional 8 player window, rather than physically resizing the player window by maximizing or pressing Ctrl-F.

How do we perform such a video-card-resizing feat? We'll be looking at that shortly. For now, let's look at Case 2.

CASE 2: DOWNLOAD AND INSTALL

You've created a killer game, full of animation and video, and you've deployed it on your Web site. It's an instant hit, and players flock from around the world to play it. Everything is fine, until one day you get an email from a dissatisfied player:

> Dear Author,
>
> I love your game, but I'm on a slow modem connection, and I'm wondering how I can go about downloading it and installing it on my computer, rather than playing it on the web?
>
> Thanks,
> Dedicated Fan.

This player has uncovered a vital problem in the combination of the Internet and games of a large file size; players on slow connections will need to be very, very patient every time they want to play your game. If we use asteroid3d.swf as an example of this (because the SWF file is very large, at over 2.5 Megabytes), we can see the necessity for a downloadable application.

What we ultimately need to do is create an "installer" that players can download and run from their personal computers, which will place an icon on their desktop that they can click on at any time to smoothly and cleanly run the game. How do we do this? Let's find out.

SWF Studio

Enter Northcode Inc. and their standalone Macromedia Flash Professional 8 wrapper, SWF Studio. As of this writing, the latest version that they offered was version 3.1 as seen in Figure 15.5. SWF Studio essentially takes a SWF file and wraps it in a Windows EXE (there is no Mac support at this time) that includes several hundred new functions and commands, thus extending the functionality of an SWF file 10-fold.

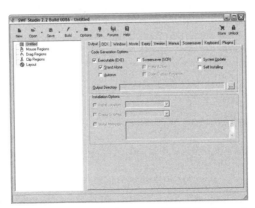

FIGURE 15.5   The default screen of SWF Studio version 3.1.

Some of the new functionality offered to Macromedia Flash Professional 8 developers is as follows:

- The ability to resize the user's screen resolution at runtime
- The ability to open several system dialog boxes including File Open and File Save
- The ability to write arbitrary data directly to the user's hard drive
- The ability to disable the right-click menu
- The ability to launch secondary applications
- The ability to play back any arbitrary video file as long as the user has the appropriate video codec installed
- The ability to confine the mouse to the bounds of the window
- Access to several pieces of system information, including the directory that the application started in, the location of the Windows system directory, and information about screen size and color depth
- Access to the user's system information including OS, processor, computer name, language information, and more
- The ability to use masks to define a window that is not restricted to rectangular shape
- A set of FTP protocols for sending and receiving files via FTP
- A complete file system including file and directory creation, deletion, and modification
- Access to the user's registry to store and retrieve any registry information or keys that might be used for application information
- A built-in email client (SMTP sender) for sending email directly from Flash without the use of an email program
- System information including Internet connection status, CPU speed, IP address, and memory size

There are many, many other features. To see a complete list, take a look at *http://www.northcode.com/V3/features.php*. The software itself must be downloaded from Northcode.com to begin with, at *http://www.northcode.com/SWF Studio/products .php*, as well as all of the plug-ins required to give the application full functionality. As of this writing, the full version was US $299, which is well worth it for all of the added functionality. This can be purchased at *http://www.northcode.com/store .php*.

EXAMPLE 1: `marsracer.exe`

Building the Project

Let's look at our first example and modify Mars Racer to allow it to run full screen, while still rendering in its base 640 × 480 window. During this development, we'll assume that you have followed the instructions at Northcode.com and have installed SWF Studio and are ready to go.

The best thing to do at this point is to copy the contents of the Chapter 15 folder on the CD-ROM to your hard drive. For the remainder of this chapter, we'll be assuming the files have been copied to `C:\CHAPTER15`*.*

The first thing to do is to define a new project in SWF Studio. Open up SWF Studio and it will begin with a new, blank project open. At the left side of the window there are several options, as shown in Figure 15.6.

FIGURE 15.6   The options at the left side of the window in SWF Studio.

At this point what we're concerned with is the option that says Layout. Select the Layout option, and you'll see the right side of the window appear as in Figure 15.7.

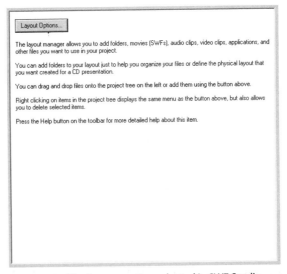

FIGURE 15.7   The Layout option selected in SWF Studio.

It is through the Layout option that we define the files that will be making up our EXE package. Click on the Layout Options button and choose the Add Movie option from the drop-down menu. In the layout at the left side of the window, there will now be a new `Movie` object added, like in Figure 15.8.

FIGURE 15.8   A new movie added to the layout.

This new movie doesn't point to any particular SWF file. We must tell it to use `marsracer.swf`, by clicking on the button with the three dots "..." next to the File text field on the right side of the screen, as shown in Figure 15.9.

FIGURE 15.9   The File button.

Clicking on the "..." button will bring up a file selection dialog box. Navigate to the `C:\CHAPTER15` folder and select `marsracer.swf`, as shown in Figure 15.10.

FIGURE 15.10   Specifying the SWF to include.

Once it is selected, click on the Open button. Now the File text field will contain the text "C:\CHAPTER15\marsracer.swf." At this point you must tell SWF Studio to use this movie as the default movie to run upon execution. In the options area at the left side of the window, click on the Untitled option (we'll be renaming this shortly) and you'll see several tabs at the right side of the window, as shown in Figure 15.11. These are how we define settings for our project.

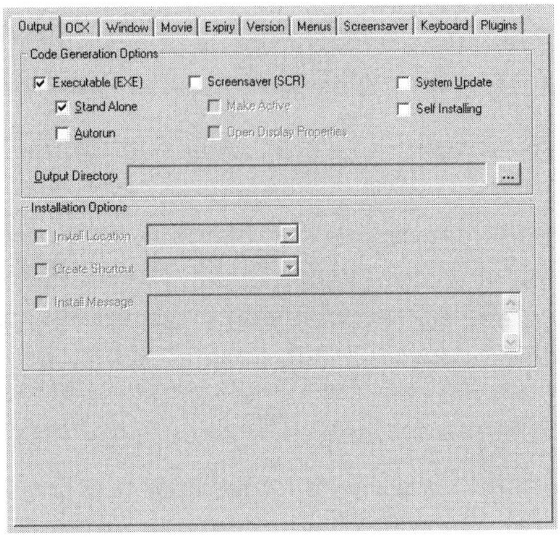

FIGURE 15.11   The Project Definition tabs.

Select the Movie tab. You'll see a drop-down menu called Main Movie at the top of the Main Movie section. From within the drop-down menu, ensure that Movie is selected, like in Figure 15.12.

FIGURE 15.12   Defining the Main Movie.

Click on the Output tab and then specify the Output Directory as C:\CHAPTER15 by clicking on the "..." button in the Code Generation Options section, as shown in Figure 15.13.

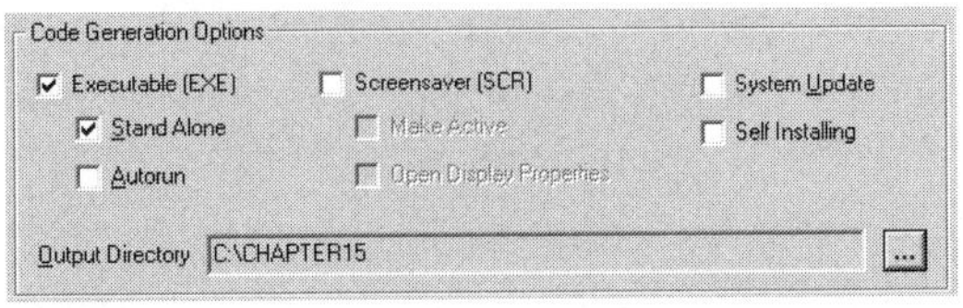

FIGURE 15.13   Specifying the Output Directory.

Finally, save the project by clicking on the Save button at the top of the window. In the Save Project As dialog box that appears, navigate to C:\CHAPTER15, name the file marsracer, and click Save, as shown in Figure 15.14.

FIGURE 15.14   Saving the project.

The name marsracer will now appear at the left side of the window, where it used to say Untitled. Click on the button that says Build, at the top of the window. SWF Studio will build the EXE file for our game. At this point, there will be a marsracer.exe file in the C:\CHAPTER15 directory.

At this point, we will want to ensure that when we make our game full-screen, there will be no window border. Click on the Window tab at the top of the SWF Studio window. Make sure your settings match those shown in Figure 15.15.

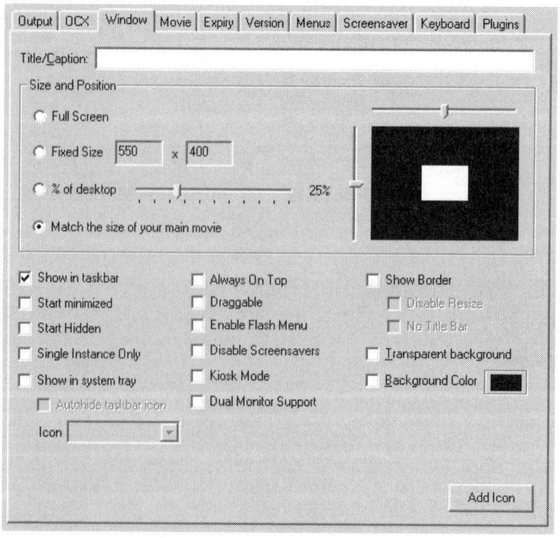

FIGURE 15.15   Setting the Window properties.

Every option should be de-selected except for the Show in Taskbar option. Build the EXE as-is and then run `marsracer.exe` from the `C:\CHAPTER15` folder, and you'll see something that looks like Figure 15.16. The game will run in a 640 × 480 window with no border, title bar, Close button, Maximize button, or Minimize button. Right-clicking on the stage will *not* display the Flash menu, and Ctrl-F will *not* cause the game to resize to full screen. Pressing Escape will cause the game to close.

FIGURE 15.16   Running the EXE file.

We're now ready to add some code to our game to change the screen resolution and bring our game to the next level.

Adding the Code

From within the `C:\CHAPTER15` directory, open the file `marsracer.fla` in Macromedia Flash Professional 8. All communication between our Actionscript code and the SWF Studio tools is accomplished through the use of the `fscommand` function. We use `fscommand` to talk to the shell that contains the SWF player. In a Web browser, `fscommand` will talk to the Web browser. With SWF Studio, however, we can use `fscommand` to pass any information to it and call its functions.

Try adding the following code to the very *end* of the code for Mars Racer. This should appear after the line `endClip.stop();`.

```
fscommand("DirectDraw.SetDisplayMode", "640, 480, 32");
fscommand("Win.SetPosition", "0,0");
```

This is *all* that is required to make our movie appear to run full screen. We're taking advantage of the DirectX functionality built into the Windows operating system. The first thing we do is set the screen resolution to 640 × 480 and 32 bits per pixel color. The next thing we do is move the game window itself to position 0, 0; the upper left corner of the screen. If we don't do this, the screen resolution *will* change, but the game will not appear to be properly positioned on screen, and we will see portions of our Windows background behind it. We must move the window to position 0, 0 to ensure that all 640 × 480 of its dimensions fill the screen perfectly.

 If you are going to use the DirectDraw functionality in a game, it's recommended that you encourage your players to download the latest DirectX drivers from Microsoft, at http://www.microsoft.com/windows/directx/downloads/default.asp.

Once this code has been entered, export the SWF by pressing Shift-F12 and then return to SWF Studio and make a new build. The file marsracer.exe should now change screen resolution and display the game full screen, even though the full screen will now be 640 × 480. The game will run noticeably faster than if you had manually converted to full screen with Ctrl-F.

Let's now look at the second project: creating a standalone EXE that includes an installable package.

EXAMPLE 2: `asteroid3d.exe`

Building the Project

This time we're going to modify asteroid3d.swf to run as a full-screen application, complete with an installer application. Initially, we set everything up almost identically to the Mars Racer EXE:

1. Import one movie: C:\CHAPTER15\asteroid3d.swf.
2. Under the Movie tab, set the Main Movie to Movie.
3. Also under the Movie tab, set the Scale mode to Stretch to Fit. We didn't do this in the Mars Racer example, because Mars Racer was exactly 640 × 480 in size. In the case of asteroid3d, the file is 550 × 400 by default.
4. Under the Output tab, set the Output Directory to C:\CHAPTER15.
5. Save the project as asteroid3d.

Adding the Code

Jump into Macromedia Flash Professional 8 and edit the asteroid3d.fla from C:\CHAPTER15 so that the following code is added to the very end:

```
fscommand("DirectDraw.SetDisplayMode", "640, 480, 32");
fscommand("Win.SetPosition", "0,0");
fscommand("Win.SetSize", "640,480");
```

As in the previous example, we're setting the screen display size to 640 × 480 and 32 bits per pixel and moving the movie to position 0, 0. We're also then resizing the window to 640 × 480, because it is designed at 550 × 400 and therefore opens up at that size to begin with.

After you've entered this code, export the SWF file by pressing Shift-F12. Return to SWF Studio and build the project. The file asteroid3d.exe will be created in the C:\CHAPTER15 folder. At this point, running it will make the game run full screen. Running `asteroid3d.swf` directly and then switching to full screen with Ctrl-F clearly shows the advantages of making these EXE files; with regular SWF full screen, the game runs so slowly that it's almost unplayable.

Make the Installer

Seeing as someone requested a downloadable application from you, it seems that the best thing to do is create an install application that places the game on the user's computer and then puts a link to it on either the desktop or the Start menu. Do the following:

1. From within SWF Studio (with the `asteroid3d` project open), switch to the Output tab and then select the Self Installing checkbox, as shown in Figure 15.17.

FIGURE 15.17   Activating the self-install.

2. Once this is activated, several other options beneath it will become editable. Edit them so that they look like the ones in Figure 15.18.

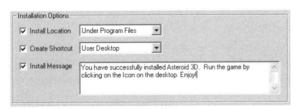

FIGURE 15.18   The self-install options.

3. Once you've done this, press the Build button. An install EXE file will be created in `C:\CHAPTER15`. This EXE will be called `asteroid3d.exe`. Running it this time, however, will not execute the game, but will execute a simple install, like in Figure 15.19.

4. Looking at the desktop, you can see that a shortcut to the application has been created, which will now be successfully installed on the user's computer, like in Figure 15.20.

FIGURE 15.19 Running the self-install.

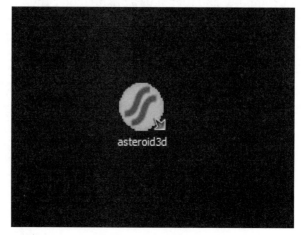

FIGURE 15.20 The shortcut to run the installed application.

5. Double-clicking on the desktop icon will run the game. That's all there is to it. We've created an application that installs on the user's hard drive and runs full screen. The user only needs to download the install EXE file.

To learn more about SWF Studio, play with it and read the help files included with the product. They cover everything from setup options and file inclusion to every function you would ever need to make use of in your games.

SUMMARY

In this chapter we looked at:

- The difference between a "professional game" and a "Flash game"
- The difference between running an SWF in the Macromedia Flash Professional 8 Flash Player and running it as a standalone EXE file
- Northcode SWF Studio as a package for creating standalone EXE files and install packages
- The interactivity and speed benefits of changing screen resolutions and modifying the game code to do so

16

PORTABLE GAMES

One of the best things about Macromedia Flash Professional 8 is its ability to create games that are cross-platform compatible. This means that they run not only on Mac and PC, but also on any system that supports the Flash Player. This presents us with the opportunity to create games that people can take with them and play on portable devices such as cell phones and PDAs.

In this chapter we're going to look at creating a game for the Pocket PC. Macromedia wisely developed the Flash Player for the Pocket PC operating system, and now any Pocket PC–powered device can be used to play our Flash games. As of this writing, however, the latest Flash Player available for Pocket PC was Flash Player 6, which means we can't take advantage of many of the new features of Flash 8, but that's okay; Flash 6 is powerful enough to create some terrific games.

In this chapter we're going to create a game that players would look at as intuitive and natural to be holding in their hand: a word search. This also means that we're going to be killing two birds with one stone in this chapter; we'll look at developing games for portable devices and we'll also look at creating a word game. This game plays equally well on both the Pocket PC and a normal desktop computer, so we can take it on the road with us or we can play it online.

DEVICE ISSUES

In general, developing for a device means we have a few limitations that we must keep in mind and some general practices that we should adhere to:

- The screen resolution on a device tends to be much lower than that of a desktop computer. On average, a large Pocket PC screen will give us about 240 × 320 pixels in resolution, compared to the *low* desktop resolution of 800 × 600.
- The CPU tends to be slower on a device. A 400-MHz Pocket PC performs about as well as a Pentium II, 266 MHz, circa late 1990s. For this reason, we have to tone back our ambitions slightly for a Pocket PC Flash game and accept that we probably won't be making full-screen motion, but rather simpler games such as word games. Mars Racer would *not* fare well on a Pocket PC.
- The amount of RAM available to a Pocket PC device compared to a desktop computer can vary greatly. On a Pocket PC we might be lucky to get 64 MB of RAM, while a modern desktop computer has a minimum of 128 MB. That doesn't sound like a huge difference until you realize that the RAM of a Pocket PC also doubles as its *storage space* for files, operating system, and, yes, our games. While a desktop computer might have hundreds of GB of hard drive space, a Pocket PC may have 16 MB available to it for files once the RAM is divided between file storage and actual *operating RAM* (the RAM used as RAM and not as file storage). For this reason, making an SWF file that contains 30 MB worth of bitmaps and sounds may be acceptable on a desktop but completely unfeasible on a device.
- The input options are substantially different on a Pocket PC and a desktop. The first, and most obvious, difference is the lack of keyboard. Don't expect to make much use of the buttons on the front of the device; most of them can't be read by Flash, and even the ones that can won't send more than one key press at a time (so you can't hold jump and run at the same time). Generally, we should design our games as if we simply have a mouse click and drag at our disposal. Even so, the drag is a risky venture because if the user's stylus leaves the screen for a fraction of a second, then the dragging is finished.

Now that our hopes of creating the next big Flash game for mobile devices are nearly crushed, let's look at things in a different light. Consider that we have access to full MP3 sound reproduction. We have a platform that performs many times better than computers of the mid-1980s, when the first computer games were coming out. We have an opportunity to get in on the ground floor of a new and growing industry with mobile gaming. We can carve niches and establish ourselves as pioneers in a world that is becoming increasingly mobile. In North America it's happening, but to truly see the potential we only need to look at markets in Asia, where mobile devices such as cell phones are practically manufactured to be bought, used, and thrown away the same day. A device with wireless Internet (WiFi) can be used to create multiplayer games or games with server connections to do things like submit high scores or chat. Imagine sitting in a café in New York, playing chess on your Pocket PC with a person who's also sitting in a café—in Paris.

We can almost think of mobile gaming as the next *it* thing—what the Internet was in the early 1990s: this big, important thing coming to us with all sorts of buzzwords and potential to change the world. And it did. All it will take is a little time, and we'll begin to see the boom of wireless devices. We're already at the point on the development curve where it starts to rise up rapidly; just look at the interest being generated by things like ring-tones, text messaging, and instant video and photos being sent to friends. Companies are investing billions of dollars in this swelling industry. Soon the devices will not just be Pocket PC *or* cell phone; they will be Pocket PC *and* cell phone (and text messenger, video camera, Dictaphone, etc.) in one device. Games are an obvious match.

THE WORD SEARCH

The word search game is a traditional word game played by young and old alike in newspapers and puzzle books. One of the things that makes a word search so enjoyable is the challenge and reward of finally finding that last word—that and the fact that it is a completely portable experience that you can sit in a comfortable chair and do on a rainy Sunday afternoon. This is why they're a natural match for the Pocket PC and all its portability.

The word search consists of a square grid of letters that can vary in size. Easier word searches have fewer letters, maybe 9 × 9, while harder word searches can be 20 × 20 in size. Figure 16.1 shows a word search (in fact, it's an image of the word search game created for this chapter).

It consists simply of the play grid, shown on the left side of the image, and the word list, which can be shown or hidden by clicking on the Wordlist button. At the right side of Figure 16.1 we can see what it looks like when the word list is turned on. The word list contains the list of words that you search for in the play grid. They're all hidden in there somewhere.

The challenge with the word search is that the words can be oriented in the grid so that they run left to right, right to left, up, or down. Figure 16.2 shows these four orientations in practice.

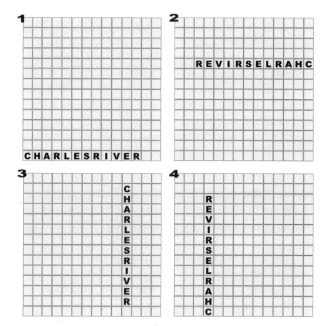

```
R B T O D C S C R I P T F C
N O J A X H T X E T N B C O
A O I S P A L T B S D Z O D
M K K E H R Y P E O E Q F E
A E A D Y L X I W N V P F M
R C U O S E F R C O E B E O
S P T H I S L C O I L Y E V
R T H R C R A S M S O T L I
A E O N S I S N P N P I S E
C K R E X V H O U E M V U C
E C U L P E M I T M E A P L
R O R G K R X T E I N R E I
R P S E G A P C R D T G R P
Z K Z G A M E A I N Q D M R
```

DX, WEB, TEXT, BOOK, GAME,
CODE, PAGES, SUPER,
SCRIPT, AUTHOR, COFFEE,
GRAVITY, FLASHMX,
COMPUTER, POCKETPC,
MOVIECLIP, MARSRACER,
DIMENSION, GLENRHODES,
DEVELOPMENT,
ACTIONSCRIPT,
CHARLESRIVER,

FIGURE 16.1   A word search, (left) with word list hidden and (right) with word list shown.

FIGURE 16.2   Four word orientations. (1) Left to right, (2)
right to left, (3) up to down, and (4) down to up.

Because of our natural inclination to read the English language from left to
right, we end up spotting words that are oriented left to right pretty quickly, but
the other orientations are difficult for us to spot. In some word searches, words
can also be placed diagonally, but in our Flash word search, we're not going to be
doing that. It makes the already-complex placement algorithm very messy, and
that difference would make it unplayable on a Pocket PC (it would take several

minutes to come up with a board that included all the words). Already we can see a limitation introduced by the development environment, but does that stop us? No. We just modify our design to include four basic orientations.

Once all of the search words have been placed in the grid, the remaining empty spaces are filled with random letters in the typical word search to make sure finding the words is challenging. The game algorithm works by placing the words, one at a time, in the grid, until all words have been placed. This can be a time-consuming process, as the algorithm is based on a random procedure whereby the computer will *try* different positions until it finds one that works. This is a bit of a brute force method, but in the Pocket PC, we don't have CPU time for elegant, university-computer-science-textbook-worthy solutions. This means Flash may try to place a word several hundred times before it finally finds a spot. The word can be placed either in blank spaces or in spaces where some of its letters intersect equivalent letters that were already placed. The board creation algorithm works like so:

1. Choose a random x, y position to start the word being placed.
2. Choose a random direction from the four possible directions.
3. Have we already tried this spot and orientation? If so, return to step 1.
4. Does the word flow off of the edge of the board? If so, return to step 1.
5. Check each letter to be placed against the corresponding space on the board, and see if either:
   a. The spaces are blank
   b. The space already contains the letter that we want to place
6. If the word does not fit (as it intersects letters that do not fit in the word), return to step 1.
7. Otherwise, place the word on the grid and make a note of its starting and ending positions, as well as all the grid positions that make up the word.
8. Proceed to the next word.
9. Return to step 1.

Also, before we begin placing the words, we begin by sorting the word list by order of longest to shortest word. This is important, because we need lots of space for the longer words, and if we start off by placing the short words all over the place, we'll have very little luck finding long, consecutive blanks for placing the long words.

As we place each word, the number of attempts required to find a good spot will increase substantially. It's possible to end up with a word that simply cannot be placed on the board. In this case, we have a limit to the number of times we'll retry a word before moving on to the next word. In our code, we've set that limit to 300. On average, the number of tries required increases as we add more words to the board. Below is a table showing the number of tries required to add each word. Notice that the beginning words required fewer tries than the later words.

NUMBER OF TRIES	WORD
7	CHARLESRIVER
8	ACTIONSCRIPT
20	DEVELOPMENT
7	GLENRHODES
2	DIMENSION
44	MARSRACER
10	MOVIECLIP
8	POCKETPC
2	COMPUTER
16	FLASHMX
7	GRAVITY
21	PHYSICS
70	COMPILE
2	COFFEE
4	AUTHOR
9	SCRIPT
25	EXPORT
58	BOUNCE
111	SUPER
81	CLICK
78	PAGES
86	CODE
17	GAME
194	OKAY
251	BOOK
54	TEXT
300	WEB
16	DX

The algorithm had to try 251 times before it found a home for BOOK, and it failed to find a position for WEB, as evidenced by the fact that it tried all allowed 300 times.

In our code once all of the words have been placed, we go through all of the remaining blank squares, and we fill them in with random letters.

Because of the random nature of this algorithm, it will be faster or slower depending on its placement success, and sometimes not all words will be successfully placed. To compare CPU differences, the whole board took about one second to complete on a P4, 1.8 GHz, but took about 10 seconds on a 400 MHz Pocket PC. Figure 16.3 shows a photograph of the Word Search game running on a Pocket PC.

FIGURE 16.3   The game
running on a Pocket PC.

Once the board has been populated, the game is ready to be played. Play is accomplished with a very simple click operation. The first click selects a letter and highlights it in yellow. This is the starting letter of the word we want to highlight and can be seen in Figure 16.4.

The next click is on the ending letter. If we've successfully selected a real word (the starting and ending letters correspond to a valid word), then the word is highlighted in green, like in Figure 16.5, and is removed from the word list.

FIGURE 16.4   Selecting the starting letter of a word.

FIGURE 16.5   A word successfully found.

In our game we're using a fixed word list, which looks like so:

```
wordlist = new Array("ACTIONSCRIPT", "DEVELOPMENT", "COMPUTER",
                     "POCKETPC", "PHYSICS", "GRAVITY",
                     "FLASHMX", "CLICK", "AUTHOR", "BOUNCE",
                     "COFFEE", "SUPER", "BOOK", "PAGES",
                     "GAME", "OKAY", "CODE", "DX", "EXPORT",
                     "COMPILE", "CHARLESRIVER", "GLENRHODES",
                     "WEB", "MARSRACER", "DIMENSION",
                     "MOVIECLIP", "SCRIPT", "TEXT");
```

It would be logical to extend this game to include dynamically generated word lists or to grab random words from a larger list, but that's an expansion you'll have to do on your own.

DEVELOPING FOR POCKET PC

Now we've seen the basics of how our word search works. Before we get into the specifics of the code, let's look at a few important concepts involved in creating Flash games for the Pocket PC.

First, you don't have to own a Pocket PC to develop games for it, but it helps quite a bit if you do. Many brands of PDA operate on the Pocket PC operating system (as opposed to the Palm operating system, which currently does not support the Flash player).

Pocket PC 2003 (the latest version) was introduced in June 2003. It's an expansion of the original Pocket PC 2002. Both versions of the operating system support the Flash 6 player. Originally, the mobile operating system developed by Microsoft was called WinCE, but it was fraught with bugs, was difficult to use, and had a high learning curve and instability. The Pocket PC operating system reinvented the wheel, so to speak, and dramatically improved Microsoft's share of the PDA market.

A great site for looking at Pocket PC devices and for general information on the Pocket PC operating system is *pdabuyersguid.com* at *http://www.pdabuyersguide .com/ppc.htm*.

Creating a Flash game for the Pocket PC is done in exactly the same manner as creating any other Flash game. The only difference will be resolution and screen size. When we're developing for the Pocket PC, we'll be using a resolution of 240 × 268, as opposed to the standard Flash resolution of 550 × 400. The Pocket PC usually has a resolution of 240 × 320, but we have to account for on-screen elements such as the title bar, address bar (as our Flash games must be run in a browser), and the application bar at the bottom. Figure 16.6 shows how our screen resolution is taken up by operating system elements.

To create a Pocket PC application in Flash, we can make use of the built-in templates that include all sorts of devices. Before we begin looking at the code for our word search game, let's look at creating a very basic movie and running it on a Pocket PC.

FIGURE 16.6   Typical Pocket PC layout, leaving us with 240 × 268 to work with.

At this point, it's a good idea to ensure that you have the Flash player installed on your Pocket PC if you're going to be using a Pocket PC rather than just testing on a PC. To get the latest Pocket PC Flash Player (version 6), go to: http://www.macromedia.com/software/flashplayer/pocketpc/2002.html. *Make sure your Pocket PC is connected to your desktop computer and download the installer and run it (the installer is run from the desktop computer, not the Pocket PC). Follow your Pocket PC instructions for more information. For those developing on a Mac, you won't be running a Pocket PC in this manner. You can still develop the games in Flash, however.*

Developing a Simple SWF for the Pocket PC

For starters, open up Macromedia Flash Professional 8. You will be presented with the introduction screen, as shown in Figure 16.7.

FIGURE 16.7   The Macromedia Flash Professional 8 introduction screen.

Near the upper-right corner of the window, underneath the section that says Create from Template, look for the option that says PDAs, shown in Figure 16.8.

FIGURE 16.8   The Mobile Devices template option.

Click on the PDAs link and you'll be taken to another dialog box that looks like the one shown in Figure 16.9. These are the templates for creating Flash for the mobile devices listed in the Templates List box. For creating a Flash game for Pocket PC, the best one we've found is the Windows Mobile—Browser link (third from the bottom, highlighted in Figure 16.9). This defaults to a 240×268 window, with all of the correct settings for HTML embedding.

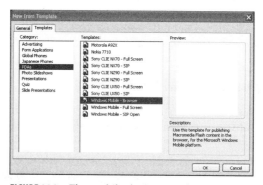

FIGURE 16.9   The mobile device templates.

With the Windows Mobile—Browser selected, click OK. Flash will create a new document with a stage that looks something like Figure 16.10. There are two layers created by default in this new movie. The top layer is called ActionScript, and the bottom layer is called Content, and this is where we can start placing items.

1. Select the Content layer and draw something simple, like a blue circle in the middle of the stage, as shown in Figure 16.11.
2. From the File menu, select Save and call the movie bluecircle.fla. Make a note of where you saved it.
3. From the File menu, choose Publish Settings.
4. In the dialog box that appears, click on the Formats tab.
5. Make sure that both the Flash (.swf) and the HTML (.html) options have their checkboxes checked.

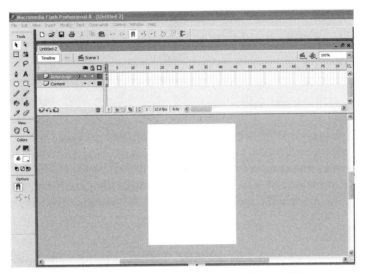

FIGURE 16.10   The new movie created by the Windows Mobile—
Browser template.

FIGURE 16.11   Drawing a blue circle
on the stage.

6. Publish this movie by pressing the Publish button at the bottom of the
   window (you can also publish the SWF and HTML file at any time by
   pressing Shift-F12.) Press OK.
7. In a regular file browser, navigate to the location where you saved the
   movie and you should see something similar to Figure 16.12.

Now, double-click on the `bluecircle.html` file and you should see the movie
open up and run in a browser. All you'll really see is a blue circle on a white Web
page. Congratulations, you've made your first Windows Mobile application and
you're able to run it on a desktop PC.

FIGURE 16.12 The files created for our new Pocket PC movie.

The real goal, however, is to run this on a Windows Mobile/Pocket PC. For this, you'll need to navigate into the files of your Pocket PC. This varies from operating system to operating system, but generally, make sure your Pocket PC is connected to your computer and look in My Computer (from the desktop or Start bar). It should appear like Figure 16.13, where at the very bottom you'll see a link for the Mobile Device.

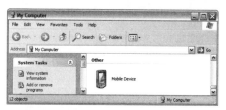

FIGURE 16.13 Accessing the Pocket PC device from My Computer.

Make sure your Pocket PC is on and connected (via either USB, Ethernet, or wirelessly) and double-click on the Mobile Device icon and from there double-click on the My Pocket PC icon. You should see the files of the device at this point, and it should look like something similar to Figure 16.14.

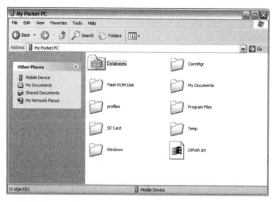

FIGURE 16.14 Accessing the Pocket PC device from My Computer.

At this point you must choose a location to copy your HTML and SWF files to. The My Documents folder is a good option, but if you have memory cards installed (which will show up as SD Card), you can copy your files there. It's up to you, just as long as you remember where you placed them. We're going to assume you've chosen My Documents.

From the window containing the `bluecircle.html` and `bluecircle.swf` files, select those two files, and drag them into the My Documents folder on the Pocket PC, as shown in Figure 16.15. Windows will automatically copy them over, and they will now be on your Pocket PC.

FIGURE 16.15   Copying from the desktop to the Pocket PC device.

Now pick up the Pocket PC device and navigate to the My Documents folder. You should see the two bluecircle files. One will have an icon that looks like an Internet Explorer icon. This is the HTML file (see Figure 16.16).

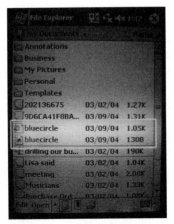

FIGURE 16.16   Navigating to the HTML file.

Click on this file with the stylus and it will run, and our movie will appear on screen. We should see the blue circle like in Figure 16.17.

FIGURE 16.17   The movie running on the Pocket PC.

Admittedly, it's not much of a game, but that's OK. We're just trying to get an idea of the process behind creating the Pocket PC movies and get them from the desktop computer onto the device.

Another important concept is this: because we're running these SWF files through HTML, we can put them online at a fixed location, for example, *http://mobilegames.hypothetical-site.com*, and anyone who has a WiFi connection with his or her Pocket PC can go to that location and play our games. This is one of the critical points behind this entire pursuit. We want to make it possible for our games to get out there. We want to be able to develop them and then FTP them up to a site that we run. That's how easy it is. Just as we ran the html directly by clicking on it, we could just as easily have typed a URL to that page, for example, *http://mobilegames.hypothetical-site.com/bluecircle.html*. It's a hypothetical address, but it shows that anyone could go there and play our blue circle game (groundbreaking game that it is). People across the globe sitting in coffee shops and Internet cafés could be looking at our blue circle within minutes of deployment.

Now that we're clear on the process of creating and uploading Flash movies for the Pocket PC, let's look specifically at our Word Search game and see how it's done.

THE WORD SEARCH GAME

By now you should be familiar with creating a movie in Macromedia Flash Professional 8 with the Windows Mobile template and then running that movie either on a desktop PC or copying it across to a Pocket PC.

In the Chapter 16 folder on the CD-ROM, locate the file called `wordsearch.fla`. This is the source file for the word search game. Open it up in Flash. Immediately you'll see that the stage looks like Figure 16.18.

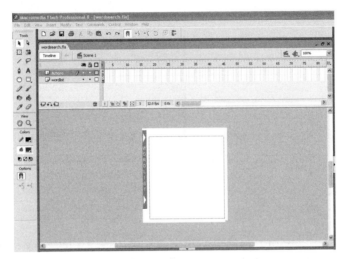

FIGURE 16.18   The stage layout of `wordsearch.fla`.

The stage is 240×268 in size, which is the standard Pocket PC layout size. We can see that the main timeline consists of two layers: `Actions` and `wordlist`. The `Actions` layer contains all of the ActionScript code for the game, and the `wordlist` layer contains the `wordbox` movie clip and a button with the instance name `showwords`. This button is used as a toggle to show or hide the `wordbox` movie clip. Because of limited screen space, we've opted to create a layout in which the word list appears only when we want to see it, rather than try to force the word list and the game grid to battle for real-estate on screen.

The `showwords` button is simply a tall, narrow button aligned with the left edge of the screen, which contains the text "WORDLIST," written vertically.

Within the `wordbox` movie clip, we have two layers: `bg` and `text`, as shown in Figure 16.19. The `bg` layer simply contains a white box with a 95% alpha value. This means the text underneath will show through very subtly. This serves no definitive function, but perhaps allows the player to see some of their game board while looking at the word list. At any rate, it looks cool.

The `text` layer contains a single, large text field of 14 point, _sans font. This text field has the instance name `words`. This is where our word list will physically be written to when it comes time.

There's one more important piece, but it's dynamically attached to the stage at runtime, so it's in the library, not on the stage. Open the library with Ctrl-L and look for a movie clip called `gridpiece`. This is set to export for linkage with the name `gridpiece`. This is the movie clip that is attached multiple times to the stage

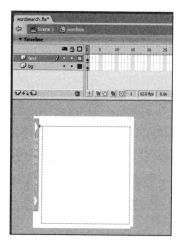

FIGURE 16.19   The layout of the
wordbox movie clip.

to create our entire grid. A grid of 10 × 10 letters will cause 100 instances of
gridpiece to be attached to the stage.

If we look inside this movie clip, we can see that it contains four layers and is
two frames long. Frame 1 is the grid piece in its normal, white state. Frame 2 is
the grid piece once it has been selected and has turned green (it is part of a found
word). The four layers, from top to bottom are:

button: This is an invisible button that is used to detect when the user clicks
on the grid piece (or presses down with a stylus, in the case of a Pocket
PC). This button has the instance name ibut.

text: This is a text field, Arial Black font, 14 point, with all basic characters
embedded. This text field has the instance name ltr, for *letter*.

highlighter: This is simply a yellow box, the same size of the grid, that turns
on and off, depending upon whether or not the grid piece is selected (to
begin selecting a word) or not. This movie clip has the instance name
highlighter.

back: The grid piece square itself. It is 15 × 15 pixels in size and it is drawn
directly on the timeline. The fill color is white on frame 1 and green on
frame 2.

The entire gridpiece movie clip can be seen in Figure 16.20.

Now that we're done looking at all of the movie clips and graphics, go back to
the main timeline and open up the actions panel for Frame 1 of the Actions layer.
This is where our code is.

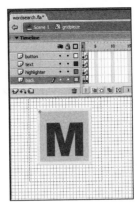

FIGURE 16.20   The layout of
the `gridpiece` movie clip.

The Code

In this game the bulk of the code is dedicated to the creation and population of the game grid, or game board. The first thing we do is physically create the movie clips and line them up on screen. While we're doing this, we're attaching code to them in order to make them respond to clicks. Let's look at the code:

```
oneSelected = false;
wordtext = new Array();
wordlist = new Array();
barray = new Array();
```

Here we're defining a variable, `oneSelected`, and setting it to `false`. This is going to be used to determine whether or not a grid piece is currently selected. Remember, game play exists in one of two states: clicking on the starting piece and clicking on the ending piece. We will be differentiating between these two modes through the use of the `oneSelected` variable.

We're also then creating three arrays: `wordtext`, `wordlist`, and `barray`. The first array, `wordtext`, is going to contain a list of all words that have been placed on the board. It will provide us with a fast way of looking to see if the user's click has selected a valid word. The `wordtext` array will not, however, use a number as its index. It will be using a string, which will be the result of the beginning letter movie clip name, concatenated with the ending letter movie clip name.

For example, let's say we have a word that runs from the upper-left corner of the grid; it's four letters long and runs horizontally. The grid pieces all have instance names "grid" plus a number, and the numbers run from 0 in the upper-left corner of the grid, so the upper-left corner grid piece has the instance name `grid0`. The next piece to the right is `grid1`, then `grid2`, `grid3`, and so on. This means that the first letter of our word is at `grid0` and the last letter is at `grid3`.

We take these two movie clip names and combine them into a string and use that as the index into the `wordtext` array. In the case of this word (let's say it's BOAT), the result would be something like this:

```
wordtext["grid0grid3"] = "BOAT";
```

That code will never actually exist anywhere like that, because it's all dynamically figured out. It's more like:

```
wordtext[startpos + endpos] = wrd;
```

The nice thing about this approach is that we can very quickly determine if the user has clicked on a valid word because we will know the two grid pieces that were clicked on and we can easily check to see if the `wordtext` array contains an entry that matches those two positions or if `wordtext` is undefined with that selection.

The second array, `wordlist`, is very similar, but this one will end up being a two-dimensional array. Each entry in the `wordlist` array contains an array of the names of all the grid pieces that make up that word. So, in the case of our previous example, where

```
wordtext["grid0grid3"] = "boat";
```

we would have the following in `wordlist`:

```
wordlist["grid0grid3"][0] = "grid0";
wordlist["grid0grid3"][1] = "grid1";
wordlist["grid0grid3"][2] = "grid2";
wordlist["grid0grid3"][3] = "grid3";
```

There are four letters, so `wordlist["grid0grid3"]` has four entries, with each entry being the name of one letter. The above example is pretty simple, but this technique becomes more helpful when we see things like vertical words running backwards:

```
wordtext["grid33grid3"] = "BOAT";
wordlist["grid33grid3"][0] = "grid33";
wordlist["grid33grid3"][1] = "grid23";
wordlist["grid33grid3"][2] = "grid13";
wordlist["grid33grid3"][3] = "grid3";
```

This means that the word BOAT runs in an upward direction, from position 33 to position 3. In order for this word to be vertical, the grid would need to be 10 × 10 in size. The following grid shows just the top left corner of what would be a 10 × 10 game grid. You can see how the word BOAT would fit into this grid.

```
grid0  grid1   grid2   grid3  T      ...
grid10 grid11  grid12  grid13 A      ...
grid20 grid21  grid22  grid23 O      ...
grid30 grid31  grid32  grid33 B      ...
```

The final array, barray, is just an array that represents the board. Each element in the barray array is a single letter, and the array is board width × board height in size. Thus, a 10 × 10 board will result in a barray that has 100 elements, each element being a letter.

After this, we have the start of our makeGrid function. This function is responsible for creating the physical game grid on the stage.

```
makeGrid = function (w)
{

    _root.createEmptyMovieClip("board", 0);

    board._x = 15;
    board._y = 5;

    size = w;

    cnt = 0;
```

The function takes one parameter, w, which is the width of the board. Since all boards are square, we don't need to specify the height. The board will simply be made w × w in size. The first thing we do is to create a new empty movie clip called board that is going to contain all of our gridpiece movie clips. We then move the board to position 15, 5, which means the board will not be flush at position 0, 0, which would be the default. We create a variable called size and set it to w. We'll be using this later. We also set a variable called cnt to 0, which we'll be using shortly. After this, we have:

```
for (var j = 0; j < w; j++)
{
    for (var i = 0; i < w; i++)
    {

        var nm = "grid" + cnt;
        board.attachMovie("gridpiece", nm, cnt);

        board[nm]._x = i * 16;
        board[nm]._y = j * 16;

        board[nm].ltr.text = "";
        board[nm].stop();
        board[nm].highlighter._visible = false;
```

This starts a nested loop to step through and create our grid. We're creating the variable nm, which will be the name of our new grid piece, grid0, grid1, grid2, and so on. We use the cnt variable for this. Then, the gridpiece movie clip is attached to the recently created board movie clip, with the instance name nm and the depth level defined by cnt. We then set the position of the grid piece within the board to i * 16, j * 16. This will cause the pieces to be placed on screen in a clean grid, where each row is 16 pixels high, and each column is 16 pixels wide.

We then set the text of the `ltr` textbox to be blank and we tell the grid piece to `stop()`, since it is two frames long. We also turn off the `highlighter` movie clip, as we only want it to be visible when the grid piece has been clicked and selected. The next code is:

```
board[nm].ibut.onRelease = function()
{
    if (!oneSelected)
    {
        oneSelected = true;
        this._parent.highlighter._visible = true;
        starting = this._parent._name;
    }
```

This is the code attached to the invisible button in the grid piece. This is our click code, triggered when the user clicks on the grid piece. First, we check to see if the `oneSelected` flag is true or false. If it's `false` (`!oneSelected`), we know that no piece is selected, so we set `oneSelected` to `true`, turn on the `highlighter` movie clip, and then set a variable called `starting` to the name of the clicked grid piece. So, if we clicked on `grid0`, then `starting` will be equal to `grid0`.

On the other hand, if `oneSelected` is already `true`, and a grid piece is therefore already selected, we do this:

```
else
{
    oneSelected = false;
    ending = this._parent._name;
    board[starting].highlighter._visible = false;

    if (wordlist[starting + ending])
    {
        for (var i = 0;
            i < wordlist[starting + ending].length;
            i++)
        {
            var nm = wordlist[starting + ending][i];
            board[nm].gotoAndStop(2);
        }

        delete wordtext[starting + ending];
        outputRemainingWords();

    }
}
```

We set `oneSelected` back to `false` and set the variable `ending` to the name of the clicked piece. We also turn off the `highlighter` on the `starting` piece. We then check our `wordlist` array to see if there is indeed a word at the `index starting + ending`. If so, we loop through every letter in the word and we tell the appropriate gridpiece movie clip on the board to go to frame 2, indicating that it is part of a found word.

We then delete that element in the wordtext array. Remember, each element in the wordtext array is simply the word at that starting/ending position. We delete this because of the way we do our updating of the word list text field. We make a call to outputRemainingWords, which, as we'll soon see, steps through the wordtext array and outputs all of the words in it to the words text field in the wordbox movie clip. That's the end of our if/else. The remaining code for the makeGrid function simply ends the loop and increments cnt for the creation of the subsequent grid piece.

```
                }

            cnt++;

        }
    }
}
```

The entire listing of the makeGrid function is as follows:

```
makeGrid = function (w)
{
    _root.createEmptyMovieClip("board", 0);

    board._x = 15;
    board._y = 5;

    size = w;

    cnt = 0;

    for (var j = 0; j < w; j++)
    {
        for (var i = 0; i < w; i++)
        {
            var nm = "grid" + cnt;
            board.attachMovie("gridpiece", nm, cnt);

            board[nm]._x = i * 16;
            board[nm]._y = j * 16;

            board[nm].ltr.text = "";
            board[nm].stop();
            board[nm].highlighter._visible = false;

            board[nm].ibut.onRelease = function()
            {
```

```
                        if (!oneSelected)
                        {
                            oneSelected = true;
                            this._parent.highlighter._visible = true;
                            starting = this._parent._name;
                        }
                        else
                        {
                            oneSelected = false;
                            ending = this._parent._name;
                            board[starting].highlighter._visible =
                                                            false;

                            if (wordlist[starting + ending])
                            {
                                for (var i = 0;
                                        i < wordlist[starting +
                                                    ending].length;
                                        i++)
                                {
                                    var nm = wordlist[starting +
                                                        ending][i];
                                    board[nm].gotoAndStop(2);
                                }

                                delete wordtext[starting + ending];
                                outputRemainingWords();

                            }
                        }
                    }

                cnt++;
            }
        }
    }
```

After this, we have a single line of code not in a function:

```
    maxtries = 50;
```

This sets the value of the maxtries variable to 50. This is the maximum number of times the game will attempt to fit each word in the grid before it will give up and move on to the next word. This number can be adjusted, but it will make the game run much slower on systems like the Pocket PC. Following this, we have the start of a function:

```
    addWord = function(wrd)
    {

        successful = false;

        if (wrd.length > size) return (false);
```

This is the start of the addWord function. This takes on parameter, wrd, which is a string that you'd like to add to the grid. We set a flag called successful to false, which we'll be using shortly. We also perform one quick check here; if the length of the word is greater than the dimension (width or height) of the grid, then it's not possible for this word to fit, so we return false. After this, we have:

```
var tries = 0;

var tried = new Array();
tried[0] = new Array();
tried[1] = new Array();
tried[2] = new Array();
tried[3] = new Array();
```

After setting a variable called tries to 0, we create an array called tried and within it create four arrays, at tried[0], tried[1], tried[2], and tried[3]. These are important arrays, and their main purpose is to ensure that when a word is being placed, it never tries to fit in a position that it has already tried and failed. If it's retrying 50 times, there's a chance it will try the same position and direction more than once. This is redundant. Each tried array corresponds to a direction. Left to right attempts are stored in tried[0], top to bottom attempts are stored in tried[1], right to left attempts are stored in tried[2], and bottom to top attempts are stored in tried[3].

For example, grid position 3 right, 3 down will correspond to grid22, which means position 22. If we try to fit a word running left to right at that position and it fails, then tried[0][22] will be set to true. If, during that same word, the computer randomly picks the same direction (0) and the same position (22), it will check and see that tried[0][22] is already true, so it has already tried this position and will try another position. Let's imagine that, though unlikely, the computer chooses position 22 again, but a different direction, 1, for a word running down. In this case tried[1][22] will not be true yet, so it will attempt to fit the word. If the word fits, the entire function would end successfully.

With these arrays created, we proceed with:

```
while (!successful && tries < maxtries)
{

    tries++;
```

If the successful is still false and the number of tries has not yet exceeded maxtries, we proceed into our main loop, where the first thing we do is increment tries. Next, we have:

```
var sx = Math.floor(Math.random() * size);
var sy = Math.floor(Math.random() * size);

dir = Math.floor(Math.random() * 4);

var spot = sx + (sy * size);
```

Here we choose a random x and y position, sx and sy, to be the starting point of our word placement attempt. We also choose a random direction value from 0 to 3 and store that in dir. We then take the value for sx and sy, convert them into a number that represents the grid index, and store that in spot. So, an sx of 0 and sy of 0 will have a spot of 0, but an sx of 0 and sy of 1 (one row down) will have a spot of 10 (assuming size was 10). spot could be any value from 0 to the total number of squares in the grid.

Next, we do the following:

```
if (tried[dir][spot] != true)
{

    tried[dir][spot] = true;
```

Here we're checking the tried array to see if this direction and location have been checked already. If not, we set the value of tried at that direction and location to true. Now we begin the process of fitting our words into the grid. This is divided into four sections, one per direction. The first direction we check, is 0, which is left to right:

```
if (dir == 0)
{
    if (sx + wrd.length < size)
    {

        successful = true;

        for (var i = 0; i < wrd.length; i++)
        {
            var num = ((i + sx) + (sy * size));
            var char = wrd.charAt(i);

            if (barray[num] != null &&
                barray[num] != char)
            {
                successful = false;
                break;
            }
        }
    }
```

The first thing we do is make sure that the word will fit into the grid, from position sx, going right. We want to make sure that sx plus the length of the word is not greater than the width of the board. We then set the successful variable to true. This is a temporary step, and any failure from here on in will cause successful to be set back to false.

We then step through the word, a character at a time. In the variable num, we store the position on the grid where we're going to try to fit the letter. The letter char will be the character in the word that we're trying to fit.

We then have a simple `if` statement. If there's already a letter in the spot `num` and that letter is not the letter we're trying to place, then this is a failed attempt. We set `successful` back to `false` and break out of the loop; there's no point in checking any more characters. In this way, if there's no letter in grid position `num` or if the letter in that position already matches the letter `char`, we continue on and check the next letter. The reason we want to see if there's already a letter there is because it's still possible for our words to intersect other words as long as they share common letters. The first few words being placed will not likely experience this kind of intersection, but as the board fills up, and we're looking for valid positions, intersecting another word may be the only way. Once we've completed checking the word, the `successful` variable will be either `true` or `false`. We proceed with the following code:

```
if (successful)
{
    var startpos = "grid" + (sx + sy * size);
    var endpos = "grid" + (sx + (wrd.length-1) + sy * size);
    wordlist[startpos + endpos] = new Array();

    for (var i = 0; i < wrd.length; i++)
    {
        var num = ((i + sx) + (sy * size));
        var nm = "grid" + num;

        wordlist[startpos + endpos][i] = nm;
        var char = wrd.charAt(i);
        board[nm].ltr.text = char;
        barray[num] = char;
    }
}
```

This is the next part of the placement attempt, for direction 0. If our `successful` variable is `true`, we know the word can be placed, so we physically place it. We first figure out the instance name of the start position grid movie clip and store that in the variable `startpos`. We then figure out the grid piece instance name of the end position and store that in the variable `endpos`. Using our concatenated string index technique (`startpos + endpos`), we create a new array at that index in `wordlist`. Remember, this array will contain a list of all the `grid` movie clips that make up this word placement.

Then we step through each letter once more, and using a temporary variable `nm`, we calculate the name of the grid piece that will be the home for each letter. We set the value of `wordlist[startpos + endpos][i]` as the name of the movie clip at position `i` in the word. We then take the letter and place it in the text field of the corresponding grid piece movie clip, and set the same letter into `barray` at the corresponding position. After this, we're done checking and placing that particular direction.

```
                 }
            }
```

The next section of code is very similar to the previous section, except that this is the code executed if `dir` is 1 instead of 0.

```
            else if (dir == 1)
            {
                if (sy + wrd.length < size)
                {

                    successful = true;

                    for (var i = 0; i < wrd.length; i++)
                    {
                        var num = (sx + ((sy + i) * size));
                        var char = wrd.charAt(i);

                        if (barray[num] != null &&
                            barray[num] != char)
                        {
                            successful = false;
                            break;
                        }
                    }

                    if (successful)
                    {

                        var startpos = "grid" +
                                    (sx + sy * size);
                        var endpos = "grid" + (sx + (sy +
                                    (wrd.length-1)) * size);
                        wordlist[startpos + endpos] =
                                    new Array();

                        for (var i = 0; i < wrd.length; i++)
                        {
                            var num = (sx + ((sy + i) * size));
                            var nm = "grid" + num;

                            wordlist[startpos + endpos][i] = nm;
                            var char = wrd.charAt(i);
                            board[nm].ltr.text = char;
                            barray[num] = char;
                        }
                    }
                }
            }
```

Everything's almost identical, but this time we're operating all of our checks along the y-axis—vertically. We check to make sure the word does not run off the bottom of the board, and then we try to place each letter vertically and make sure, like last time, that it is on a blank space or the same letter. If everything is successful, we place the word on the board, set up our `wordlist` array, and we're done. The next section of code checks the right to left direction, `dir` of 2.

```
else if (dir == 2)
{
    if (sx - wrd.length > 0)
    {
        successful = true;

        for (var i = 0; i < wrd.length; i++)
        {
            var num = ((sx - i) + (sy * size));
            var char = wrd.charAt(i);

            if (barray[num] != null &&
                barray[num] != char)
            {
                successful = false;
                break;
            }
        }

        if (successful)
        {
            var startpos = "grid" +
                            (sx + sy * size);
            var endpos = "grid" + ((sx-(wrd.length-
                            1)) + sy * size);
            wordlist[startpos + endpos] =
                            new Array();

            for (var i = 0; i < wrd.length; i++)
            {
                var num = ((sx - i) + (sy * size));
                var nm = "grid" + num;

                wordlist[startpos + endpos][i] = nm;
                var char = wrd.charAt(i);
                board[nm].ltr.text = char;
                barray[num] = char;
            }
        }
    }
}
```

Everything's the same yet again, except for a few things. Now we're making sure the word doesn't run off the board to the left by making sure that sx - wrd. length is greater than 0. After this, we proceed to place the word, running right to left, checking for valid spaces, in a similar manner. If it was successful, we populate the board with this backward word and move on.

The last check is for `dir` 3:

```
else if (dir == 3)
{
    if (sy - wrd.length > 0)
    {

        successful = true;

        for (var i = 0; i < wrd.length; i++)
        {
            var num = (sx + ((sy - i) * size));
            var char = wrd.charAt(i);

            if (barray[num] != null &&
                barray[num] != char)
            {
                successful = false;
                break;
            }
        }

        if (successful)
        {

            var startpos = "grid" + (sx + sy *
                            size);
            var endpos = "grid" + (sx + (sy --
                        (wrd.length -1)) * size);
            wordlist[startpos + endpos] =
                        new Array();

            for (var i = 0; i < wrd.length; i++)
            {
                var num = (sx + ((sy - i) * size));
                var nm = "grid" + num;

                wordlist[startpos + endpos][i] = nm;
                var char = wrd.charAt(i);
                board[nm].ltr.text = char;
                barray[num] = char;
            }
        }
    }
}
```

This direction involves the word running upward on screen. We check to make sure the end of the word is not higher than the top of the grid and then we proceed to try the usual placement. If `successful` is `true`, we place the word on the board.

Those are all of the placement checks. After this we have some code for the end of the function:

```
        }
    }

    if (tries < maxtries)
    {
        wordtext[startpos + endpos] = wrd;
        return (true)
    }
    else
    {
        // Couldn't fit the word in
        return (false);
    }

}
```

This code represents the end of the while loop. Remember, the while loop will end if successful is true or tries has exceeded maxtries. As long as tries is less than maxtries, we store the word in the wordtext array at position startpos + endpos. Otherwise, if tries is not less than maxtries, we know that placement failed, and we return false. The entire code for the addWord function is as follows:

```
addWord = function(wrd)
{

    successful = false;

    if (wrd.length > size) return (false);

    var tries = 0;

    var tried = new Array();
    tried[0] = new Array();
    tried[1] = new Array();
    tried[2] = new Array();
    tried[3] = new Array();

    while (!successful && tries < maxtries)
    {

        tries++;

        var sx = Math.floor(Math.random() * size);
        var sy = Math.floor(Math.random() * size);

        dir = Math.floor(Math.random() * 4);

        var spot = sx + (sy * size);
```

```
if (tried[dir][spot] != true)
{

    tried[dir][spot] = true;

    if (dir == 0)
    {
        if (sx + wrd.length < size)
        {

            successful = true;

            for (var i = 0; i < wrd.length; i++)
            {
                var num = ((i + sx) + (sy * size));
                var char = wrd.charAt(i);

                if (barray[num] != null &&
                    barray[num] != char)
                {
                    successful = false;
                    break;
                }
            }

            if (successful)
            {
                var startpos = "grid" + (sx + sy *
                            size);
                var endpos = "grid" + (sx + (wrd.length-
                            1) + sy * size);
                wordlist[startpos + endpos] =
                            new Array();

                for (var i = 0; i < wrd.length; i++)
                {
                    var num = ((i + sx) + (sy * size));
                    var nm = "grid" + num;

                    wordlist[startpos + endpos][i] = nm;
                    var char = wrd.charAt(i);
                    board[nm].ltr.text = char;
                    barray[num] = char;
                }
            }
        }
    }
    else if (dir == 1)
    {
        if (sy + wrd.length < size)
        {
```

```
            successful = true;

            for (var i = 0; i < wrd.length; i++)
            {
                var num = (sx + ((sy + i) * size));
                var char = wrd.charAt(i);

                if (barray[num] != null &&
                    barray[num] != char)
                {
                    successful = false;
                    break;
                }
            }

            if (successful)
            {

                var startpos = "grid" +
                                (sx + sy * size);
                var endpos = "grid" + (sx + (sy +
                                (wrd.length-1)) * size);
                wordlist[startpos + endpos] =
                                new Array();

                for (var i = 0; i < wrd.length; i++)
                {
                    var num = (sx + ((sy + i) * size));
                    var nm = "grid" + num;

                    wordlist[startpos + endpos][i] = nm;
                    var char = wrd.charAt(i);
                    board[nm].ltr.text = char;
                    barray[num] = char;
                }
            }
        }
    }
}
else if (dir == 2)
{
    if (sx - wrd.length > 0)
    {

        successful = true;

        for (var i = 0; i < wrd.length; i++)
        {
            var num = ((sx - i) + (sy * size));
            var char = wrd.charAt(i);

            if (barray[num] != null &&
                barray[num] != char)
            {
```

```
                                successful = false;
                                break;
                            }
                        }

                        if (successful)
                        {
                            var startpos = "grid" +
                                        (sx + sy * size);
                            var endpos = "grid" + ((sx-(wrd.length-
                                        1)) + sy * size);
                            wordlist[startpos + endpos] =
                                        new Array();

                            for (var i = 0; i < wrd.length; i++)
                            {
                                var num = ((sx - i) + (sy * size));
                                var nm = "grid" + num;

                                wordlist[startpos + endpos][i] = nm;
                                var char = wrd.charAt(i);
                                board[nm].ltr.text = char;
                                barray[num] = char;
                            }
                        }
                    }
                }
                else if (dir == 3)
                {
                    if (sy - wrd.length > 0)
                    {

                        successful = true;

                        for (var i = 0; i < wrd.length; i++)
                        {
                            var num = (sx + ((sy - i) * size));
                            var char = wrd.charAt(i);

                            if (barray[num] != null &&
                                barray[num] != char)
                            {
                                successful = false;
                                break;
                            }
                        }

                        if (successful)
                        {

                            var startpos = "grid" + (sx + sy *
                                        size);
                            var endpos = "grid" + (sx + (sy --
```

```
                                      (wrd.length -1)) * size);
                   wordlist[startpos + endpos] =
                                      new Array();

                   for (var i = 0; i < wrd.length; i++)
                   {
                       var num = (sx + ((sy - i) * size));
                       var nm = "grid" + num;

                       wordlist[startpos + endpos][i] = nm;
                       var char = wrd.charAt(i);
                       board[nm].ltr.text = char;
                       barray[num] = char;
                   }
               }
           }
       }
   }

   if (tries < maxtries)
   {
       wordtext[startpos + endpos] = wrd;
       return (true)
   }
   else
   {
       // Couldn't fit the word in
       return (false);
   }

}
```

After this, we have another function:

```
fillInBlanks = function()
{
    for (var i = 0; i < cnt; i++)
    {
        var nm = "grid" + i;
        if (board[nm].ltr.text == "")
            board[nm].ltr.text = chr(random(26) + ord("A"));
    }
}
```

This function is called after the board has been fully populated, and its sole responsibility is to step through all the squares and fill in any pieces that were not filled with letters from a word. We go through and check to see if the ltr text field of any of the grid pieces is blank, and if so we place a random letter from A to Z in it. The cnt variable will be set to the total number of grid pieces, from the very point that the grid is created. After this, we have another short function:

```
outputRemainingWords = function()
{
    wordbox.words.text = "";
    for (var i in wordtext)
    {
        wordbox.words.text += wordtext[i] + ", ";
    }
}
```

This steps through our wordtext array, which contains a list of all words on the board, and outputs it to the words text field into the wordbox movie clip. The words are output as a comma-separated list. If you recall, when the user uncovers a word, it is then deleted from the wordtext array. This ensures that any call to outputRemainingWords (which is called when the word is deleted) will not include this found word.

Next we have the general function we call to begin board population:

```
populateBoard = function()
{
    wordlist.sort(orderByLength);

    for (var i = 0; i < wordlist.length; i++)
    {
        addWord(wordlist[i]);
    }
}
```

The first thing we do is to sort an array called wordlist, using the sort method of the Array class. This method will sort any array by any criteria we specify. By default, this is sorted alphanumerically, but we've provided our own custom sorting function, orderByLength. This will sort the wordlist array by length, so the longer words are at the beginning of the array. We'll be looking at the orderByLength function next, but first we'll cover the wordlist array, which is the array of words we want to include in our word search. You may recall us talking about this at the very beginning of this chapter.

We sort from longest to shortest, as it's easier to add long words first because early on there's more room on the board and longer words are harder to place. Once the array is sorted, we step through it, one element at a time, and add the element (which is a string word) to the board, by calling the addWord function. The next function we have is the orderByLength function:

```
orderByLength = function(w1, w2)
{
    var val1 = w1.length;
    var val2 = w2.length;

    if (val1 < val2)
    {
        return 1;
```

```
    }
    else if (val1 > val2)
    {
        return -1;
    }
    else
    {
        return 0;
    }
}
```

Any custom sorting function, used by the `Array.sort` method, simply works by taking in two parameters. It compares them and returns 1, 0, or –1, depending upon the result of that comparison. In the `orderByLength` function we'll automatically be passed two words. We calculate and store their lengths in `val1` and `val2`. We then compare these two values, and if `val1` is shorter than `val2` we return 1. If `val1` is longer than `val2`, we return –1. If the two words were the same length we return 0.

This is all we need to do to use our custom sorting function. We then have one more function:

```
showwords.onRelease = function()
{
    wordbox._visible = !wordbox._visible;
}
```

This is the code to control the clicking of the `showwords` button. When it's clicked, we simply toggle the visibility of the `wordbox` movie clip. That's the last function. The remaining code is responsible for initializing the game:

```
wordbox.swapDepths(3);
```

This moves the `wordbox` movie clip to depth layer 3, which is on top of the `board` movie clip.

```
makeGrid(14);
```

We then make a call to the `makeGrid` function, passing in 14. This means our game grid will be 14 × 14 grid squares in size. Next, we define our word list:

```
wordlist = new Array("ACTIONSCRIPT", "DEVELOPMENT", "COMPUTER",
                "POCKETPC", "PHYSICS", "GRAVITY",
                "FLASHMX", "CLICK", "AUTHOR", "BOUNCE",
                "COFFEE", "SUPER", "BOOK", "PAGES",
                "GAME", "OKAY", "CODE", "DX", "EXPORT",
                "COMPILE", "CHARLESRIVER", "GLENRHODES",
                "WEB", "MARSRACER", "DIMENSION",
                "MOVIECLIP", "SCRIPT", "TEXT");
```

These are the words we'd like to have on the board. They won't all necessarily end up being placed. It depends on random luck, to see if they'll all fit. Next we have the final three lines of code:

```
populateBoard();
fillInBlanks();
outputRemainingWords();
```

Here we populate the board, fill in all the remaining blanks, and then output the words to the wordbox. That's the end of the code. Once this has been run, the game will be ready to play. We'll have a great Pocket PC classic ready to go!

EXTENDING THE GAME

How could you extend this game? The first thing is to remember how to keep it performing well within the confines of the Pocket PC. Be careful about doing things like adding complex graphics and animation. You could:

- Add support for diagonal words
- Modify the engine so it's a crossword instead of a word search

SUMMARY

In this chapter we looked at:

- The advantage of portable games and the Flash player
- Issues surrounding the devices and their limitations
- The wireless possibilities (WiFi)
- Creating a word search game
- Working with the Pocket PC to:
    1. Create a Flash game from scratch with the mobile templates
    2. Install the Flash player on the Pocket PC
    3. Transfer files across from the desktop to the Pocket PC
- The programming techniques surrounding grid-based word games

ENTERING THE THIRD DIMENSION

One of the final frontiers in a game developer's learning journey is the third dimension. Once we've mastered up and down and left and right, we inevitably start to think about forward and backward, or *in* to the screen, and *out* of the screen.

However, it's important to remember that we *are* indeed talking about a *screen*, and therefore the third dimension can only ever be simulated. The screen does have physical width and height, which provides us with two true dimensions (x and y), but it's not as if our screen also somehow extends two feet from its surface to provide us with the third dimension of depth. Everything we do that looks 3D is merely a "picture of 3D" projected onto a flat, 2D screen.

The third dimension is often referred to as "z," and when it comes to displaying three dimensions on a flat screen, we must inevitably find a way of representing x, y, and z by using only x and y, or _x and _y. This process is known as *projection*, and we'll be looking at it in this chapter.

We're now going to look at a few of the tricks used to create 3D effects. What we're not going to do is get into full-blown 3D modeling, with matrices and rotation. There are plenty of books on that topic, and we're really dealing with a medium that requires us to cheat to create our effects with maximal performance. So we're going to be creating the *impression* of full-blown 3D without actually doing all of the really complex math associated with it. Our most complex equation will be projection, which we'll look at shortly.

PARALLAX SCROLLING

The third dimension is all about *depth*. We understand this from real life. There are three visual cues that we're used to reading to tell us of an object's relative distance. First, objects farther away from us appear smaller. Figure 17.1 shows this very simple principle. The caveman closest to us is the biggest, and the smaller caveman is the farthest away.

FIGURE 17.1   Farther away equals smaller.

Second, objects that are farther away tend to move slower than objects that are closer to us. This doesn't mean the objects in the distance are physically covering less ground; it just means we see more space around them, so they move slower relative to that space. Figure 17.2 shows this motion in practice. The caveman closest to us covers the most distance on screen, indicated by the size of his black arrow. The caveman in the far distance covers less distance on screen, but the same distance relative to the ground as the closest caveman.

The third cue that we're used to using to determine depth is stereoscopic differentiation. That is, our two eyes perceive slightly different images and our brain interprets these *differences* and then uses them to measure depth. When we look at a mountain in the distance, our two eyes see essentially the exact same thing. This is because the mountain is so far away that the spacing between our eyes is not enough to cause differences in the image of the mountain; a mountain ten miles away looks the same from one point and another point two inches to the right (the distance from one eye pupil to the other eye pupil).

FIGURE 17.2   Farther away equals slower.

Hold a small box in front of your face, however, and your left eye will see the left side of the box, while your right eye will see the right side of the box. In Figure 17.3 we're looking down from above at a person who's looking at a little box. We can see how each eye, because of its vantage point, sees a slightly different image of the box.

Looking at Figure 17.4, we can see the actual image that each eye will see. These two images are very different, but our brain handles this difference by adequately telling us that this box has depth.

In fact, it's possible to look at the image in Figure 17.4, and let your eyes converge so that the two halves of the box overlap perfectly. When they do, the box will appear to become 3D; your brain will interpret the difference between the two images as a false sense of depth.

FIGURE 17.3   Viewing a small box close up.

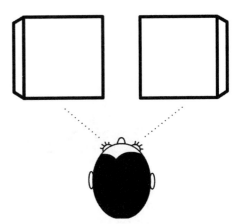

FIGURE 17.4   The two views that the eyes see.

This is real life we're talking about. In computers, we don't really have a way of causing each eye to see a different image, because both eyes are looking at the same screen. There are some ways, for example 3D glasses that send slightly different images to each eye, but for our purposes, this is not an option. We have to assume that the average player of our games won't just be sitting there wearing a pair of 3D glasses. So we're left with the first two options—size and speed—to bring our players into the third dimension.

Parallax Planes

One of the easiest ways to create depth in our games is to scroll elements in the background in parallax to each other. We've already seen this done at a very basic level in Mars Racer (Chapter 14). In that game we had two planes: the mountains and the foreground terrain. The motion difference was extreme; the background wasn't moving at all, while the terrain was whipping by.

ON THE CD

We can find an example of parallax scrolling in the file `parallax.fla`, in the Chapter 17 folder on the CD-ROM. This movie consists of five layers, or planes, and when you move the mouse around, they respond accordingly by all moving at different rates. Each layer is simply a movie clip, and they have instance names `layer0`, `layer1`, `layer2`, and `layer3`. The farthest layer (the clouds) does not have an instance name because it does not move. Figure 17.5 shows the stage for this movie.

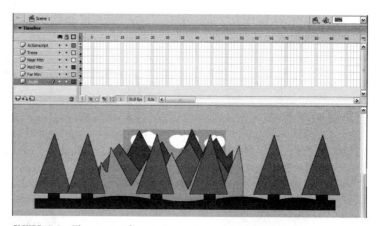

FIGURE 17.5   The stage of `parallax.fla`.

Each layer has a different width, and it is this width that is used to determine the layer's scroll speed. The five layers associated with this, from closest to farthest are:

The trees: `layer0`; width of 1646.
The near mountains: `layer1`; width of 807.

The middle mountains: `layer2`; width of 711.
The far mountains: `layer3`; width of 588.
The clouds: These do not move.

Notice that the difference in width between the trees and the first layer of mountains is quite substantial. This is because the supposed distance between the nearest mountains and the trees is quite far. The rate at which things move as they get farther away decreases exponentially with distance. For example, an object that is 10 feet away appears to move twice as fast as an object that is 20 feet away, four times as fast as an object that is 30 feet away, eight times as fast as an object that is 40 feet away, and so on (these are not the *actual* numbers, but are used to illustrate the point).

The technical explanation behind this is the way light moves and decreases in strength and intensity at a rate that is inversely proportional to the square of the distance. This is known as the inverse square rule, but that's about as far as we're going to go into it. All we really care about are the effects we're trying to create.

On frame 1 of our movie, we have the following code:

```
scrollMe = function()
{
    var xperc = _root._xmouse / 550;
    this._x = -xperc * (this._width - 550);
}

layer0.onEnterFrame = scrollMe;
layer1.onEnterFrame = scrollMe;
layer2.onEnterFrame = scrollMe;
layer3.onEnterFrame = scrollMe;
```

That's all that is required to bring this effect to life. Make sure to run this movie first and see what's happening. The parallax effect is difficult to capture in the pages of this book, but what we're essentially doing is moving each layer based on the position of the mouse cursor relative to the screen. The function called `scrollMe` is a generic function that can be used to parallax scroll any movie clip.

The first thing we do is to compute what percentage of the way across the screen the mouse cursor is. We know that the screen is 550 in width, so by taking `_root._xmouse` and dividing it by 550, we are left with a number between 0 and 1. We store this in the variable `xperc`. Once we've figured out `xperc` then we set the `_x` position of `this` to the exact percentage of the total width of `this`, minus 550. We must subtract 550 so that when `xperc` is 1 (mouse is at the far right edge of the screen), `this` will be aligned flush with the right edge.

The idea is that the mouse position is used to scroll the entire extent of every movie clip. So, we have trees with a width of 1646. Moving the mouse to the left edge of the screen must allow you to see the absolute left edge of the trees, while moving the mouse to the right edge must allow you to see the absolute right edge of the screen. Though we've only moved the mouse 550 pixels, we've moved the trees by 1096 pixels (1646 minus 550).

We set the `onEnterFrame` function of each of the `layer` movie clips to `scrollMe`, and each layer will respond according to its own width. Assuming that each layer progressively farther back is also progressively *less* wide, we will be left with a satisfying parallax effect. If, for some reason, we were to make one of the layers *less* wide than the layers farther away, we would be left with the very confusing effect of something closer moving slower than something farther, which would destroy the parallax distance effect.

Parallax Objects

ON THE CD

We can extend the concept of parallax scrolling and rather than performing this scroll on several planes, we can perform it on individual objects instead. The result is that we can get a much greater sense of depth. For example, we can have a screen full of stars, each one moving at a different speed. Take a look at `starfield.fla` in the Chapoter 17 folder. Give it a go, and you should see something that looks like Figure 17.6.

FIGURE 17.6   `starfield.fla` in action.

What you can't tell by looking at Figure 17.6 is that all the stars are streaking by at different speeds. The larger, brighter stars are moving relatively fast, while the dimmer, smaller stars are hardly moving at all.

All of these stars are moving in parallax; we can think of each star as its own parallax plane. This file generates 250 randomly placed stars, so it's as if we're looking at 250 planes of parallax. Their speed is governed by a very simple formula:

screen speed = standard speed/distance from viewer

We're assuming here that all of these stars are moving at the exact same speed (like our cavemen from earlier). It's easier to think of the way it would probably be in a game: the stars would not be moving; the player would be moving, and the stars would be streaking past. Therefore, all stars would be moving at the exact opposite speed to the player's speed.

So, if we take this standard speed and divide it by the star's distance, we'll be left with a number that we can use to determine how fast to move the star across the screen. This is critical, because we can also use this relationship to determine another factor: scale. Remember, farther objects must appear smaller, so we have another, similar formula:

$$\text{size on screen} = \text{standard scale/distance from viewer}$$

It's very similar to the speed equation, but this time we're using a "standard scale," or in other words, the *actual* size of the star. We're assuming that every star is exactly the same size; otherwise, we would have to factor that into the equation as well (which we'll be seeing in the next chapter).

In `starfield.fla` we have one graphic in the library. It's simply a white circle, 4×4 in size, and it's set with a linkage name star.

On frame 1 of the main timeline, we have the following code:

```
for (var i = 0; i < 250; i++)
{
    var nm = "star" + i;
    _root.attachMovie("star", nm, i);

    _root[nm]._x = Math.random() * 550;
    _root[nm]._y = Math.random() * 400;

    _root[nm].distance = Math.random() * 200 + 1;

    _root[nm]._xscale = 1000 / _root[nm].distance;
    _root[nm]._yscale = 1000 / _root[nm].distance;

    _root[nm].speed = 20 / _root[nm].distance;

    _root[nm].onEnterFrame = function()
    {
        this._x += this.speed;
        if (this._x > 550) this._x = 0;
    }
}
```

We're creating 250 instances of the star movie clip and instance naming them star0, star1, star2, and so on, up to star249. Once each star is created, it is placed at a random _x and _y location on the screen. After this, the magic distance variable is randomly set. This will be a number from 1 to 201. A distance of 1 would be very close, and a distance of 201 would be very far away.

After this, we calculate our scale variables (we must set _xscale *and* _yscale because we have to adjust both of these in order to properly scale an object evenly down in size). We're using the same formula as before:

size on screen = standard scale/distance from viewer

is equal to:

```
_root[nm]._xscale = 1000 / _root[nm].distance;
_root[nm]._yscale = 1000 / _root[nm].distance;
```

Our standard scale is 1000, and the larger the distance, the smaller the star will be scaled to. What does this mean? Well, technically it means that the biggest star will be 40 × 40 in size (when distance is 1, _xscale will be 1000, which is 10 times the movie clip size of 4 × 4 pixels). This also means that a distance of 10 will be where we see the true 4 × 4 star (1000/10 = 100%). What it really means is that we have to figure these numbers out based on what looks right. If we wanted smaller stars, we would increase the number 1000, whereas if we wanted bigger, brighter stars, we would decrease the number 1000.

After computing scale, we compute speed, based on our speed formula of

screen speed = standard speed/distance from viewer

which equates to

```
_root[nm].speed = 20 / _root[nm].distance;
```

We can think of it as though the viewer is moving at a rate of 20, so that 20 is our standard speed. The larger the distance, the slower the value of speed will be. For example:

DISTANCE	EQUATION (20 / DISTANCE)	RESULTANT SPEED
10	20/10	2
50	20/50	0.4
100	20/100	0.2
200	20/200	0.1

This means that a star with a distance of 10 will be moving along the screen at a rate of 2, which translates to 2 pixels every frame. A star with a distance of 200 will only be moving at a rate of 0.1, or 1/10th of a pixel every frame; it will take 10 frames to move one pixel.

Notice the exponential nature of the equation? A difference in distance of 100, between 100 and 200, results in a speed difference of only 0.1. A difference in distance of 40, between 10 and 50, results in a speed difference of 1.6.

Finally, after all of the speeds and scales have been calculated, we have the following code:

```
_root[nm].onEnterFrame = function()
{
    this._x += this.speed;
    if (this._x > 550) this._x = 0;
}
```

This causes the star to move along the _x axis (horizontally) by its speed every frame. The last line of code simply returns the star to the left side of the screen, should it happen to fly off the right side of the screen. This causes a continually cycling effect so that our space appears to go on forever.

Now, we've been looking at the variable distance, and what it represents makes perfect sense to us. What we should probably also realize at this point is that the distance we're referring to is called (in the world of 3D graphics), z. That's right, we're already using the z variable without even realizing it—we're already thinking in terms of x, y, and z.

Let's expand our repertoire at this point and take a look at *projection*.

Projection

To think of projection, it helps to understand what it is that we're *projecting*. In terms of the real world, projection is the process by which light hits our eyes, or hits a surface of some sort. For our purposes, we can think of projection as the process of taking a 3D image, and making it 2D.

Think of it like this. Imagine you're standing in a room with several boxes and teapots within it. This room might look something like Figure 17.7.

You then take a large piece of glass and place it on an easel at one end of the room, like in Figure 17.8.

FIGURE 17.7   The hypothetical room.

FIGURE 17.8   Placing glass at one end.

After this, you stand directly in front of the glass and do not move. Looking through the glass, you see the room beyond, like in Figure 17.9.

With a magic marker in one hand you reach up to the glass and begin to trace, onto the glass, exactly what you see *through* the glass, like in Figure 17.10. You would have to be careful to not move your head, and it would be best to trace with one eye closed.

FIGURE 17.9   Looking through the glass.

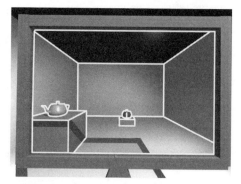

FIGURE 17.10   Drawing on the glass.

Once you're completely finished, you take the glass off the easel and lay it down on a flat white surface and then color the lines in black. You would be left with something like Figure 17.11.

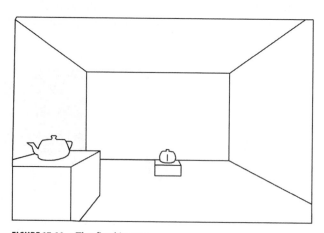

FIGURE 17.11   The final image.

Congratulations, you have just performed 3D projection, and you didn't use a single line of code. You now have a perfect 2D rendering of what was actually a 3D scene. This is not an artist's conception of a scene; this image is a physical *tracing* of a real 3D scene.

This is exactly how we do things with code when we want to project a 3D image onto the screen. You can think of the monitor screen as the piece of glass and the 3D scene as imaginary, existing only as a 2D projection.

If you imagine moving your eye closer to the piece of glass before you start tracing, you would see more of the scene within the frame of the glass. Conversely, the farther back from the glass you stand (imagine you have a 10 foot arm with which to trace), you would see less of the scene through the glass.

This is a very important concept, and it refers to a number known as the *view distance*. This is defined as the distance between the viewer and the plane upon which the image is being projected. The view distance, referred to in code as d, will affect the look of the final projection in some dramatic ways. Take a look at Figure 17.12 for a very short view distance and Figure 17.13 for a long view distance. In both images, we've cropped things so that the picture frame takes up the full image, regardless of how close we are to the pane of glass.

FIGURE 17.12   Short view distance.

FIGURE 17.13   Long view distance.

Keep in mind that this doesn't necessarily refer to how close you are to the glass when *viewing* the final, traced image (or how close you are to the monitor when viewing a 3D game). This refers to the distance that you are from the glass while you're *tracing* the image (or while the computer is rendering the scene).

This may seem abstract at the moment, but it will make more sense when we look at the projection code and see exactly how view distance factors in.

x, y, z

On a 2D surface all points are represented with two variables x and y. In the 3D world, all things are represented by three coordinates: x, y, and z—width, height, and depth.

We just saw how projection is the method by which 3D images are placed on a 2D surface. To that end, we're ultimately looking at how we convert x, y, and z, into simply sx and sy—screen coordinates. We're factoring out the z, and this is how we do it:

$$zfactor = d/z$$
$$sx = x * zfactor + centerX$$
$$sy = y * zfactor + centerY$$

That is the meat of it, and it's how we project any arbitrary point from the 3D world onto a 2D surface. For each point, the variable `zfactor` is calculated by taking the `d` variable (which is the view distance we discussed earlier) and dividing it by the `z` of the point. The `zfactor` is simply a number by which the x and y values of a point are multiplied to result in a scaled, modified x and y in screen space.

By multiplying x times `zfactor` we get an `sx` value for the screen coordinate, and multiplying y times `zfactor` gives us an `sy` value for the screen coordinate. As objects recede into the distance, they must also scale down in size. We accomplish this by performing a similar equation:

$$scale = 100 * zfactor$$

Remember, 100 is the *actual* scale of the object (which seems almost too logical, but it's true), and therefore multiplying 100 by `zfactor` will give us a new value by which this object will be scaled so that it appears to be the correct *size* on screen.

Once we have `sx` and `sy`, we must add `centerX` and `centerY` to the values. This is because our projection is going to be working based on zero, meaning that our objects will all recede into the distance toward the `sx`, `sy` point of 0, 0. This means that all of our 3D scenes will be top and left aligned with the screen. Take a look at Figure 17.14. It's a long string of spheres in a cosine wave shape, without the addition of `centerX` and `centerY`. Notice that they all recede toward position 0, 0, which is the upper-left corner of the screen.

In Figure 17.15, on the other hand, we've added `centerX` and `centerY`, and we can see now that the string of spheres recedes properly toward the center of the screen. The center of screen can be thought of as the *vanishing point*—an artistic term that refers to the point to which all objects in a 3D scene converge.

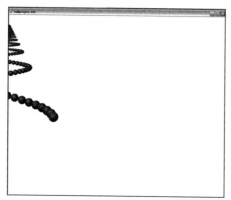

FIGURE 17.14 Projection without proper centering.

FIGURE 17.15 Projection with proper centering.

To figure out the values for `centerX` and `centerY`, we simply take the screen width and height and divide by two.

$$centerX = \text{screen width}/2$$
$$centerY = \text{screen height}/2$$

To see the FLA for the string of spheres, open up `sphereproject.fla` from the Chapter 17 folder on the CD-ROM. In it, we have only one item in the library: a movie clip called `sphere`, with the linkage name `sphere`. This sphere is 43 × 43 pixels in size. Our string contains 1250 spheres, and we can find the following code on frame 1 of the main timeline. First we have:

```
d = 800;
centerX = 275;
centerY = 200;
```

This code is where we're defining our initial variables `d`, `centerX`, and `centerY`. A value of 800 for `d` creates a fairly realistic scale that mimics real-life perspective as our eyes expect to see them. This value means that a sphere whose z value is 800 would appear exactly 43 × 43 on screen; at 800, `zfactor` will be 800/800, which is 1, and therefore scale will be 100 * 1, which is still 100. Continuing on, we have:

```
ang = 0;
for (var i = 0; i < 1250; i++)
{
    var nm = "sphere" + i;
    _root.attachMovie("sphere", nm, i);
```

First we define a variable called `ang` and set it to 0 to begin with. This is what we're going to be using to cycle through our cosine wave.

After this, we create our 1250 sphere movie clips, with instance names of `sphere0`, `sphere1`, `sphere2`, and so on. We attach them to the _root, and for now their depth levels are simply defined by `i`. Their depths will be changed later to accurately reflect the layering that we would expect to see, based on their z value. After this, we have:

```
    _root[nm].x = Math.cos(ang) * 200;
    ang += 0.2;
    _root[nm].y = 400;
```

This is how we create our cosine wave. We're setting the x position of each sphere to `Math.cos(ang) * 200`, which will mean that x will be a number between −200 and 200, cycling back and forth as we increase `ang` by 0.2 with each successively created sphere. The faster we increase `ang`, the more times the wave will cycle back and forth.

We're also setting y to 400, so that we can see the string of spheres from a raised elevation, rather than head on. If we don't set y to 400, and instead set it to 0, we'll see something like Figure 17.16.

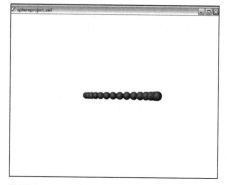

FIGURE 17.16 The string of spheres with y values of 0.

Notice that the x and y variables are called x and y, and not _x and _y. Remember, these are virtual positions in 3D space, not screen coordinates—not yet anyway. Next we have this line of code:

```
_root[nm].z = (i * 50) + 1400;
var zfactor = d / _root[nm].z;
```

Here we're calculating our z variable. In this case, z is created as a multiple of i * 50 plus 1400, which means the first sphere will be at 1400, the next at 1450, then 1500, 1550, 1600, and so on. This means our wave will recede evenly and smoothly into the distance. We're also computing zfactor here, using the equation discussed earlier: dividing d by the z value of the sphere. Once we've computed zfactor, we can calculate the actual screen position of the sphere, with:

```
_root[nm]._x = _root[nm].x * zfactor + centerX;
_root[nm]._y = _root[nm].y * zfactor + centerY;
```

Once we do this, our sphere will be moved to the correct position on screen. After this, we have the following:

```
_root[nm]._xscale = 100 * zfactor;
_root[nm]._yscale = 100 * zfactor;
```

This is how we correctly scale the sphere so that it recedes into the distance. Hypothetically, if we didn't perform this scale operation, every sphere would be 100% scale, and the final scene would look something like Figure 17.17.

After this we have the following, final line of code:

```
_root[nm].swapDepths(Math.floor(100000
                - _root[nm].z));
}
```

FIGURE 17.17　The projected sphere string without scaling.

This is how we cause the rendering engine to layer things properly so that objects farther away appear behind objects that are closer. It works by simply setting the depth level of each sphere to 100,000 minus its z value. We have to do this subtraction operation because we want the spheres with higher z values to have lower depths, thus causing them to be drawn *beneath* other objects. A sphere with a huge z value of 100,000 would be drawn at depth level 0, which is 100,000 minus 100,000. This means that the farthest away an object can be is 100,000.

If we were to disable this `swapDepths` function, we would have an image that looks something like Figure 17.18. Notice that the farther spheres are actually layered in *front* of the closer spheres. This creates a very confusing look.

FIGURE 17.18　The projected sphere string without swapping depths.

Here is the entire source code for this example:

```
d = 800;
centerX = 275;
centerY = 200;

ang = 0;
```

```
for (var i = 0; i < 1250; i++)
{
    var nm = "sphere" + i;
    _root.attachMovie("sphere", nm, i);

    _root[nm].x = Math.cos(ang) * 200;
    ang += 0.2;
    _root[nm].y = 400;

    _root[nm].z = (i * 50) + 1400;

    var zfactor = d / _root[nm].z;
    _root[nm]._x = _root[nm].x * zfactor + centerX;
    _root[nm]._y = _root[nm].y * zfactor + centerY;

    _root[nm]._xscale = 100 * zfactor;
    _root[nm]._yscale = 100 * zfactor;

    _root[nm].swapDepths(Math.floor(100000 - _root[nm].z));
}
```

A Dynamic Scene

In the previous example we looked at creating a static 3D scene. In other words, the position, scale, and depth of all the spheres was calculated once, when they were created, and then all calculation was finished.

What if we want our scene to be dynamic, and instead of everything being calculated once, we want to make our scene dynamic in any of the following ways?

- The ability to move objects in the scene physically in 3D space
- The ability to move the viewpoint up, down, left, right, forward, or backward

The first example moves the viewer, and the second example moves the objects being viewed. Let's look at both.

Moving the Spheres

In order to move the spheres dynamically, in an animated fashion, we will need to change the point at which our calculations are performed, and rather than performing them once, we'll need to perform them every frame that the object moves.

This has one big ramification: we're not going to be able to support 1250 spheres and keep any sort of acceptable real-time performance when all of them are moving and all of them have onEnterFrame functions attached to them. We're going to have to reduce the number of spheres, so we'll be using 40. Open up sphereproject2.fla from the Chapter 17 folder on the CD-ROM. When we run this as is, we'll see a much shorter string of spheres, but this time they'll be mov-

ON THE CD

ing upward on screen, in proper 3D perspective; the farther spheres will move slower than the closer spheres. Figures 17.19 and 17.20 show the scene at the beginning of execution and after several seconds of execution.

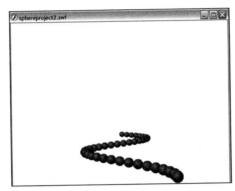

FIGURE 17.19   The dynamic spheres initially.

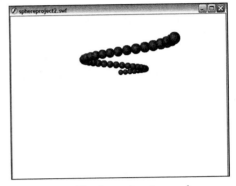

FIGURE 17.20   The dynamic spheres after several seconds.

To do this is very simple. All we're doing is decreasing the y value for each sphere, every frame, and then reprojecting the scene. That's right. We're *decreasing* the y value to move *up* because a point that is higher on screen has a smaller y value, and a lower screen point has a larger y value. To facilitate this, we create a new function called `project`, and assign it to each sphere.

The code in this example is similar to the previous example, with a few small changes. It's located on frame 1 of the main timeline, so let's look at it now. First, we have:

```
d = 1000;
centerX = 275;
centerY = 200;

ang = 0;
```

This is exactly like the previous example, but note the new value for d. We've done this because we have fewer spheres on screen. A value of 1000 makes things bigger on screen, with a less exaggerated depth recession. For comparison, look at Figures 17.21 and 17.22. The first figure has a d value of 1000, while the second figure has a d value of only 100. Notice that the second figure seems much deeper and more exaggerated.

After these first three lines of code, we have the following:

```
function project()
{
```

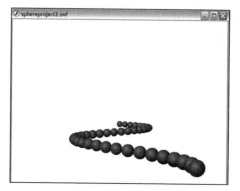

FIGURE 17.21   d value of 1000.

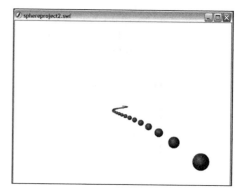

FIGURE 17.22   d value of 100.

This is where we start our new `project` function. Inside this we have:

```
if (this.z < 40)
{
    this._visible = false;
}
```

We're performing an important check here. If the z value of an object is less than 40, we consider it to be physically behind the user, so we don't draw it at all. Imagine the sphere coming toward us; at what point do we say, "OK, the sphere has passed us and is now behind us so we can't see it"? Well, it seems that 40 in our case is a good z value. We don't want to say `if (this.z < 0)`, because when a sphere reaches zero it is so infinitesimally close to the viewer that it would appear to be nearly infinite in size; it would be *touching* your eyeball. At position 40 the sphere appears quite big and close, so we would be able to believe that is the point at which we pass it.

If z is not less than 40, however, we have the following code:

```
else
{
    this._visible = true;
    var zfactor = d / this.z;
```

We set the sphere to visible, just in case it had previously been behind our head, and then we calculate `zfactor`, as usual. We're using a lot of `this` now because this function will be attached to each sphere, so `this` refers to the movie clip itself. Then, as expected, we have:

```
this._x = this.x * zfactor + centerX;
this._y = this.y * zfactor + centerY;
```

We move the sphere to the correct position on screen. Finally, we scale the sphere and swap its depth level, as we looked at in the last example.

```
this._xscale = 100 * zfactor;
this._yscale = 100 * zfactor;

this.swapDepths(Math.floor(100000 - this.z));
    }
}
```

That's the entire `project` function. After this, we create our spheres, as before:

```
for (var i = 0; i < 40; i++)
{
    var nm = "sphere" + i;
    _root.attachMovie("sphere", nm, i);

    _root[nm].x = Math.cos(ang) * 200;
    ang += 0.2;
    _root[nm].y = 400;

    _root[nm].z = (i * 50) + d;
```

All of the above code is exactly the same as the previous example, except that here you can see that we're creating 40 spheres instead of 1250. Also, notice that we're adding d to `_root[nm].z`, rather than the number 1400 as in the previous examples. This is because as we decrease d, spheres that are farther away on the z-axis than the actual value of d become increasingly smaller and smaller. If we were to keep 1400 there while decreasing d to 100, the spheres would hardly be seen.

Next we have:

```
_root[nm].project = project;
```

This attaches the `project` function to the `sphere` movie clip, under the name `project`. Now, to cause a sphere to reposition, scale, and layer itself we simply call *sphere*.`project()`, where *sphere* refers to the instance of the sphere we want to re-draw. We won't be calling this function on an individual basis, per sphere. Instead we'll create an `onEnterFrame` function for each sphere, which causes the sphere to re-project itself:

```
_root[nm].onEnterFrame = function()
{
    this.y --;
    this.project();
    }
}
```

This is where we make things dynamic. First we decrease the y value of each sphere, and then we call each sphere's `project` function, causing the screen to be updated.

To recap, the entire contents of this movie's code is:

```
d = 1000;
centerX = 275;
centerY = 200;

ang = 0;

function project()
{
    if (this.z < 40)
    {
        this._visible = false;
    }
    else
    {
        this._visible = true;
        var zfactor = d / this.z;
        this._x = this.x * zfactor + centerX;
        this._y = this.y * zfactor + centerY;

        this._xscale = 100 * zfactor;
        this._yscale = 100 * zfactor;

        this.swapDepths(Math.floor(100000 - this.z));
    }
}

for (var i = 0; i < 40; i++)
{
    var nm = "sphere" + i;
    _root.attachMovie("sphere", nm, i);

    _root[nm].x = Math.cos(ang) * 200;
    ang += 0.2;
    _root[nm].y = 400;

    _root[nm].z = (i * 50) + d;
    _root[nm].project = project;

    _root[nm].onEnterFrame = function()
    {
        this.y --;
        this.project();
    }
}
```

Try changing the line

```
this.y --;
```

to

```
this.x --;
```

Instead of the string of spheres moving up, now they'll be moving to the left. The difference between these two can be seen in Figure 17.23 and Figure 17.24. The spheres that are closer move faster to the left, while the far spheres move slower. For the figures, the y value of each sphere was changed to 200 from 400, so that more of the string of spheres would be seen on screen.

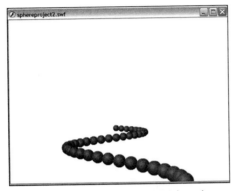

FIGURE 17.23   Spheres at their initial x values.

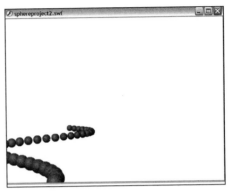

FIGURE 17.24   The spheres after moving left for several seconds, by decreasing their x values.

Finally, let's try changing `this.x --` to `this.z ++`. Now our string will be moving into the screen, as shown in Figure 17.25 and Figure 17.26. We can really feel the spheres moving into the third dimension.

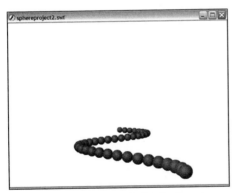

FIGURE 17.25   Spheres at their initial z values.

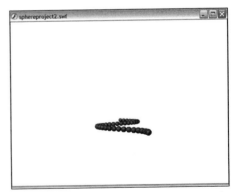

FIGURE 17.26   The spheres after moving "in" for several seconds, by increasing their z values.

ON THE CD

If you open `sphereproject3.fla` in the Chapter 17 folder, you'll see an even more dynamic example of motion in the third dimension. In this example we've created the cosine wave along the x-axis, as before, but now we're also *animating* a cosine wave along the y-axis. The result is a very interesting motion with a high degree of depth and dimension as illustrated in Figures 17.27 and 17.28.

FIGURE 17.27   sphereproject3.fla.

FIGURE 17.28   sphereproject3.fla.

To create this effect, we have the same code as the previous example, with a few small changes:

```
d = 1000;
centerX = 275;
centerY = 200;

ang = 0;

function project()
{
    if (this.z < 40)
    {
        this._visible = false;
    }
    else
    {
        this._visible = true;
        var zfactor = d / this.z;
        this._x = this.x * zfactor + centerX;
        this._y = this.y * zfactor + centerY;

        this._xscale = 100 * zfactor;
        this._yscale = 100 * zfactor;

        this.swapDepths(Math.floor(100000 - this.z));
    }
}

for (var i = 0; i < 40; i++)
{
    var nm = "sphere" + i;
    _root.attachMovie("sphere", nm, i);

    _root[nm].x = Math.cos(ang) * 200;
    ang += 0.2;

    _root[nm].z = (i * 50) + d;
    _root[nm].project = project;

    _root[nm].myAngle = i;
```

```
_root[nm].onEnterFrame = function()
{
    this.y = 100 + Math.cos(this.myAngle / 3) * 100;
    this.myAngle -= 0.4;
    this.project();
}
}
```

Each sphere is given a variable called myAngle, which is simply set to the value of i as each sphere is created. This is used to give each sphere a position along the y-axis cosine wave. In the onEnterFrame function, we use the value of this.myAngle to set the y position, and then by decreasing this.myAngle, we cause each sphere to move up and down in a wave pattern.

Moving the Viewpoint

Now that we've looked at moving the objects, let's look at how we can go about moving the entire view so that the user's perspective seems to move, and the objects remain stationary, rather than the objects moving while the user remains stationary.

ON THE CD

Take a look at sphereproject4.fla from the Chapter 17 folder on the CD-ROM. In this example, you'll see the same string of spheres as in the previous example, but this time they will not be rising and falling. They'll be frozen in space. However, moving the mouse around the screen will cause the view to shift so that you see the spheres from different vantage points. We're using the new mouse scroll wheel functionality built into Macromedia Flash Professional 8 so that scrolling the mouse wheel will move the viewer forward into and out of z. Figures 17.29, 17.30, and 17.31 show the effect of moving around from various different positions.

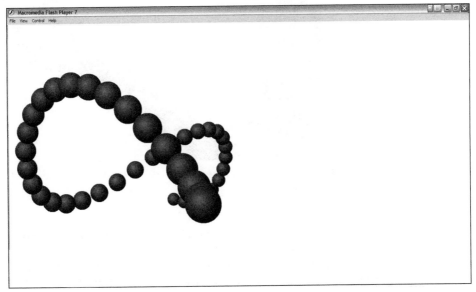

FIGURE 17.29   sphereproject4.fla with the mouse in the lower-right corner of the screen.

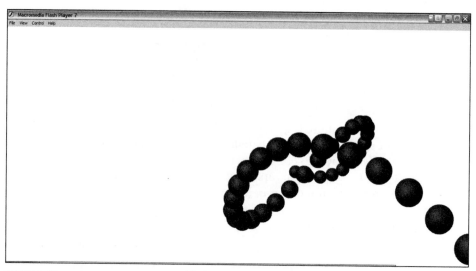

FIGURE 17.30 sphereproject4.fla with the mouse in the upper-left corner of the screen.

FIGURE 17.31 sphereproject4.fla with the mouse in the center of the screen, zoomed in.

When running this example, notice also that if you zoom in so that you move *past* any spheres on the z-axis, they are no longer drawn as if they are assumed to be *behind* you. We saw this functionality earlier, with the check if (this.z < 40), but this is the first time we're actually able to see it working.

Note that in order for the scroll wheel to work, you must be running this movie in a standalone player window, or a browser, and not from within the Macromedia Flash Professional 8 development environment.

This movie has the following code on frame 1 of the main timeline.

```
xoff = 0;
yoff = 0;
zoff = 0;

d = 1000;
centerX = 275;
centerY = 200;

ang = 0;
```

This is the initialization of our variables. Notice that we're creating three new variables: xoff, yoff, and zoff. These are the variables that are used to determine where we're standing when we look at the world. We can think of these three variables as being used to represent the user's position relative to the world, as we'll be seeing in the next piece of code:

```
function project()
{
    if ((this.z - zoff) < 40)
    {
        this._visible = false;
    }
    else
    {
        this._visible = true;
        var zfactor = d / (this.z - zoff);
        this._x = (this.x - xoff) * zfactor + centerX;
        this._y = (this.y - yoff) * zfactor + centerY;

        this._xscale = 100 * zfactor;
        this._yscale = 100 * zfactor;

        this.swapDepths(Math.floor(100000 -
                       (this.z - zoff)));
    }
}
```

This is our familiar project function, but with a few differences, highlighted in bold. Since the view position variables xoff, yoff, and zoff, are used to modify the rendering of a scene, they're applied during the project phase. Everywhere we have a reference to a position (this.x, this.y, or this.z), we have added in an adjustment for xoff, yoff, and zoff by subtracting these variables from the positions.

It's important to understand that we make these adjustments during the project phase, and *not* during the creation of the spheres. The actual x, y, and z values of each sphere do *not* change; they're merely adjusted as they're projected onto the screen. The projection and the offset of the viewer's position is independent of the actual position of the spheres. We could have the spheres moving around on their own, within their own motion system (for example, the wave motion from the previous example), and at the same time, be moving through and around that system with our mouse motion.

After this, we have the following code:

```
        for (var i = 0; i < 40; i++)
    {
        var nm = "sphere" + i;
        _root.attachMovie("sphere", nm, i);

        _root[nm].x = Math.cos(ang) * 200;
        ang += 0.2;
        _root[nm].y = 100 + Math.cos(i / 3) * 100;

        _root[nm].z = (i * 50) + d;
        _root[nm].project = project;

        _root[nm].onEnterFrame = project;
    }
```

This is very similar to our previous sphere creation and placement code. Notice, however, that we're determining the y value only once, even though it's the same cosine wave code as we used in the moving example. The only thing happening within the onEnterFrame function in this example is the project function, and as a result, we've simply set the onEnterFrame function to *be* the project function. By constantly calling project, we ensure that any changes to xoff, yoff, and zoff are immediately represented on screen.

Next we have some new code: the mouse listener code:

```
    mouseListener = new Object();
```

First we create a new object called mouseListener. Next,

```
    mouseListener.onMouseWheel = function(diff)
    {
        zoff += (diff * 50);
    }
```

Here we create a new function on the mouseListener object called onMouseWheel. This function is called whenever the user moves the mouse wheel. Currently, this only works on Windows machines. When the mouse wheel is scrolled, a variable called diff is passed in to the onMouseWheel function, and it contains the *amount* of scrolling that took place. Scrolling faster produces a larger value for diff. Scrolling the wheel upward produces a positive number for diff, while scrolling the wheel downward produces a negative number for diff. This means that scrolling up increases zoff and therefore zooms in, while scrolling down decreases zoff and therefore zooms out.

Generally, diff will be 1, 2, 3, –1, –2, or –3. We multiply it by 50 to cause the scrolling to have a dramatic enough affect on the zoff variable (and thus adjust the z variables upon projection). Next, we have:

```
mouseListener.onMouseMove = function()
{
    xoff = _xmouse - centerX;
    yoff = _ymouse - centerY;
}
```

This function is triggered every time the user moves the mouse. Upon motion, we take the current position of the mouse cursor and use it to adjust xoff and yoff. We subtract centerX from _xmouse and centerY from _ymouse because we want to use the center of the screen as our zero point; when the user has the cursor in the dead center of the screen, xoff and yoff should be zero, which will cause the 3D scene to be perfectly centered.

Finally, we have the following code:

```
Mouse.addListener(mouseListener);
```

This is required to make the mouse begin listening for the events defined in our mouseListener object.

To recap, here's the entire code listing for sphereproject4.fla.

```
xoff = 0;
yoff = 0;
zoff = 0;

d = 1000;
centerX = 275;
centerY = 200;

ang = 0;

function project()
{
    if ((this.z - zoff) < 40)
    {
        this._visible = false;
    }
    else
    {
        this._visible = true;
        var zfactor = d / (this.z - zoff);
        this._x = (this.x - xoff) * zfactor + centerX;
        this._y = (this.y - yoff) * zfactor + centerY;

        this._xscale = 100 * zfactor;
        this._yscale = 100 * zfactor;
```

```
                        this.swapDepths(Math.floor(100000 -
                                              (this.z - zoff)));
            }
        }

        for (var i = 0; i < 40; i++)
        {
            var nm = "sphere" + i;
            _root.attachMovie("sphere", nm, i);

            _root[nm].x = Math.cos(ang) * 200;
            ang += 0.2;
            _root[nm].y = 100 + Math.cos(i / 3) * 100;

            _root[nm].z = (i * 50) + d;
            _root[nm].project = project;

            _root[nm].onEnterFrame = project;

        }

        mouseListener = new Object();
        mouseListener.onMouseWheel = function(diff)
        {
            zoff += (diff * 50);
        }

        mouseListener.onMouseMove = function()
        {
            xoff = _xmouse - centerX;
            yoff = _ymouse - centerY;
        }

        Mouse.addListener(mouseListener);
```

Now, to demonstrate that we can mix the two modes and have object movement peacefully coexist alongside viewpoint movement, open up sphereproject5.fla in the Chapter 17 folder. In this movie we have our old wave motion back from sphereproject3.fla. However, we also have our mouse motion code and viewpoint adjustment code (with xoff, yoff, and zoff) in this movie. The result is something very pleasing to the eye, with the multiple layers of motion overlapping in a seamless manner that is both natural and acceptable to our eyes. This effect is difficult to capture in print, so it's best if you run this movie to experience it.

Here's the entire code body for sphereproject5.fla, with the key elements highlighted in bold.

```
        xoff = 0;
        yoff = 0;
        zoff = 0;
```

```
d = 1000;
centerX = 275;
centerY = 200;

ang = 0;

function project()
{
    if ((this.z - zoff) < 40)
    {
        this._visible = false;
    }
    else
    {
        this._visible = true;
        var zfactor = d / (this.z - zoff);
        this._x = (this.x - xoff) * zfactor + centerX;
        this._y = (this.y - yoff) * zfactor + centerY;

        this._xscale = 100 * zfactor;
        this._yscale = 100 * zfactor;

        this.swapDepths(Math.floor(100000 -
                                    (this.z - zoff)));
    }
}

for (var i = 0; i < 40; i++)
{
    var nm = "sphere" + i;
    _root.attachMovie("sphere", nm, i);

    _root[nm].x = Math.cos(ang) * 200;
    ang += 0.2;

    _root[nm].z = (i * 50) + d;
    _root[nm].project = project;

    _root[nm].myAngle = i;

    _root[nm].onEnterFrame = function()
    {
        this.y = 100 + Math.cos(this.myAngle / 3) * 100;
        this.myAngle -= 0.4;
        this.project();
    }
}

mouseListener = new Object();
mouseListener.onMouseWheel = function(diff)
{
    zoff += (diff * 50);
}
```

```
mouseListener.onMouseMove = function()
{
    xoff = _xmouse - centerX;
    yoff = _ymouse - centerY;
}

Mouse.addListener(mouseListener);
```

As you can see, it's the perfect combination of sphereproject3.fla and sphere-project4.fla. Next, we're going to look at a few techniques for really enhancing the 3D effect by adjusting the objects themselves, and using "fake 3D" to bring the scene to life.

FAKE 3D

In the previous example we moved spheres around the screen. The spheres were simply circles with gradient fills in them to create the illusion of depth. These spheres work such that you can look at them from any vantage point and they'll always appear uniform and 3D.

In the effort to expand upon our 3D effect repertoire, without actually getting into using advanced 3D modeling that is rendered in real time, we must look at ways to create convincing 3D with prerendered images. The first, and obvious, move is to take the sphere from the previous example and replace it with a rendered bitmap image. For this example, open up fake3D1.fla from the Chapter 17 folder on the CD-ROM. This file is exactly the same as sphereproject5.fla, but with one key difference, as seen in Figure 17.32.

ON THE CD

FIGURE 17.32   fake3D1.fla.

This time, rather than simply using a vector sphere, we're using a rendered bitmap of an asteroid. The effect is that we appear to have a 3D stone snake swimming on the spot. By using a 3D image that is prerendered, we give the impression that our game is doing quite a bit more work than it actually is. While the projection and layering of the object are 3D, the object itself is still a flat image, but with the addition of a rendered 3D flat image our scene looks much more convincing.

Code-wise, this file is *exactly* the same as the previous example, but with the addition of one line of code at the very bottom of the code listing:

```
_quality = "LOW";
```

Because the new image uses an alpha channel to create a transparent edge around the asteroid, the rendering engine has quite a bit more work to do to cleanly overlay all of the instances of the bitmap. To this end, we set the quality to low because we don't want the rendering engine to have to antialias all of the pixels in the bitmap, for two reasons:

- Because the bitmap itself was rendered out in a program that already applied antialiasing to the final image.
- Because the edge of the image uses pixels with alpha values of less than 100%, so it already has smoothness to it that antialiasing will not augment. If we were using crisp vector images, we would want antialiasing to smooth the edges of the vector to blend it with the background. When we use bitmap images with alpha values, our edges are already going to blend with the background. To see this in practice, take a look at Figure 17.33. Notice that the edges of the asteroid in the extreme foreground are partially see-through, and beneath those edge pixels the farther asteroids can be seen. This is the antialiasing provided by the 3D rendering software, built intrinsically into the image itself, and therefore _quality does not need to be "HIGH", allowing us to make things more optimized. If we didn't use bitmaps that had alpha edges, we would see something more like Figure 17.34. Notice that the edges are much choppier and seem less integrated into the background.

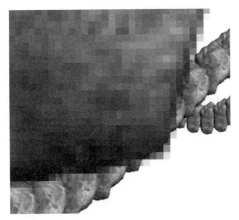 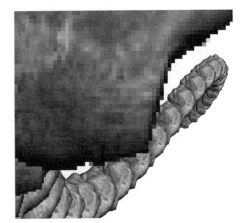

FIGURE 17.33 Alpha-based antialiasing contained within the image.

FIGURE 17.34 No alpha-based antialiasing contained within the image.

Depth Shading

One of the best ways to emulate 3D is with the use of lighting. Along with objects decreasing in size and speed with distance, objects tend to get darker to our eyes because the light has more opportunity to dissipate before it reaches us. For us, this is made possible with the use of the `Color` class built into Macromedia Flash 8.

ON THE CD

An example of depth shading can be found in the file `fake3D2.fla`, in the Chapter 17 folder on the CD-ROM. The code for this movie is very similar to the code listing for `sphereproject5.fla`, with a few differences. The effect of depth shading can be seen in Figure 17.35.

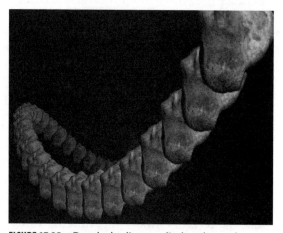

FIGURE 17.35   Depth shading applied to the snake.

Here is the entire code listing with the differences highlighted in bold.

```
xoff = 0;
yoff = 0;
zoff = 0;

d = 1000;
centerX = 275;
centerY = 200;

ang = 0;

function project()
{
    if ((this.z - zoff) < 40)
    {
        this._visible = false;
    }
    else
    {
        this._visible = true;
```

```
            var zfactor = d / (this.z - zoff);
            this._x = (this.x - xoff) * zfactor + centerX;
            this._y = (this.y - yoff) * zfactor + centerY;

            this._xscale = 100 * zfactor;
            this._yscale = 100 * zfactor;

            this.swapDepths(Math.floor(100000 -
                                      (this.z - zoff)));
        }
}

for (var i = 0; i < 40; i++)
{
    var nm = "sphere" + i;
    _root.attachMovie("sphere", nm, i);

    _root[nm].x = Math.cos(ang) * 200;
    ang += 0.2;

    _root[nm].z = (i * 50) + d;
    _root[nm].project = project;

    _root[nm].myAngle = i;

    var percentage = 100 - (i / 40 * 80);

    _root[nm].c = new Color(_root[nm]);
    _root[nm].ctrans = new Object();
    _root[nm].ctrans.ra = percentage;
    _root[nm].ctrans.ga = percentage;
    _root[nm].ctrans.ba = percentage;
    _root[nm].c.setTransform(_root[nm].ctrans);

    _root[nm].onEnterFrame = function()
    {
        this.y = 100 + Math.cos(this.myAngle / 3) * 100;
        this.myAngle -= 0.4;
        this.project();
    }
}


mouseListener = new Object();
mouseListener.onMouseWheel = function(diff)
{
    zoff += (diff * 50);
}

mouseListener.onMouseMove = function()
{
    xoff = _xmouse - centerX;
    yoff = _ymouse - centerY;
```

```
}

Mouse.addListener(mouseListener);

_quality = "LOW";
```

The new code consists simply of the `Color` class instance that is created and attached to each instance of the movie clip. When we compute the shade level, the first thing we need to do is figure out a percentage from 0 to 100 that indicates how dark each instance should be.

```
var percentage = 100 - (i / 40 * 80);
```

By using the value `i` and dividing by 40 we know what percentage of the way through the snake each movie clip is, since the snake is 40 segments long. For example, segment number 20 would be halfway along the snake, and in this case `i` is 20, which means that `i / 40` is 20/40, which equals 0.5. Once we've arrived at that number, we multiply it by 80, to get a number from 0 to 80. We don't want our farthest segment to be pitch black, so we're only going to have 80 degrees of shade. When we have this number, we subtract it from 100, which means that our nearest segment would have a `percentage` variable of 100, and our farthest segment would have a `percentage` variable of 20.

We then create a new `Color`, called `c`, on each movie clip and a color transform object called `ctrans`.

```
_root[nm].c = new Color(_root[nm]);
_root[nm].ctrans = new Object();
_root[nm].ctrans.ra = percentage;
_root[nm].ctrans.ga = percentage;
_root[nm].ctrans.ba = percentage;
_root[nm].c.setTransform(_root[nm].ctrans);
```

We set the values of `ra`, `ga`, and `ba` in the `ctrans` object to be equal to `percentage`. Since `ra`, `ga`, and `ba` are defined as percentages by which to scale red, green, and blue, setting these to the value of `percentage` will achieve the exact effect we want to achieve. We then apply a `setTransform` on the `Color` `c`, and then that segment takes on the appropriate level of darkening.

ON THE CD

If we take a look at `fake3D3.fla` in the Chapter 17 folder, we can see that things look the same, but this time we're doing the darkening in a slightly different manner, namely, the way in which percentage is calculated. This time we calculate it like so:

```
var percentage = 100 - (_root[nm].z / 2000 * 100);
```

This time we use the `z` variable of the movie clip to calculate the light level. This more accurately simulates light and the way light fades into the distance. The number 2000 in that line of code can be thought of as the far distance where the light will fall. Anything beyond a z position of 2000 will not be visible.

The main thing this allows us to do is accomplish something like the effect in `fake3D4.fla` in the Chapter 17 folder, where the light levels can be changed dynamically as you move the scroll wheel and modify `zoff`. This is the best way to do things, because the light level is then strictly tied to the user's position and therefore the user's viewpoint. It's as if the user is using a flashlight to illuminate the scene ahead. This effect can be seen in Figure 17.36, Figure 17.37, and Figure 17.38.

FIGURE 17.36   Approaching the dark snake.

FIGURE 17.37   Illuminating more of the snake upon approach.

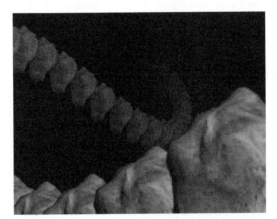

FIGURE 17.38   Moving farther along the snake, illuminating farther.

To accomplish this dynamic lighting, a small change has to be made to the `project` function from `fake3D4.fla`:

```
function project()
{
    if ((this.z - zoff) < 40)
    {
```

```
            this._visible = false;
        }
        else
        {
            this._visible = true;
            var zfactor = d / (this.z - zoff);
            this._x = (this.x - xoff) * zfactor + centerX;
            this._y = (this.y - yoff) * zfactor + centerY;

            this._xscale = 100 * zfactor;
            this._yscale = 100 * zfactor;

            this.swapDepths(Math.floor(100000 -
                                    (this.z - zoff)));

            var percentage = 100 - ((this.z - zoff) /
                                2000 * 100);
            this.ctrans.ra = percentage;
            this.ctrans.ga = percentage;
            this.ctrans.ba = percentage;
            this.c.setTransform(this.ctrans);
        }
    }
```

The new code is highlighted in bold. We're now calculating the value of percentage dynamically on the fly. Once we've calculated this, we apply it to the ctrans object and then set the color transform using setTransform. This is done every frame.

Reflection

Another very effective 3D technique is known as reflection. This is the process by which light from an object is bounced off of a reflective surface such as a mirror or a shiny floor and then that reflection is rendered into the view. Load up fake3D5.fla in the Chapter 17 folder, and run the file. You should see something that appears like in Figure 17.39. Reflected on the ground is a darkened version of the snake.

ON THE CD

To accomplish this effect, we have to do a few things:

- Each segment of the snake requires an identical segment that will be used as the object in the mirror.
- Each mirrored segment must be drawn darker than its source.
- Each mirrored segment must be set at an x and a z value that is identical to its source.
- Each mirrored segment must be set at a y value that is exactly opposite the source's y value, on either side of an imaginary line called floor.
- Each mirrored segment must be rendered upside down (_yscale flipped).

FIGURE 17.39   Reflecting the snake off the floor.

Most of the code is the same as the nonreflected version (`fake3D4.fla`), but there are a few critical differences. This code is found in frame 1 of the main time-line. First of all, we have this:

```
xoff = 0;
yoff = 0;
zoff = 0;

floor = 500;

d = 1000;
centerX = 275;
centerY = 200;

ang = 0;
```

That's all very familiar to us, except for the highlighted line. With that line we're defining the position of the floor at a y value of 500. This means that each reflected segment is drawn exactly equidistant from 500, in the opposite direction as its source segment. When we say *source*, we're referring to the segment that each reflection segment is representing. After this, we have our project function with some changes.

```
function project()
{
    if ((this.z - zoff) < 40)
    {
        this._visible = false;
    }
}
```

```
        else
        {
            this._visible = true;
            var zfactor = d / (this.z - zoff);
            this._x = (this.x - xoff) * zfactor + centerX;
            this._y = (this.y - yoff) * zfactor + centerY;

            this._xscale = 100 * zfactor;
            this._yscale = 100 * zfactor * this.flip;

            this.swapDepths(Math.floor(100000 -
                                    (this.z - zoff)));

            var percentage = (100 - ((this.z - zoff)
                            / 2000 * 100)) * this.pscale;
            this.ctrans.ra = percentage;
            this.ctrans.ga = percentage;
            this.ctrans.ba = percentage;
            this.c.setTransform(this.ctrans);
        }
    }
```

This time, each movie clip has a value called flip, which is multiplied into the calculation for _yscale. The flip variable will either be 1 or −1, depending on whether it's a reflection, or a source.

Second, the calculation for the light percentage will now make use of a variable called pscale. This is responsible for adjusting the final result of percentage in order to scale it further. Generally, our reflections will use a pscale of 0.5, which means they'll be exactly half as bright as their source image's brightness.

After this, we have:

```
_root.createEmptyMovieClip("sourceSpheres", 1);
_root.createEmptyMovieClip("reflection", 0);
```

We're now splitting our reflection movie clips and our source movie clips into two different parent movie clips: reflection and sourceSpheres. This makes organization easier and helps us ensure that the source segments will always be rendered on top of the reflection segments. Our segment creation code is nearly identical, except that instead of attaching things to the _root, we attach our source segments to sourceSpheres, like so:

```
for (var i = 0; i < 40; i++)
{
    var nm = "sphere" + i;
    sourceSpheres.attachMovie("sphere", nm, i);

    sourceSpheres[nm].x = Math.cos(ang) * 200;
    ang += 0.2;

    sourceSpheres[nm].z = (i * 50) + d;
    sourceSpheres[nm].project = project;
```

```
sourceSpheres[nm].myAngle = i;
sourceSpheres[nm].pscale = 1;
sourceSpheres[nm].flip = 1;

var percentage = 100 - (sourceSpheres[nm].z /
                       2000 * 100);

sourceSpheres[nm].c = new Color(sourceSpheres[nm]);
sourceSpheres[nm].ctrans = new Object();
sourceSpheres[nm].ctrans.ra = percentage;
sourceSpheres[nm].ctrans.ga = percentage;
sourceSpheres[nm].ctrans.ba = percentage;
sourceSpheres[nm].c.setTransform(
                       sourceSpheres[nm].ctrans);

sourceSpheres[nm].onEnterFrame = function()
{
    this.y = 100 + Math.cos(this.myAngle / 3) * 100;
    this.myAngle -= 0.4;
    this.project();
}
```

Ignoring all the obvious differences between `_root` and `sourceSpheres`, the two main differences here are in the highlighted lines. We're assigning `pscale` and `flip` to each segment and setting them both to 1. This means the light will not be dimmed and the segments will be rendered right-side up.

The remaining code inside the `for` loop is all new:

```
var nm = "ref" + i;
reflection.attachMovie("sphere", nm, i);

reflection[nm].project = project;
reflection[nm].mySource = sourceSpheres["sphere" + i];

reflection[nm].x = reflection[nm].mySource.x;
reflection[nm].z = reflection[nm].mySource.z;

reflection[nm].pscale = .5;
reflection[nm].flip = -1;

reflection[nm].c = new Color(reflection[nm]);
reflection[nm].ctrans = new Object();

reflection[nm].onEnterFrame = function()
{
    this.y = floor - this.mySource.y;
    this.project();
}
}
```

For each movie clip we create inside of `sourceSpheres`, we create one inside of `reflection`. We attach the same movie clip from the library, and we attach to it the same `project` function. We also create a variable on each reflection segment called `mySource`. This is a reference to the movie clip that is this reflection's source segment.

We then set the x and z variables to be the same as the x and z variables defined by `mySource`. We set `pscale` to 0.5, which means that our brightness calculation in `project` will be scaled down exactly 50%, making the reflection darker than the source. After that, we set `flip` to –1, which will cause the movie clip to be flipped upside down.

Beyond that, we simply create a new `Color` class instance and a new `ctrans` object, exactly like we do in the source segment movie clip. We then set the `onEnterFrame` for the reflection segment.

```
reflection[nm].onEnterFrame = function()
{
    this.y = floor - this.mySource.y;
    this.project();
}
```

This will set the y value of the reflection to be exactly the opposite value of the y value of `mySource`, on the other side of `floor`. This means that when the source segment rises up, the reflection segment will drop down, and vice versa. This is exactly the behavior of a reflection. Once this value of y has been calculated, we tell the reflection segment to `project` itself.

The rest of the code is identical to the previous example:

```
mouseListener = new Object();
mouseListener.onMouseWheel = function(diff)
{
    zoff += (diff * 50);
}

mouseListener.onMouseMove = function()
{
    xoff = _xmouse - centerX;
    yoff = _ymouse - centerY;
}

Mouse.addListener(mouseListener);

_quality = "LOW";
```

Shadow

Another 3D effect that has to do with light being cast is none other than the cast-shadow. Unlike depth fading, which simply adjusts the color to simulate distance fading, what we're talking about here is the actual shape of the movie clip being cast down onto the ground, as though the light rays were forming the shadow on the ground.

We're going to assume that all light is coming directly from above, pointing straight down. There will be no light shining from any arbitrary angle.

Fundamentally, the cast-shadow is very similar to the reflection, except that rather than being reflected across `floor`, it rests *at* `floor`. When done right, the effects are similar to Figure 17.40 and Figure 17.41, which show shadows being cast onto the floor, with the viewpoint at two differing height levels. The first figure has a high viewpoint, and the second figure has a low viewpoint.

FIGURE 17.41   Viewing the shadow from near ground level.

FIGURE 17.40   Viewing the shadow from higher up.

The shadow, like the reflection, is made up of segments, each one being paired up with a source object. This time, however, the shadow is not the actual image reflected. Rather, we're using a symmetrical 50% alpha black circle, which is approximately the same size as the width of one of the main asteroid units. This movie clip is embedded in the library, and it is set to export with the linkage name `shad`. This can be seen in Figure 17.42.

The code to create this cast-shadow effect can be found in the file `fake3D6.fla` in the Chapter 17 folder on the CD-ROM. It's attached to frame 1 of the main timeline, and it looks like this:

ON THE CD

```
xoff = 0;
yoff = 0;
zoff = 0;

floor = 400;

d = 1000;
centerX = 275;
centerY = 200;

ang = 0;
```

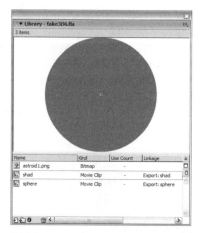

FIGURE 17.42 The shadow movie clip, shad.

The first thing we do is set our usual variables, including a floor, which is at y position 400. Next, we start our project function, as usual:

```
function project()
{
    if ((this.z - zoff) < 40)
    {
        this._visible = false;
    }
    else
    {
```

In the next few lines, we have our new code:

```
        this._visible = true;
        var zfactor = d / (this.z - zoff);
        this._x = (this.x - xoff) * zfactor + centerX;
        this._y = (this.y - yoff) * zfactor + centerY;

        this._xscale = 100 * zfactor * this.resizeval;
        this._yscale = 100 * zfactor * this.resizeval *
                                      this.ysize;

        this.swapDepths(Math.floor(100000 -
                                   (this.z - zoff)));
    }
}
```

The lines of code that have changed are highlighted. We have two size modifiers now: resizeval and ysize. resizeval is used to adjust the overall size of the shadow segment, depending on how close its source movie clip is, physically. Generally, as an object gets closer to a surface, its shadow becomes clearer, more defined, and smaller. Conversely, as an object is lifted away from a surface, its shadow grows in size and decreases in opaqueness. We will see shortly that the `resizeval` variable is set every frame for each shadow segment, depending on the distance between the floor and the source object.

The second variable, `ysize`, is used to determine the level of squash applied to the shadow, to facilitate the projection onto the floor surface, and the way it gets thinner as the viewpoint gets closer to the floor.

Next, we create the two container movie clips:

```
_root.createEmptyMovieClip("sourceSpheres", 1);
_root.createEmptyMovieClip("shadowSphere", 0);
```

We create one movie clip now called `shadowSphere` to hold our shadows. The next few lines of code are similar to the previous example:

```
for (var i = 0; i < 40; i++)
{
    var nm = "sphere" + i;
    sourceSpheres.attachMovie("sphere", nm, i);

    sourceSpheres[nm].x = Math.cos(ang) * 200;
    ang += 0.2;

    sourceSpheres[nm].z = (i * 50) + d;
    sourceSpheres[nm].project = project;

    sourceSpheres[nm].myAngle = i;
    sourceSpheres[nm].resizeval = 1;
    sourceSpheres[nm].ysize = 1;

    sourceSpheres[nm].onEnterFrame = function()
    {
        this.y = 100 + Math.cos(this.myAngle / 3) * 100;
        this.myAngle+= 0.1;
        this.project();
    }
```

The two changed lines are highlighted. We're setting `resizeval` and `ysize` to 1 so that they will have no effect on the movie clip during projection. Remember, these two variables are strictly for the shadow.

After this, we have:

```
var nm = "shad" + i;
shadowSphere.attachMovie("shad", nm, i);

shadowSphere[nm].project = project;
shadowSphere[nm].mySource = sourceSpheres["sphere"
                                                + i];

shadowSphere[nm].x = shadowSphere[nm].mySource.x;
shadowSphere[nm].z = shadowSphere[nm].mySource.z;
```

```
shadowSphere[nm].onEnterFrame = function()
{
    this.y = floor;

    var ydist = this.y - this.mySource.y;
    this.resizeval = ydist / 300;
    this._alpha = 150 - (this.resizeval * 100);
    this.ysize = ((this.y - yoff) / 1000);
    this.project();
}
}
```

Here we're creating an instance of the shad movie clip for every instance of the main segment and setting that shadow clip's mySource variable to that main segment piece. We're also setting each shadow's position to be the same x and z values as its mySource.

The biggest changes from the previous example are in the highlighted lines of code. Because shadows exist on the floor, we immediately set the y value of this instance to simply floor. From this, we determine the vertical (y) distance between mySource and this. This will tell us how high the instance of the object whose shadow we're casting is. Once we have calculated ydist, we determine the value of resizeval based on dividing ydist by 300. The number 300 was arrived at by trial and error.

We then set the _alpha value of the shadow so that higher segments produce dimmer shadows, which will also be larger because the value of resizeval will be larger—usually a number between 0.3 and 1. By applying resizeval to the formula 150 - (this.resizeval * 100), we end up with _alpha values that range anywhere from about 50 to 130. This will cause the closer shadows to be darker and the higher shadows to be dimmer.

We also determine the amount of y squash (ysize) to apply to the shadow movie clip based on the distance that the viewpoint is vertically from the floor. We divide that distance by 1000, which results in our ysize. This was also arrived at through trial and error, and it tends to produce the most realistic results.

The remaining code is the same, with the creation of mouse listeners and setting the _quality to "LOW". Our final code for the entire shadow example, fake3D6.fla, is:

```
xoff = 0;
yoff = 0;
zoff = 0;

floor = 400;

d = 1000;
centerX = 275;
centerY = 200;

ang = 0;
```

```
function project()
{
    if ((this.z - zoff) < 40)
    {
        this._visible = false;
    }
    else
    {
        this._visible = true;
        var zfactor = d / (this.z - zoff);
        this._x = (this.x - xoff) * zfactor + centerX;
        this._y = (this.y - yoff) * zfactor + centerY;

        this._xscale = 100 * zfactor * this.resizeval;
        this._yscale = 100 * zfactor * this.resizeval
                                    * this.ysize;

        this.swapDepths(Math.floor(100000 -
                                 (this.z - zoff)));
    }
}

_root.createEmptyMovieClip("sourceSpheres", 1);
_root.createEmptyMovieClip("shadowSphere", 0);

for (var i = 0; i < 40; i++)
{
    var nm = "sphere" + i;
    sourceSpheres.attachMovie("sphere", nm, i);

    sourceSpheres[nm].x = Math.cos(ang) * 200;
    ang += 0.2;

    sourceSpheres[nm].z = (i * 50) + d;
    sourceSpheres[nm].project = project;

    sourceSpheres[nm].myAngle = i;
    sourceSpheres[nm].resizeval = 1;
    sourceSpheres[nm].ysize = 1;

    sourceSpheres[nm].onEnterFrame = function()
    {
        this.y = 100 + Math.cos(this.myAngle / 3) * 100;
        this.myAngle+= 0.1;
        this.project();
    }

    var nm = "shad" + i;
    shadowSphere.attachMovie("shad", nm, i);

    shadowSphere[nm].project = project;
    shadowSphere[nm].mySource = sourceSpheres["sphere"
                                            + i];
```

```
            shadowSphere[nm].x = shadowSphere[nm].mySource.x;
            shadowSphere[nm].z = shadowSphere[nm].mySource.z;

            shadowSphere[nm].onEnterFrame = function()
            {
                this.y = floor;

                var ydist = this.y - this.mySource.y;
                this.resizeval = ydist / 300;
                this._alpha = 150 - (this.resizeval * 100);
                this.ysize = ((this.y - yoff) / 1000);
                this.project();
            }
        }

        mouseListener = new Object();
        mouseListener.onMouseWheel = function(diff)
        {
            zoff += (diff) * 50;
        }

        mouseListener.onMouseMove = function()
        {
            xoff = _xmouse - centerX;
            yoff = _ymouse - centerY;
        }

        Mouse.addListener(mouseListener);

        _quality = "LOW";
```

That brings us to the end of this chapter. In the next chapter we'll be looking at applying most of the effects we just covered in a very advanced game.

SUMMARY

In this chapter we've seen several ways in which the effect of 3D can be created. We've covered:

- Parallax scrolling with planes
- Parallax scrolling with objects
- Projection of a 3D scene onto a 2D surface
- Projecting x, y, and z coordinates into screen x and screen y
- Dynamically moving items in 3D around a scene
- Dynamically moving the viewpoint through a 3D scene
- Using prerendered items to create enhanced 3D effects
- Using shading to add to the depth effect
- Using reflections to add to the 3D effect

THE 3D GAME: ASTEROID RUN

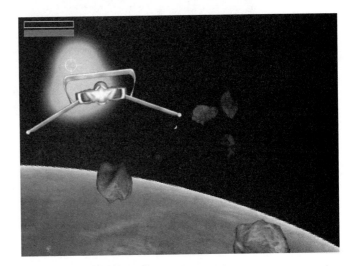

Now we're going to take everything that we looked at in the previous chapter, and apply it to the game for this chapter: Asteroid Run. This is the most graphically intensive game of the book, and as a result will require the most out of your CPU. Unfortunately, readers with slower CPUs may notice a performance hit.

In Asteroid Run you play a space ranger whose job it is to fly around the Earth destroying the asteroids that threaten to plummet to the ground and wreak havoc on the inhabitants below. While destroying the asteroids, your secondary goal is to collect enough radioactive space fuel to fill your reservoir tank so you can bring it home and put it to good use on the Earth.

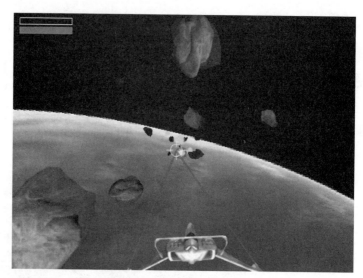

FIGURE 18.1   Asteroid Run in progress.

As you fly, you gradually circle the entire Earth, and with each complete circle around the planet, you gradually move further south, as illustrated in Figures 18.2, 18.3, and 18.4.

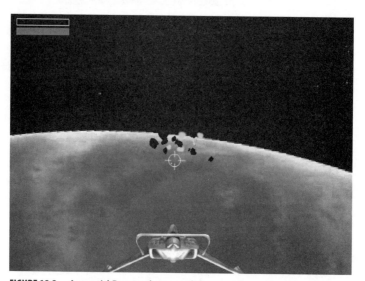

FIGURE 18.2   Asteroid Run at the top of the world.

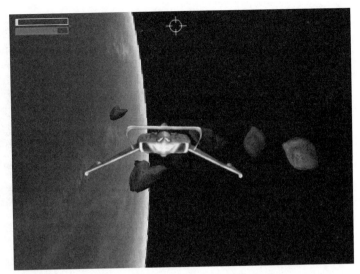

FIGURE 18.3   At the equator.

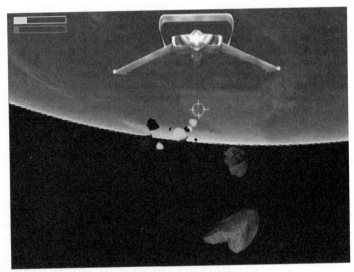

FIGURE 18.4   At the bottom of the world.

As you fly, you have to be careful to not be hit by the asteroids zooming toward you. Every time an asteroid hits your hull, a percentage of your hull integrity is lost. The hull integrity is represented by the lower of the two bars in the upper-left corner of the screen. When all of your hull integrity is lost, it is game over, like in Figure 18.5.

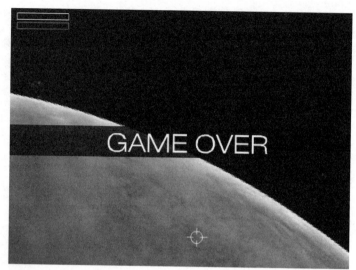

FIGURE 18.5   Game over.

Flying and steering are accomplished by simply moving the mouse around the screen. This will move the crosshairs on screen, and the ship will always bank and fly toward the crosshairs, as shown in Figure 18.6.

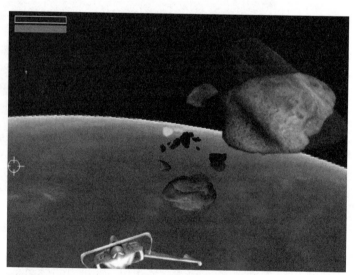

FIGURE 18.6   Steering toward the crosshairs.

The crosshairs also have the secondary function of targeting and firing your lasers. When you click the left mouse button, the lasers will fire toward the crosshairs, like in Figure 18.7.

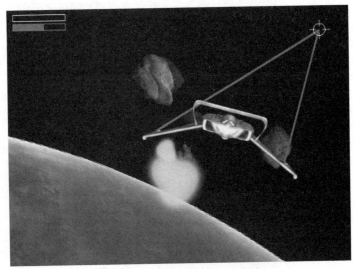

FIGURE 18.7   Firing the lasers toward the crosshairs.

When you move the crosshairs over an asteroid and then you fire the lasers, the asteroid will be destroyed. You must do this to remove the asteroids as a threat to the Earth and to avoid colliding with them, like in Figure 18.8.

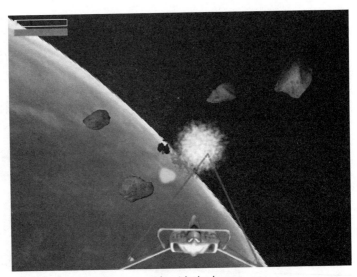

FIGURE 18.8 Destroying asteroids with the lasers.

As you proceed, you must collect as much green radioactive space fuel as you can. Unlike the asteroids, which you must avoid colliding with, you have to fly into the radioactive space fuel to pick it up, like in Figure 18.9.

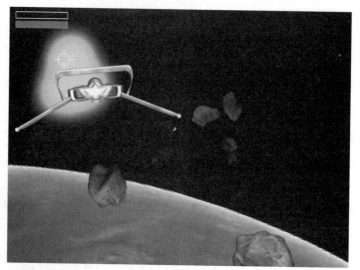

FIGURE 18.9   Picking up radioactive space fuel.

Be careful, though; don't shoot the radioactive space fuel, or you will destroy it. When you collect the radioactive space fuel, your fuel reservoir will fill up. This is the top green bar located in the upper-left corner of the screen. When you have completely filled the bar, you have won the game, like in Figure 18.10.

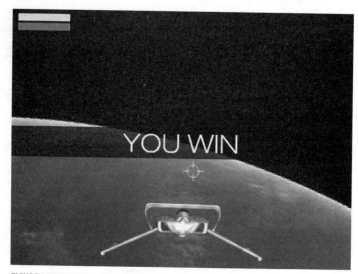

FIGURE 18.10   Winning the game.

The overall effect of this game is a very smooth and interactive 3D experience with high levels of action. All of the graphics in the game were rendered using a 3D rendering program, so they look extremely real and highly 3D, including the ship, which will always be shown from one of 30 different angles, depending on its screen position.

The earth is a 620-frame looping movie, rendered in a 3D rendering program. The movie is one complete orbit of the planet. As this movie plays, it is scaled, rotated, and moved on screen, depending on the position of the ship, giving a very effective and dynamic parallax effect.

The asteroids were rendered in the same 3D rendering program, and there are a total of 14 asteroid images of varying shape and size. We also apply a lighting effect on the asteroids as they approach from the distance. The farther away they are, the darker they appear. The green radioactive fuel, on the other hand, has no lighting applied to it and thus always appears to glow brightly.

Because of the complexity of this game, rather than create the graphics from scratch in this chapter, we'll be working with a completed movie file with embedded graphics and going through it step by step to understand what all of the graphics do and how all of the code works.

THE GRAPHICS

ON THE CD

Start by opening the movie file `asteroid3d.fla` in Macromedia Flash Professional 8. This file is located in the Chapter 18 folder on the CD-ROM. You should see a stage that looks something like Figure 18.11.

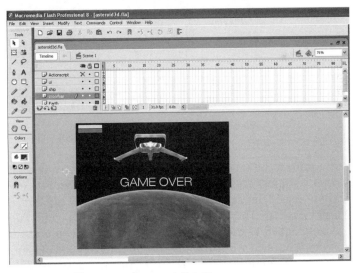

FIGURE 18.11   The stage of `asteroid3d.fla`.

The main timeline consists of five layers. From top to bottom, these are:

Actionscript: The code for the game on Frame 1
UI: Contains all user interface elements including fuel bar, hull integrity bar, and "Game Over" and "You Win" text
Ship: The `ship` movie clip
Crosshair: The `crosshair` movie clip
Earth: The 620-frame Earth animation in a movie clip

Let's look at the layers in detail. We'll be looking at the `Actionscript` layer in the next section, when we start looking at the code, so let's start with the `UI` layer.

The UI Layer

On the `UI` layer we have two movie clips. The first one is an instance of the `meters` movie clip, with the instance name `meters`. The second one is an instance of the `textDisplays` movie clip, with the instance name `textDisplays`. The layer looks like Figure 18.12.

FIGURE 18.12   The `UI` layer.

Within the `meters` movie clip, there are two layers. The top layer has two colored outlines, and the bottom layer has the rectangles that fill these outlines. These rectangles are instances of the `bar` movie clip, with instance names `fuelBar` and `healthBar`. These movie clips are 83.8 pixels wide. They each have a tint color effect applied to them so that the `fuelBar` is green and `healthBar` is red. The color effect is applied from the properties panel when the movie clip is selected. The chosen color effect is Tint, like in Figure 18.13, where the `fuelBar` is shown with a tint of R:153, G:255, and B:102.

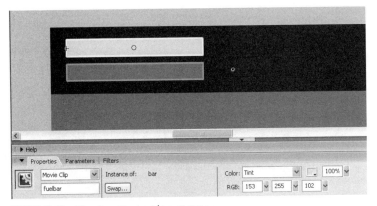

FIGURE 18.13 The `fuelBar` and `healthBar`.

To reflect the player's hull integrity (`healthBar`) or radioactive space fuel (`fuel-Bar`), we simply adjust the _xscale of either of these bars. Since _xscale is a number based on 100 being full size, in our game (where we have fuel and health levels of 0 to 100), we simply need to set the _xscale of the appropriate bar to *that* exact number, and the display will be accurate.

The other movie clip that we have on the UI layer is the `textDisplays` movie clip. Within it, we'll see that there are two frames. Frame 1 contains text that reads, "GAME OVER" (Figure 18.14), and frame 2 contains text that reads, "YOU WIN" (Figure 18.15). Underneath both of these text displays, spanning two frames, is a black bar that nicely frames the text.

FIGURE 18.14 The "Game Over" text in the `textDisplays` movie clip.

There is also a line of code on frame 1 of this movie clip, which says simply:

```
stop();
```

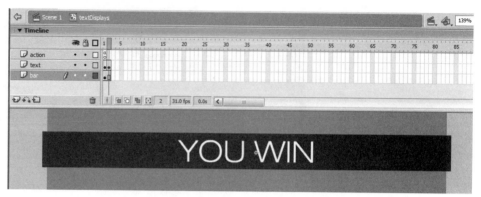

FIGURE 18.15 The "You Win" text in the `textDisplays` movie clip.

This ensures that the `textDisplays` movie clip doesn't loop between the two frames, over and over. Even though it will be hidden, we don't want Macromedia Flash Professional 8 to be doing all that work in the background.

The `Ship` Layer

The next layer down on the main timeline contains one movie clip. This movie clip is an instance of the `ship` movie clip, and it has the instance name `ship`. The layer looks like Figure 18.16.

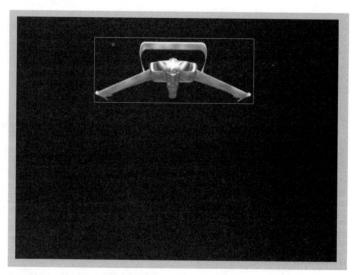

FIGURE 18.16 The ship layer.

The `ship` movie clip is 32 frames in length, and it consists of three layers:

Ship

This layer (the bottom-most layer) contains 31 distinct rendered frames of the 3D ship. The first frame is the ship rendered from a high angle, and the last frame is the ship rendered from a low angle. Figures 18.17 through 18.21 show the ship rendered at various frames starting from frame 1 and ending at frame 31.

FIGURE 18.17   The ship: frame 1.

FIGURE 18.18   The ship: frame 7.

FIGURE 18.19   The ship: frame 15.

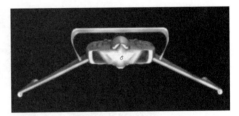

FIGURE 18.20   The ship: frame 24.

FIGURE 18.21   The ship: frame 31.

Each of the rendered frames of the ship was originally taken from a PNG image, exported from a 3D rendering program with the alpha values preserved. In the previous chapter we learned that PNG images with alpha values create images with smooth edges that the background shows through.

The reason we have rendered this ship from so many subtly different angles is to maximize the 3D effect we want to create. When the ship is near the top of the screen, we want to see more of its underside, but when the ship is near the bottom of the screen, we want to see more of its upper side. The decision as to which frame to show is made with code at runtime, which we'll see later. The last frame of this movie clip, frame 32, is blank at this point, and contains no ship picture. This is used for the explosion and death of the player, which we'll see under the explosion heading, a littler farther down.

Gun Tips

The next layer up (the middle layer) contains two movie clips, which are the gun tips. The ship has laser guns at the ends of its wings, and the lasers shoot out of the tips of the guns. As the currently displayed frame of the ship changes, so too does the position of the gun tips. For this reason, we cannot simply use a fixed position determined with code. We must instead position two empty movie clips at the tip of the guns on each frame. We use the position of these movie clips to derive a starting point for our lasers.

Looking at Figures 18.22 and 18.23, we can see how the gun tip movie clip has moved up on screen at different ship frames. The figures show frame 1 and frame 30. The gun tip is the small white circle at the end of the gun.

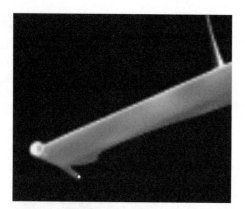
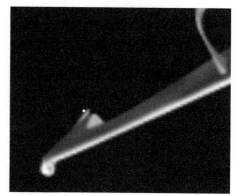

FIGURE 18.22 The gun tip: frame 1.   **FIGURE 18.23** The gun tip: frame 30.

The gun tips are instances of the blank movie `guntip`. The left gun tip movie clip has the instance name `gun0`, and the right gun tip (which differentiates its position from frame to frame, in exactly the same manner) has the instance name `gun1`.

Using this method we could, if we wanted to, add as many guns as desired, and the lasers would always appear to originate from the correct spot, where they would terminate at the position of the crosshairs.

Explosion

The top layer of the `ship` movie clip contains a single movie clip called `explosion`, with the instance name `explosion`, centered on the main body of the ship graphic.

This is an animation of an explosion. When the player dies, this animation plays, and when the explosion crescendos to its height, the ship movie clip is moved to frame 32, which has no ship frame—only the explosion movie clip. This way, as the fireball dies down, the ship appears to have disintegrated in the explosion.

The explosion movie clip is reused many times throughout the game, as we'll be seeing later. It consists of 14 frames of animation, starting from a tiny fireball, which swells to a large fireball that eventually dissipates and fades away. This animation was rendered in a 3D rendering program, and three of its frames can be seen in Figures 18.24, 18.25, and 18.26.

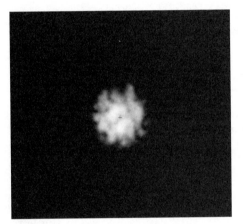

FIGURE 18.24   The explosion movie clip: frame 2.

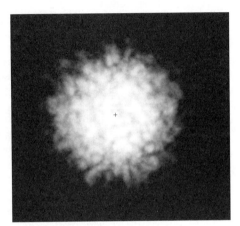

FIGURE 18.25   The explosion movie clip: frame 8.

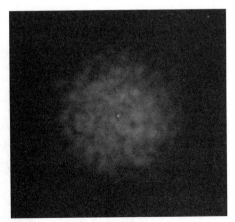

FIGURE 18.26   The explosion movie clip: frame 11.

Frame 2 of the explosion movie clip is blank, and this is the frame that it sits on most of the time while attached to asteroids and the ship. This way, the explosion is ready to be called up at a moments notice, as it's technically already there.

There is some code attached to the explosion animation as well. In frame 1 we have the familiar stop(); action, which prevents the animation from playing right away. Frame 16, on the other hand, has a more complex block of code:

```
if (_parent._name != "ship")
{
    _parent.z += 10000;
    _parent.dr = (Math.random() * 6) - 3;
    _parent.scoff = (Math.random() * 200) + 100;
    _parent.x = (Math.random() * 2000) - 1000;
    _parent.y = (Math.random() * 1000) - 500;
    _parent.hitting = false;
    _parent.exploding = false;
    _parent.gotoAndStop(Math.ceil(Math.random() * 15));
}
```

Explaining that code now would be premature. We'll come back to it when we've looked at more of the main game code.

That's it for the ship, and the ship layer.

The Crosshair Layer

This is probably the simplest layer. It consists only of a movie clip called crosshair, with the instance name crosshair, sitting just off stage to the left, as shown in Figure 18.27.

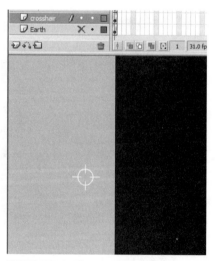

FIGURE 18.27   The crosshair layer.

This movie clip is a graphic of a crosshair that consists of a circle, two vertical ticks, and two horizontal ticks. At game time, this movie clip follows the mouse cursor around, and the mouse cursor itself is hidden, so the crosshair effectively *becomes* the mouse cursor.

The center point of the crosshair movie clip is in the dead center of the circle, which corresponds to the position of the hot spot of the mouse cursor. This means that aiming the crosshairs at something and clicking is exactly the same as moving the mouse cursor over something and clicking. We'll be using this click event later as an easy way to handle the firing of the laser.

The Earth Layer

This layer contains a single movie clip called backMovie, with the instance name backMovie. This movie is a 620-frame movie clip, and it contains a single instance of an embedded video that is 550 × 400 in size. This movie is the most graphically intensive aspect of our game, as it necessitates a full-screen update absolutely every frame. However, this is the nature of a parallax background layer. The layer can be seen in Figure 18.28.

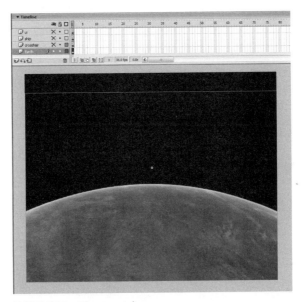

FIGURE 18.28 The Earth layer.

The embedded video was animated and exported from a 3D rendering program as an uncompressed AVI file that was approximately 360 megabytes in size. From here, it was converted into a Macromedia Flash MX 2004 FLV movie file with the program Sorenson Squeeze, as shown in Figure 18.29. Sorenson Squeeze is a great utility for compressing video into a small format, although Macromedia

Flash Professional 8 has an advanced video import interface that makes use of the On2 VP6 video codec to greatly compress video.

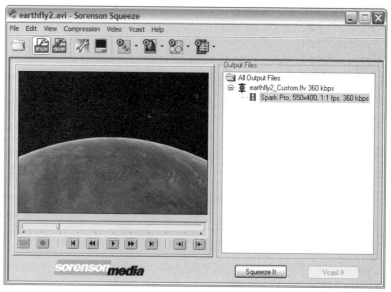

FIGURE 18.29 Converting to FLV with Sorenson Squeeze (*http://www.sorenson.com*).

The FLV created is 1.9 megabytes, which is a dramatic reduction in size from the original 360 megabytes. The nice thing about using the external program Sorenson Squeeze is that you can try several different compression settings to see what looks best, without having to import to Macromedia Flash Professional 8 each time. The other advantage is in batch processing. If you have a service that has many movies being created and updated on a regular basis (like a news media site), it's often easier to create FLV files and then load those FLV files at runtime using the NetConnection class. For more information on this, see "Working with Video" under the "Using Flash" section in the Macromedia Flash Professional 8 help system.

In Asteroid Run we're not playing this FLV file back externally, however. Once the FLV was created, we imported it directly into the backMovie movie clip so that we could place it properly on stage and have it loop continually in a seamless fashion.

The embedded video object is not centered perfectly in the backMovie movie clip. It's positioned about 40 pixels below center so that when the backMovie is scaled and rotated during the game, we never see the "bottom edge" of backMovie. This would look very strange, as the earth would appear to come to an abrupt end. By having the embedded video 40 pixels down, we ensure that the only edge we ever see is the top edge, which is already black and will therefore blend almost seamlessly with the black background of the movie stage.

We'll look again at backMovie when we look at the code.

That's it for the layers that are on the main timeline, but that's not all the graphics we have to look at. We have one more movie clip that is embedded in the library, set up for linkage.

Embedded Clip: Asteroid

In the library we have one movie clip that is set up for external embedding. It's called asteroid, and its linkage name is asteroid. The movie clip is 17 frames long and looks something like Figure 18.30.

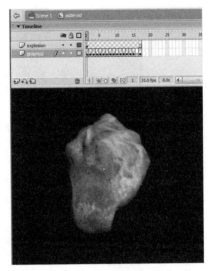

FIGURE 18.30   The asteroid movie clip.

Each of the first 14 frames of the asteroid movie clip contains a different rendering of an asteroid in the exact same position on the stage. The variety exists so that the game never appears to be repeating the same asteroid twice. The asteroids vary greatly, as depicted in Figure 18.31.

Frame 15 of the asteroid movie clip contains a single-frame rendering of the radioactive space fuel, as shown in Figure 18.32.

Frame 16 of the asteroid movie clip is blank. This is the frame we switch to when an asteroid is destroyed and the explosion animation is playing. The explosion animation is, of course, on the top layer of the asteroid movie clip. It spans the entire timeline, exactly like in the ship movie clip, and it has the instance name explosion.

Frame 17 contains a special rendition of the radioactive space fuel image stretched to 200% of its normal width. We do this to create a special effect when the player grabs the radioactive space fuel. We switch to this frame to indicate a

FIGURE 18.31   The differing shapes and sizes of asteroids.

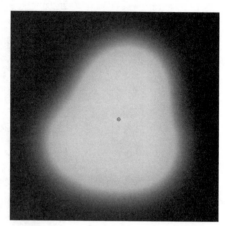

FIGURE 18.32   Frame 15 of the `asteroid` movie clip: the radioactive space fuel.

successful pickup. We can't do this stretch with code, because the `_xscale` and `_yscale` of our asteroids are tightly controlled by the `project` function (like in the previous chapter).

As we see soon, the destruction of an asteroid with the laser is performed with a mouse click, which relies upon the shape of the movie clip. As a result, the default rectangular shape of each asteroid bitmap will not suffice. As Figure 18.33 shows, the actual shape of the bitmap is a rectangle that is larger than the physical representation of the asteroid itself.

We don't want all of that white space around the asteroid to be considered clickable. As a result, we go through the `asteroid` movie clip and break apart all of the bitmap images by selecting each bitmap and pressing Ctrl-B. Once they're broken, we use the eraser tool (Figure 18.34) to carefully erase as much "blank"

FIGURE 18.34   The eraser tool.

FIGURE 18.33   The bounding box of the asteroid.

space as possible, leaving something that looks like Figure 18.35. Notice that the shaded area represents what has been left behind and that there is an outline remaining to make it a little bit easier to click on the asteroids. What we're ultimately erasing are pixels that have an alpha value of zero, which means they're not seen anyway.

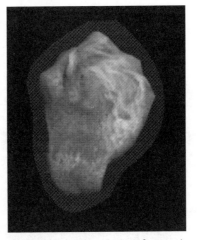

FIGURE 18.35   The remains after erasing.

With each frame carefully sculpted, we're done with the asteroid movie clip and finished with all of the graphics for the game.

THE CODE

Fundamentally, the code for this game is very simple and makes use of many of the concepts discussed in the previous chapter. Because of this, it's highly recommended that you read the previous chapter before proceeding with this code. Some of the 3D concepts will not be covered in explicit detail, as an understanding of them is assumed at this point: specifically, the understanding of x, y, and z, and the projection functions.

The code for this game is found on frame 1 of the Actionscript layer, on the main timeline. The first thing we have is this:

```
backMovie._xscale = 200;
backMovie._yscale = 200;
```

What we're doing here is immediately resizing the background Earth movie to 200% of its original size. We do this because, as you'll see soon, we use the position of the ship to pan around the background to create the parallax effect. When the ship moves to the right on screen, the Earth moves to the left, and when the ship moves to the left, the Earth moves to the right. This creates the effect that there's a camera behind the ship that is panning left and right as the ship moves. This greatly increases the 3D effect. Figure 18.36 shows how the backMovie movie clip will position itself when the ship is in the upper-left corner of the screen, and Figure 18.37 shows how the backMovie movie clip will position itself when the ship is in the lower-right corner of the screen. The white box represents the game window that the player sees, and it remains stationary on screen while the background pans around based on the player's position.

FIGURE 18.36 Panning the backMovie movie clip down and to the right.

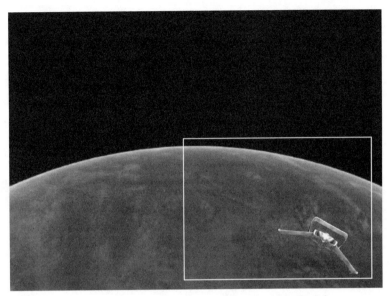

FIGURE 18.37   Panning the `backMovie` movie clip up and to the left.

After this, we have:

```
_root.xoff = 0;
_root.yoff = 0;
_root.zoff = 0;
```

Here we're setting the first variables for the 3D engine. These are the camera offset (the player's position) variables that we covered in the previous chapter. These are used in the `project` function. Next, we have the following code:

```
project = function ()
  {
```

We're starting our `project` function, which is similar in most ways to the previous chapter's `project` functions, except for a few additions. Next we have:

```
if ((this.z - _root.zoff) > 40)
    {
```

Here we're checking to make sure that the object being projected is not closer than 40 units to the player. Otherwise, this is considered to be *behind* the player. Following this is:

```
this._visible = true;
var zt = 300 / (this.z - _root.zoff);
```

```
this._x = ((this.x - _root.xoff) * zt) + 275;
this._y = ((this.y - _root.yoff) * zt) + 200;

this._xscale = this._yscale = this.scoff * zt;
this.swapDepths(10000 - (this.z - _root.zoff));
```

This is all the standard projection code that we saw in the previous chapter. The one main difference is in the computation of _xscale and _yscale for the object being projected. Rather than just using the number 100, we're using a variable called scoff, which represents *scale offset*. We do this because we want the asteroids to have varying sizes, rather than be all the same size. So, when they're created, we randomly set the value of scoff, which we'll see shortly. Next, we have:

```
var cperc = ((this.z - _root.zoff) / 5000)
              * 100;

if (this.exploding || this._currentframe == 15)
    cperc = 0;

if (this.hitting) cperc = -400;
```

This is how we handle the darkening of the projected movie clips. The first thing we do is set the variable cperc to a number between 0 and 100, where anything at a z distance of 5000 will have a cperc of 100, and everything between 0 and 5000 will have a cperc from 0 to 100, respectively. A movie clip with a cperc of 0 will not be darkened at all; and a movie clip with a cperc of 100 will be pitch black.

We then check to see if the flag this.exploding is true or if this._currentframe == 15. In both these cases, we manually reset cperc to 0. When cperc is 0, no darkening is applied. In the first case this.exploding will be true only in asteroids that have been shot with the lasers. We want to ensure that they don't have any darkening applied to them because they are exploding, and explosions generate their own light (it looks very strange to see a darkened explosion). In the second case a _currentframe of 15 means it's a glob of radioactive space fuel and therefore it glows and should not be darkened.

When this.hitting is true, we set cperc to –400, which will cause the movie clip to glow *very* brightly—almost to the point of being white. This is how we indicate to the player that he has been hit, and which asteroid hit him.

After this, we have:

```
this.cobj.ra = this.cobj.ga = this.cobj.ba =
    100 - cperc;

this.c.setTransform(this.cobj);
```

This is where we set the values of the color transform objects ra, ga, and ba to 100 - cperc. This means that anything that had a cperc of 100 would now set the color transforms to 100 – 100, which is 0. Conversely, a cperc of 0 would produce a color transform of 100 – 0, which is 100.

Once the color transform has been set, we apply it to the `Color` class instance c, using the `setTransform` method. After this, we close off the `project` function, like so:

```
        }
        else
        {
            this._visible = false;
        }
    }
```

This `else` refers to the alternative of the `if ((this.z - _root.zoff) > 40)` line. This is what we do to when the projected object has passed behind the player and is therefore invisible. The entire code of our `project` function is as follows:

```
project = function ()
{
    if ((this.z - _root.zoff) > 40)
    {
        this._visible = true;
        var zt = 300 / (this.z - _root.zoff);

        this._x = ((this.x - _root.xoff) * zt) + 275;
        this._y = ((this.y - _root.yoff) * zt) + 200;

        this._xscale = this._yscale = this.scoff * zt;
        this.swapDepths(10000 - (this.z - _root.zoff));

        var cperc = ((this.z - _root.zoff) / 5000)
                        * 100;

        if (this.exploding || this._currentframe == 15)
            cperc = 0;

        if (this.hitting) cperc = -400;

        this.cobj.ra = this.cobj.ga = this.cobj.ba =
            100 - cperc;

        this.c.setTransform(this.cobj);
    }
    else
    {
        this._visible = false;
    }
}
```

After this, we have:

```
_root.createEmptyMovieClip("asteroids", 4);
_root.createEmptyMovieClip("laser", 5);
```

Here we create two empty movie clips on the stage, asteroids and laser, at depth levels 4 and 5, respectively. Both of them will be sitting, by default, at position _x = 0, _y = 0 on screen, meaning that they perfectly match the coordinate system of the _root timeline. Once this is done, we have:

```
for (var i = 0; i < 20; i++)
{
```

This is where we begin creating our asteroid movie clips on screen. We will be creating 20 in total. That is all we need to produce a very intense action game, as they move back into the distance once they pass you, giving the impression that there are an infinite number of asteroids. Next, we have:

```
var nm = "ast" + i;
asteroids.attachMovie("asteroid", nm, i);
```

We will be creating 20 instances of the embedded movie clip asteroid, named ast0, ast1, ast2, and so on, to ast19. Next:

```
asteroids[nm].project = project;
```

We're creating a function called project on each asteroid and setting it to the project function we created above. Next we have:

```
asteroids[nm].x = (Math.random() * 2000) - 1000;
asteroids[nm].y = (Math.random() * 1000) - 500;
asteroids[nm].z = i * 500 + 13000;
```

Here we're setting the x, y, and z position of each asteroid as it's created. The x and y positions are based on a random range, of −1000 to +1000 along x, and −500 to +500 along y. This will cause our asteroid field to be wider than it is high, but this is how we want the asteroid field to seem—as if it's flat like a ring orbiting the planet. We simply set the z variable to a multiple of 500, using i as the multiplier. Each asteroid will be evenly spaced along z, exactly 500 units apart. We also add 13,000 to each asteroid's z value so the player will start off with no asteroids in front of him. The asteroids will start quite far in the distance, and the player will have a moment to get the feel of the control before he enters the asteroid field. Our first asteroid will be at a z of 13000, the next at 13500, the next at 14000, 14500, 15000, and so on.

Next, we have:

```
asteroids[nm].scoff = (Math.random() * 200) + 100;
asteroids[nm].dr = (Math.random() * 6) - 3;
```

This creates two more variables on each asteroid: scoff and dr. The value of scoff will be a number between 100 and 300. This is used as the scale value for the asteroid, so the smallest asteroid will be 100% of its natural scale, and the largest will be 300% of its natural scale.

The dr variable will be a number between −3 and +3. This is used to determine the rate at which the asteroid rotates around its center as it approaches the player. We do this because asteroids in space are not stationary, but they tend to have a rotational motion. The dr variable is that rate of rotation. A negative number will cause the asteroid to rotate in a counterclockwise direction, and a positive number will cause the asteroid to rotate in a clockwise direction. The larger the number in either direction, the faster the asteroid will rotate.

The motion that the player sees appears to be a very advanced 3D rotation. In truth, all we're doing is adjusting the _rotation value of the asteroid movie clip by dr every frame. This way, we only need a single frame for each asteroid type, because the rotational motion is on an axis that is perpendicular to the viewing plane. After this, we have:

```
asteroids[nm].gotoAndStop(Math.ceil(Math.random()
                * 15));
```

This will cause the new asteroid to go to a random frame from 1 to 15. By doing this, we get any of 15 random asteroids, including frame 15, which is the radioactive space fuel. Math.random() * 15 will technically return a number between 0 and 14.9999. By using the Math.ceil function, we will cause that to evaluate to an even number between 1 and 15. We can use this directly as a frame number to go to. Next is:

```
asteroids[nm].c = new Color(asteroids[nm]);
asteroids[nm].cobj = new Object();
```

We're creating the instances of the Color class, c, on each asteroid, and applying that Color to the asteroid itself by passing asteroids[nm] into the new Color constructor. We then create a new object called cobj, which we'll be using as our color transform object in the project function, as we saw before. After this we have:

```
asteroids[nm].project();
```

Here we run the project function once on the asteroid, so that it will move itself into position on screen, scale itself, swap to the right depth level, and so on. We have to do this immediately; otherwise, if we wait for the onEnterFrame function, there will be one frame at the beginning where all the asteroids are sitting in their default position of _x = 0, _y = 0, at 100% scale. Next:

```
asteroids[nm].onPress = function()
{
    this.exploding = true;
    this.gotoAndStop(16);
    this.explosion.play();
}
```

This is the deceptively simple code that handles the destruction of an asteroid (or radioactive space fuel). When the user presses the mouse button down while the crosshair is over of an asteroid, that asteroid's onPress function will be triggered. When this happens, the player has destroyed the asteroid, and we set its exploding flag to true. This flag is used in the project function to ensure that no darkening is applied, among other things. We also tell the asteroid to gotoAndStop frame 16, which is the frame with no asteroid bitmap at all—only an explosion. We then tell that explosion to play.

Remember the code at the end of the explosion animation? Let's look at it again now:

```
if (_parent._name != "ship")
{
    _parent.z += 10000;
    _parent.dr = (Math.random() * 6) - 3;
    _parent.scoff = (Math.random() * 200) + 100;
    _parent.x = (Math.random() * 2000) - 1000;
    _parent.y = (Math.random() * 1000) - 500;
    _parent.hitting = false;
    _parent.exploding = false;
    _parent.gotoAndStop(Math.ceil(Math.random() * 15));
}
```

This code executes at the *end* of the explosion animation, after the explosion has finished playing. At this point, we assume that the asteroid has been completely obliterated, so we reuse the asteroid movie clip and bring it back into action. Because the explosion is *inside* the asteroid movie clip, referring to _parent references the asteroid movie clip itself. Notice that we check to make sure the _name of the _parent is not ship, because the ship movie clip also contains an explosion, and we don't want any of these adjustments performed on the ship movie clip (at which point the ship would be destroyed and the game would be over anyhow).

So, assuming the _parent is not the ship, we move forward along z by 10,000. This will push the asteroid far into the distance. Next we give it a new rate of rotation (dr), a new scale size (scoff), and a new x and y position, and then we set the hitting and the exploding flags to false. Finally, we bring it back to a frame that contains an asteroid bitmap, using the same gotoAndStop statement that we used earlier.

Back to the main code now. Next, we have:

```
asteroids[nm].onEnterFrame = function()
{
```

This is where we begin the onEnterFrame of the new asteroid. This onEnterFrame function will handle all of the motion and action of the asteroid. Inside this, we have:

```
if (!this.exploding) this.z -= flyspeed;
```

We have to first check to make sure the asteroid is not currently `exploding`. If it is not `exploding`, we move it along `z` by the variable `flyspeed`. If it is `exploding`, we won't be moving this asteroid, as we want to see the explosions and don't want them flying toward us. We'll look at `flyspeed` later.

Notice how we're moving the *asteroids*, and not the *player* (which we would do by changing `zoff`). In essence, the player remains motionless while the asteroids zoom toward him. The motion gives the appearance of the player zooming through space, but by keeping the player in one z position, we don't have to perform a `project` function on the `ship` movie clip. This also helps keep our numbers lower for calculating the `swapDepths` of movie clips. Next, we have:

```
this.project();
```

This is the call to the `project` function, executed every frame, responsible for updating the screen display of the asteroid according to its new 3D position. After this, we have:

```
this._rotation += this.dr;
```

This rotates the `asteroid` movie clip by its `dr` value, which was randomly determined earlier. Next we have

```
if (this.z < 400)
{
```

The contents of this `if` statement are triggered if the asteroid has reached a z value of less than 400. This is the point where the asteroid is considered to be close enough to have physical contact with the `ship`, so, logically, we have the next statement:

```
if (this.hitTest(ship._x, ship._y, false)
    && this.z > 300 && !this.exploding)
{
```

We use `hitTest` to check if the `ship` movie clip is touching the asteroid by checking to see if the `_x` and `_y` position of the `ship` (the center of the `ship` movie clip) is overlapping the bounding area of the asteroid. This is a faster version of the `hitTest` function than if we were to change the `false` to `true` and checks only the solid areas of the asteroid. This method was arrived at through trial and error, and it seems to yield the most realistic and expected results.

Unfortunately, `hitTest` doesn't do the ideal collision check, whereby we would want to check if the *solid* areas of the `ship` are colliding with the *solid* areas of the asteroid. The only way we can check for collision between two movie clips is to check if both movie clips' bounding boxes are overlapping like so: `if (this.hitTest(ship))`. Unfortunately, this is far too inaccurate and produces hits when the `ship` and the offending asteroid are not visibly touching. By using the screen-point-to-movie-clip's-bounding-box `hitTest`, we have the best and most realistic results.

Back to the code: if the `hitTest` is true, then we also want the z point of the asteroid to be greater than 300. This is because we're assuming that the `ship` is floating out at about a z value of 300, so if the asteroid has passed below 300 (`this.z < 300`), the asteroid is past the `ship` (but not past the camera).

Finally, we also want to ensure that the asteroid is not already `exploding`, either by having been shot or by having hit the player in the previous frame. We don't want the same asteroid hitting and causing damage to the player more than once.

If all of these conditions are met (`hitTest`, z value greater than 300, and not `exploding` already), we have the following code:

```
if (this._currentframe < 15)
{
```

This ensures that it's an asteroid, not a glob of radioactive space fuel. If so,

```
this.exploding = true;
this.gotoAndStop(16);
this.explosion.play();
health-=10;
meters.healthbar._xscale = health;
```

We set the `exploding` flag of this asteroid to `true`, `gotoAndStop` frame 16, which has no asteroid bitmap, and tell the `explosion` animation to `play`. This is the same code we executed when the asteroid was successfully shot by the player. In this case, however, the asteroid has struck the `ship`, and the player loses 10 units of `health`. The `health` is then reflected in the `healthbar`, by setting its `_xscale` to the value of `health`. Immediately after this, we have:

```
if (health <= 0)
{
```

We're checking to make sure that asteroid didn't kill the player. If it did, we perform the following code:

```
ship.gotoAndStop(32);
ship.explosion.play();
delete _root.onEnterFrame;
delete crosshair.onEnterFrame;
_root.createEmptyMovieClip(
        "asteroids", 4);
_root.createEmptyMovieClip(
        "laser", 5);
Mouse.show();
textDisplays._visible = true;
textDisplays.gotoAndStop(1);
```

We tell the ship to `gotoAndStop` frame 32, which is the blank frame that contains no ship bitmap. We also tell the `explosion` within the `ship` movie clip to `play`. We then delete `_root.onEnterFrame` and `crosshair.onEnterFrame` (which we'll be covering soon) to halt all game play. We also kill *all* the asteroid movie clips and any on-screen `laser` shots by quickly re-creating their container movie clips, `asteroids` and `laser`. Hierarchically, this is a very quick way to delete a large number of movie clips. We also then make the mouse cursor (which is hidden at game time) visible again with `Mouse.show`. Last, we make the `textDisplays` movie clip visible, and we tell it to `gotoAndStop` frame 1, which is the frame with the text, "GAME OVER."

Next, we have:

```
        }
```

This is the closing to our zero health check. Next, we have:

```
        }
        else
        {
```

This is the `else` that will be `true` if the player has collided with an asteroid whose `_currentframe` is 15, meaning that it's a glob of radioactive space fuel. In this case, we do the following:

```
        energy += 5;
        meters.fuelbar._xscale = energy;
        this.hitting = true;
```

We add 5 to the player's energy level, and then we set the `_xscale` of the `fuelBar` movie clip to that new value. We also set the `hitting` flag of the movie clip to `true` to ensure that the `project` function will draw it brightly (because `cperc` will be set to –400 in `project` when `hitting` is true). After this, we have:

```
        if (energy >= 100)
        {
            delete _root.onEnterFrame;
            delete crosshair.onEnterFrame;
            _root.createEmptyMovieClip(
                    "asteroids", 4);
            _root.createEmptyMovieClip(
                    "laser", 5);
            Mouse.show();
            textDisplays._visible = true;
            textDisplays.gotoAndStop(2);
        }
```

This is similar to the check to see if the player has been killed, but instead we're checking to see if the player has filled his fuel reservoir and has won the game. If energy is 100 or more, he has won, so we delete the `_root.onEnterFrame` and `crosshair.onEnterFrame` like in player death. We also re-create the `asteroids` and `laser` movie clips to remove all asteroids and laser shots from existence. We then show the mouse cursor and cause the `textDisplays` to be visible and on frame 2, which contains the text, "YOU WIN." Next, we have:

```
                this.gotoAndStop(17);
        }
    }
```

This will cause the `asteroid` movie clip to go to the frame that contains the stretched version of the radioactive space fuel, which is used to quickly indicate to the player that he's successfully picked it up. It will continue to animate and fly toward the camera in this state, because nothing has yet told it to reset and move back into the distance. That functionality comes next, with:

```
    if (this.z < 200)
    {
```

This is the point at which we consider the asteroid to be past the camera. Though our `project` function will allow us to display asteroids up to a z of 40, there's no reason for us to take them that far. At this point, we do the following:

```
        this.z += 10000;
        this.dr = (Math.random() * 6) - 3;
        this.scoff = (Math.random() * 200)
                        + 100;
        this.x = (Math.random() * 2000) - 1000;
        this.y = (Math.random() * 1000) - 500;
        this._xscale = 0;
        this.gotoAndStop(Math.ceil(
                        Math.random() * 15));
        this.hitting = false;
        this.exploding = false;
        this.explosion.gotoAndStop(1);
```

We move the asteroid forward into space by 10,000 and give it a new `dr` and a new `scoff`. We also give it a completely new x and y value. We then set the `_xscale` of the movie clip to 0, which will cause it to not be invisible for one frame, while the `project` function catches up and shows it in the correct location. If we don't do this, then we'll see the movie clip "pop" into a new frame, with the `gotoAndStop` code. We then set `hitting` and `exploding` variables to `false` and tell the `explosion` animation to return to its blank frame 1. Finally, we finish off the asteroid creation with:

```
            }
        }
    }
}
```

At this point, all of our asteroids will exist and they'll be moving through space toward the camera. For reference, the entire code for the asteroid creation is as follows:

```
for (var i = 0; i < 20; i++)
{
    var nm = "ast" + i;
    asteroids.attachMovie("asteroid", nm, i);

    asteroids[nm].project = project;

    asteroids[nm].x = (Math.random() * 2000) - 1000;
    asteroids[nm].y = (Math.random() * 1000) - 500;
    asteroids[nm].z = i * 500 + 13000;

    asteroids[nm].scoff = (Math.random() * 200) + 100;
    asteroids[nm].dr = (Math.random() * 6) - 3;

    asteroids[nm].gotoAndStop(Math.ceil(Math.random()
                             * 15));

    asteroids[nm].c = new Color(asteroids[nm]);
    asteroids[nm].cobj = new Object();

    asteroids[nm].project();

    asteroids[nm].onPress = function()
    {
        this.exploding = true;
        this.gotoAndStop(16);
        this.explosion.play();
    }

    asteroids[nm].onEnterFrame = function()
    {
        if (!this.exploding) this.z -= flyspeed;
        this.project();

        this._rotation += this.dr;

        if (this.z < 400)
        {
            if (this.hitTest(ship._x, ship._y, false)
                && this.z > 300 && !this.exploding)
            {
                if (this._currentframe < 15)
                {
                    this.exploding = true;
                    this.gotoAndStop(16);
                    this.explosion.play();
                    health-=10;
                    meters.healthbar._xscale = health;
```

```
if (health <= 0)
{
    ship.gotoAndStop(32);
    ship.explosion.play();
    delete _root.onEnterFrame;
    delete crosshair.onEnterFrame;
    _root.createEmptyMovieClip(
            "asteroids", 4);
    _root.createEmptyMovieClip(
            "laser", 5);
    Mouse.show();
    textDisplays._visible = true;
    textDisplays.gotoAndStop(1);
}

}
else
{
    energy += 5;
    meters.fuelbar._xscale = energy;
    this.hitting = true;

    if (energy >= 100)
    {
        delete _root.onEnterFrame;
        delete crosshair.onEnterFrame;
        _root.createEmptyMovieClip(
                "asteroids", 4);
        _root.createEmptyMovieClip(
                "laser", 5);
        Mouse.show();
        textDisplays._visible = true;
        textDisplays.gotoAndStop(2);
    }

    this.gotoAndStop(17);
}
}

if (this.z < 200)
{
    this.z += 10000;
    this.dr = (Math.random() * 6) - 3;
    this.scoff = (Math.random() * 200)
            + 100;
    this.x = (Math.random() * 2000) - 1000;
    this.y = (Math.random() * 1000) - 500;
    this._xscale = 0;
    this.gotoAndStop(Math.ceil(
            Math.random() * 15));
    this.hitting = false;
    this.exploding = false;
    this.explosion.gotoAndStop(1);
}
```

```
            }
        }
    }
```

Next, we have the following code:

```
_root.onEnterFrame = function()
{
```

This is our main `onEnterFrame` function, and we're attaching it to the `_root`. One of the things the game does is adjust the `xoff` and `yoff` variables based on the position of the `ship`. This causes all of the asteroids in the distance to be drawn from a slightly different angle, as `xoff` and `yoff` are factored in to the `project` function. To this end, first:

```
var destx = _xmouse - 275;
var desty = _ymouse - 200;
```

We calculate temporary variables `destx` and `desty`, which are screen coordinates based on the position of the mouse, but offset relative to the center of the screen, rather than the upper-left corner (which is the location from which `_xmouse` and `_ymouse` are naturally measured). Once we've calculated these values, we do the following:

```
_root.xoff += (destx - _root.xoff) * .05;
_root.yoff += (desty - _root.yoff) * .05;
```

We increment `xoff` by the difference between `destx` and `xoff`, multiplied by 0.05. This means that every frame, `xoff` will move toward `destx` by moving 0.05, or 5% of the difference. This will cause `xoff` to gradually slide toward `destx` and therefore gradually slide into its new position. The same logic is applied to `desty` and `yoff`. Figure 18.38 shows how the `xoff` and `yoff` would gradually slide into place every frame.

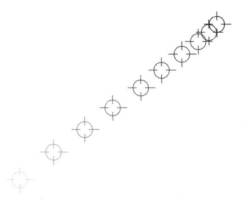

FIGURE 18.38   `xoff` and `yoff` sliding gradually into place.

After this, we have the following code:

```
var diffx = _xmouse - ship._x;
```

This calculates the difference between the current x position of the mouse and the _x position of the `ship` and stores a temporary variable called `diffx`. If the `ship` was at _x position 25 and _xmouse was 125, then `diffx` would be 100. If the `ship` was at _x position 200 and _xmouse was 100, then `diffx` would be −100. This will be used shortly for several different functions, including moving the `ship` to a new position on screen based on the mouse (which is visually the `crosshair`).

Next we do the following:

```
var tempy = ((_ymouse - 200) * 5) + 200;
if (tempy < 10) tempy = 10;
if (tempy > 390) tempy = 390;
var diffy = (tempy) - ship._y;
```

The ultimate purpose of this code is to compute `diffy`, but the way in which we compute it is not as straightforward as computing `diffx`. Rather than computing `diffy` from _ymouse directly, we compute `diffy` from a variable called `tempy`. We use _ymouse in computing `tempy`.

Basically, what we're doing is making the ship favor either the top or the bottom of the screen by setting its position to a multiple of 5 times _ymouse. We're subtracting and then adding 200 to make the middle of the screen be the center point around which this position is calculated. So, if the _ymouse is at 210, then `tempy` will be 250, because 210 − 200 is 10 and 10 * 5 is 50. Then we re-add 200, giving us 250. This means that when you place the mouse cursor at exactly 200, the `ship` will sit at exactly 200.

Figure 18.39 shows this principle in action. The farther away from a y position of 200 the mouse cursor moves, the farther away (by a factor of 5) the `ship` moves from the _y position of 200. This causes an accelerated vertical motion away from the screen's center.

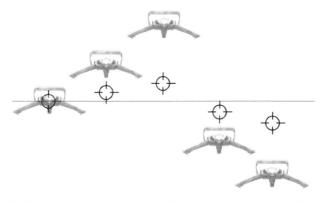

FIGURE 18.39 Accelerating vertically away from center, based on the position of the crosshair.

Of course, if the mouse cursor was 50 pixels away from the centerline, that would take the ship 250 pixels away from the centerline, which would be off screen, as the screen is only 400 high. In this case we have the two if statements to make sure that tempy is not less than 10 or greater than 390.

The reason we want the ship to be, most of the time, away from the screen's center is that we don't want the ship to obscure the crosshair and thus make it very difficult to see the asteroids that we're shooting at. This also gives the impression that the crosshair is indeed an object in 3D space that we're aiming toward and therefore gives us an exaggerated sense of depth.

The next code we have is:

```
ship._rotation = diffx / 10;
```

This takes the _rotation of the ship and sets it to the value of diffx divided by 10. This makes the ship bank into the motion, and depending upon how extreme the motion (the larger the value of diffx), the greater the bank will be. Also, depending on the direction of diffx (negative to the left, positive to the right), the bank angle will either be left or right. Figure 18.40 shows that the greater diffx is to the right, the larger the bank angle will be to the right. Figure 18.41 shows the opposite of this; the greater diffx is to the left, the greater the bank to the left will be.

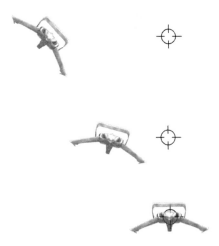

FIGURE 18.40   diffx > 0; ship banks to the right.

The next code we have is:

```
var shipframe = (ship._y / 400) * 30 - (diffy
                / 20);
```

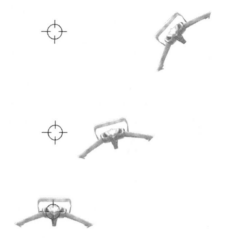

FIGURE 18.41 `diffx < 0`; ship banks to the left.

Here we compute the frame to display the `ship` from the 31 different frames of the movie clip. The first part of the equation is simple; we take `ship._y` and divide it by 400, which is the screen height. This will give us a percentage of how far up the screen the `ship` is. Then we multiply this by 30 to give us a number between 0 and 30. A ship at the top of the screen will favor lower frame numbers (where we see the bottom of the ship), and a ship at the bottom of the screen will favor higher frame numbers (where we see the top of the ship).

We then apply a slight modification to this number by subtracting (`diffy / 20`) from it. This adjusts the visible `ship` frame based on the vertical speed at which it's moving. In other words, when the `ship` is zooming up toward the top of the screen, we want to see more of the top of it, even if it's already near the top of the screen; if the `ship` is moving downward, we want to see the bottom of it, no matter where it is. The effect that this creates is, of course, that the `ship` is *pitching* its nose up and down as it flies from vertical position to vertical position on screen. Figure 18.42 shows how the `ship` favors the downward-facing frames when it is descending on screen, even though it is already lower than the middle of the screen. Only when it finally starts to come to rest do we start to see the correct frame as determined by (`ship._y / 400) * 30`.

The next code we have is:

```
if (shipframe > 31) shipframe = 31;
if (shipframe < 1) shipframe = 1;
ship.gotoAndStop(Math.floor(shipframe));
```

Here we're taking `shipframe` and making sure it's not greater than 31 or less than 1. Once we've brought it back within the right range, we tell the `ship` movie

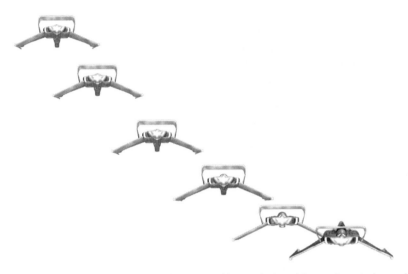

FIGURE 18.42   The ship frame is determined by vertical position and vertical speed.

clip to gotoAndStop on the calculated frame. We apply a Math.floor to the value of shipframe because we cannot pass a fractional number to the gotoAndStop function, and our shipframe will most definitely be a fractional number. Next, we have:

```
ship._x += (diffx) * .03;
ship._y += (diffy) * .03;
```

Here's where we physically move the ship on screen. Once we've carefully determined diffx and diffy, we move the ship by only 3% of that, which means the ship will always decelerate gently into position, rather than jumping there instantaneously. This creates a much more realistic motion that's based on smoothly changing direction and flying from position to position. After this we have:

```
backMovie._x = 275 - ((ship._x - 275) / 2);
backMovie._y = 200 - ((ship._y - 200) / 2);
```

This takes the backMovie movie clip (the animated earth) and sets its position according to the position of the ship. It is with this code that we cause the backMovie to move in parallax to the ship, where the backMovie moves down and to the right while the ship moves up and to the left, and vice versa, always moving in the opposite direction of the ship. It also moves at exactly half the rate of the ship, giving it a greater sense of distance and depth. Next, we have:

```
backMovie._rotation += 0.05;
}
```

This causes the `backMovie` to slowly rotate around its center point. This is how we achieve the very effective impression that the `ship` is gradually flying around the globe, going from north to south and back again. This rotation dramatically enhances the overall effect of the game.

That's the entire `_root.onEnterFrame` function. To recap, here's the code in whole:

```
_root.onEnterFrame = function()
{
    var destx = _xmouse - 275;
    var desty = _ymouse - 200;

    _root.xoff += (destx - _root.xoff) * .05;
    _root.yoff += (desty - _root.yoff) * .05;

    var diffx = _xmouse - ship._x;
    var tempy = ((_ymouse - 200) * 5) + 200;
    if (tempy < 10) tempy = 10;
    if (tempy > 390) tempy = 390;
    var diffy = (tempy) - ship._y;

    ship._rotation = diffx / 10;
    var shipframe = (ship._y / 400) * 30 - (diffy
                        / 20);
    if (shipframe > 31) shipframe = 31;
    if (shipframe < 1) shipframe = 1;
    ship.gotoAndStop(Math.floor(shipframe));

    ship._x += (diffx) * .03;
    ship._y += (diffy) * .03;

    backMovie._x = 275 - ((ship._x - 275) / 2);
    backMovie._y = 200 - ((ship._y - 200) / 2);

    backMovie._rotation += 0.05;
}
```

The next code we have is:

```
crosshair.onMouseDown = function()
{
```

This function contains code that will be triggered whenever the player presses the mouse button, regardless of whether or not he has clicked on an asteroid or just the background movie. This function contains:

```
targx = crosshair._x;
targy = crosshair._y;
```

First, we set the value of the two variables `targx` and `targy` to the _x and _y position of the `crosshair` movie clip. We'll be using this shortly in the rendering of our laser shots. The next code is:

```
        startshoot = true;
        delete laser.onEnterFrame;
        laser.onEnterFrame = function()
        {
            this._alpha *= .6;
        }
    }
```

This is the remainder of the `crosshair.onMouseDown` function. We set the `startshoot` variable to `true`, and then we delete the current `onEnterFrame` function of the `laser` movie clip. We then re-create that `onEnterFrame` function, which contains one simple instruction to decrease the `_alpha` value of the `laser` movie clip by 40%, each frame. This will cause the laser to fade out once it's fired.

The entire function is:

```
crosshair.onMouseDown = function()
{
    targx = crosshair._x;
    targy = crosshair._y;
    startshoot = true;
    delete laser.onEnterFrame;
    laser.onEnterFrame = function()
    {
        this._alpha *= .6;
    }
}
```

After this, we have the following code:

```
crosshair.onEnterFrame = function()
{
```

Here we begin the `onEnterFrame` function of the `crosshair` movie clip. This is where we handle the motion of the `crosshair` relative to the mouse cursor, as well as the firing of the laser shots. Next, we have:

```
        this._x = _xmouse;
        this._y = _ymouse;
```

We immediately set the `_x` and `_y` position of the `crosshair` to that of the mouse cursor. There is no delay or deceleration here; we want the `crosshair` to be an instantly reacting entity. Next:

```
        var point = new Object();
        point.x = ship.gun0._x;
        point.y = ship.gun0._y;
```

We create a new object called `point`, and within it we create two variables, `x` and `y`, which we set to the `_x` and `_y` position of the left gun tip, `gun0`, on the `ship`. From there, we have:

```
ship.localToGlobal(point);
```

This takes the x and y value in point, which will be relative to the ship movie clip, and converts it to a global value that is relative to the main stage. We'll need this to render our laser lines, which come next:

```
laser.clear();
laser.moveTo(point.x, point.y);
laser.lineStyle(3, 0xFF0000, 100);
laser.lineTo(targx, targy);
```

We're using the draw API to draw our laser shots, and we're drawing them within the laser movie clip. The first thing we do is clear the laser from the previous frame by issuing the draw API's clear method. We then move the starting point of the draw operation to the newly calculated point.x and point.y. We then define our line style to be a 3-point thick red line (color 0xFF0000) with an alpha value of 100%. Finally, we complete the draw operation by drawing a line to targx, targy, which was defined in the crosshair.onMouseDown function.

Redrawing the laser line like this, every frame, ensures that as the ship moves from frame to frame, the laser will always be drawn to the same target location as it fades out. After this, we compute and draw the other laser:

```
var point = new Object();
point.x = ship.gun1._x;
point.y = ship.gun1._y;
ship.localToGlobal(point);
laser.moveTo(point.x, point.y);
laser.lineStyle(3, 0xFF0000, 100);
laser.lineTo(targx, targy);
```

This is identical to the first laser line, but we're using the position of the right gun tip (gun1) and we're not clearing the laser movie clip with the draw API's clear method.

At this point we will have two clean laser lines drawn from the tips of both guns to the position defined by targx, targy. This will be drawn every single frame, regardless of whether or not the laser movie clip is actually visible. Doing this provides a consistent performance level, where the game never slows down, because we're always making it draw the laser lines, even if we don't see them. After this, we have:

```
if (startshoot)
{
    startshoot = false;
    laser._alpha = 100;
}

}
```

We check the value of the startshoot flag, and if it's true, we set it to false, and then we set the _alpha value of the laser movie clip to 100. This makes our laser lines visible, where they will then immediately begin to fade out. Remember that startshoot is set to true in the crosshair.onMouseDown function. This creates the overall effect of firing the lasers at the crosshair whenever you click with the left mouse button on screen.

To recap, the entire crosshair.onEnterFrame function is as follows:

```
crosshair.onEnterFrame = function()
{
    this._x = _xmouse;
    this._y = _ymouse;

    var point = new Object();
    point.x = ship.gun0._x;
    point.y = ship.gun0._y;
    ship.localToGlobal(point);
    laser.clear();
    laser.moveTo(point.x, point.y);
    laser.lineStyle(3, 0xFF0000, 100);
    laser.lineTo(targx, targy);

    var point = new Object();
    point.x = ship.gun1._x;
    point.y = ship.gun1._y;
    ship.localToGlobal(point);
    laser.moveTo(point.x, point.y);
    laser.lineStyle(3, 0xFF0000, 100);
    laser.lineTo(targx, targy);

    if (startshoot)
    {
        startshoot = false;
        laser._alpha = 100;
    }

}
```

Those are all the functions of the game. The remaining code is responsible for setting a few initial variables:

```
laser._alpha = 0;
flyspeed = 80;
```

We set the _alpha value of the laser movie clip to 0, so that it begins invisible. We then set the flyspeed variable to 80. This is the variable used to determine how fast the asteroids fly toward the player. Increasing this number makes them move faster but may jeopardize the collision detection, as the asteroid may never fall within the collision zone, along the z-axis.

```
energy = 0;
health = 100;

meters.fuelbar._xscale = energy;
meters.healthbar._xscale = health;
```

Next, we set the `energy` variable to 0 and the `health` variable to 100, and then reflect these initial values in the `fuelbar` and `healthbar` meters through the use of their `_xscale` properties.

```
_quality = "MEDIUM";
crosshair.swapDepths(6);
ship.swapDepths(7);
```

We set the game rendering `_quality` to `"MEDIUM"`, which will cause the game to run faster. We also perform a `swapDepths` on the `crosshair` movie clip and the `ship` movie clip. Placing the `crosshair` movie clip at depth level 6 ensures that it will be on top of all the background items (asteroids, Earth), while at the same time being below the `ship` movie clip, which we `swapDepths` to level 7.

```
textDisplays.swapDepths(8);
textDisplays._visible = false;

Mouse.hide();
```

Finally, we swap the `textDisplays` movie clip to depth level 8, making it higher than everything else, and then we make it invisible for the time being. After this, we hide the mouse cursor by calling the `hide` method of the `Mouse` class.

That's all there is to the game. With the graphics and code that we covered in this chapter, we have the makings of a very exciting space game that could be expanded in any number of directions.

EXPANDING THE GAME

There are many ways to expand this game and take it in new directions. Some of these are:

- Add sound and music. Nothing calls for killer sound effects and high-intensity action music more than a space battle scene.
- Divide the game into levels. Rather than make it one long level that is simply win or die, divide the game up into distinct stages; perhaps arriving at an orbiting star base signals the end of one level and the beginning of another.
- Add enemies. How about some of those asteroids firing back at you, or perhaps adjusting their x and y positions so that they hone in on you.
- Add scoring. The fuel meter provides a sense of scoring, but what about adding a distinct point system for asteroids destroyed.

SUMMARY

In this chapter we looked at the following concepts:

- Using a movie clip as the mouse cursor
- Implementing 3D projection code in a game setting
- Using embedded video to create more dynamic animation
- Using the position of game objects as parameters for things like object rotation and background parallax position
- Using a multiframed 3D rendering of an object and choosing the correct frame from that object based on its position on screen
- Implementing simple techniques to emulate more advanced functionality, for example, rather than firing a complex 3D laser system, simply using the onPress event to detect for hits or using the _rotation property to add to the impression of movement in 3D space
- Using invisible movie clips to act as anchors used in other processes; using the gun tips to control the origin of the laser blasts

ACTIONSCRIPT FOR GAMES PRIMER

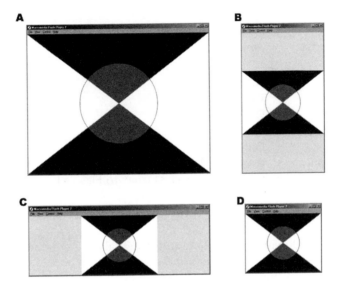

The purpose of this chapter is to provide a reference for some of the basic, most important ActionScript concepts used in the development of Macromedia Flash 8 games. We're not going to be delving into semi-game-related things like the XML class, Date class, or Microphone class (although these could probably find their way into games nonetheless). Instead, we'll be looking at those fundamentals and some classes that are most frequently used to create good, solid Flash games.

If you're new to ActionScript, or want to brush up, this chapter should help you get on your way. For a full reference, however, it's best to refer to the Macromedia Flash Professional 8 help included with the development system. This covers the entire ActionScript 1.0 and 2.0 language.

We'll take a look at a few of the fundamentals including:

- ActionScript 1.0 versus ActionScript 2.0 (and why we've chosen to code this book with ActionScript 1.0)
- `trace`
- Variables

Comments

- Comparisons and conditions
- Loops
- Functions
- Relative paths and objects

The classes we'll be looking at are:

- The `MovieClip` class
- The `Key` class
- The `Mouse` class
- The `Stage` class
- The `Math` class
- The `Array` class
- The `BitmapData` class (new to Flash 8)

FUNDAMENTALS

Following are the bare fundamentals of ActionScript necessary to get you up to speed with the games and projects in this book.

When it comes to typing code in like the samples to follow, the best way is to open up a new, blank movie, click on frame 1 of the timeline, and type the code in the Actions window. You can compile and run the code by pressing Ctrl-Enter or choosing Control > Test Movie.

ActionScript 2.0 versus ActionScript 1.0

You may have heard about ActionScript 2.0. The purpose of ActionScript 2.0 was to make the ActionScript language ECMAScript 4 compliant. In truth, ActionScript 2.0 is 98% ActionScript 1.0, according to the Macromedia Web site (*http://www .macromedia.com/support/flash/ts/documents/presalesfaq.htm*). What ActionScript 2.0 provides is:

- The ability (and requirement) to declare variables by name and type before using them
- The strictness of variable names (case sensitivity)
- True class inheritance

It's important to remember that Macromedia Flash Professional 8 is not synonymous with ActionScript 2.0. Macromedia Flash Professional 8 is simply a series of new components, an expanded ActionScript language (with more functions, classes, and objects that are all ActionScript 1.0 *and* 2.0 compatible), a better compiler that exports faster swf files, a new development environment, and a new player: Flash Player 8.

In this book we use ActionScript 1.0 because we don't need to support the custom class structure. Yes, we *will* be consistent with our variable names (we won't interchange case of variables in the middle of the code) and we *will* declare them before using them. However, the custom class structure introduces overhead in performance that we don't want in our games. Instead we're going to be using the traditional object structure, with events, methods, and properties, while at the same time taking advantage of the classes of Flash Professional 8. Yes, we can use these classes even though we're not using ActionScript 2.0. The Object structure itself is inherently class-like, and before ActionScript 2.0 was created, objects were considered the classes of Flash MX. For example, the Math class in Flash 8 was referred to as the Math object in Flash MX, even though they're identical in every way from Flash MX to Flash 8.

We're interested in optimal performance, so we're going to do what we have to do to ensure that we achieve it. Complex class hierarchy is good for some applications, but not for our games that rely on fast visuals and faster data manipulation.

trace

In the Macromedia Flash Professional 8 development environment, we can make good use of the `trace` function. With `trace`, we can display any text we want in the output window. The output window is simply an empty window that appears when we run a movie from within the development environment. This means that if we want to determine whether or not Flash is actually executing a certain section of code, we could say something like:

```
trace ("I am executing this section now");
```

When we ran the movie, Flash would display "I am executing this section now" in the output window as soon as it reached that line of code, as shown in Figure 19.1.

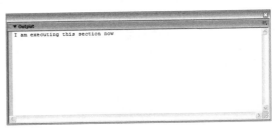

FIGURE 19.1   The `trace` output window.

The trace statement is also very useful for showing the value of variables at any given time, with something like this:

```
trace (i);
```

or

```
trace ("The value of i is " + i);
```

In the first case, if i was 7, then the number 7 would appear in the output window when that line of code was reached. In the second case, "The value of i is 7" would appear in the output window.

 If you put trace statements in and they don't seem to be appearing in the output window, press F2 to force the output window to appear. If your output window is blank, make sure your trace statements are indeed being reached.

Variables

In ActionScript we can create and manipulate variables much like in any other ECMA (European Computer Manufacturers Association)–compatible programming language. By default, if you refer to a variable before it has been defined, it will return the value undefined.

Numbers

At the core, variables are defined by simply setting a value to a variable name, like so:

```
j = 5;
trace ("The value of j is " + j);
```

This would place the number value 5 in the variable j and then display The value of j is 5 in the output window. In this case, j is a *number* and it can be adjusted with code like any number variable can be adjusted. For example,

```
j = 5;
trace ("The next value of j is " + (j + 1));
```

This would display the output, The next value of j is 6, because we're outputting (j + 1) and not merely j.

In most programming languages numbers are specified as either integer or decimal. In ActionScript, you don't have to specify. Simply setting the variable will do the required work. So you can say

```
j = 5;
```

and that's just as valid as saying

```
j = 5.1;
```

In both cases j will be a number, but in the second case it will contain the decimal number 5.1 (also called a floating point number).

Numbers can be manipulated in many ways. We can perform all of the basic arithmetic operations on them:

DESCRIPTION	CODE (ASSUME THAT j = 5)	VALUE OF k
Addition	k = j + 1;	6
Subtraction	k = j - 1;	4
Multiplication	k = j * 2;	10
Division	k = j / 2;	2.5

Also, we can modify a number by simply adjusting its value with the increment and decrement operators:

DESCRIPTION	CODE (ASSUME THAT j = 5)	VALUE OF j
Increment by 1	j ++;	6
Increment by anything	k = 5;	
	j += k;	10
Decrement by 1 (with two minus signs)	j --;	4
Decrement by anything	k = 5;	
	j -= k;	0

It's important to know that incrementing with j ++ is faster and more optimized than incrementing with

```
j = j + 1;
```

and decrementing with j -- is more optimized than decrementing with

```
j = j - 1;
```

Strings

Strings are how we store words, letters, and sentences. Yes, we can also store numbers as a string if we wanted to. The default way to create a string is very much like creating a number variable, except that we use quotes, like so:

```
s = "Hello World";
trace (s);
```

When run, this code would display the text "Hello World" in the output window. Unlike a number, we cannot perform any arithmetic on a string, but we can "add" strings together, like so:

```
s = "Hello";
t = "World";
trace (s + t);
```

This code would display the text "HelloWorld" (with no space between the two words). To place a space, we'd have to modify the code like so:

```
s = "Hello";
t = "World";
trace (s + " " + t);
```

Alternatively, we could have included the space character in the string, like so:

```
s = "Hello ";
t = "World";
trace (s + t);
```

When we use the + operator between two strings, then what we're doing is known as concatenation. We're concatenating the strings together into one long string. If we add a string and a number, we get a concatenation only:

```
k = "Hello";
g = 3;
trace (k + g);
```

This will send the text "Hello3" to the output window, even though g is a number and not a string. If we declare two variables that are both strings that contain numbers, the concatenation will still take place:

```
k = "5";
g = "3";
trace (k + g);
```

This would trace 53 to the output window, not 8, because the 5 and the 3 are both strings, as they are defined with quotes, so they are simply placed next to each other—concatenated.

Booleans

A boolean variable is a variable that has one of two values, true or false. A boolean variable is used to keep track of states of things, for example, has the player collected the magic ring? We might have a boolean variable called hasRing, and it will be false until the player collects the ring, at which point hasRing will be set to true. Booleans are assigned and created like so:

```
hasRing = true;
```

or

```
hasRing = false;
```

No quotes are placed around the true or false, as they're not strings. They're treated specially by Flash. Generally, we can safely think of a Boolean as either zero or nonzero, where zero always evaluates to false, and anything nonzero evaluates to true.

The result of any comparison always returns a Boolean value, but we'll look at this shortly.

Comments

Any time you want to put text in your code that you do not want to execute, you can convert it into a comment. These are only readable by the developer, and they're ignored by the compiler. To place a comment, simply precede the line in the code with //.

For example,

```
k = 4;
// this is a comment
k ++;
```

The line this is a comment has no bearing on the execution of the other two lines of code. It's strictly there to make the code clearer to the reader. One of the useful applications of comments is to "comment out" a line of code if you temporarily don't want it to execute. You could take the above code and do this:

```
k = 4;
// this is a comment
// k ++;
```

Now k will not be incremented, because the line of code k ++ will be ignored and skipped.

You can also comment out larger blocks of code by using a comment block. A comment block contains an opener /* and a closer */. Anything between the opener and closer will not be run. For example,

```
k = 5;

/*
j = 4;
k += j;
*/

trace (k);
```

While k would have been incremented by j, which was 4, it will not now because we have commented out the two middle lines of code. All that will happen now is that k will trace out as 5.

Comparisons and Conditions

In ActionScript we have all of the standard comparisons and conditions that are in other programming languages. By using the if statement, we can perform any logic that will, in turn, affect the flow of our program.

if

At its core, the if statement works on the Boolean principle. It's structured like this:

```
if (true)
{
    // This code will execute
}

if (false)
{
    // this code will not execute
}
```

You can structure your if *statement in a few different ways. Some people prefer to put the opening curly brace on the same line as the* if, *like so:*

```
if (condition) {
}
```

and some people prefer to put the opening curly brace on the next line, like so:

```
if (condition)
{
}
```

When you only have one line of code running based on the if, *then you don't even need curly braces:*

```
if (condition)
    trace ("My single line of output");
```

Now, we don't normally put the straight values true and false inside an if statement. We normally put *conditions* in the if statement, which in turn evaluate to Boolean true or false. For example we could say this:

```
k = 5;
if (k == 5)
{
    trace ("k is indeed 5");
}
```

The condition is k == 5, which means, "k must be equal to 5." If it is (and it will be because we've set k to 5 just the line before) then the text "k is indeed 5" will trace to the output window. Remember, a condition results in a Boolean—true or false. So, if we do this:

```
k = 5;
trace (k == 5);
```

What will happen? The word true will appear in the output window. We don't need an if statement to evaluate a condition. On the other hand, we can say:

```
k = 5;
trace (k == 6);
```

This will trace the word false to the output window, because the condition is false; k does not equal 6. Following are a list of conditions.

ACTIONSCRIPT	DESCRIPTION	EXAMPLE OF TRUE CASE

a == b	Equals. Evaluates to **true** if **a** is equal to **b**.	a = 4;
		b = 4;
		if (a == b)
		{
		}

$\rightarrow$

ACTIONSCRIPT	DESCRIPTION	EXAMPLE OF TRUE CASE

a != b	Not equal to. Evaluates to **true** if **a** is not equal to **b**.	a = 4;
		b = 5;
		if (a != b)
		{
		}

a < b	Less than. Evaluates to **true** if **a** is less than **b**.	a = 4;
		b = 5;
		if (a < b)
		{
		}

a <= b	Less than or equal to. Evaluates to **true** if **a** is less than, or equal to **b**.	a = 4;
		b = 5;
		if (a <= b)
		{
		}

		a = 5;
		b = 5;
		if (a <= b)
		{
		}

a > b	Greater than. Evaluates to **true** if **a** is greater than **b**.	a = 6;
		b = 5;
		if (a > b)
		{
		}

a >= b	Greater than or equal to. Evaluates to **true** if **a** is greater than or equal to **b**.	a = 6;
		b = 5;
		if (a >= b)
		{
		}

		a = 5;
		b = 5;
		if (a >= b)
		{
		}

All of these comparisons can be performed with either numbers or strings. For example,

```
s = "Hello";
t = "Hello";
if (s == t)
{
```

```
        trace ("They're Equal Hellos");
    }
```

and

```
    s = "Hello";
    t = "Goodbye";
    if (s != t)
    {
        trace ("Hello is not goodbye");
    }
```

When it comes to using greater than, less than, greater than or equal to, and less than or equal to, the conditions evaluate based on alphabetical ordering. So,

```
    s = "Apple";
    t = "Zebra";
    if (s < t)
    {
        trace ("Apple is less than zebra");
    }
```

and

```
    s = "Zebra";
    t = "Apple";
    if (s > t)
    {
        trace ("Zebra is greater than apple");
    }
```

We can also combine conditions by using the AND and OR operators. The AND operator is specified like so:

```
    if (condition1 && condition2)
    {
    }
```

The OR operator is specified like so:

```
    if (condition1 || condition2)
    {
    }
```

Those are two vertical "pipes," typed by pressing Shift and then pressing the backslash key (beneath the Backspace key). These operators work very much the same way they would in real life:

"If you finish your homework AND you eat five carrots, we will go to the movies." It is clear that both of these conditions must be satisfied in order for the movie trip to occur. In code this could be written like so:

```
    homeWorkFinished = true;
    carrots = 5;
    if (homeWorkFinished && carrots == 5)
    {
        trace ("Let's go to the movies");
    }
```

Notice that we *don't* need to say

<code>if (homeWorkFinished == true …</code>

The <code>if</code> statement takes the Boolean value, and since <code>homeWorkFinished</code> is already a Boolean value, we simply need to AND it against the condition <code>carrots == 5</code> to get our overall condition. In other words, <code>true && true</code> results in a <code>true</code>. Consider this alternative:

```
homeWorkFinished = true;
carrots = 4;
if (homeWorkFinished && carrots == 5)
{
    trace ("Let's go to the movies");
}
```

There's no movie for this person, who only ate four carrots. Both conditions are not satisfied as <code>true</code>, so the overall <code>if</code> statement does not evaluate to <code>true</code>. It evaluates to <code>false</code>.

On the other hand, imagine this statement. "If you get an A+ or you win the contest, you will get to go to the theme park." The code is as follows:

```
grade = "A+";
contestWinner = false;

if (grade == "A+" || contestWinner)
{
    trace ("You're going to the theme park");
}
```

Would this person be going to the theme park? Yes. Even though he lost the contest, he got the right grade. The first condition evaluates to <code>true</code>, and the second condition evaluates to <code>false</code>, but <code>true || false</code> evaluates overall to <code>true</code>. Notice that we're using a string to represent A+. Consider this alternative:

```
grade = "B-";
contestWinner = true;

if (grade == "A+" || contestWinner)
{
    trace ("You're going to the theme park");
}
```

He's still going to the theme park, because he won the contest. How about this version?

```
grade = "B-";
contestWinner = false;

if (grade == "A+" || contestWinner)
{
    trace ("You're going to the theme park");
}
```

OK, now this person is not going to the theme park because neither the grade is right, nor is he a contest winner. Finally, how about this?

```
grade = "A+";
contestWinner = true;

if (grade == "A+" || contestWinner)
{
    trace ("You're going to the theme park");
}
```

He's a contest winner and he got the right grade. So, should he get to go to the theme park? Of course. If both conditions are true, the || operator will still evaluate to true.

In the following table you can see the definitive results of the Boolean conditional operations:

CONDITION 1	OPERATOR	CONDITION 2	RESULT
true	&&	true	true
true	&&	false	false
false	&&	false	false
true	||	true	true
true	||	false	true
false	||	false	true

It's also possible to use the NOT operator to reverse the results of any Boolean condition, so true becomes false, and false becomes true, so:

```
k = 5;
if (k == 5)
{
    trace ("k is 5");
}
```

However, we can make the condition evaluate to false, if we do this:

```
k = 5;
if (!(k == 5))
{
    trace ("k is 5");
}
```

So, even though k is indeed equal to 5, the condition will fail, because our condition will succeed only if k is NOT equal to 5. We could also write it like this:

```
if (k != 5)
```

but the use of the NOT operator becomes more applicable when we want to use a Boolean variable like so:

```
paidTicket = false;
if (!paidTicket)
{
    trace ("You haven't paid your ticket");
}
```

In the above example, the text "You haven't paid your ticket" *would* be traced to the output window, because `paidTicket` is `false`, meaning that `NOT paidTicket` is `true`, because `NOT false` *is* `true`. (When is a `false` not a `false`? When it's a `true`.)

else and `else if`

Along with the `if` statement, we also have the `else` statement. When we say `else`, it's like we're saying *otherwise*. Imagine this statement. "If you start the fire, you will be warm. *Otherwise*, you will be cold." In code we would write this like so:

```
fire = false;
if (fire)
{
    trace ("You are warm");
}
else
{
    trace ("You are cold");
}
```

The `else` statement follows the last curly brace of the `if` statement, or, if it only has one instruction, then `else` comes immediately after that instruction.

```
if (condition)
    instruction;
else
    instruction;
```

We can, if we want, have *more* than two conditions by using the `else if` statement. Imagine this statement. "If you have a chicken, you will have chicken eggs. Otherwise if you have a goose, you will have goose eggs. Otherwise you will have nothing." In code, this would be:

```
haveChicken = false;
haveGoose = false;
if (haveChicken)
{
    trace ("You have a chicken, and chicken eggs.");
}
else if (haveGoose)
{
    trace ("You don't have a chicken, but you do have" +
        " a goose and its eggs");
}
else
{
    trace ("You have neither chicken nor goose eggs");
}
```

In the above example `You have neither chicken nor goose eggs` would appear in the output window. However, consider this version:

```
haveChicken = true;
haveGoose = true;
if (haveChicken)
{
```

```
    trace ("You have a chicken, and chicken eggs.");
}
else if (haveGoose)
{
    trace ("You don't have a chicken, but you do have" +
           " a goose and its eggs");
}
else
{
    trace ("You have neither chicken nor goose eggs");
}
```

What would you expect to happen here? Would it tell us that we had both chicken and goose eggs? The answer is no, it would evaluate true with haveChicken and would not bother checking the haveGoose variable. It would simply state that we had chicken eggs. The nature of if / else / else if is that it will only move on to the next condition if the previous condition is not satisfied. If we wanted to handle a case where we reported having both chicken and goose eggs, we'd have to do this:

```
haveChicken = true;
haveGoose = true;

if (haveChicken && haveGoose)
{
trace ("You have chicken and goose eggs.");
}
else if (haveChicken)
{
    trace ("You have a chicken, and chicken eggs.");
}
else if (haveGoose)
{
    trace ("You don't have a chicken, but you do have" +
           " a goose and its eggs");
}
else
{
    trace ("You have neither chicken nor goose eggs");
}
```

We have to perform an AND check to see if both haveChicken and haveGoose are true. If we adjusted the code like so:

```
haveChicken = false;
haveGoose = true;

if (haveChicken && haveGoose)
{
trace ("You have chicken and goose eggs.");
}
else if (haveChicken)
{
    trace ("You have a chicken, and chicken eggs.");
}
else if (haveGoose)
{
```

```
        trace ("You don't have a chicken, but you do have" +
                " a goose and its eggs");
    }
    else
    {
        trace ("You have neither chicken nor goose eggs");
    }
```

we would be told "You don't have a chicken, but you do have a goose and its eggs." This is because the first `if` evaluates to `false` and then the second `if` evaluates to `false`. Given that all of this code has one-line results, we could always do things like this:

```
    haveChicken = false;
    haveGoose = true;

    if (haveChicken && haveGoose)
        trace ("You have chicken and goose eggs.");
    else if (haveChicken)
        trace ("You have a chicken, and chicken eggs.");
    else if (haveGoose)
        trace ("You don't have a chicken, but you do have" +
                " a goose and its eggs");
    else
        trace ("You have neither chicken nor goose eggs");
```

We don't actually require the curly braces because our statements are only one line long. (The third trace statement is broken over two lines, but that doesn't count. It's not a separate statement; it's still the same statement.).

`if` statements, when you've written a lot of them, become second nature. They can get incredibly long and complex, in fact. For example,

```
    if ((!aUser && aGuest || (aVisitor || !aClient)) &&
        age < 25 && (height >= 5 || height < 2) && name=="BOB")
        trace ("What a condition!");
```

Can you see the thinking here? If you're not a user but you are a guest OR you're a visitor and not a client and your age is less than 25 and your height is greater than or equal to 5, or less than 2, and your name is BOB, then the condition is satisfied.

Remember though, all of that boils down to Boolean logic. Let's assume that the values are set like so:

```
    aUser = false;
    aGuest = true;
    aVisitor = true;
    aClient = false;
    age = 21;
    height = 6;
    name = "BOB";
```

Then the `if` statement results in this logic taking place:

```
    if ((!false && true || (true || !false)) &&
        true && (true || false) && true)
        trace ("What a condition!");
```

which would simplify down to

```
if ((true || true) && true && (true) && true)
    trace ("What a condition!");
```

which, simpler still is

```
if (true && true && true && true)
    trace ("What a condition!");
```

The end result would be

```
if (true)
    trace ("What a condition!");
```

Loops

The purpose of a loop in ActionScript is to provide us with a mechanism for repeating an action as many times as we want, without needing to rewrite that action in code over and over. We're interested in two types of loops for this primer: for loops and while loops.

for Loops

In a for loop, we're essentially telling Flash to do something "for" a certain number of times. Jus t as we would say to someone, "walk forward, for 15 steps," we could represent this action with ActionScript like so:

```
step = 0;
trace ("Taking step number " + (step++));
trace ("Taking step number " + (step++));
trace ("Taking step number " + (step++));
trace ("Taking step number " + (step++));
trace ("Taking step number " + (step++));
trace ("Taking step number " + (step++));
trace ("Taking step number " + (step++));
trace ("Taking step number " + (step++));
trace ("Taking step number " + (step++));
trace ("Taking step number " + (step++));
trace ("Taking step number " + (step++));
trace ("Taking step number " + (step++));
trace ("Taking step number " + (step++));
trace ("Taking step number " + (step++));
trace ("Taking step number " + (step++));
```

That code would produce the following output in the output window:

```
Taking step number 0
Taking step number 1
Taking step number 2
Taking step number 3
Taking step number 4
Taking step number 5
Taking step number 6
Taking step number 7
Taking step number 8
Taking step number 9
Taking step number 10
```

```
Taking step number 11
Taking step number 12
Taking step number 13
Taking step number 14
```

Notice that we've repeated the same line of code 15 times, and that we've also embedded the ++ increment within the line of code itself. We're allowed to do this; the value of step will be incremented *after* it is used in the trace statement. If we wanted the value of step to be increased and *then* used in the trace statement we could say:

```
trace ("Taking step number " + (++step));
```

It's important to notice that it's doing the code 15 times, even though the last step is number 14. This is because the first step is step 0, so it's 15 steps total, starting with step 0 and ending with step 14.

It's pretty clear that there has to be a better way of doing this. What if we wanted to take 150 steps, or 1500 steps? Would we write the code 1500 times? No. We tell ActionScript to do something repeatedly this way:

```
for (step = 0; step < 15; step++)
{
    trace ("Taking step number " + step);
}
```

This will produce the exact same results as the previous example, but it has three lines of code rather than 15. The format of the for statement is as follows:

```
for (run this once; this must evaluate to true; do this every loop
iteration)
```

So, in our example, the first thing (before the first semicolon) is to set the value of step to 0. Then, before the second semicolon, we perform a check that must evaluate to true in order to proceed with the loop. Our check is simply the condition step < 15. This will only evaluate true as long as step is less than 15 (from 0 to 14 are true). Finally, the last part, after the second semicolon, is the code we want the loop to run each time it iterates. This usually revolves around incrementing, or in some way changing, the loop variable. In our example, we're incrementing step.

Much like the if statement, we can place our opening curly braces on the same line as, or on the next line after, the for statement, like so:

```
for (step = 0; step < 15; step++) {
    trace ("Taking step number " + step);
}
```

or

```
for (step = 0; step < 15; step++)
{
    trace ("Taking step number " + step);
}
```

If there's only one line of code inside the loop, we can eliminate the curly braces and say

```
for (step = 0; step < 15; step++)
    trace ("Taking step number " + step);
```

Here are a few useful loop setups and what they mean.

CODE	DESCRIPTION
for (k = 0; k < 10; k++)	k will count up from 0 to 9.
for (k = 0; k <= 10; k++)	k will count up from 0 to 10.
for (k = 9; k >= 0; k--)	k will count down from 9 to 0.
for (k = 20; k >= 0; k-=2)	k will count down from 20 to 0, in steps of 2.
for (k = 0; k < 100; k+=2)	k will count from 0 to 99, incrementing by 2 each time (0, 2, 4, 6, 8, etc.).
for (k = 10; k <= 100; k+=10)	k will begin at 10 and will increment by 10 until it reaches 100.
for (k = 100; k > 2; k /= 2)	k will begin at 100 and will divide in half until k is less than 2. This will cause k to be 100, 50, 25, 12.5, 6.25, 3.125.

The while Loop

The other type of loop is known as the while loop. It's analogous to saying, "Walk east *while* the sun is still shining." We would write this like so:

```
while (minutesOfSunRemaining > 0)
{
    trace ("The sun is still shining");
    minutesOfSunRemaining--;
}
```

The while loop very simply evaluates a condition.

```
while (true)
{
    trace ("doing this code forever and forever");
}
```

or

```
while (false)
{
    trace ("will never see this trace");
}
```

 If we were to run the first example, while(true), we would be stuck in what's known as an infinite loop. There's no way that condition, simply true, would ever, ever evaluate to false in order to end the loop. The Flash Player would keep this up for about 15 seconds before presenting a dialog box that says, "A script in this movie is causing the Flash Player to run slowly. If it continues to run, your computer may become unresponsive. Do you want to abort the script?" as shown in Figure 19.2.

FIGURE 19.2   The dialog box presented after 15 seconds of closed code execution.

This warning message appears when Flash has been executing code, without proceeding to a new frame, for at least 15 seconds. This is to give the users of our movies a way to save their computer. During this code execution (our infinite loop, for example), Flash will be consuming 100% of the user's CPU. It is wise of Flash to prevent the computer from being completely overtaken. However, this can sometimes become an annoyance when you have legitimate code that is long and complex and genuinely needs more than 15 seconds to compute. Flash will dutifully present the error message and the user will be given the incorrect impression that your code has crashed.

Even if you had text on screen that said something like, "Please wait, this will take 60 seconds to compute," Flash will still intercede. It seems that the only way around this is to ensure that your code is able to run in 15 seconds or less, or you can spread your code over multiple frames. Either way, this can be a challenge, but this error message generally only appears when Flash has entered an infinite loop.

The `while` loop is best used in situations where we just don't know how long we're going to be doing something and therefore need to constantly evaluate the condition. Consider, for example, a series of variables called `ball0`, `ball1`, `ball2`, `ball3`, `ball4`, and so on. We could have four variables or we could have 400. Let's say the variables were passed in from a server script in some way, so we just don't know how many there are. We could do something like this:

```
k = 0;
while (this["ball" + k] != undefined)
{
    trace ("ball" + k + " exists");
    k++;
}
```

Don't worry about what `this` means; we'll be looking at that in the next section, "Relative Paths and Objects." What we're doing here is, starting with `ball0`, checking to see if the variable indeed exists. We keep going `while` the variables exist, tracing out the message. If there were four variables declared, like so,

```
ball0 = 1;
ball1 = 1;
ball2 = 1;
ball3 = 1;
```

then the total code would be

```
ball0 = 1;
ball1 = 1;
ball2 = 1;
ball3 = 1;
```

```
k = 0;
while (this["ball" + k] != undefined)
{
    trace ("ball" + k + " is valid");
    k++;
}
```

When run, this would write the following text in the output window.

```
ball0 is valid
ball1 is valid
ball2 is valid
ball3 is valid
```

This means we successfully determined how many ball variables there were, and that number will now be stored in k upon completion of the while loop.

Functions

So far, all the code we've looked at has been placed directly on frame 1 of the main timeline, and when we run the movie, the code executes in linear order, from top to bottom. Because our movie has been one frame in length, Flash does not loop the code, and instead only executes it once, and then everything finishes up nicely.

If we want, we can "package" code into a discreet container known as a function. For example,

```
k = 0;
trace ("k is " + k);
```

This code sets the value of k to 0 and then traces k is 0 to the output window. What if we wanted to be able to run that code many times throughout our program? What if we wanted to almost think of it as a task of "zeroing k?" We could place it inside a function, like so:

```
function zeroK()
{
    k = 0;
    trace ("k is " + k);
}
```

That's known as a *function definition*. Now, anywhere we want in our code (in the same timeline block—we'll be looking at this next), we can simply "call" that function by saying

```
zeroK();
```

That's known as a *function call*. Wrapping code in a function allows us to call it as many times as we want, while not forcing us to write the actual code contents of the function more than once. We have a two-line function with zeroK, but we could also create a 2000-line function that would be called in the same manner.

The function above performs a specific task and then ends. One of the other things we can do with a function is have it perform a specific task and then return a value back to the code that called it. For example,

```
function returnFive()
{
    return 5;
}

k = returnFive();
```

In this case k would be set to 5, because k would be set to the return value of the function, and the return *value* of a function is simply the data that it returns. This is a fairly useless function, as it's easier to just set k to 5 manually with k = 5, but we could put a spin on things like so:

```
function double(n)
{
    return n * 2
}

k = double(10);
```

What we're seeing here is a function called double that takes one *parameter*. The parameter is specified in the brackets during the function definition, and in there we specify the variable name (n) to use inside the function for the *value* (10) that is passed in when the function is called.

When we *call* the double function, we're passing in a value of 10, which is seen inside the brackets of the function call itself. With this, the function will be called, and n will be set to 10 for the duration of the call. By returning n * 2, we're doubling the result and then passing it back out into k.

We could do this:

```
function double(n)
{
    return n * 2
}

trace ("10 doubled is " + double(10));
```

This would trace out the text "0 doubled is 20."

It's also possible for a function to take more than one parameter. For example,

```
function addThemUp(a, b)
{
    return (a + b);
}

k = addThemUp(15, 5);
trace (k);
```

In this function, addThemUp, we're passing in two parameters, a and b, and then we're adding them together and returning the result. Multiple parameters are defined in the brackets, by simply separating each parameter with a comma. We then call the function with 15 and 5 and place that value in k. By tracing out k, we'll see the number "20" appear in the output window.

We can create a function that returns a true or a false Boolean value, like so:

```
function hasMoney(balance)
{
    if (balance > 0)
        return (true);
    else
        return (false);
}

myMoney = 43;

if (hasMoney(myMoney))
    trace ("You have money!");
else
    trace ("You're broke.");
```

The `hasMoney` function simply checks to see if the `balance` passed in is greater than zero. If it is, we pass back `true`; otherwise, we pass back `false`. We're using the results of the `hasMoney` function inside an `if` statement to determine what text to display on screen. What will ultimately happen is this: if `balance` is greater than zero, we'll see "You have money!" Otherwise, we'll see "You're broke."

Interestingly, we could modify the `hasMoney` function like so:

```
function hasMoney(balance)
{
    return (balance > 0);
}
```

All we need to do is check to see if the `balance` is greater than zero, and since that's a condition, we can return the result of the condition directly. If `balance` is indeed greater than zero, then `balance > 0` will return `true`. Otherwise, `balance > 0` will return `false`; there's no need for the `if` statement inside the function.

Relative Paths and Objects

So far, we've looked at creating variables, conditions, loops, and functions all within frame 1 of the main timeline. This means that all of this code will be attached to what is known as the _root timeline.

It's important to understand that everything in ActionScript is contained within something else. Everything has a "parent," and we refer to objects via their paths using a method known as dot notation. For example, if we have this code in frame 1 of the main timeline,

```
k = 0;
```

that's the same as saying

```
_root.k = 0;
```

The original line is being written in the _root timeline. Think of it like the *address* of the variable. We can place variables *inside* of ActionScript variables known as objects. The _root timeline is essentially an object, but we can also create our own and place variables inside of them, like so:

```
myObj = new Object();
myObj.k = 0;
myObj.s = "Hello";
```

Now, the object called `myObj` contains two variables: `k` and `s`. When a variable is attached to an object, it is usually referred to as a *property*. If we placed that code on the main timeline, frame 1, then `myObj` could also be referred to as `_root.myObj`.

 The reason for referring to `_root` becomes more obvious in a little while when we get into movie clips, which contain their own timelines.

We can also place functions inside of objects, like so:

```
myObj = new Object();
myObj.addThemUp = function(a, b)
{
    return (a + b);
}

trace (myObj.addThemUp(3, 5));
```

This would display the number 8 in the output window. When a function is attached to an object, it is usually referred to as a *method*. We can make an object refer to its own properties by using the `this` keyword:

```
myObj = new Object();
myObj.k = 5;
myObj.displayMyK = function()
{
    trace (this.k);
}

myObj.displayMyK();
```

We've created `myObj` and inside it set the property `k` to 5 and then created a `displayMyK` method. When we call `myObj.displayMyK`, it will trace the number 5 to the output window. When the word `this` is used within an object, it means "referring to myself." Consider this situation:

```
k = 9;

myObj = new Object();
myObj.k = 5;

myObj.displayMyK = function()
{
    trace (k);
}

myObj.displayMyK();
```

What will be displayed here? The answer is 9. When we don't specify `this` inside an object method, we're telling ActionScript to refer to the `k` on the timeline that *contains* the function definition itself. We can fix the code:

```
k = 9;

myObj = new Object();
myObj.k = 5;

myObj.displayMyK = function()
{
    trace (k);
    trace (this.k);
}

myObj.displayMyK();
```

This code will first trace 9, and then below that it will trace 5. Even though the variable is called k in both cases, the two k's have different containers. The k that is 9 has _root as its container. The k that is 5 has myObj as its container.

Because of the nested nature of ActionScript objects, it's possible to create objects within objects, like so:

```
myObj = new Object();
myObj.innerObj = new Object();
myObj.innerObj.k = 5;
```

Now, one of the properties of myObj is another object, called innerObj. This hierarchy is an important concept to understand. Think of it like this:

```
myCountry = new Object();
myCountry.name = "Canada";
myCountry.myCity = new Object();
myCountry.myCity.name = "Toronto";
myCountry.myCity.myStreet = new Object();
myCountry.myCity.myStreet.name = "Main Street";

trace (myCountry.name);
trace (myCountry.myCity.name);
trace (myCountry.myCity.myStreet.name);
```

The objects are arranged hierarchically so that the street is *inside* of the city, and the city is inside of the country. This is a logical arrangement that mimics the way we would think of this real-life situation. We could also create a generic function that handled the printout of the name, like so:

```
function printMyName()
{
    trace (this.name);
}

myCountry = new Object();
myCountry.name = "Canada";
myCountry.printName = printMyName;

myCountry.myCity = new Object();
myCountry.myCity.name = "Toronto";
myCountry.myCity.printName = printMyName;

myCountry.myCity.myStreet = new Object();
myCountry.myCity.myStreet.name = "Main Street";
myCountry.myCity.myStreet.printName = printMyName;
```

```
myCountry.printName();
myCountry.myCity.printName();
myCountry.myCity.myStreet.printName();
```

We're creating a generic function called `printMyName`, which simply traces out `this.name`. We can then create methods inside of the objects and set those methods to be the `printMyName` function. That's right, we're using a single function as the template for methods in three different places. When we assign one function to a variable name like this, we don't need to use the brackets—we don't say `printName = printMyName();`—because we're not *calling* the function; we're simply assigning a reference to it. Since we're using the `this` operator, every time the method is called it will smartly refer to the `name` property of the object whose method is being called. So, `myCountry.printName()` will display "Canada," while `myCountry.myCity.myStreet.printName()` will display "Main Street."

That's it for the basic fundamentals of ActionScript. Those aren't *all* the fundamentals of the language, by far, but this is just a primer. For now, let's move on to the next section: the ActionScript classes that are game related.

THE ACTIONSCRIPT CLASSES FOR GAMES

In the previous section we looked briefly at creating objects and then attaching methods and properties to them. We looked at creating functions that perform specific tasks of our choosing. If we want to really expand and do anything else in ActionScript, then we need to use the classes built into ActionScript. These are essentially objects, but they contain methods and properties that come with ActionScript.

There are many, many ActionScript classes, but let's look at the ones that most closely pertain to game development.

The `MovieClip` Class

The `MovieClip` class is the class of methods and properties that are associated with movie clip objects: the objects that have a visual presence on the stage and are designated as movie clips and have instance names.

In the Macromedia Flash Professional 8 development environment, a movie clip object is created by simply drawing something on the stage, selecting it, pressing F8 to convert it to a movie clip, and then giving that new movie clip a name.

When a movie clip is on stage, we must give it an *instance name* in order to refer to it with code—to use the methods and properties of the `MovieClip` class. For all of these samples, we're going to assume that you have a movie clip sitting on the stage and that it has an instance name `my_mc`. The steps to create it are:

1. Open a new, blank Flash movie.
2. Use a drawing tool such as the circle or box and draw a shape on the stage.

3. With the Selection tool, select the entire shape.
4. Press F8 to bring up the Convert to Symbol dialog box.
5. Make sure the Behavior is set to Movie Clip in the dialog box. In the Name field type my_mc. This does not refer to instance name; this is only the movie clip name as it appears in the library. We'll be setting the instance name elsewhere.
6. Click OK.
7. The new movie clip will now be sitting on the stage. Make sure it is selected.
8. Find the Properties panel or press Ctrl-F3 if it's not on screen.
9. In the Instance Name text field in the Properties panel, type the text my_mc.
10. Press Enter

We now have a movie clip on screen, and that movie clip is an instance of the MovieClip class. This is automatic. Every movie clip is an instance of the MovieClip class.

Now any more code that you type in will be in frame 1 of the main timeline. Make sure frame 1 is selected before entering code. Do not enter code in the Actions panel if the movie clip itself is the only thing selected.

We can, if we want, place movie clips within movie clips. These are said to be encapsulated movie clips, and their naming and hierarchy are very much like the objects within objects from the previous section.

We can use the properties of the MovieClip class to adjust many things about our movie clip. For example,

```
my_mc._x = 0;
my_mc._y = 0;
```

Here we're setting the _x and _y properties of my_mc to 0. This will move the movie clip to the upper-left corner of the stage, so that it is sitting at position 0, 0. That is, the *registration point* of the movie clip (the little + symbol inside the movie clip) will be positioned at stage position 0, 0. Here's a list of valid MovieClip properties and what they do:

_x

```
my_mc._x = 100;
```

This is the _x (horizontal) position of the movie clip. It is relative to the movie clip that encapsulates it. If it's sitting on the main _root timeline, then the _x position will be relative to the stage, which has its _x of zero at the left edge of the screen.

_y

```
my_mc._y = 100;
```

This is the _y (vertical) position of the movie clip. It is relative to the movie clip that encapsulates it. If it's sitting on the main _root timeline, then the _y position will be relative to the stage, which has its _y of zero at the top edge of the screen.

_rotation

```
my_mc._rotation = 90;
```

This is the rotation angle of the movie clip. It is relative to the movie clip that encapsulates it, meaning that the rotation is compounded with the rotation of any encapsulating movie clip. If it's sitting on the main _root timeline, then the _rotation will be relative to the stage, which usually has a _rotation value of zero.

The _rotation property is measured in degrees from 0 to 359.

_xscale

```
my_mc._xscale = 50;
```

This is the percentage that the movie clip is scaled along the x (horizontal) axis. This scale is compounded with the scale value of any movie clip that encapsulates it. So, a movie clip with an _xscale value of 200 (which is 200%), which contains a movie clip with an _xscale value of 50 (which is 50%), will appear to have its _xscale at 100%.

_xscale is a number where 100 is unaffected; anything less than 100 is scaled down, and anything greater than 100 is scaled up. It's possible to horizontally flip a movie clip by using an _xscale value that is a negative number.

_yscale

```
my_mc._yscale = 50;
```

This is the percentage that the movie clip is scaled along the y (vertical) axis. This scale is compounded with the scale value of any movie clip that encapsulates it. So, a movie clip with a _yscale value of 200 (which is 200%), which contains a movie clip with a _yscale value of 50 (which is 50%), will appear to have its _yscale at 100%.

_yscale is a number where 100 is unaffected; anything less than 100 is scaled down, and anything greater than 100 is scaled up. It's also possible to vertically flip a movie clip by using a _yscale value that is a negative number.

_height

```
h = my_mc._height;
```

This is the actual height, in pixels, of the movie clip.

_width

```
w = my_mc._width;
```

This is the actual width, in pixels, of the movie clip.

_alpha

```
my_mc._alpha = 10;
```

This is the semitransparency value of a movie clip. This is a number from 0 to 100, where 100 is solid and unaffected, and 0 is completely transparent. It's possible to use the _alpha value to make a movie clip look transparent and glass-like.

_name

```
trace (my_mc._name);
```

This is the instance name of the movie clip. This is a read-only property returned as a string.

_currentframe

```
b=my_mc._currentframe;
```

This is the current frame that the movie clip's playhead is at within the movie clip's timeline. A movie clip can have any number of frames within it, which will play independently of our ActionScript manipulations of the movie clip object itself.

_totalframes

```
b=my_mc._totalframes;
```

This is the total number of frames in the timeline of the movie clip.

_visible

```
my_mc._visible = true;
my_mc._visible = false;
```

This is the visibility state of the movie clip. By changing the _visible property, we can cause Flash to render or not render the movie clip. Setting _visible to false will make the movie clip disappear. Setting _visible to true will make the movie clip reappear.

_xmouse

```
xp = my_mc._xmouse;
```

This is the current x (horizontal) position of the mouse cursor, in pixels, relative to the center point of the movie clip. If you want the x position of the mouse cursor to be relative to the stage, you must say

```
xp = _root._xmouse;
```

_ymouse

```
yp = my_mc._ymouse;
```

This is the current y (vertical) position of the mouse cursor, in pixels, relative to the center point of the movie clip. If you want the y position of the mouse cursor to be relative to the stage, you must say

```
yp = _root._ymouse;
```

The `MovieClip` class also has a few dozen methods and events associated with it that we can make use of in our development. One of the most useful of these methods is the `createEmptyMovieClip` method. This allows us to create a new, blank movie clip from scratch at runtime. This movie clip will have no graphics associated with it. An example usage is

```
_root.createEmptyMovieClip("my_mc", 0);
```

Here we're creating a new movie clip on the `_root` `timeline`, and the instance name of this new movie clip will be `my_mc`. The 0 specifies that we're creating it on depth level 0. Depth levels are used to specify drawing order; the higher the number, the more "on top" the movie clip is. So,

```
_root.createEmptyMovieClip("my_mc1", 0);
_root.createEmptyMovieClip("my_mc2", 1);
```

In this case `my_mc2` would be rendered on top of `my_mc1`. We can also create movie clips inside of other movie clips, like so:

```
_root.createEmptyMovieClip("myNew_mc", 0);
my_mc.createEmptyMovieClip("inner_mc", 0);
```

Any properties or methods would be accessed via dot notation:

```
myNew_mc._rotation = 90;
my_mc.inner_mc._rotation = 90;
```

Remember, the `inner_mc` will inherit the position, rotation, and scale adjustments of `myNew_mc`. In the above example `inner_mc` will appear to be rotated 180 degrees on screen, because it is rotated 90 degrees within `myNew_mc`, which is *also* rotated 90 degrees.

In the case of empty movie clips, one of the best things we do with them is to make use of their `onEnterFrame` functions. The `onEnterFrame` is an event that is triggered each time Flash advances the overall playhead by one frame. If our movie frame rate is set to 30 frames per second, then the `onEnterFrame` function of the `MovieClip` class will be executed 30 times per second. Think of it like this:

```
_root.createEmptyMovieClip("myNew_mc", 0);

myNew_mc.onEnterFrame = function()
{
    trace ("Frame code!");
}
```

If you copy this to frame 1 of the main timeline and run it, you'll see the words "Frame code!" appear in the output window over and over at a rate that matches the frame rate of the movie. We use these `onEnterFrame` functions as the basis for most of our games. The `onEnterFrame` function is a nice solid way for us to do game animation and control logic code that we want to execute at a regular interval. Throughout the book we make extensive use of the onEnterFrame function.

 It's important to realize that Flash sees the _root as a movie clip, which exists by default. This is why we could say _root.createEmptyMovieClip, even though createEmpty-MovieClip *is a method of the* MovieClip *class.*

Another thing we can do with movie clips is attach them to other movie clips using the attachMovie method. This takes a movie clip from the library and creates an instance of it at a location that we specify. Before we look at the code, though, we have to understand how movie clips are set up in the library so that they can be used in this manner.

From our previous example, you should have a movie clip in the library right now called my_mc. We're not talking about the instance on the stage, but the actual movie clip in the library.

1. Open up the library by pressing Ctrl-L.
2. You should see a window with the movie clip inside it. (If not, go back to the previous step-by-step instructions and create a movie clip.)
3. Select the movie clip in the library by clicking on it.
4. Right-click on the movie clip and select Linkage from the menu that pops up.
5. In the box that appears, type linked_mc in the Linkage Identifier text box and make sure that Export for ActionScript and Export in First Frame are both checked. Leave the AS 2.0 Class text box empty.
6. Press OK.

Now we can use the attachMovie method, like so:

```
_root.attachMovie("linked_mc", "my_mc", 0);
```

The first parameter we pass into the function is the linkage name (which we just defined in the library), the second parameter is the instance name we want to use for the new movie clip instance, and the third parameter is the depth level.

This is very similar to createEmptyMovieClip, except that it's not empty. We don't need to use createEmptyMovieClip *and* attachMovie. One or the other will suffice, depending on our goals. If we just want an empty movie clip for its onEnterFrame function, we can use createEmptyMovieClip. On the other hand, if we want an actual game graphic, we'll need to use attachMovie or have it already on the stage to begin with. We'll be seeing many more examples of this throughout the book.

When we're done with an empty movie clip, or a movie clip that has been attached with attachMovie, we can remove it from existence by saying,

```
my_mc.removeMovieClip();
```

This method only works with movie clips that have been created at runtime, not with movie clips that were placed on the stage at design time.

It's important to see that the this term is very important with movie clips. If we want a movie clip to take care of its own motion, for example, we could use its onEnterFrame function, like so:

```
_root.attachMovie("linked_mc", "my_mc", 0);

my_mc.onEnterFrame = function()
{
    this._rotation ++;
    this._alpha--;
}
```

What would happen here? The movie clip, my_mc, would appear on screen and it would begin to rotate clockwise. As it was doing so, it would also be fading out because the _alpha value refers to transparency and is decreasing by 1 each frame. Again, we'll be seeing many more examples of movie clip onEnterFrame code throughout the book.

The following is a list of the major events that we can put code into with the MovieClip class. For a complete list, refer to the ActionScript dictionary included with the Macromedia Flash Professional 8 development system.

onEnterFrame

```
my_mc.onEnterFrame = function()
{
    this._x++;
}
```

The onEnterFrame function is triggered every frame at the frame rate specified in the Document Properties dialog box.

onPress

```
my_mc.onPress = function()
{
    trace ("pressed");
}
```

This can be used to detect the user pressing the mouse button down anywhere on the movie clip. Any solid areas will be clickable, and the cursor will change to a hand on roll-over if this function is defined.

onRelease

```
my_mc.onRelease = funtion()
{
    trace ("released");
}
```

onRelease can be used to detect the user releasing the mouse button anywhere on the movie clip. Any solid areas will be clickable, and the cursor will change to a hand on roll-over if this function is defined.

onReleaseOutside

```
my_mc.onReleaseOutside = function()
{
    trace ("released outside");
}
```

This is triggered when the user releases the mouse button with the cursor no longer over the movie clip. If the user clicks down on the movie clip and moves off the movie clip and then releases, onReleaseOutside will be triggered.

onMouseDown

```
my_mc.onMouseDown = function()
{
    trace ("Mouse down");
}
```

This is invoked when the mouse button is pressed anywhere on the stage. The cursor does not need to be touching the movie clip for this function to be triggered.

onMouseUp

```
my_mc.onMouseUp = function()
{
    trace ("Mouse Up");
}
```

onMouseUp is invoked when the mouse button is released anywhere on the stage, not just over the movie clip.

onRollOver

```
my_mc.onRollOver = function()
{
    trace ("rolled over");
}
```

This is invoked when the user moves the mouse cursor over the movie clip.

onRollOut

```
my_mc.onRollOut = function()
{
    trace ("rolled out");
}
```

This is invoked when the user moves the mouse cursor *off* of the movie clip.

When it comes to the methods of the MovieClip class, we have a wide array of them to choose from. We've already looked at three methods: createEmpty-MovieClip, attachMovie, and removeMovieClip. What else do we have?

- We have methods available to us to affect the playback of animation inside movies with more than one frame.

- We have methods to load external swfs and jpegs into empty movie clips so we can use external graphics for our games.
- We have methods to determine what percentage of that external data is loaded so we can make Flash wait until a movie clip is fully loaded and even display a progress bar.
- We have methods to determine whether or not two movie clips are touching or whether an arbitrary x, y point on screen touches a movie clip. This collision detection is especially useful in games.
- We have methods to use one movie clip as a mask for another movie clip. This will allow us to only see certain areas of the movie clip, as defined by the solid parts of the mask movie clip.
- We have methods to start and stop dragging of a movie clip so that the mouse can be used to easily move a movie clip around the screen.
- We have methods to allow us to detect and change the depth level of a movie clip at any time so we can force it to move in front of or behind other movie clips on the stage.

Let's look at these in detail. The first methods we're going to look at are the methods that control the playback of a movie clip's timeline.

stop

```
my_mc.stop();
```

stop causes the timeline of a movie clip to stop playing if the movie clip is a multiframed animation. By default, any movie clip that contains more than one frame in its timeline will start off playing by default and will loop back to the beginning when it reaches the last frame. When we call the stop method, the movie clip will stop playing at whatever frame it's currently on.

play

```
my_mc.play();
```

This causes the timeline of a movie clip to start playing if the movie clip is a multiframed animation. A movie clip will start playing by default when the main movie is run, but if we have stopped a movie clip with the stop command, we can use the play command to resume the animation.

gotoAndStop

```
my_mc.gotoAndStop(frame);
```

This causes the timeline of a movie clip to go to a particular frame number, or frame label, specified by frame, and then stop on that frame.

gotoAndPlay

```
my_mc.gotoAndPlay(frame);
```

`gotoAndPlay` causes the timeline of a movie clip to go to a particular frame number, or frame label, specified by `frame`, and then play the movie clip's timeline from there.

nextFrame

```
my_mc.nextFrame();
```

Calling the `nextFrame` method will cause the timeline of the movie clip to advance to the next frame, where it will then stop. If the playhead is on the last frame, then `nextFrame` will have no effect (it will not loop back to the first frame).

prevFrame

```
my_mc.prevFrame();
```

Calling the `prevFrame` method will cause the timeline of the movie clip to advance to the previous frame, where it will then stop. If the playhead is on the first frame, `prevFrame` will have no effect (it will not loop to the last frame of the timeline).

prevFrame

```
my_mc.prevFrame();
```

Calling the `prevFrame` method will cause the timeline of the movie clip to advance to the previous frame, where it will then stop. If the playhead is on the first frame, `prevFrame` will have no effect (it will not loop to the last frame of the timeline).

All of the preceding playhead methods can also be written on the `_root time-line` without any dot notation, like so:

```
stop();
```

Placing this method on the first frame of any timeline (be it `_root` or inside a movie clip, on *its* first frame) will cause that timeline to stop playing.

The next methods we're going to look at are the methods concerned with loading external images and graphics into a movie clip.

loadMovie

```
my_mc.loadMovie(swfName);
```

or

```
my_mc.loadMovie(jpegName);
```

We can use the `loadMovie` method to bring external swf and jpeg files into a movie clip. The external file will be loaded so that its upper-left corner is positioned on top of the registration point of the movie clip. For example, we could do something like this:

```
_root.createEmptyMovieClip("title", 0);
title.loadMovie("titlepicture.jpg");
```

By default, the movie clip `title` would be created so that its registration point was positioned in the upper-left corner of the _root timeline (the stage). Then, the picture `titlepicture.jpg` would be loaded and its upper-left corner would be aligned with the registration point of the `title` movie clip. The end result? The `title-picture.jpg` image would appear lined up with the upper-left corner of the stage.

unloadMovie

```
my_mc.unloadMovie();
```

We use the `unloadMovie` method to clear the contents of a movie that has been filled with the `loadMovie` method. We could do this:

```
_root.createEmptyMovieClip("title", 0);
title.loadMovie("titlepicture.jpg");
```

Then, later in our code, when we're done with the title picture:

```
title.unloadMovie();
title.removeMovieClip();
```

We don't technically need to do the `unloadMovie` in that case, because the `removeMovieClip` would take care of both the unloading and removal of the movie clip, but it's good practice to see how things are working.

getBytesTotal

```
my_mc.getBytesTotal();
```

When we load an external movie into a movie clip, we can call the `getBytes-Total` method to determine how big the incoming movie is going to be. This is used along with the next method, `getBytesLoaded`, to determine the total percentage loaded of any movie clip.

getBytesLoaded

```
my_mc.getBytesLoaded();
```

The `getBytesLoaded` method tells us the number of bytes of an externally loaded movie clip that have been loaded. When we load large images or files into movie clips, the process might take a while, and it's a good idea to keep track of where things are. Look at the following code:

```
_root.createEmptyMovieClip("loader", 0);
_root.createEmptyMovieClip("my_mc", 1);

my_mc.loadMovie("biganimation.swf");

loader.onEnterFrame = function()
{
    percentage = (my_mc.getBytesLoaded() /
                 my_mc.getBytesTotal()) * 100;
    trace ("The percentage loaded is: " + percentage + " %");
}
```

We're creating two movie clips: One, `loader`, whose `onEnterFrame` event we'll be using to check the status of the other one, `my_mc`, into which we'll be loading the animation, `biganimation.swf`. The reason we don't simply use the `onEnterFrame` of the `my_mc` movie clip is because when external movies and images are loaded into a movie clip, all methods and properties contained within the movie clip are erased and reset.

In the above code the loader movie clip's `onEnterFrame` will be running and constantly tracing out "The percentage loaded is:" and then the actual percentage value loaded. This value is simply the number of bytes loaded, divided by the number of bytes total, multiplied by 100.

Next, we have a method that is used to test collision with a movie clip.

hitTest

```
my_mc.hitTest(another_mc);
```

or

```
my_mc.hitTest(x, y, shapeFlag);
```

In the first usage, `hitTest` will return `true` if the two movie clips specified (`my_mc` and `another_mc`) are overlapping in any way. This simply takes the largest extents of both movie clips (the area in which a single box could encompass every pixel of the movie clip; the bounding box) and compares them to see if they're overlapping.

The second usage determines if the point specified by `x`, `y` is physically being touched by the movie clip. The `shapeFlag` parameter is used to specify whether we want to check only the bounding box area of the movie clip (pass in `false`) or whether we want to look at the intricacies of the shape of the movie clip and use the `hitTest` to determine if the position `x`, `y` is touching only solid pixels of the movie clip (pass in `true`).

For example,

```
if (my_mc.hitTest(50, 50, true))
{
    trace ("Screen position 50, 50 has pixels my_mc");
}
```

or

```
if (!my_mc.hitTest(another_mc))
{
    trace ("my_mc and another_mc are not touching");
}
```

setMask

```
my_mc.setMask(mask_mc);
```

This method causes `my_mc` to be masked by `mask_mc`. When a movie clip is masked, the movie clip can *only* be seen when overlaid by solid areas of the mask movie clip. As soon as `setMask` is called, the `mask_mc` is no longer seen. This is the same functionality as using mask layers at design time, but we're doing things with code here. If the `mask_mc` contains animation and a timeline, the mask will appear animated as well. This is great for motion graphics.

To clear a mask that has been applied, simply call `setMask` with `null` as the parameter, like so:

```
my_mc.setMask(null);
```

startDrag

```
my_mc.startDrag();
```

or

```
my_mc.startDrag(lock, x1, y1, x2, y2);
```

This method will cause the movie clip `my_mc` to be dragged automatically by the mouse cursor. The first usage simply starts dragging the movie clip, relative to the mouse cursor's position.

The second usage starts dragging the movie clip but allows us to specify its behavior. If `lock` is set to `true`, the movie clip will "snap" so that its registration point is lined up with the tip of the mouse cursor. If `lock` is `false`, the movie clip will be dragged, but relative to the position of the mouse cursor when `startDrag` was called.

The `x1`, `y1`, `x2`, and `y2` variables specify the left, top, right, and bottom limits of the movie clip's movement. This means that even if the mouse cursor moves outside of this range, the movie clip will not.

Look at this code:

```
_root.attachMovie("ball", "my_mc", 0);
my_mc.onPress = function()
{
    this.startDrag();
}
```

This will attach a ball to the stage, with the instance name `my_mc`, and, when the user clicks the mouse button down while over the movie clip, it will begin dragging the movie clip.

stopDrag

```
my_mc.stopDrag();
```

This method will cause the movie clip `my_mc` to stop being dragged. If it currently is not being dragged, this code will do nothing. Look at this example:

```
_root.attachMovie("ball", "my_mc", 0);
my_mc.onPress = function()
{
    this.startDrag();
}
```

```
my_mc.onRelease = function()
{
    this.stopDrag();
}
```

This will create an instance of the `ball` movie clip, `my_mc`, and when the user clicks and drags it, it will move with the mouse cursor, but when the user releases the mouse button, the movie clip will stop being dragged.

Finally, we have methods that allow us to affect the depth level at which a movie clip is being drawn.

swapDepths

```
my_mc.swapDepths(depth);
```

This will cause the movie clip `my_mc` to switch to depth level `depth` in its rendering order. We must use a `swapDepths` rather than something hypothetical such as "setDepth," because no two movie clips can occupy the same depth level at the same time, so we must *swap* the depths of two movie clips. Most often, it's possible to just swap to a depth level that doesn't actually contain another movie clip, in which case it's almost as if you were doing the hypothetical setDepth.

getDepth

```
my_mc.getDepth();
```

This method returns a number that corresponds to the depth level that `my_mc` currently occupies.

getNextHighestDepth

```
my_mc.getNextHighestDepth();
```

This returns the next highest unused depth level *within* the movie clip `my_mc`, which then allows us to create an empty movie clip at this depth level. Consider the following code:

```
dep = _root.getNextHighestDepth();
_root.createEmptyMovieClip("my_mc", dep);
```

No matter where this code is placed, you know that `my_mc` will be on top of all other movie clips on the _root timeline, because we've *determined* the highest free depth level *on* the _root timeline.

That's it for the overview of the `MovieClip` class. For more information, see the ActionScript dictionary included with Macromedia Flash Professional 8.

The Key Class

Unlike the `MovieClip` class, we don't create instances of the `Key` class. There is only one, global instance that we make use of at any time. The `Key` class allows us to interface with the keyboard by detecting key presses and releases and allows us to detect the general state of any key at any time.

The `Key` class is made up of several properties, methods, and events known as *listeners*. To use the `Key` class, we simply need to refer to it by name. For example, one of the methods of the `Key` class is the `getCode` method, which returns the keyboard code of the last key pressed. This is simply accessed like so:

```
lastCode = Key.getCode();
```

The `Key` class has several properties, which are essentially constants that correspond to certain keys on the keyboard. These properties are:

ACTIONSCRIPT	DESCRIPTION
`Key.BACKSPACE`	Key code value for the Backspace key
`Key.CAPSLOCK`	Key code value for the Caps Lock key
`Key.CONTROL`	Key code value for the Control key
`Key.DELETEKEY`	Key code value for the Delete key
`Key.DOWN`	Key code value for the Down Arrow key
`Key.END`	Key code value for the End key
`Key.ENTER`	Key code value for the Enter key
`Key.ESCAPE`	Key code value for the Escape key
`Key.HOME`	Key code value for the Home key
`Key.INSERT`	Key code value for the Insert key
`Key.LEFT`	Key code value for the Left Arrow key
`Key.PGDN`	Key code value for the Page Down key
`Key.PGUP`	Key code value for the Page Up key
`Key.RIGHT`	Key code value for the Right Arrow key
`Key.SHIFT`	Key code value for the Shift key
`Key.SPACE`	Key code value for the Spacebar
`Key.TAB`	Key code value for the Tab key
`Key.UP`	Key code value for the Up Arrow key

For a complete list of key codes for every key on the keyboard, see Appendix A. To see if the last key pressed was the up arrow, we would say

```
if (Key.getCode() == Key.UP))
```

Several methods are associated with the `Key` class. We can use these methods in various ways to get information about the keyboard.

Key.isDown

```
Key.isDown(keycode);
```

This method returns `true` if the `keycode` specified is being held down. Let's imagine the following game loop.

```
_root.onEnterFrame = function()
{
    if (Key.isDown(Key.RIGHT))
```

```
            ball._x ++;
        else if (Key.isDown(Key.LEFT))
            ball._x --;
}
```

That code runs on a constant `onEnterFrame` event on the _root timeline. We're assuming there's a movie clip with the instance name `ball` on the _root as well. The code is simple. Every frame we check to see if the right arrow key is being held. If so, then we move the `ball` to the right by one pixel, by incrementing its _x property. Otherwise, if the left arrow key is being held down, we move the ball to the left by decrementing its _x property.

This is what we'll be using most often when doing key control for games in this book.

Key.addListener

```
    Key.addListener(listenerObject);
```

This method is used to set up a listener on the `Key` class. A listener is a function that sits and *listens* for events and triggers when specific events occur. There are two events in the `Key` class:

Key.onKeyDown: Triggered whenever a key is pressed down

Key.onKeyUp: Triggered whenever a pressed key is released

We define these listener functions through the use of a generic object, like so:

```
    my_listener = new Object();
    my_listener.onKeyDown = function()
    {
        trace ("You Pressed a Key");
    }

    my_listener.onKeyUp = function()
    {
        trace ("You Released a Key");
    }

    Key.addListener(my_listener);
```

If we run this code and then press keys, we'll see the text "You Pressed a Key" whenever we press a key down (or when we hold a key down for a certain amount of time), and we'll see the text "You Released a Key" whenever a held key is released.

Key.removeListener

```
    code = Key.removeListener(listenerObject);
```

This method removes the listener object `listenerObject` from the `Key` class. Calling this will cause the `onKeyUp` and `onKeyDown` functions inside `listenerObject` to stop being called when keys are pressed and released.

Key.getCode

```
code = Key.getCode();
```

This method returns the key code of the last key pressed. It's important to understand that a key code is different from a character (or ASCII) code. Appendix B contains all of the ASCII codes for the standard characters, and Appendix A contains all of the key codes for the keys. Two keys that produce the same *character* do not produce the same *key code*. See the two following appendices for more information. Look at this sample code:

```
my_listener = new Object();
my_listener.onKeyDown = function()
{
    code = Key.getCode();
    trace ("You Pressed the key with code " + code);
}

my_listener.onKeyUp = function()
{
    code = Key.getCode();
    trace ("You Released the key with code " + code);
}

Key.addListener(my_listener);
```

Key.getAscii

```
ascii = Key.getAscii();
```

This method returns the ASCII character code of the last key pressed. Pressing keys such as Shift and Control, which do not have ASCII codes, cause getAscii to return 0. Look at this sample code:

```
my_listener = new Object();
my_listener.onKeyDown = function()
{
    ascii = Key.getAscii();
    trace ("You Pressed the key with ascii " + ascii);
}

my_listener.onKeyUp = function()
{
    ascii = Key.getAscii();
    trace ("You Released the key with ascii " + ascii);
}

Key.addListener(my_listener);
```

If we press and release the A key with the Shift key held down, we'll see the text:

```
You Pressed the key with ascii 65
You Released the key with ascii 65
```

If, on the other hand, Shift is not pressed, or Caps Lock is off, we'll see:

```
You Pressed the key with ascii 97
You Released the key with ascii 97
```

These correspond to the ASCII codes for uppercase and lowercase A. The getCode method, on the other hand, will always return the same code when the A key is pressed, no matter what the status of the Shift key is. In other words, getCode is tied to a *key*, while getAscii is tied to the *character* produced by a key press.

Key.isToggled

```
capsDown = Key.isToggled(20);
```

or

```
numLockDown = Key.isToggled(144);
```

This method returns a true or a false indicating whether or not the Caps Lock key (20), or the Num Lock key (144) is currently toggled on or off. This method is special because unlike Key.isDown, Caps Lock and Num Lock can be in one of two states regardless of whether or not they're being pressed manually with a finger when Key.isToggled is called.

The Mouse Class

The Mouse class provides us with access to the mouse and presents us with a few listener events and methods that we can use to perform some mouse-related tasks.

Mouse.hide

```
Mouse.hide();
```

This method will turn the mouse cursor off. Be careful about doing that. If you do, and don't somehow indicate where the mouse cursor is (by perhaps using a startDrag method), the user will have great difficulty navigating your interface. To use a custom cursor, you would have to do something like this:

```
customCursor._visible = true;
customCursor.startDrag(true);
Mouse.hide();
```

Assuming you have a movie clip with the instance name customCursor on the stage or have previously attached it with attachMovie, this will cause that to become the mouse cursor. It will automatically be dragged by the position of the invisible mouse cursor.

Mouse.show

```
Mouse.show();
```

This turns the mouse cursor back on when we're ready to start seeing it again.

`Mouse.addListener` and `Mouse.removeListener`

```
Mouse.addListener(listenerObject);
Mouse.removeListener(listenerObject);
```

In addition to `Mouse.hide` and `Mouse.show`, we have `Mouse.addListener` and `Mouse.removeListener`, which are very similar to the `Key.addListener` and `Key.removeListener`. The listener events at our disposal are:

`Mouse.onMouseDown`: Triggered whenever the mouse button is pressed down

`Mouse.onMouseUp`: Triggered whenever the mouse button is released

`Mouse.onMouseMove`: Triggered when the mouse is moved

`Mouse.onMouseWheel`: Triggered when the user rolls the mouse wheel

For example,

```
my_listener = new Object();
my_listener.onMouseDown = function()
{
    trace ("You Pressed the mouse button");
}

my_listener.onMouseUp = function()
{
    trace ("You Released the mouse button");
}

my_listener.onMouseMove = function()
{
    trace ("You moved the mouse");
}

my_listener.onMouseWheel = function(delta)
{
    trace ("You moved the mouse wheel by " + delta);
}

Mouse.addListener(my_listener);
```

The first three events, onMouseDown, onMouseUp, and onMouseMove receive no parameters. They're merely triggered when the respective event occurs. The onMouseWheel event, however, receives a value, delta, which is the amount and direction that the mouse wheel was rolled. Rolling the wheel up (away from your arm) produces a positive delta. Rolling the wheel down (toward your arm) produces a negative delta. The value of delta depends upon how fast the wheel is scrolled.

Look at the following trace output from scrolling up and down, first slowly, then quickly:

```
You moved the mouse wheel by 3
You moved the mouse wheel by 3
You moved the mouse wheel by 3
You moved the mouse wheel by -3
You moved the mouse wheel by -3
You moved the mouse wheel by -3
You moved the mouse wheel by 6
You moved the mouse wheel by 6
```

```
You moved the mouse wheel by 9
You moved the mouse wheel by -6
You moved the mouse wheel by -6
You moved the mouse wheel by -9
```

The Stage Class

We have access to several important pieces of information about the stage via the Stage class. The stage is the area that is visible by default in our Flash movies. In the design environment it's the large area usually indicated by a white box (by default), and it's surrounded by the gray area that is considered to be *off stage*. When we edit the document properties in Flash, we can set the width, height, and background color of the stage.

With the Stage class, we can use code to determine the width and height of the stage, as well as set the scale and alignment mode of the stage. Let's look at the properties individually.

Stage.scaleMode

```
Stage.scaleMode = "showAll";
```

or

```
Stage.scaleMode = "exactFit";
```

or

```
Stage.scaleMode = "noBorder";
```

or

```
Stage.scaleMode = "noScale";
```

The Stage.scaleMode property adjusts the way the stage is resized and positioned to fit within the Flash window. Does it zoom to fit? Does it squash when the window is resized? If so, does it scale evenly, or can it become distorted away from its original aspect ratio? The breakdown is as follows:

MODE	DESCRIPTION	EXAMPLE
showAll	As the window is resized, the stage resizes to grow or shrink to fit but maintains its initial aspect ratio. The stage scales down to fit the shortest window edge.	See Figure 19.3
exactFit	As the window is resized, the stage resizes to grow or shrink to fit but resizes so that the stage will stretch horizontally or vertically to fill the entire window.	See Figure 19.4
noBorder	As the window is resized, the stage stays its original size until both horizontally and vertically scrolled. The stage scales up to fit the longest window edge.	See Figure 19.5
noScale	As the window is resized, the stage stays its original size. It is not scaled up or down to match the window.	See Figure 19.6

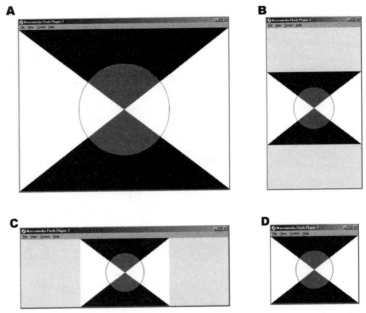

FIGURE 19.3 scaleMode showAll. (A) Unchanged window. (B) Scaled 50% horizontally. (C) Scaled 50% vertically. (D) 50% scale on both axes.

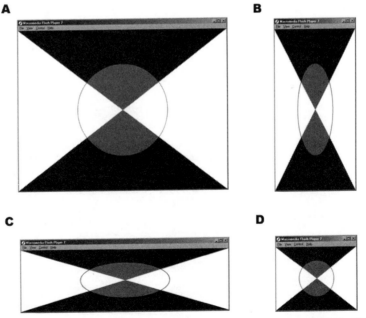

FIGURE 19.4 scaleMode exactFit. (A) Unchanged window. (B) Scaled 50% horizontally. (C) Scaled 50% vertically. (D) 50% scale on both axes.

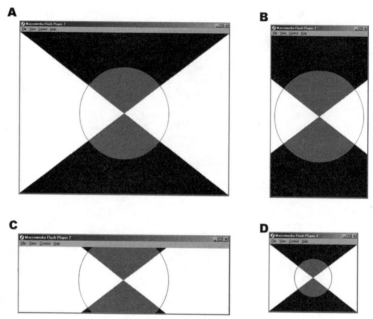

FIGURE 19.5 `scaleMode noBorder`. (A) Unchanged window. (B) Scaled 50% horizontally. (C) Scaled 50% vertically. (D) 50% scale on both axes.

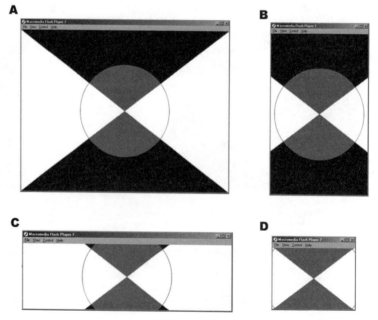

FIGURES 19.6 `scaleMode noScale`. (A) Unchanged window. (B) Scaled 50% horizontally. (C) Scaled 50% vertically. (D) 50% scale on both axes.

`Stage.align`

```
Stage.align = alignmentValue;
```

The `Stage.align` property allows us to specify how the stage will be aligned within the *window*. In the `scaleMode`, such as `exactFit`, the `Stage.align` property has no effect because the stage is always centered in the window. The valid values for `Stage.align` are:

VALUE	STAGE VERTICAL ALIGNMENT	STAGE HORIZONTAL ALIGNMENT
"T"	Top	Center
"B"	Bottom	Center
"L"	Center	Left
"R"	Center	Right
"TL"	Top	Left
"TR"	Top	Right
"BL"	Bottom	Left
"BR"	Bottom	Right

So, if we were to say

```
Stage.align = "TL";
Stage.scaleMode = "noScale";
```

then our entire stage would be left aligned, and resizing it would allow us to see more or less off the right side and bottom of the screen. The advantage of this becomes clear with the next two properties.

`Stage.width` and `Stage.height`

```
w = Stage.width;
h = Stage.height;
```

We can use the `Stage.width` and `Stage.height` properties to determine the width and height of the stage. The thing to remember with these two properties is that depending on the scale mode they'll reflect different things. When `Stage.scaleMode` is set to `showAll`, `noBorder`, or `exactFit`, then `Stage.width` and `Stage.height` will always be the exact height that was specified in the document properties at design time. Even when the window is resized, they'll always equal the exact dimensions specified at design time. This is because although the window is resizing, the stage is not technically changing in width and height—it's merely scaling, and its coordinate system remains the same.

The only `Stage.scaleMode` that accurately reflects the *window* size is `noScale`. In this mode we can use the `Stage.width` and `Stage.height` properties to see how large the window is on screen. That, combined with setting `Stage.align` to `"TL"` provides us with some powerful functionality.

Let's assume you have a movie clip on screen, with the instance name box. Let's also assume that the registration point of box is in the dead center of the movie clip. Put the following code on frame 1 of the main timeline.

```
Stage.align = "TL";
Stage.scaleMode = "noScale";

_root.onEnterFrame = function()
{
    box._x = Stage.width - (box._width / 2);
    box._y = Stage.height - (box._height / 2);
}
```

This allows us to position any movie clip at any location relative to the upper left corner of the *window*, not just the stage. If you run the above code, you'll see that the box will always be flush aligned with the lower-right corner of the window, even as the window is resized. This allows us to make some powerful interfaces that automatically realign themselves to the stage as you adjust and resize it. For example, how about a game that is resizable, but in which the scoreboard always lines up with the right edge of the window or a health bar that's always at the bottom of the window.

Stage.addListener

```
Stage.addListener(listenerObject);
```

Stage.addListener is a method that allows us to add to the stage a listener that listens for an event. There is only one event that is ever passed to the stage object:

onResize: This event is triggered when the stage is resized, and remember, the stage is only actually "resized" (Stage.width and Stage.height change) when the Stage.scaleMode is set to noScale.

We can expand on our previous example, and instead of using _root.onEnterFrame, let's use the onResize event:

```
Stage.align = "TL";
Stage.scaleMode = "noScale"

listenerObject = new Object();

listenerObject.onResize = function ()
{
    box._x = Stage.width - (box._width / 2);
    box._y = Stage.height - (box._height / 2);
}

Stage.addListener(listenerObject);

listenerObject.onResize();
```

Every time the window is resized, the stage width and height will also be changed. When that happens, onResize will be triggered and the box will be moved. We have to make one manual call to listenerObject.onResize() at the bottom of the code, the stage `onResize` function will not be called until the first time the user resizes the window.

Stage.removeListener

```
Stage.removeListener(listenerObject);
```

This method simply removes any stage listener that was set up previously:

```
Stage.align = "TL";
Stage.scaleMode = "noScale"

listenerObject = new Object();

listenerObject.onResize = function ()
{
    box._x = Stage.width - (box._width / 2);
    box._y = Stage.height - (box._height / 2);
}

Stage.addListener(listenerObject);

listenerObject.onResize();

exitButton.onRelease = function()
{
    Stage.removeListener(listenerObject);
}
```

The Math Class

The `Math` class (which should not be confused with a 60-minute time slot at school) contains several dozen methods that we can use to perform all sorts of mathematical functions, just like at the beginning of this primer, when we created a function `addThemUp`:

```
function addThemUp(a, b)
{
    return (a + b);
}

k = addThemUp(15, 5);
```

The `Math` class has many methods that we call in the same manner. The nice thing is, we don't need to see or care how these methods work. We just call them, pass parameters to them, and get the results we expect. The `Math` class also has several properties that correspond to popular mathematical constants such as pi.

Math.abs()

```
a = Math.abs(n);
```

This method calculates the absolute value of n. The value of a will be n, without the sign.

```
a = Math.abs(22);
```

a will be 22.

```
a = Math.abs(-22);
```

a will be 22.

Math.acos()

```
a = Math.acos(n);
```

This calculates the arc cosine value of n and returns the result in radians.

Math.asin()

```
a = Math.asin(n);
```

Math.asin() calculates the arc sine value of n and returns the result in radians.

Math.atan()

```
a = Math.atan(n);
```

This calculates the arc tangent value of n and returns the result in radians.

Math.atan2()

```
a = Math.atan2(y, x);
```

This method calculates the arc tangent value, which is the angle formed when measuring counterclockwise from the x axis up to the point formed by x, y.

```
x = 5;
y = 5;
a = Math.atan2(y, x);
trace ("The angle to point is " + a);
```

Note that y is passed in before x. This function essentially calls Math.atan, because Math.atan simply takes a value of y / x.

Math.ceil()

```
a = Math.ceil(n);
```

This calculates the value of n, rounded up to the nearest whole number.

```
a = Math.ceil(2.5);
```

a will be 3.

```
a = Math.ceil(8.1);
```

a will be 9.

Math.cos()

```
a = Math.cos(n);
```

`Math.cos()` calculates the cosine value of n.

Math.exp()

```
a = Math.exp(n);
```

This calculates the base of the natural logarithm, *e*, to the power of the exponent, n.

Math.floor()

```
a = Math.floor(n);
```

This method calculates the value of n, rounded down to the nearest whole number.

```
a = Math.floor(2.9);
```

a will be 2.

```
a = Math.floor(8.1);
```

a will be 8.

Math.log()

```
a = Math.log();
```

`Math.log()` calculates the logarithm value of n.

Math.max()

```
a = Math.max(m, n);
```

This method returns the maximum (larger number) value between m and n.

```
a = Math.max(6, 7);
```

a will be 7.

```
a = Math.max (-5, -9);
```

a will be −5.

Math.min()

```
a = Math.min(m, n);
```

This returns the minimum (smaller number) value between m and n.

```
a = Math.min(6, 7);
```

a will be 6.

```
a = Math.min(-5, -9);
```

a will be –9.

Math.pow()

```
a = Math.pow(m, n);
```

Math.pow() computes m raised to the power of n.

```
a = Math.pow(2, 3);
```

a will be 2 * 2 * 2, which multiplies out to 8.

```
a = Math.pow(5, 2);
```

a will be 5 * 5, which multiplies out to 25.

Math.random()

```
a = Math.random();
```

This method returns a random number between 0.0 and 1.0. This number can be multiplied by any number to modify the return range. For example,

```
a = Math.random();
```

a will be a random number between 0.0 and 1.0.

```
a = Math.random() * 7;
```

a will be a random number between 0.0 and 7.0.

```
a = Math.random() * -15;
```

a will be a random number between 0.0 and –15.0.

```
a = Math.random() * 5 + 2;
```

a will be a random number between 2.0 and 7.0.

Math.round()

```
a = Math.round(n);
```

Math.round() rounds the number, n, to the nearest whole number.

```
a = Math.round(2.9);
```

a will be 3.

```
a = Math.round(8.1);
```

a will be 8.

```
a = Math.round(4.5);
```

a will be 5.

Math.sin()

```
a = Math.sin(n);
```

This method calculates the cosine value of n.

Math.sqrt()

```
a = Math.sqrt(n);
```

This method calculates the square root of n.

Math.tan()

```
a = Math.tan(n);
```

This calculates the tangent of n.

The Math class also has several properties built in. Here are the most popular mathematical constants:

Math.E

```
a = Math.E;
```

The mathematical constant e is known as Euler's constant. It is the base of natural logarithms—approximately 2.718281828.

Math.LN2

```
a = Math.LN2;
```

This is the natural logarithm of 2—approximately 0.693147181.

Math.LOG2E

```
a = Math.LOG2E;
```

This is the base 2 logarithm of e—approximately 1.442695041.

Math.LN10

```
a = Math.LN10;
```

This is the natural logarithm of 10—approximately 2.302585093.

Math.LOG10E

```
a = Math.LOG10E;
```

This is the base 10 logarithm of e—approximately 0.434294482.

Math.PI

```
a = Math.PI;
```

`Math.PI` radians is the number of radians in 180 degrees. It is also the ratio of the circumference of a circle to its diameter—approximately 3.141592654.

Math.SQRT1_2

```
a = Math.SQRT1_2;
```

This is the reciprocal of the square root of 1/2—approximately 0.707106781.

Math.SQRT2

```
a = Math.SQRT2;
```

This is the square root of 2—approximately 1.414213562.

The Array Class

One of the most important concepts for us to understand when programming games in ActionScript is the concept of the array and the intricacies of the `Array` class. Through the array we're able to associate data in logical groups, almost like a list. In real life we might say, "The names of our gerbils are Herbie, Gordie, Lemmie, Sammie, Gummie and Kimmie." Without the use of arrays, we might write this as

```
gerbilName1 = "Herbie";
gerbilName2 = "Gordie";
gerbilName3 = "Lemmie";
gerbilName4 = "Sammie";
gerbilName5 = "Gummie";
gerbilName6 = "Kimmie";
```

Now, let's imagine that we want to add the word "Gerbil" to the beginning of each of the `gerbilName` variables. So, we say this:

```
gerbilName1 = "Gerbil " + gerbilName1;
gerbilName2 = "Gerbil " + gerbilName2;
gerbilName3 = "Gerbil " + gerbilName3;
gerbilName4 = "Gerbil " + gerbilName4;
gerbilName5 = "Gerbil " + gerbilName5;
gerbilName6 = "Gerbil " + gerbilName6;
```

Each variable will contain the values like so:

VARIABLE NAME	VALUE
gerbilName1	Gerbil Herbie
gerbilName2	Gerbil Gordie
gerbilName3	Gerbil Lemmie
gerbilName4	Gerbil Sammie
gerbilName5	Gerbil Gummie
gerbilName6	Gerbil Kimmie

This is easy enough, but what would happen if we didn't have six gerbils, but instead we had 600 gerbils? How could we organize this kind of data without creating 600 individual string variables? Enter the array.

With the array, we can assign our gerbil names like so:

```
gerbilName = new Array("Herbie", "Gordie", "Lemmie",
                       "Sammie", "Gummie", "Kimmie");
```

Now, there's only one variable, `gerbilName`, which contains every gerbil name. How do we access a particular gerbil's name? We use something called an *index*.

```
trace(arrayName[index]);
```

or, with our gerbils:

```
trace (gerbilName[0]);
```

This traces out Herbie, since the first index in our array is index 0; that is, index 0 refers to the first gerbil in the list. If we wanted to see the last gerbil in this list, that would be index 5:

```
trace (gerbilName[5]);
```

This would trace out Kimmie.

Remember that arrays start with index 0, so our `gerbilName` array contains gerbil names at indexes 0, 1, 2, 3, 4, and 5—that's 6 total.

The nice thing about the array is that we can make the index a variable, so we could display all six (or 600) gerbil names like so:

```
for (k = 0; k < gerbilName.length; k++)
{
    trace ("Gerbil number " + k + " is named " + gerbilName[k]);
}
```

In the output window we would see the following:

```
Gerbil number 0 is named Herbie
Gerbil number 1 is named Gordie
Gerbil number 2 is named Lemmie
Gerbil number 3 is named Sammie
Gerbil number 4 is named Gummie
Gerbil number 5 is named Kimmie
```

If we wanted to do our original task of adding "Gerbil" to the name, we'd say this:

```
for (k = 0; k < gerbilName.length; k++)
{
    gerbilName[k] = "Gerbil " + gerbilName[k];
    trace ("Gerbil number " + k + " is named " + gerbilName[k]);
}
```

This would result in

```
Gerbil number 0 is named Gerbil Herbie
Gerbil number 1 is named Gerbil Gordie
Gerbil number 2 is named Gerbil Lemmie
Gerbil number 3 is named Gerbil Sammie
Gerbil number 4 is named Gerbil Gummie
Gerbil number 5 is named Gerbil Kimmie
```

Each item in the array is known as an *element*. Notice that we're not specifying an exact number of elements, but rather we're using `gerbilName.length`. The length property returns the number of elements in an array. In the case of our `gerbilName` array, that will be 6. By using `gerbilName.length`, it's as if we said

```
for (k = 0; k < 6; k++)
{
    gerbilName[k] = "Gerbil " + gerbilName[k];
    trace ("Gerbil number " + k + " is named " + gerbilName[k]);
}
```

It's also possible to create an array in steps, rather than in one line like the gerbil names were. If you wanted to create an array with 5000 random numbers, you could do this:

```
randomNums = new Array();
for (k = 0; k < 5000; k ++)
{
    randomNums[k] = Math.random() * 100;
}
```

This would fill the `randomNums` array with 5000 numbers, each number being between 0.0 and 100.0.

Besides strings and numbers, an array can also contain objects and can even contain other arrays. We could create an array of 200 objects like so:

```
objectArray = new Array();

for (k = 0; k < 200; k ++)
{
    objectArray[k] = new Object();
    objectArray[k].owner = "Human";
    objectArray[k].height = Math.random() * 7;
    objectArray[k].age = Math.random() * 99;
}
```

This would create an array of 200 objects called `objectArray`, and each object will contain a string, `owner`, and two random numbers, `height` and `age`. On the other hand, you could do this:

```
objectArray = new Array();

for (k = 0; k < 200; k ++)
{
    objectArray[k] = new Array();
}
```

This would create an array of arrays, and any element could be referred to as

```
objectArray[j][k];
```

This is also what we call a multidimensional array. Rather than just one row of data, like just the gerbil names, you can create a grid of data. So, imagine we have gerbil ages and the names of gerbils that are that age:

AGE 0	AGE 1	AGE 2	AGE 3
Roy	Pickle	Ham	Jumper
Dave	Fuzzers	Cheese	
Bob		Twitch	

From the standpoint of a multidimensional array (in this case a two-dimensional array), we would represent the data like so:

```
gerbilName = new Array();

for (k = 0; k < 4; k ++)
{
    gerbilName[k] = new Array();
}

gerbilName[0][0] = "Roy";
gerbilName[0][1] = "Dave";
gerbilName[0][2] = "Bob";

gerbilName[1][0] = "Pickle";
gerbilName[1][1] = "Fuzzers";

gerbilName[2][0] = "Ham";
gerbilName[2][1] = "Cheese";
gerbilName[2][2] = "Twitch";

gerbilName[3][0] = "Jumper";
```

The first element in the array is the year (the first square brackets), and the second element is the gerbil number (the second square brackets). In games two-dimensional arrays are often used to represent game grids. Imagine the following 10×10 game grid, where each position of the grid contains either a 0 or a 1, for solid or hollow:

```
gameGrid = new Array();

for (k = 0; k < 10; k ++)
{
    gameGrid[k] = new Array();

    for (j = 0; j < 10; j++)
    {
        gameGrid[k][j] = Math.floor(Math.random() * 2);
    }
}
```

This would fill each element of the grid with a random number, 0 or 1.

It's also possible to use nonnumbers as the elements in arrays. You can use a string, for example, so rather than saying

```
colorList = new Array();
colorList[0] = 0xFF0000;
colorList[1] = 0x00FF00;
colorList[2] = 0x0000FF;
```

you could say

```
colorList = new Array();
colorList["red"] = 0xFF0000;
colorList["green"] = 0x00FF00;
colorList["blue"] = 0x0000FF;
```

Rather than having to know which element in the array corresponded to which color, you could simply say something like

```
myColorToUse = colorList["red"];
```

This would set the variable myColorToUse to 0xFF0000, which is the hexadecimal value for the RGB color red.

Several methods can be used to modify arrays in various ways. We can use these methods to join arrays and split them and add and remove elements and sort them. Some of them are as follows.

Array.concat()

```
newArray = oldArray.concat(item1, item2, item3);
```

The Array.concat method takes any number of parameters and combines them into an array. You can use this to combine arrays of numbers, strings, or arrays. For example,

```
array1 = new Array ("hi", "bye");
array2 = new Array(1, 2, 3);
array3 = new Array(9, 8, 7);

newArray = array1.concat(array2, array3);
```

newArray now contains hi, bye, 1, 2, 3, 9, 8, 7.

Array.join()

```
newString = myArray.join(",");
```

This takes all of the elements in an array and joins them into one string, each element being separated by the parameter passed into the join method. For example,

```
myArray = new Array("One", "Two", "Three");
joined = myArray.join("*");
```

This would create the string joined, looking like: One*Two*Three. If you specify no separator, the words will be joined with no separator:

```
myArray = new Array("One", "Two", "Three");
joined = myArray.join("");
```

`joined` would be OneTwoThree.

`Array.reverse()`

```
myArray.reverse();
```

This method reverses the direction of an array. So, 6,7,8,9 would become 9,8,7,6.

`Array.sort()`

```
myArray.sort();
```

This sorts an array alphanumerically. For example,

```
myArray = new Array("Zebra", "Bob", "Tim", "Goat");
myArray.sort();
```

`myArray` would then be: Bob, Goat, Tim, Zebra.

The `BitmapData` Class

The `BitmapData` class is brand new to Macromedia Flash Professional 8 and gives us a powerful new set of tools to use in the manipulation of high-speed blocks of memory specifically designed to handle bitmap images. This is a boon for game developers, as it streamlines game performance by optimizing the graphics pipeline and putting the "flow of pixels" in our hands.

To start with, always make sure to have the following code at the top of any program that makes use of the `BitmapData` class:

```
import flash.display.BitmapData;
```

This is necessary to make use of any of the `BitmapData` methods and to avoid having to write extremely long path names when using the constructor.

Constructor

At its core, the `BitmapData` class is used to create rectangular areas of pixels. We then extend that functionality to load images into those areas, modify pixels, apply filters, copy pixels, and more. To create a new instance of a the `BitmapData` class, we would say

```
my_bitmap:BitmapData = new BitmapData(640, 480,
                              true, 0x00000000);
```

This is the basic constructor that creates a `BitmapData` object with a width of 640 and height of 480 and makes use of transparent pixels, with the object initially filled with blank, transparent pixels. The constructor looks like so:

```
new BitmapData(width, height, transparent, fillColor)
```

If `transparent` is set to `true`, the `fillColor` must be in the format `0xAARRGGBB`, where the `AA` is a number from `00` to `FF`, representing a level of transparency. With `alpha`, `00` is completely transparent, and `FF` is completely solid. So, for a completely solid, perfect blue box, we would use the color `0xFF0000FF`, where the first `FF` refers to the alpha (solid) and the last `FF` is for the blue portion of the number.

If, on the other hand, we pass in `false` for the `transparent` parameter, the color only needs to be a traditional `0xRRGGBB` format. The maximum width and height of a `BitmapData` object is 2880×2880 pixels in size.

BitmapData.setPixel and BitmapData.setPixel32

If we want to directly change pixels in a `BitmapData` object, we must make use of the `setPixel` or the `setPixel32` method. Both of these have the exact same structure:

```
BitmapData.setPixel(x, y, color);
BitmapData.setPixel32(x, y, color);
```

The only difference between these two methods is the format of the color. In `setPixel` a color of the type RRGGBB is expected, while in `setPixel32`, a color of type AARRGGBB is expected. We therefore choose our method based on the way the `BitmapData` object was initialized to begin with. To set the pixel at position 10, 10 to solid red, on a nontransparent `BitmapData` object, we would say

```
my_bitmap.setPixel(10, 10, 0xFF0000);
```

To set pixel 140, 221 to 50% alpha green, we would say

```
my_bitmap.setPixel32(140, 221, 0x7F00FF00);
```

BitmapData.getPixel and BitmapData.getPixel32

The `getPixel` and `getPixel32` methods are very similar to the `setPixel` and the `setPixel32` methods, but they only take an x and a y parameter, and the value they return *is* the color at that given coordinate.

For the nontransparent `BitmapData` object:

```
theColor = my_bitmap.getPixel(10, 10);
```

For the `BitmapData` object that includes an alpha channel:

```
theColor = my_bitmap.getPixel32(10, 10);
```

BitmapData.fillRect

This method fills a rectangular area of a `BitmapData` object with a specific color. This is the fastest way to change a large area of pixels. The function looks like so:

```
BitmapData.fillRect(rect, color)
```

The first thing to make note of is that we will need to declare a rectangle to fill, and in order to do that, we should include the geometry classes, like so:

```
import flash.geom.*;
```

Then we declare a rectangular area:

```
my_rect = new Rectangle(0, 0, 320, 240);
```

This would define a rectangle that was 320 wide, 240 high, and had its upper-left corner at 0, 0. Then we could use the `fillRect` method:

```
my_bitmap.fillRect(my_rect, 0x000000);
```

This would make a black rectangle on `my_bitmap` that encompassed the region from 0,0 to 319, 239.

BitmapData.draw

This function is one of the most important tools for getting graphics and images actually *into* the pixels of a `BitmapData` object. The draw method takes a source object, which can be a movie clip, video, button, another `BitmapData` object, and so on, and renders that object, using the Flash vector renderer, onto a destination `BitmapData` object.

The most basic use of this method is

```
my_bitmap.draw(source_mc);
```

This will simply draw `source_mc` onto `my_bitmap`, with no transformations applied. Note that any transformations that may have been applied to `source_mc` with code will *not* be carried over to the rendered version in `my_bitmap`.

The draw method does, however, have a much larger set of optional parameters:

```
BitmapData.draw(source:Object, [matrix:Matrix],
[colorTransform:ColorTransform], [blendMode:Object], [clipRect:Rectangle],
[smooth:Boolean])
```

The matrix parameter is used to define any transformations we want applied to the source object, such as scale, rotation, or translation. The `colorTransform` object performs any color adjustments to the source object. This allows you to adjust the various levels of red, green, and blue.

The `blendMode` parameter defines how the source object will be drawn over the top of the currently existing contents of the `BitmapData` object. The valid values for the `blendMode` parameter are:

- `"normal"`
- `"layer"`
- `"multiply"`
- `"screen"`
- `"lighten"`
- `"darken"`
- `"difference"`
- `"add"`
- `"subtract"`
- `"invert"`
- `"alpha"`

- "erase"
- "overlay"
- "hardlight"

For more details on what each of these blend modes does, see the "blendMode" section under "ActionScript 2.0 Language Reference" in the Flash 8 IDE help.

The `clipRect` object defines how the source will be clipped (cut off) against the `BitmapData` object so it would be possible to draw only a small piece of the source object if the `clipRect` was very small.

The `smooth` parameter is a Boolean value that specifies whether or not the source object should be smoothed when scaled, using the built-in Flash bitmap smoothing algorithm. Use this if you're passing in a bitmap image as your source and scaling it up past 100% and you don't want it to look pixelated or blocky.

For example, the following code would draw the movie clip `source_mc` onto the `BitmapData` object `my_bitmap`. The `source_mc` movie clip would be scaled to 200% both horizontally and vertically and rotated to 1.22 radians. The `col_trans` Color-Transform object used is a default constructed `ColorTransform`. No color adjustments will actually be performed.

```
import flash.display.BitmapData;
import flash.geom.*;

my_bitmap:BitmapData = new BitmapData(500,500,false,0);

trans_mat = new Matrix();
trans_mat.scale(2, 2);
trans_mat.rotate(1.22);

col_trans = new ColorTransform();

clip_rect = new Rectangle(0, 0, 300, 200);

my_bitmap.draw(source_mc, trans_mat, col_trans,
               "add", clip_rect, false);
```

BitmapData.copyPixels

This is a fast method to perform pixel manipulation between images with no stretching, rotation, or color effects. This method copies a rectangular area of a source image to a rectangular area of the same size at the destination point of the destination `BitmapData` object. For example,

```
import flash.display.BitmapData;
import flash.geom.*;

src_rect = new Rectangle(0, 0, 32, 32);
dest_pt = new Point(34, 35);
```

... later, after the `BitmapData` objects have been defined:

```
my_bitmap.copyPixels(src_bitmap, src_rect, dest_pt);
```

This would copy the pixels encompassed by `src_rect`, from the `src_bitmap` `BitmapData` object and place the upper-left corner of those copied pixels at the point defined by `dest_pt` in `my_bitmap`.

This method is used heavily in the Chapter 11 and 12 examples.

BitmapData.loadBitmap

This is a static method that creates a new instance of a `BitmapData` object, and into it loads a bitmap image from the library, using a specific linkage ID as the source image. For example, if we had a bitmap image in the library, with the linkage ID `cloudyday`, we could create a new `BitmapData` object and fill it with the contents of `cloudyday`, like so:

```
my_bitmap:BitmapData = BitmapData.load("cloudyday");
```

MovieClip.attachBitmap

This is a method of the `MovieClip` class, but it is more applicable in context to the `BitmapData` object, so we're placing it here. This method is how we get our `Bitmap-Data` objects to be seen, visually, on screen. Using this method, we give our `Bitmap-Data` objects a home in the visual world. This works by attaching the `BitmapData` object to a movie clip at a specific depth level so it is drawn on screen at the position of the movie clip.

```
holder_mc.attachBitmap(my_bitmap, 0);
```

This would attach the `BitmapData` object `my_bitmap` to depth level 0 of the `holder_mc` movie clip. Just like that, any changes we made to `my_bitmap` would now appear on screen.

SUMMARY

All that we've talked about here represents but a small portion of ActionScript. This has been meant to get you up to speed with what you'll basically need to know to program the games in this book.

There are other things that are touched on as we proceed through the book, for example, the Draw API, which is a set of drawing tools that are methods of the `MovieClip` class and can be used to create graphics at runtime with things such as lines and fills. Another topic is the `Sound` class. We've dedicated an entire chapter to the `Sound` class, which provides us with the ability to play music and sound effects as events or as streams.

To truly get deep into the ActionScript language, you should consult (heavily) the ActionScript reference and dictionary that comes with the Macromedia Flash Professional 8 development environment. It's thorough and cross referenced in so many ways that it's highly usable.

In this chapter we looked at:

- ActionScript 1.0 versus ActionScript 2.0 (and why we've chosen to code this book with ActionScript 1.0)
- `trace`
- Variables
- Comparisons and conditions
- Loops
- Functions
- Relative paths and objects
- The `MovieClip` class
- The `Key` class
- The `Mouse` class
- The `Stage` class
- The `Math` class
- The `Array` class
- The `BitmapData` class

20

THE FUTURE OF GAMES

Where do we go from here? That really depends upon what we, as game developers, do with the tools and software packages at our disposal. As we continue to push the envelope and make Macromedia Flash do bigger and better things, we will, accordingly, promote the growth and enhancement of Flash.

Macromedia Flash could continue to grow in several ways:

- The rendering engine could become faster and more optimized, thus allowing us to do more with the current tool set.
- Macromedia could expand the tool set itself, giving us more functionality to do things such as:
  1. Create true polygon-based 3D graphics that make use of hardware rendering engines built into most computers today.
  2. Allow more interfacing with hardware such as joysticks and other input devices.
  3. Allow users to apply advanced physics principles such as gravity, motion, inverse kinematics, and collision to games.

- The ActionScript language, although it has evolved by leaps and bounds in the past few versions, could continue to be strengthened with an even greater set of classes and functions. Such improvements remain to be seen in upcoming versions, including the new ActionScript 3.0.

With the evolution of the Web, more and more people have access to high-speed connections. What this means for us as Macromedia Flash developers is that we have the opportunity to use more media in our games. We can feel freer to use larger and more detailed images, more complex sound effects and music, and even full-motion video.

How can you further your skills as a game programmer?

Practice: The best way to learn a concept, and indeed a trade, is by continually practicing and doing. Once you have seen a particularly devious bug pop up several times, you will begin to recognize it immediately and you'll be able to easily fix it. Also, once you've written the physics code for 3D motion for the hundredth time, that code will become second nature to you.

Learn: If you find a great game programming book that is written for a language other than ActionScipt, read it. Most game programming concepts are universal, and most programming languages are similar enough that if you understand one, you can understand them all. Never stop learning. There are hundreds of authors and programmers out there with new and original ways of doing things. These are your most valuable resources. It is the interaction among programmers in the game development community that ultimately leads to tomorrow's innovations.

Experiment: If you have even the seed of an idea but you're not sure if it would work, give it a try. There is nothing to be lost and an immeasurable amount to be gained. It is when you experiment that you end up accidentally doing things that turn into great pieces of code and even great games.

Computer games are more than just idle entertainment; they are a means of expression, exploration, creativity, and self-discovery. The worlds that we create as game developers will be personal to us and will provide hours of engagement and enjoyment to those who explore them. When we find players developing an emotional attachment to our games, we have accomplished what the great directors and musicians of our time have been accomplishing for many years. Ultimately, the future of games will be in the fusion of all creative media, and computer games will and have become an established part of our past, present, and future.

KEY CODES

In Macromedia Flash Professional 8, we have access to a very powerful Key class. We can use this class to determine the state of almost any key on the keyboard, which is great for game development where we need to react to the state of keys like the arrows and the space bar. We can almost think of the key codes as a map, in much the same way that joystick buttons are mapped with ID numbers in a DirectX game to determine the state of the joystick. The keyboard becomes a very large joystick for us.

To check the state of any particular key, simply use the following code:

```
if (Key.isDown(code))
```

So, to see if the right arrow key is being held down, you can use the ActionScript:

```
if (Key.isDown(39))
```

This will evaluate to true if the right arrow key is being held down. For more detail on the Key object, see Chapter 19, the ActionScript for Games primer. In the key chart that follows, you can see the keyboard layout, with the key value, and the code that represents it. Note that key codes and ASCII codes are *not* the same thing. The ASCII code for the - (minus) will be the same no matter which key is used to create it (as there are two keys on the keyboard that create a minus key), however, the key code will be different depending upon which minus key you press (189 or 109). Note that the ALT key does not have a key code (it opens the drop down menus in browsers instead).

Main keyboard:

esc 27	F1 112	F2 113	F3 114	F4 115	F5 116	F6 117	F7 118	F8 119	F9 120	F10 121	F11 122	F12 123
~ 192	1 49	2 50	3 51	4 52	5 53	6 54	7 55	8 56	9 57	0 48	- 189	=+ 187
Tab 9	Q 81	W 87	E 69	R 82	T 84	Y 89	U 85	I 73	O 79	P 80	{[219	}] 221
Capslock 20	A 65	S 83	D 68	F 70	G 71	H 72	J 74	K 75	L 76	:; 186	"' 222	
Shft 16	Z 90	X 88	C 67	V 86	B 66	N 78	M 77	<, 188	>. 190	?/ 191	Shft 16	
Ctrl 17	Win 91				Space 32							

BkSpc 8 · \| 220 · Enter 13

Navigation / editing cluster:

Home 36	PgUp 33
End 35	PgDn 34
Del 46	Ins 45

Left 37	Up 38	Right 39
	Down 40	

Numeric keypad:

Numlck 47	/ 111	* 106	- 109
7 103	8 104	9 105	+ 107
4 100	5 101	6 102	
1 97	2 98	3 99	Ent 13
0 96		. 110	

ASCII CHARACTER CHART

The ASCII (American Standard Code for Information Interchange) character chart is a chart that contains all of the base standard letters, numbers, punctuation and special characters used in computers today. This is a helpful guide, and an invaluable resource to keep by your side.

The chr function

In Macromedia Flash Professional 8, we can determine the ASCII character, from an ASCII code, by using the chr function, like so:

```
char = chr(code);
```

So, if we were to use a code of 65, which corresponds to uppercase A, then we'd be saying:

```
code = 65;
char = chr(code);
```

This would cause char to be equal to A. It's necessary to pass a value directly into the chr function via a variable, rather than directly. For example, ASCII character 241 is the ñ character. However, if we trace out chr(241), we get an output that contains a small box, and no character. We must set a variable to 241 first, and then pass that into the function, like so:

```
code = 241;
trace (chr(code));
```

This will output ñ in the trace output window. The reason that we must not pass 241 in directly is because Flash seems to treat it as if it's a string, rather than a number. If we say:

```
trace (chr(Number(code)));
```

Then ñ will be successfully displayed.

The ord function

Conversely, we can supply a character, and use the ord function to determine the ASCII code for it, like so:

```
code = ord(char);
```

If we were to supply the letter A, then code would be 65, like so:

```
char = "A";
code = ord(char);
```

The first 32 ASCII characters (0 to 31) are special characters, that do not have a character representation, per se. These are characters that are used to specify line breaks, page breaks, and other various pieces of information to monitors, printers, etc. The screen may not be able to visually display the Form Feed character (ASCII code 12), but if that is sent to a printer then the printer will eject a sheet of paper. The ASCII characters have many different applications beyond displaying numbers and letters on screen.

The ASCII Chart

ASCII CODE (CODE)	ASCII CODE IN HEXADECIMAL PRODUCED WITH CHR(CODE)	CHARACTER VALUE
	0x00	Null
1	0x01	Header Start
2	0x02	Text Start
3	0x03	Text End
4	0x04	Transmission End
5	0x05	Enquiry
6	0x06	Acknowledgment
7	0x07	Bell Sound
8	0x08	Backspace (backspace key produces this)
9	0x09	Tab (tab key produces this)
10	0x0A	Line Feed
11	0x0B	Vertical Tab
12	0x0C	Form Feed
13	0x0D	Carriage Return (enter key produces this)
14	0x0E	Shift Out
15	0x0F	Shift In

ASCII CODE (CODE)	ASCII CODE IN HEXADECIMAL PRODUCED WITH CHR(CODE)	CHARACTER VALUE
16	0x10	Data Link Escape
17	0x11	Device Control 1
18	0x12	Device Control 2
19	0x13	Device Control 3
20	0x14	Device Control 4
21	0x15	Negative Acknowledge
22	0x16	Synch Character
23	0x17	Transmission Block End
24	0x18	Cancel
25	0x19	Message End
26	0x1A	Substitute
27	0x1B	Escape (escape key produces this)
28	0x1C	File Separator
29	0x1D	Group Separator
30	0x1E	Record Separator
31	0x1F	Unit Separator
32	0x20	Space (space bar produces this)
33	0x21	!
34	0x22	"
35	0x23	#
36	0x24	$
37	0x25	%
38	0x26	&
39	0x27	'
40	0x28	(
41	0x29	)
42	0x2A	*
43	0x2B	+
44	0x2C	,
45	0x2D	-
46	0x2E	.
47	0x2F	/
48	0x30	0
49	0x31	1
50	0x32	2
51	0x33	3
52	0x34	4
53	0x35	5
54	0x36	6

ASCII CODE (CODE)	ASCII CODE IN HEXADECIMAL PRODUCED WITH CHR(CODE)	CHARACTER VALUE
55	0x37	7
56	0x38	8
57	0x39	9
58	0x3A	:
59	0x3B	;
60	0x3C	<
61	0x3D	=
62	0x3E	>
63	0x3F	?
64	0x40	@
65	0x41	A
66	0x42	B
67	0x43	C
68	0x44	D
69	0x45	E
70	0x46	F
71	0x47	G
72	0x48	H
73	0x49	I
74	0x4A	J
75	0x4B	K
76	0x4C	L
77	0x4D	M
78	0x4E	N
79	0x4F	O
80	0x50	P
81	0x51	Q
82	0x52	R
83	0x53	S
84	0x54	T
85	0x55	U
86	0x56	V
87	0x57	W
88	0x58	X
89	0x59	Y
90	0x5A	Z
91	0x5B	[
92	0x5C	\
93	0x5D	]

ASCII CODE (CODE)	ASCII CODE IN HEXADECIMAL PRODUCED WITH CHR(CODE)	CHARACTER VALUE
94	0x5E	^
95	0x5F	_
96	0x60	`
97	0x61	a
98	0x62	b
99	0x63	c
100	0x64	d
101	0x65	e
102	0x66	f
103	0x67	g
104	0x68	h
105	0x69	i
106	0x6A	j
107	0x6B	k
108	0x6C	l
109	0x6D	m
110	0x6E	n
111	0x6F	o
112	0x70	p
113	0x71	q
114	0x72	r
115	0x73	s
116	0x74	t
117	0x75	u
118	0x76	v
119	0x77	w
120	0x78	x
121	0x79	y
122	0x7A	z
123	0x7B	{
124	0x7C		
125	0x7D	}
126	0x7E	~
127	0x7F	Delete (delete key produces this)

The characters that follow are known as the "extended characters", and are not standardized and therefore tend to be different from font to font. The ones below are probably the most common set (and are produced by the output window in Flash).

ASCII CODE (CODE)	ASCII CODE IN HEXADECIMAL PRODUCED WITH CHR(CODE)	CHARACTER VALUE
128	0x80	Ç
129	0x81	ü
130	0x82	‚é
131	0x83	ƒ
132	0x84	„
133	0x85	…
134	0x86	†
135	0x87	‡
136	0x88	ˆ
137	0x89	‰
138	0x8A	Ŝ
139	0x8B	‹
140	0x8C	Œ
141	0x8D	ì
142	0x8E	Ä
143	0x8F	Å
144	0x90	É
145	0x91	'
146	0x92	'
147	0x93	"
148	0x94	"
149	0x95	•
150	0x96	–
151	0x97	—
152	0x98	~
153	0x99	™
154	0x9A	ŝ
155	0x9B	›
156	0x9C	œ
157	0x9D	¥
158	0x9E	▯
159	0x9F	Ÿ
160	0xA0	á
161	0xA1	¡
162	0xA2	¢
163	0xA3	£
164	0xA4	¤
165	0xA5	¥
166	0xA6	¦

ASCII CODE (CODE)	ASCII CODE IN HEXADECIMAL PRODUCED WITH CHR(CODE)	CHARACTER VALUE
167	0xA7	§
168	0xA8	¨
169	0xA9	©
170	0xAA	ª
171	0xAB	«
172	0xAC	¬
173	0xAD	–
174	0xAE	®
175	0xAF	¯
176	0xB0	°
177	0xB1	±
178	0xB2	²
179	0xB3	³
180	0xB4	´
181	0xB5	µ
182	0xB6	¶
183	0xB7	·
184	0xB8	¸
185	0xB9	¹
186	0xBA	º
187	0xBB	»
188	0xBC	¼
189	0xBD	½
190	0xBE	¾
191	0xBF	¿
192	0xC0	À
193	0xC1	Á
194	0xC2	Â
195	0xC3	Ã
196	0xC4	Ä
197	0xC5	Å
198	0xC6	Æ
199	0xC7	Ç
200	0xC8	È
201	0xC9	É
202	0xCA	
203	0xCB	Ë
204	0xCC	Ì
205	0xCD	Í

ASCII CODE (CODE)	ASCII CODE IN HEXADECIMAL PRODUCED WITH CHR(CODE)	CHARACTER VALUE
206	0xCE	Î
207	0xCF	Ï
208	0xD0	Đ
209	0xD1	Ñ
210	0xD2	Ò
211	0xD3	Ó
212	0xD4	Ô
213	0xD5	Õ
214	0xD6	Ö
215	0xD7	×
216	0xD8	Ø
217	0xD9	Ù
218	0xDA	Ú
219	0xDB	Û
220	0xDC	Ü
221	0xDD	Ý
222	0xDE	Þ
223	0xDF	ß
224	0xE0	à
225	0xE1	á
226	0xE2	â
227	0xE3	ã
228	0xE4	ä
229	0xE5	å
230	0xE6	æ
231	0xE7	ç
232	0xE8	è
233	0xE9	é
234	0xEA	ê
235	0xEB	ë
236	0xEC	ì
237	0xED	í
238	0xEE	î
239	0xEF	ï
240	0xF0	
241	0xF1	ñ
242	0xF2	ò
243	0xF3	ó
244	0xF4	ô

245	0xF5	õ
246	0xF6	ö
247	0xF7	÷
248	0xF8	ø
249	0xF9	ù
250	0xFA	ú
251	0xFB	û
252	0xFC	ü
253	0xFD	ý
254	0xFE	þ
255	0xFF	ÿ

ABOUT THE CD-ROM

The CD-ROM included with *Macromedia Flash Professional 8 Game Development* includes all of files necessary to complete the tutorials in the book.

CD FOLDERS

- **CHAPTERS:** All of the files necessary to complete the tutorials in the book including, game images and SWF/FLA files. They are set up in chapter folders that correspond to the appropriate chapter in the book. Each chapter folder also includes a subfolder called Images, which contains all of the images from that chapter printed in the book.
- **DEMOS:** These are located in the folder called Trials. We have included a demo of Northcode SWF Studio to use in developing standalone Macromedia Flash Professional 8 games. We have also included a demo of Macromedia Flash Professional 8 itself, which can be used to get you going developing games right away.
- This is a demo version of Northcode SWF Studio (PC Only). The software is merely a trial mode, and therefore has a few limitations. Check the product documentation for more information. The CD-ROM also includes all of the necessary plug-ins to make Northcode SWF Studio as powerful and feature-rich as possible.
- The demo version of Macromedia Flash 8 Professional will expire after 30 days. See the program for purchase / upgrade instructions.

SYSTEM REQUIREMENTS

- Windows 2000 or Windows XP
- 600 MHz Pentium III processor
- 128 MB RAM (256 MB recommended)
- OLE_LINK1100 MB free disk space (to copy all files to the hard drive)
- OLE_LINK1
- Mac OS X 10.26+
- 600 MHz PowerPC G3 processor
- 128 MB RAM (256 MB recommended)
- 100 MB free disk space (to copy all files to the hard drive)

In addition, you will need to have a copy of Macromedia Flash Professional 8 installed on your computer.

INSTALLATION

To use the chapter files on this CD, simply copy the files and folders onto your hard drive. You may or may not want to copy the book images as well. These are inside of each chapter folder, in a subfolder called Images.

To install Northcode SWF Studio, double click on the setup.exe file, located in the "Northcode SWFStudio" folder, inside the Trials folder. Once you have installed the main program, you can install the plugins by running plugins.exe, which is located in the same folder as setup.exe

To install the trial version of Macromedia Flash 8 Professional , look in the Trials folder on the CD, and choose either " Flash 8 Professional Mac", or " Flash 8 Professional Windows." Inside the appropriate folder, open either the DMG (Mac) or EXE (PC) file, and run the installer.

INDEX